# REVISITING REFLEXIVITY

## Liveable Worlds in Research and Beyond

Edited by
Sarah R. Davies, Andrea Schikowitz,
Fredy Mora-Gámez, Elaine Goldberg,
Esther Dessewffy, Bao-Chau Pham,
Ariadne Avkıran and Kathleen Gregory

BRISTOL
UNIVERSITY
PRESS

First published in Great Britain in 2025 by

Bristol University Press
University of Bristol
1–9 Old Park Hill
Bristol
BS2 8BB
UK
t: +44 (0)117 374 6645
e: bup-info@bristol.ac.uk

Details of international sales and distribution partners are available at bristoluniversitypress.co.uk

© Sarah R. Davies, Andrea Schikowitz, Fredy Mora-Gámez, Elaine Goldberg,
Esther Dessewffy, Bao-Chau Pham, Ariadne Avkıran, Kathleen Gregory 2025.
Individual chapters © their respective authors 2025

The digital PDF and ePub versions of this title are available open access and distributed under the
terms of the Creative Commons Attribution-NonCommercial-NoDerivatives 4.0 International licence
(https://creativecommons.org/licenses/by-nc-nd/4.0/) which permits reproduction and distribution for
non-commercial use without further permission provided the original work is attributed.

British Library Cataloguing in Publication Data
A catalogue record for this book is available from the British Library

ISBN 978-1-5292-4487-8 paperback
ISBN 978-1-5292-4488-5 ePub
ISBN 978-1-5292-4489-2 ePdf

The right of Sarah R. Davies, Andrea Schikowitz, Fredy Mora-Gámez, Elaine Goldberg, Esther
Dessewffy, Bao-Chau Pham, Ariadne Avkıran and Kathleen Gregory to be identified as editors of this
work has been asserted by them in accordance with the Copyright, Designs and Patents Act 1988.

All rights reserved: no part of this publication may be reproduced, stored in a retrieval system, or
transmitted in any form or by any means, electronic, mechanical, photocopying, recording, or
otherwise without the prior permission of Bristol University Press.

Every reasonable effort has been made to obtain permission to reproduce copyrighted material.
If, however, anyone knows of an oversight, please contact the publisher.

The statements and opinions contained within this publication are solely those of the editors and
contributors and not of the University of Bristol or Bristol University Press. The University
of Bristol and Bristol University Press disclaim responsibility for any injury to persons
or property resulting from any material published in this publication.

Bristol University Press works to counter discrimination on grounds of gender,
race, disability, age and sexuality.

Cover design: Andrew Corbett
Front cover image: Alamy/Shutterbug33
Bristol University Press uses environmentally responsible print partners.
Printed and bound in Great Britain by CPI Group (UK) Ltd, Croydon, CR0 4YY

Bristol University Press' authorised representative in the European Union is:
Easy Access System Europe, Mustamäe tee 50, 10621 Tallinn, Estonia,
Email: gpsr.requests@easproject.com

# Dis-positions: Troubling Methods and Theory in STS

*Series Editors*: **Mike Michael**, University of Exeter
and **Alex Wilkie, Goldsmiths**, University of London

Turning the mirror on science and technology studies, this pioneering
book series explores the pivotal changes in the discipline. It occupies a
unique position in the field as a platform for adventurous projects that
redraw the disciplinary boundaries of STS.

## Also available in the series:

*1000 Platforms,*
by **Adrian Mackenzie**

*More-Than-Human Aesthetics,*
edited by **Melanie Sehgal** and **Alex Wilkie**

*Ecological Reparation,*
edited by **Dimitris Papadopoulos, Maria Puig de
la Bellacasa** and **Maddalena Tacchetti**

## Find out more at:
bristoluniversitypress.co.uk/dis-positions

# Dis-positions: Troubling Methods and Theory in STS

*Series Editors*: **Mike Michael**, University of Exeter
and **Alex Wilkie, Goldsmiths**, University of London

Turning the mirror on science and technology studies, this pioneering book series explores the pivotal changes in the discipline. It occupies a unique position in the field as a platform for adventurous projects that redraw the disciplinary boundaries of STS.

## International Advisory Board

**Itty Abraham**, National University of Singapore
**Ben Anderson**, Durham University, UK
**Casper Bruun-Jensen**, Kyoto University, Japan
**Nerea Calvillo**, University of Warwick, UK
**Tomás Sánchez Criado**, Humboldt-University of Berlin, Germany
**Didier Debaise**, Free University of Brussels, Belgium
**Marisol de la Cadena**, University of California, Davis, US
**Carl DiSalvo**, Georgia Tech, US
**Miquel Domènech**, Autonomous University of Barcelona, Spain
**Ignacio Farías**, Humboldt-University of Berlin, Germany
**Michael Guggenheim**, Goldsmiths, University of London, UK
**Michael Halewood**, University of Essex, UK
**Gay Hawkins**, Western Sydney University, Australia
**Christopher M. Kelty**, University of California, Los Angeles, US
**Daniel López Gómez**, Open University of Catalonia, Spain
**Celia Lury**, University of Warwick, UK
**Patrice Maniglier**, Université Paris Nanterre, France
**Noortje Marres**, University of Warwick, UK
**Amade M'charek**, University of Amsterdam, Netherlands
**Atsuro Morita**, Osaka University, Japan
**Fabian Muniesa**, Paris Mines School, France
**Dimitris Papadopoulos**, University of Nottingham, UK
**Kavita Philip**, University of British Columbia, Canada
**Maria Puig de la Bellacasa**, University of Warwick, UK
**Kane Race**, University of Sydney, Australia

## Find out more at:

bristoluniversitypress.co.uk/dis-positions

# Contents

## PART III    Experimenting



## PART IV    Institutionalizing

# Series Editors' Preface

*Mike Michael, University of Exeter*
*Alex Wilkie, Goldsmiths, University of London*

The aim of the Dis-Positions book series is to bring together recent work in the emerging intersections of such disciplines as sociology, anthropology, history, geography, design and philosophy, not least as they bear on the broad field of science and technology studies (STS). Conversely, if STS is undergoing major shifts in how it engages with 'the social' and the question of 'societies', it raises vital matters of concern for these various disciplines and their inter-connections. Dis-Positions thus provides a platform on which varieties of generative mutualities across these areas of scholarship can be presented.

In this respect, Dis-Positions is undergirded by a desire to promote novel fields of inquiry, adventurous theoretical and empirical projects and inventive methodological practices. It seeks to encourage authors to address live debates, while drawing on and interrogating developments across academic areas, in the process disturbing and repatterning STS. In pursuing this ethos, Dis-Positions comprises a consolidated, rigorous and proactive space through which creative and critical new perspectives in STS and beyond can find a voice. Under this rubric fall: discussions of the posthuman, post-colonial, affective and aesthetic; methodological inventions that incorporate speculative, engaged, entangled, and sociomaterial practices; empirical novelty that ranges from emergent technoscientific innovations to reformulations of the ordinary; and conceptually creative and critical developments that capture processual and pluralistic thought, extensions of assemblage and practice theories, and the turns to affect and post-performativity.

We are very pleased indeed to welcome as the latest publication in the Dis-positions series the volume *Revisiting Reflexivity: Liveable Worlds in Research and Beyond*. Edited by Sarah R. Davies, Andrea Schikowitz, Fredy Mora-Gámez, Elaine Goldberg, Esther Dessewffy, Bao-Chau Pham, Ariadne Avkıran and Kathleen Gregory, this collection brilliantly revisits the seemingly defunct debates around reflexivity that occupied STS in the late 1980s and early 1990s. If the 'reflexive turn' was marked by a preoccupation with the ironic promises and epistemic limitations of social constructionism, *Revisiting Reflexivity: Liveable Worlds in Research and Beyond* thoroughly (re-)ignites the conversation on reflexivity in light of the transformations of STS in the last 30 years or so. These transformations have taken place on a number of levels that exceed the strictly academic and epistemic. As the volume amply demonstrates, reflexivity now encompasses the ontological – how does research methodology (in the widest sense and in multiple innovative guises) compose its object of study, but also the subject who studies? What are the practices and conditions whereby research questions and their researchers co-emerge with the researched? Set alongside these reflections are ethico-political questions. Who and what are excluded in the doing and making of STS research and how might these be better embraced and cared for (even if such care risks a 'dark side' and must itself be open to critical reflection)? In this regard, *Revisiting Reflexivity* sits interestingly within contemporary decolonializing and more-than-human efforts to rethink the relations of Western scholarship to its others: 'interestingly' not least because reflexivity might turn out to be an 'indulgence' or a 'privilege' that reflects the very conditions it sets out to critique. Moreover, and perhaps most inventively, the editors situate reflexivity in its institutional context. Reflexivity is not the same thing for those at different stages of their career, researching and teaching in different disciplines, working in different university systems. If the shape reflexivity can take varies under these variable circumstances, there are nevertheless questions that the pursuit of reflexivity prompts, questions such as: What sort of spaces are needed to allow reflexivity to flourish within increasingly commodified, managerialist, standardized and surveilled scholarly institutions? How can reflexive methods inform the crafting of more liveable worlds for academics and beyond?

*Revisiting Reflexivity* explores and elaborates reflexivity not only from multiple substantive angles, but also in terms of its form. Produced through a collective, deploying and juxtaposing multiple genres and media, drawing from contributors at different points in their development and from contrasting academic perspectives, suggesting alternative modes for navigating the volume as a whole, *Revisiting Reflexivity* embodies and enacts a range of reflexivities that, at minimum, further open up questions on what a scholarly publication can look and feel like.

The editors must be congratulated in successfully bringing all these qualities together in a single volume. *Revisiting Reflexivity: Liveable Worlds in Research and Beyond* invites and incites a creative and critical revisioning of thinking and practice – making and doing – in STS, and elsewhere. As such, it comprises an invaluable addition to the Dis-Positions book series.

# List of Figures

# Notes on Contributors

**Doris Allhutter** is Senior Scientist at the Institute of Technology Assessment, Austrian Academy of Sciences and teaches Science and Technology Studies (STS) at the University of Vienna and the Johannes Kepler University Linz. Her research focuses on the reconfiguration of welfare through automation and datafication, intersectional inequality and the normativity of computing practices in machine learning.

**Ruth Anderwald** and **Leonhard Grond**, artist-researchers, have been exhibited internationally, including at Centre Pompidou, Paris, Himalayas Art Museum, Shanghai, Tate Modern and Whitechapel Gallery, London. Their artistic research projects include the EU-funded *The Arts of Resistance* (2024–2025) and *ART WORKS!* (2019–2021), as well as *Iliggocene – The Age of Dizziness* (2025–2028, KSB Kulturstiftung des Bundes), *Navigating Dizziness Together* (2020–2024, Austrian Science Fund, FWF PEEK AR 598) and *Dizziness-A Resource* (2014–2017, Austrian Science Fund, FWF PEEK AR 244). With K. Feyertag, they edited the volume *Dizziness: A Resource* with Sternberg Press (2019).

**Malcolm Ashmore** is author of *The Reflexive Thesis* (University of Chicago Press, 1989) and co-author of *Health and Efficiency* (Open University Press, 1989). Within STS he has researched reflexivity, the debunking of scientific fraud, the false/recovered memory controversy and, with Olga Restrepo Forero, the ironies of state documentary practices, particularly in Colombia. He is Honorary Fellow in the Department of Social Sciences, Loughborough University, UK, and is now virtually retired.

**Ariadne Avkıran** is a PhD student and sowi:doc fellow 2023 at the Department of Science and Technology Studies, University of Vienna. With a background in Translation Studies, her interdisciplinary research interest lies at the cross-section between co-production, societal involvement in knowledge production and sociology of translation.

**Anne Beaulieu** holds the Aletta Jacobs Chair of Knowledge Infrastructures at the University of Groningen, The Netherlands and her work contributes to shaping knowledge infrastructures, especially those dedicated to climate and ecology, as detailed in her book *Revealing Relations: Knowledge Infrastructures for Liveable Futures* (Bristol University Press, 2026).

**Jane Calvert** is Professor of Science and Technology Studies at the University of Edinburgh. Her research is on the social studies of the life sciences, particularly synthetic biology. She works in close collaboration with scientists, engineers, policy makers, artists and designers. Her book *A Place for Science and Technology Studies* was published Open Access by MIT Press in 2024.

**Camilo Castillo** is a postdoc researcher at the School of Global Studies, University of Gothenburg. His work is situated at the interface between STS, anthropology and sociology, from there he has researched the tensions around biodiversity conservation in the Colombian Andes and more recently the management of plant diseases in agriculture and the development of quantum technologies.

**Sarah R. Davies** is Professor of Technosciences, Materiality, and Digital Cultures at the Department of Science and Technology Studies, University of Vienna. Her current work explores the intersections between digital and epistemic practices and forms of life.

**Esther Dessewffy** is a PhD candidate at the Department of Science and Technology Studies at the University of Vienna. Esther researches the more-than-human practices and materialities engaged in making computer simulations for architecture and spatial planning in academic contexts.

**Joshua D. Evans** is Senior Researcher and Group Leader at the Danish Technical University's Center for Biosustainability. His group, Sustainable Food Innovation, brings together social science, natural science, and culinary research and development to cultivate more sustainable food systems and transdisciplinary research around food, sustainability and flavour. His own work focuses on fermentation, investigating how the pursuit of new flavours shapes microbial ecology and evolution, facilitates new relationships among humans and between humans and microbes, and offers new theoretical opportunities across STS, more-than-human geography and environmental humanities.

**Elaine Goldberg** is a researcher and filmmaker. Until 2024, she was a research assistant at the Department of Science and Technology Studies and a research associate in the Department of Cultural and Social Anthropology, University of Vienna. Her focus is on audio-visual exploration of the mutual shaping of technology, space and epistemic practices.

**Kathleen Gregory** is a social scientist working at the Centre for Science and Technology Studies (CWTS) at Leiden University. Her research focuses on scholarly communication practices and infrastructures, including those related to open science, data, and research evaluation.

**Karen Kastenhofer** is Senior Scientist at the Austrian Academy of Sciences' Institute of Technology Assessment and teaches STS at the University of Vienna. Her work focuses on diverse/changing epistemic cultures, technoscience-in-society and the governance of controversial technologies.

**Dimas D. Laksmana** is Lecturer at the Sociology Department, Universitas Indonesia, Indonesia. He coordinates *Warung Ilmiah Lapangan* (Science Field Shops), a long-term education programme that integrates agrometeorology, social sciences and farmers' knowledge to support farmers' capacity for designing climate change responsive strategies. He is currently developing a new research agenda that links social studies of soil (microorganism) with the history of soil science in Indonesia.

**Ewa Łączkowska** is an independent researcher, sociologist and multidisciplinary artist. Her work integrates scientific and artistic research practices, putting specific emphasis on embodied inquiry and somatic understanding of knowledge production spaces. In that, she is especially interested in perception, translations of various modes of knowing in communicative forms, as well as the human relationship with the world they study and the influence of that relationship on enacted realities.

**Katja Mayer**, a sociologist at the University of Vienna, studies the politics of open science and data, with a focus on citizen science, computational social sciences and artificial intelligence. She teaches Critical Data Studies. In her other role as senior scientist at the Center for Social Innovation, she has led international research projects and advised policy makers, science diplomats and scientific institutions.

**Reuben Message** is Research Fellow in Responsible Research and Innovation in the Science, Technology and Innovation Studies (STIS) subject area at the University of Edinburgh. He works on the application of engineering biology to the development of cell and gene therapies and has a special interest in the role of time in research practices and cultures.

**Mike Michael** is a sociologist of science and technology, and Professor of Sociology at the University of Exeter, UK. Latterly, he has worked on lay metrology, design and speculative methodology. Recent major publications include *Actor-Network Theory: Trials, Trails and Translations* (SAGE, 2017) and *The Research Event: Towards Prospective Methodologies in Sociology* (Routledge, 2021).

**Mirjana Mitrović** is a media artist and researcher. Currently, she works as a research associate at the Vilém Flusser Archive and is doing a PhD about the flâneuse and the digitalization of urban space at Berlin University of the Arts. She studied Cultural Studies, Spanish Philology and Interdisciplinary Latin American Studies and was a fellow at the Institute for Advanced Studies on Science, Technology and Society, TU Graz, among others. She combines artistic and academic practices, focusing on new technologies, especially the internet and smartphones; the lifeworlds of women★ and feminist activism; geographical, physical and mental borders and their transgression.

**Fredy Mora-Gámez** is a postdoctoral researcher at the Department of Science and Technology Studies, University of Vienna, and a senior lecturer (docent/habil) at the Department of Thematic Studies (Division of Gender Studies), Linköping University. His research concerns questions about borders and migration, everyday materiality and creative methods. His current work explores the (dis)encounters between STS, decolonial feminisms and scholarship on social movements.

**Barbara Morsello** is Assistant Professor in Sociology at the University of Padova and is a member of the Padova Science, Technology, and Innovation Studies (PaSTIS) Research Unit. Her research interests revolve around the relationship between biomedical innovation, everyday life and clinical practices, with a particular emphasis on knowledge co-production. Recently, she has explored the production of refused knowledge in pro-vaccine choice communities during COVID-19 and contributed to a FET-Horizon 2020 project on the clinical and social implications of intelligent neuroprostheses.

**Ekat Osipova** is a PhD researcher at the TU Wien Human-Computer Interaction Group. Their research explores technologically-mediated intimacies from a neurodivergent standpoint.

**Annie Y. Patrick** is an interdisciplinary researcher and scholar in applied STS. Her research integrates her experience and knowledge in technology and innovation, care work, community engagement, engineering studies, healthcare and social justice within STEM, higher education and international development.

**Michael Penkler** is Senior Lecturer at the Institute for Scientific Methodology and Market Research at the University of Applied Sciences Wiener Neustadt. His work centres on questions of embodiment and care in biomedicine and health as well as on qualitative methodology. He is co-editor of the *Handbook of DOHaD & Society: Past, Present and Future Directions of Biosocial Collaboration* (Cambridge University Press, 2024).

**Bao-Chau Pham** is a PhD candidate at the Department of Science and Technology Studies, University of Vienna. Her doctoral research explores the co-production of artificial intelligence, society and security, with a focus on discourses around artificial intelligence policy in the European Union.

**Nikolaus Poechhacker** is a postdoc researcher at the IDea_Lab, University of Graz and research fellow at the Department of Innovation and Digitalisation in Law, University of Vienna. In his work he researches the relationship between democratic institutions, law, social order and algorithmic systems in various domains, bringing together perspectives from sociology, STS and computer science.

**Olga Restrepo Forero** is Professor at Departamento de Sociología, Universidad Nacional de Colombia, Bogotá. She has published on Darwinism in Colombia and on the historiography of Darwinism in Latin America, on scientific writing and scientific rhetoric. She has also researched, with Malcolm Ashmore, institutional settings that produce and negotiate trust relationships, such as notaries and identification cards, and their uses in Colombian society. From 2010 to 2013, she directed and published an enormous research project called 'Ensamblado en Colombia: producción de saberes y construcción de ciudadanías' ('Assembling Colombia: Producing Knowledges and Constructing Citizenships'). Most of her previously published work is in Spanish.

**Andrea Schikowitz** is a senior postdoc researcher at the Department of Science and Technology Studies, University of Vienna. She works on (digital) knowledge practices and infrastructures in distributed urban planning and controversies.

**Sarah Schönbauer** is a postdoc at the Department of Science and Technology Studies, Technical University of Munich and former Erwin Schrödinger scholar (Austrian Science fund). She has a two-pronged interest: the relationship of scientists with environmental crises with a focus on marine science; and the social and political dimensions of small and big plastic particles, which she studies as a member of the German waste network 'Waste in Motion'.

**marissa micah schut** is a Rotterdam-based queercrip transdisciplinary poet, (artistic) researcher and somatics student/teacher. They graduated from the MA Gender Studies programme at Utrecht University in 2022. Generally, their work is informed by queer/crip theory, Black feminist practice, ancestral futurism and hydrofeminism.

**Rob Smith** is Lecturer (Assistant Professor) in Science and Technology Studies at the University of Edinburgh. His research examines the social, political and policy dimensions of biological engineering, particularly the ways in which they are made and governed. He is currently examining attempts to engineer life at the genome scale and the role of research funding organizations as a site for democratically governing science.

**Erika Szymanski** is Associate Professor of Rhetoric of Science in the English Department and the microbiome cluster at Colorado State University. Her work primarily concerns words as scientific tools for constructing microbe–human and other multispecies relationships through contemporary biotechnologies.

**Sanderien Verstappen** is Associate Professor in Social and Cultural Anthropology with a focus on Visual Anthropology at the University of Vienna. She is head of the Vienna Visual Anthropology Lab, which supports ethnographic media practices in academic research and teaching.

**Maria Vlachou** is an independent researcher in gender studies, particularly focusing on the intersections between decolonial feminisms and critical migration studies. Vlachou is a passionate advocate of collective, processual, creative and slow research that takes as its entry point embodied everyday experiences and memory. She is also a yoga teacher and a dance lover.

**Lisa Weasel** is Professor of Environmental Science and Management in the School of Earth, Environment and Society, and Affiliate Faculty in Women, Gender and Sexuality Studies in the School of Gender, Race and Nations, at Portland State University. Her interdisciplinary work seeks to connect science and social justice and to transform laboratory practice using feminist and queer approaches.

**Alex Wilkie** is Professor of Design and Societies at Goldsmiths, University of London. His work bridges design, STS and empirical philosophy and his recent research has focused on exploring the proposition and possibilities of a more-than-human aesthetics for sociomaterial and knowledge practices amidst ecological crisis.

**Steve Woolgar** is Professor Emeritus at Oxford University (Marketing) and Linköping University (Science and Technology Studies). His favourite recent publication is *The Imposter as Social Theory: Thinking with Gatecrashers, Cheats and Charlatans* (with Else Vogel, David Moats and C.F. Helgesson, Bristol, 2021). Current projects include *AI in Surgery* (with Emma Dahlin) and *Managing Eternity: Accountability Relations in Nuclear Waste Disposal* (with Thomas Keating). He continues to work on his long-awaited magnum opus on the nature and limits of provocation – *It Could Be Otherwise*.

**Sally Wyatt** is Professor of Digital Cultures with the Maastricht University Science, Technology and Society (MUSTS) research programme. She studied in Canada and worked in England, before moving to the Netherlands in 1999. For many years, the main focus of her work has been on the development and use of digital technologies. She has also dabbled in questions of STS methodology and representation.

# PART I

# Navigating

1

# Introduction

*Sarah R. Davies, Elaine Goldberg, Andrea Schikowitz
and Fredy Mora-Gámez*

---

### Vignette 1

*During a workshop that we organized to develop this book and discuss the chapters, a discussion arose that I remember very vividly and that, up to today, encapsulates for me much of the controversies that are part of this project. Erika Szymanski wrote her chapter by hand. The handwriting, the size of the font, the inaccuracies, the print quality all present difficulties. For readers, part of the task is guesswork. You cannot annotate or highlight, you cannot skim, you don't have a summary in an abstract, you don't know what you're getting into, whether you even need to read it carefully. ... You cannot prepare for anything, and every sentence takes time to become comprehensible.*

*[...]*

*While I argued how enriching I found it not to be given an abstract in advance and not to be able to basically skim the rest of the text, others also saw this as a problem. At the time, it was easy for me to devote the whole day to this text. But if you have a full-time job and a family at home, you don't have the opportunity to read a few pages in peace for eight hours. So, who was this text written for? Who can afford spending a day with one article? Who has this privilege?*

---

| Sarah: | What content do we need to cover in the introductory chapter? |
|---|---|
| Elaine: | • Why the notion of reflexivity? What is its importance in today's academic and non-academic research worlds? Why do we think this term needs to be revisited? |

Andrea:

- Development/process/journey of bringing the volume together.

- Address the relations (hitherto and potentially) between reflexivity and liveability (and care), and also the limits of this.
- Write a bit about the 'dark sides' of reflexivity.

Fredy:

- What do we mean exactly with 'liveable worlds' and for whom do they become 'more liveable'?
- I feel it is important to mention the collective spirit of the book.

Welcome! After some text that has set the scene in terms of the kinds of writing you can expect from this volume, you have reached a section written in a more traditional academic voice. Here we write as an editorial collective – a 'we' that, while it is not a voice from nowhere (we'll explain who we are later in the text), still retains a sense of being disembodied and authoritative. Depending on your preferences, you may find this pleasingly familiar and easier to engage with, or irritating, maybe even disingenuous. In any case, in this introductory chapter this style of writing will continue to be interspersed with vignettes and other reflections or conversations that disaggregate the authorial 'we', and that highlight the choices that have been made in constructing this chapter and the volume as a whole.

What is this book about? As a whole, we have always wanted this collection to be messy, complex, provocative, diverse, and ~~contradictory~~ polyambivalent. These characteristics seem to us to be central if the book is to speak to experiences and reflections on reflexivity, from ourselves and others. At the same time, it is useful to know what you are about to encounter as you engage with the volume. So here are some central statements concerning the topics and ideas this collection focuses on:

- Reflexivity involves turning one's analytical gaze and tools upon one's own situation, practices and research activities.
- This has been presented as a central virtue in academic scholarship, one that enables robust research and that *situates* our knowledge claims (Haraway 1988).
- It is also associated with creativity and experimentation in making those knowledge claims, and in crafting scholarly representations (Ashmore 1989). Being attentive to our research practices means observing the formats, genres and rhetorics through which we make arguments, and acknowledging that these could be different. Indeed, maybe they *should*

be different if they are to point to aspects of the world that are not readily captured by abstracted text and the universalized Euroamerican traditions of academic argument that dominate social science (Molinari 2022).

- Relatedly, paying attention to our own practices, privileges and struggles can raise questions about the conditions under which we work and the impacts that we have in and through our research. This is where the notion of liveability comes from. In this collection we therefore engage with what difference reflexivity can make, to our own lives as researchers and to the sites and people that we engage with.

If that is the topline, now on to the detail. As suggested by our brainstorming, in what follows we move through a number of sections: (1) we answer the question 'why reflexivity?', briefly introducing our interest in this term and its significance to Science and Technology Studies (STS) research; (2) we reflect on how it relates to what we are calling liveability – the possibility to live as well as possible in the different worlds of which we are a part; and (3) we tell something of the story of the book, and how the content in it has come together. These sections are intertwined with text fragments and reflections that offer more creative, intimate or oppositional insights into the themes and ideas that they cover.

---

## Vignette 2

*At the workshop mentioned earlier, I began by giving a presentation that introduced the background to the book project and how we had come to imagine it. We were, I explained, a newly formed research group who came together during the COVID-19 pandemic and who had faced practical problems because of this. First, access to our usual fieldwork sites had become complicated, and sometimes impossible. Second, we were at the same time trying to figure out what it meant to be a (or, better,* this*) research collective at the University of Vienna. How should we work together, and what were the norms and practices at what was, for almost all of us, a new institutional and national context?*

*As a response to these challenges, we began an autoethnographic project that explored our own knowledge-producing practices, particularly with regard to digital tools. This allowed us both to carry out empirical research and to reflect on how we were working together and how we wished to do so in the future. Indeed, it quickly became apparent that we could not study epistemic practice without also studying care and the ways in which we sought to intervene in academic culture. This was how we became interested in reflexive methods and how they are used to create more liveable worlds, in academia but also more broadly, leading to a conference panel in 2022, and then to the workshop and book project.*

*I prepared this kick-off presentation rather hurriedly, and did so in the format easiest for me, using Google Slides and clicking through the text as I presented. Later, one of the participants commented that there was an irony in starting a workshop that sought to reflect on our methods and approaches, and that had encouraged 'contributions that experiment with the form and presentation of their scholarly argumentation' and would use 'interactive and creative methods and formats', in such a traditional way. Can we ever escape the confines of standardized formats and modes, especially when time (and sometimes imagination) is short?*

## 1. Reflexivity in Science and Technology Studies thought

Reflexivity – turning one's analytical gaze upon one's own position and research – has been presented as a core methodological virtue in both STS and social research generally. From its position as a founding principle in the sociology of scientific knowledge (Bloor 1991 [1976]) to being the object of intense attention, discussion and literary experimentation in the 1990s (Woolgar 1991), it is now a taken-for-granted, even mundane, aspect of research (Felt et al 2017). There is not scope here to review the now vast body of interdisciplinary literature that reflects on reflexivity (see Lumsden [2019] for one extended account), so instead we will, in this section, highlight some of the specific texts and discussions that have been the context to our own interest in it. This work primarily comes from STS, and indeed, in our view the notion of reflexivity has been central to the development of STS as a field.

What is reflexivity? One answer is that it is one of the founding tenets of early STS scholarship. Bloor's four principles of the 'Strong Programme' of the sociology of scientific knowledge included the need to 'be reflexive. In principle [the programme's] patterns of explanation would have to be applicable to sociology itself. ... It is an obvious requirement of principle because otherwise sociology would be a standing refutation of its own theories' (Bloor 1991 [1976], 5). Such a sociology of scientific knowledge should thus not shy away from studying its own practices, developing theories and modes of explanation that apply to its own results as much as to other disciplines. Quite rapidly, however, a focus on reflexivity turned into an interest in the forms and genres of scholarly representation. In Steve Woolgar's words, 'reflexivity is the ethnographer of the text', involving deconstruction of academic books and articles to acknowledge that 'representation and object are not distinct' (1991, 22). The 1980s and 1990s therefore saw a variety of efforts to draw attention to this interconnectedness, and to 'make visible ... some of the work (questions, doubts, anxieties) involved in producing that text' (Woolgar 1991, 123). Fiction, dialogues and different kinds of typography were all used to create such visibility and to '*show* the mutual constitution of form and content' (Ashmore et al 1994, 322, emphasis in original).

Later work both offered critique of these efforts and, in doing so, continued to reflect on and theorize the nature of reflexivity (for instance, see Lynch [2000], who offers a catalogue of different forms of reflexivity). With regard to critique, STS experiments with reflexivity and with what were termed 'new literary forms' have variously been described as self-defeating, self-indulgent, depoliticized, involving 'superfluous epistemological hairsplitting or pretentious self-positioning' (Knuuttila 2002, para 27), and, tellingly, as not actually having 'much impact on the way STS scholars write' (Knuuttila 2002, para 27; see also Lumsden 2019; Barla 2023). For Knuuttila (2002), for example, the additional work required of readers in interpreting experimental or creative forms can result in 'irritation', and is in part the reason that such experiments have largely 'petered out' (para 26; para 7). Perhaps most substantively, the notion of reflexivity has been criticized as hewing too closely to concepts of reflection and representation, and thereby in practice reinforcing a distinction – and separation – between the knower and the known. 'For Haraway and even more so for Barad', writes Barla:

> reflection and reflexivity are insufficient not only because they are based on the belief that our senses and methods have a direct access to the objects or referents of representation, but also because they assume that our methods and practices of representation have no effect on the phenomena they purport to represent. (Barla 2023, 447)

In contexts influenced by feminist new materialism and in particular by the work of Trinh, Barad and Haraway, the notion of diffraction is therefore understood as providing a more fruitful means of understanding the place of the researcher in the research. For Haraway, 'reflexivity, like reflection, only displaces the same elsewhere, setting up the worries about copy and original and the search for the authentic and really real' (2018, 16), whereas diffraction 'is an optical metaphor for the effort to make a difference in the world' (2018, 16). For these authors and others who use the metaphor, diffraction thus offers a more explicit means of emphasizing the relations between researchers and the worlds we engage with – a way of both acknowledging and making difference. 'What we need', Haraway suggests, 'is to make a difference in material-semiotic apparatuses, to diffract the rays of technoscience so that we get more promising interference patterns on the recording films of our lives and bodies' (2018, 16).

Should we then speak of diffraction and not reflexivity? While the answer to this question is to some degree split along disciplinary and theoretical lines, we would agree with Lumsden (2019) that at least some arguments for diffraction have 'caricatured' reflexivity (2019, 49), ignoring the ways in which it has, in many of its iterations, been described exactly in terms that emphasize its potential for intervention and difference. If '[s]eeing and thinking diffractively … implies a self-accountable, critical, and responsible engagement with the world' (Geerts and van der Tuin 2021, 175), it is not clear that this is a form of engagement categorically different from that of reflexive research more generally, and the potential that this holds for similar forms of accountability and change. We therefore take a 'non-oppositional' reading of the relation between reflexivity and diffraction (Barla 2023, 450) and have chosen to stay with the language of reflexivity (of course, convenience, disciplinary affiliation and simplicity also play a role in this decision).

Discussions of the relation between reflexivity and diffraction further draw attention to the fact that there are multiple languages for, and ways of framing, the practices involved in what we understand as reflexive research. Thus while the experiments with form that flourished during the 1990s have to some extent fallen from view, concern with the situatedness of research and researchers, and the need to reflect on this, has continued to be instantiated in diverse ways over the last decades. Reflexivity has been framed as not only epistemically but also morally fruitful: it enables work that is of higher analytical quality (by exploring how knowledge is situated [Haraway 1988]), while integrating reflection on the ethics and impacts of scholarship. Reflexivity therefore helps to interrogate the role that research plays in constituting, rather than merely describing, the worlds that we engage with (Law 2004), and to query what could and should be otherwise in empirical sites and relations. In the context of STS, the term and the practices associated with it have therefore transformed from an interest in form to a broader concern with method and its ontological politics (Law 2004; Lury and Wakeford 2012; Michael 2021). As such, recent accounts of reflexivity have sought to respond to critiques of earlier work as disembodied and inattentive to gender, racialized identities and other positionalities (for example, Gluzman 2021).

Most recently, we recognize interest in reflexivity reflected in the body of STS work termed 'making and doing' (Downey and Zuiderent-Jerak 2017; 2021). While, interestingly, accounts of making and doing are presented as emerging from STS studies of public engagement and policy interventions as much as from theorizations of reflexivity, the movement represents 'a mode of scholarship that involves attending not only to what the scholar makes and does but also to how the scholar and the scholarship get made and done in the process' (Downey and Zuiderent-Jerak 2017, 225). Significantly, it is oriented to 'scholarly projects that extend beyond the academic article or book' (Downey and Zuiderent-Jerak 2021, 2) and thus incorporates research activities from policy briefs to online games, resources for activists, art projects, and inclusive and participatory processes for engagement with technoscientific issues (Downey and Zuiderent-Jerak 2017; 2021). Similarly, the 2020 collection *Transmissions* (edited by Kat Jungnickel) showcases accounts of moments in which 'invention meets dissemination' in research, framing the outputs of scholarship in their various forms as intrinsically tied to the doing of that research, and positioning experimentation in and reflection on research communication as one aspect of wider attentiveness to method in STS (see Law 2004; Lury and Wakeford 2012; Michael 2021). In presenting projects that involve creative writing, video games, sewing and crafts, and exhibitions (among others), the volume highlights the interconnectedness of knowing, doing, making and telling.

Similarly, drawing on Black studies and anticolonial thought, Katherine McKittrick's *Dear Science and Other Stories* offers a creative and compelling account of the nature of research, focusing on stories and storytelling as involving:

> methodological practices wherein we read, live, hear, groove, create, and write across a range of temporalities, places, texts, and ideas that build on existing liberatory practices and pursue ways of living the world that are uncomfortably generous and provisional and practical and, as well, imprecise and unrealized. ... The practice of bringing together multiple texts, stories, songs, and places involves the difficult work of thinking and learning across many sites, and thus coming to know, generously, varying and shifting worlds and ideas. (McKittrick 2021, 5)

McKittrick's writing is at once deeply theoretical and simultaneously personal and creative, merging – or, better, realizing – conceptual argument with letters, vignettes, lists, remixes and images to argue for the continuing relevance of 'the question of *where* we know science from' (2021, 131, emphasis in original). This body of work thus insists on the ongoing importance of examining the situatedness of knowledge alongside the need for interdisciplinary approaches to representing that knowledge – because 'thinking and writing and imagining across a range of texts, disciplines, histories, and genres unsettles suffocating and dismal and insular racial logics' (McKittrick 2021, 4).

There is therefore a wide range of contemporary work that continues to foreground reflexivity, in the sense of highlighting the situated nature of (our) knowledge claims, reflecting on methods and approaches, and mobilizing different genres and forms to articulate research. Interestingly, however, relatively little of this recent work frames itself specifically through the notion of reflexivity, being more commonly oriented, as we have seen, to notions of 'making and doing' or of method. In addition, while reflexivity may be a taken-for-granted virtue in STS scholarship, this means that it has in practice become rather diffuse, something to be mentioned but not specified. Hence our sense, in this volume, that it is a fitting moment to 'revisit' reflexivity – to take it as a focus in and of itself, and to explore connections between the rich landscape of current experiment with form and method and earlier STS work on the nature of reflexivity in research.

| | |
|---|---|
| Elaine: | Something that has been bothering me lately is the feeling that academics think they can do everything. Now that we have realized that there are epistemic values in art and craft, we suddenly think we can do everything: knitting, painting, filming, dancing. There is also a certain hubris in this. These are professions that people spend years learning. It can understandably make any professional group angry when academics come along and think – ah yes, I'm making films now too! I think that's an interesting point of contention: what can we do as academics and how do we put that into an appreciative dialogue with other intellectual and material work? |
| Sarah: | Yes! And a kind of colonial logic in the sense of appropriating other (knowledge) traditions. It also reminds me of the cliche of the natural scientist who decides they can do social research or history – the assumption that these practices are easy and don't require expertise or training. |
| Andrea: | The question here is also one of boundary work and the enactment of expertise: who gets to decide who can do what? Where does borrowing and taking inspiration end, and where does extraction start? |

## Vignette 3

*There is discomfort and a feeling of exposure involved in reflexivity. If you do it honestly, you need to put things on the table you are ashamed of, where you did wrong by others or where you took your privileges for granted. It is even necessary to feel uncomfortable in order to be able to learn from such instances. I certainly did wrong by others sometimes, even if I meant well and tried to be careful. I certainly*

> *learned from it. However, I would not like to expose that in public. For protecting myself. And for protecting others that were involved. Does that hinder reflexivity? How much of it needs to be done in public, collectively, to be of value? And who is in the position of doing it in public without too high costs for themselves and those they are responsible for?*

## 2. Liveability and the 'dark sides' of reflexivity

Even as the term moves between being more or less the explicit focus of scholarly discussion (as section 1 has charted), the practice of reflexivity continues to be understood as central to robust (as in, situated) research. Indeed, for some commentators it is a trope that is almost meaningless, a 'buzzword' that has become an empty signifier (Goldthorpe 2000). It is thus vital not only to call for reflexivity, or to argue for its value to research, but to critically describe and reflect on what it means in practice. What does reflexivity look and feel like in different contexts?

While the volume as a whole offers a diverse set of responses to this question (and while we will reflect on it further in the concluding chapter), some immediate and important answers are suggested by Vignette 3. Here, reflexivity is experienced as uncomfortable, perhaps even dangerous, albeit productive. It necessitates vulnerability and thereby engenders insecurity – the need to protect oneself and others from (potential) public criticism or censure. It also hints at the fact that vulnerability and learning from failure feels out of place in contemporary academia, in which 'excellence' needs to be permanently performed. The vignette thus opens up an aspect of reflexivity that we find essential: that it is not a straightforwardly positive practice, one that is all sweetness and light and productive research outcomes, but something that may itself involve harm or risks – risks that are, moreover, not distributed evenly, but may affect some more than others. As the vignette suggests, reflexivity – here in the context of reflecting on and learning from one's actions in academic contexts – is not a universal but a situated activity, one that is shaped by positionality and role. The reflections in the vignette thus raise central questions. Who is responsible for reflexivity, who can afford it, and who profits from it? Does calling for reflexivity serve to individualize responsibility for it? Does it function to compensate for institutional shortcomings, or to further expose those who are already vulnerable? In short: can calling for reflexivity be careless or harmful?

In talking of the 'dark sides', complexities, and ambivalences of how reflexivity is realized we take inspiration from work on care, which has similarly been presented as both an object of study and as an ethos for scholarship (Puig de la Bellacasa 2011). Scholars of care have emphasized that, while it is vital to notice and acknowledge care work and the ways in which this enables the mundane functionings of lives, care should not be romanticized or presented as purely or necessarily positive (Mol et al 2010). Care has its 'darker sides' (Martin et al 2015), not least 'the violence committed in its name' (Martin et al 2015, 627). Care further involves selection and exclusion: in caring for some things, we choose not to care for others, and those decisions are shot through with power relations (some have more agency over what and who they care for, and how they become the object of care, than others). Lisa Lindén and Doris Lydahl therefore call for 'a double vision of care' in which scholarship is 'both situated and critical, staying with the practices, specificities and potentialities of care while simultaneously critically interrogating those practices when needed' (2021, 8). This double vision entails maintaining an interest in and commitment to the emancipatory and ethical potential of care while also charting, clear-eyed, its violences and injustices. Attention to care may thus give visibility to 'devalued ordinary labours' (Puig de la Bellacasa 2011, 93), but also reveal how care 'can render a receiver powerless or otherwise limit their power' (Martin et al 2015, 627).

Engaging with reflexivity as an aspect of research practice similarly demands honesty regarding its situated realization, the inequities that may emerge in and through it, and its potential challenges and harms. The parallel with what Lindén and Lydahl (2021) call STS 'care studies' is an important one, not only because it draws attention to the situated nature and 'dark sides' of reflexivity but because it further flags the connection to themes of liveability – and how to enhance this – that both strands of scholarship entail. The darker sides of care are important to notice exactly because of the vital and valuable capacity of care practices to 'maintain, continue, and repair our world so that we can live in it as well as possible' (Tronto 1998, 16); similarly, we should be attentive to the harms that reflexivity may entail because of its promise to nurture liveability – to bring about not just better research, but better lives for those involved in or touched by that research.

This is, as we have already noted, a central starting point for this volume – the idea that it is important to revisit reflexivity not just because of its illustrious history as a central concept in STS scholarship, but because reflexive research holds the potential to help create more liveable worlds, in academia and beyond. Just as care is an 'ethico-political issue' as well as an epistemic one (Puig de la Bellacasa 2011, 86), reflexivity can be construed as an ethical and political practice that has the potential to call attention to conditions of diverse lives, and thereby to intervene in them. For reasons connected to the history of this volume (already hinted at in Vignette 2), we have been particularly concerned with how reflexivity can serve as a practice for nurturing more liveable academic lives. For instance, attention to our research and how it is realized can open up questions about the conditions under which we work, and the ways in which these are differently experienced by each of us. Making our concerns and experiences visible and reflecting on how they shape our knowledge practices can open up spaces of collective conversation and vulnerability; these spaces are, indeed, where the notion of liveability comes from, as a means of imagining and envisioning other possible ways of doing research and of intervening in the worlds we engage with.

Liveability in academia is thus both a central issue for us and inextricably entangled with the 'dark sides' of reflexivity that we have already mentioned. Vignette 3 points to the vulnerabilities entailed by reflexivity, but it is also important to note that reflexivity is work, requiring emotional and intellectual effort and the investment of time and energy. Do demands for reflexivity put even more pressure on scholars who, in the context of academic capitalism (Hackett 2014), already need to be innovative, relevant, responsible and engaging? Is reflexivity rewarded by recruitment, evaluation and promotion systems, and if not, who bears the cost of this? How can reflexivity be realized in the context of neoliberal institutions to which logics of quantifiable evaluation are central (Fochler 2016; Fochler et al 2016; Müller and de Rijcke 2017), and where many academics may have limited scope to effect change? Is it ever possible to institutionalize reflexivity, and if not, does it become an individual responsibility alongside that of developing our careers and capacities as 'human resources' (Loveday 2017)? Ultimately, how does reflexivity demand and imply extra layers of labour that are then made invisible in academic canons?

These questions interest and animate us, but we do not have satisfying or stable answers to them. They set the frame for the contributions that follow, and indeed many of the contributors to this volume are also concerned with them, in that they are interested in the conditions of academic work and in how we, as academics in different positions and with varying backgrounds and interests, navigate these. But it is not clear that these (and related) questions are really answerable, not least because they are dependent not only on the specific contexts of academic life and work in which we are embedded, but on particular choices regarding how we wish to exist within these. The possibilities and priorities of a senior scholar with a permanent job are different to those of a student assistant with a six-month contract. Not the least important aspect of reflexivity is noticing and acknowledging this, and allowing it to shape what reflexivity could and should look like in practice within diverse research contexts.

Still, despite these dark sides and ambiguities we do not wish to entirely abandon or lay aside our claim that reflexivity can nurture liveability. One aspect of this connects to the link between reflexivity and the experiments with form, genre, and style described earlier. For early STS scholars, such experimentation drew attention to the constructedness of knowledge and to the ways in which (re)presentation and its objects were never distinct (Woolgar 1991), resulting in questioning *why* academic writing is as it is. John Law asks, for example:

> Why do the books fall into two heaps, the novels on the one hand, and
> the academic volumes on the other? Why do the novels get themselves

read at the weekends, or on holidays, or in the ten minutes before falling asleep at night? Why do the work-books get read in the day, at prime times? (Law 2004, 11)

Recent work has also been attentive to the question of whose voices, and which ways of knowing, may be being silenced through an insistence on conventional academic forms. Enhancing liveability in academia thus means opening up space for the coexistence of those conventional forms with others that incorporate other modalities and forms of inquiry. For Julia Molinari (2022), for instance, it is essential to disrupt taken-for-granted and often invisibilized assumptions concerning the nature of 'good' academic writing. Speaking from long experience of teaching academic writing skills, she argues that 'the modern-day imaginary of what makes writing "academic" celebrates objectivity, linearity, some linguistic standards rather than others, prose and impersonality at the expense of other epistemic virtues, such as creativity, public and popular engagement (to democratize knowledge), recursiveness and composition, multilingualism and multimodality' (Molinari 2022, 57).

Importantly, this isn't only an issue for the *quality* of scholarly writing – the ways in which an emphasis on 'linearity' and 'impersonality' results in texts that are experienced as 'a formulaic product stripped of love, emotion and feeling' (Molinari 2022, 32 – compare with John Law's question regarding the difference between novels and 'work-books'). It is also a problem of epistemic injustice, in which the knowing of certain groups is excised from academic knowledge. 'Reductive approaches to writing', Molinari writes, 'have undesirable aesthetic, socio-cultural and ethical implications, including the denial of a writer's humanity, understood in terms of the literacies, backgrounds and range of knowledge repertoires that they (could) bring to their academic texts' (2022, 163). Moving away from standardized norms and forms therefore opens up the possibility for academics of diverse backgrounds to articulate their knowing in the ways best fitted to that knowledge, whether that involves non-standard English, images or other forms of multimodality, or creative forms such as poetry.

More generally we can tie openness regarding the forms that academic knowledge takes to the (urgent) need to render the academy more friendly to diverse epistemologies, those that do not present knowing as solely emerging from Western, White, male, cisgender, wealthy positionalities (Bhambra et al 2018). While the mobilization of different genres and approaches to knowledge expression is not in and of itself a decolonial effort, experimental approaches to form are at least aligned with scholarship that has sought to disrupt imaginations of academia as necessarily predicated on 'an ethnocentrism that has privileged the questions, experiences, and knowledges of Western scholars and societies at the expense of their non-Western equivalents' (Moosavi 2023, 137). 'The critical pedagogy of decolonization', write Vivetha Thambinathan and Elizabeth Anne Kinsella, 'consists of transforming our colonized views and holding alternative knowledges' (2021, 2). Enabling academic environments in which knowledge and arguments can be presented in diverse, provocative and unconventional (compared to standard academic writing) forms can certainly aid the inclusion of such 'alternative knowledges' (although, again, such experimentation is in no way sufficient as an effort towards undoing colonial logics and their ongoing impacts). Indeed, reflexivity is often presented as central to efforts towards decolonization. For Leon Moosavi, 'decolonial reflexivity' involves 'drawing upon theoretical discussions about academic decolonisation to introspectively locate the inadequacies, limitations, and contradictions within our own efforts at academic decolonisation, particularly in relation to the potential for us to inadvertently perpetuate coloniality rather than dismantle it' (2023, 138–139). We might thus suggest that the possibility for diverse bodies to live well in academia is enhanced both by reflexivity in general – which supports critical engagement with the conditions of academic work, including who is able to access this – and by diversifying the forms and genres through which we represent our knowledge in particular, as a means of allowing multiple epistemologies, logics, and ways of knowing to gain visibility within academic discourse.

Perhaps the preceding sentence can stand as a tentative conclusion to this section. It ties together reflexivity, liveability and experimentation with form, and thereby offers a concise starting point for the volume as a whole. It also connects, less obviously, with our interest in reflexivity's dark sides by implying a further question: liveability for whom?

---

## Vignette 4

*One thing that has stuck with me as a memory of this project over the last years is the way in which ideas end up being disciplined by admin. As a group of authors and editors we were (and are) committed to experimentation, creativity, and exceeding the genres and voices that were in some cases very familiar to us. Indeed, at the workshop devoted to work-in-progress contributions we brainstormed everything from a pop-up book to one covered in fur. One take-home point was 'avoid boring'.*

*This collection is not boring, but it's also clear that all of the organization involved in creating such a project (putting a proposal together, getting chapters from authors, arranging peer review, finding funding) means that at times the intellectual content ends up being secondary to simply making things happen – or at least something that you don't have as much space as you would like to develop. It's also apparent that to many of us as authors, it is just easier to fall back into familiar genres and styles. Why write poetry when you could write a paragraph in the passive voice? In this respect I think it's fair to say that this volume is, as a whole, more traditional than we had originally thought it might be. Perhaps part of the reason for this is that it is also something that has been created in time carved out from other projects, and is nobody's central research project or focus (the thing that they are primarily paid to do). When is there ever time and space enough to realize the best, the strangest, the most provocative of our imaginings?*

|             |                                                                                     |
|-------------|-------------------------------------------------------------------------------------|
| Andrea:     | To be discussed: should we also include some utopian visions of more liveable worlds – how things could be otherwise? And how could that be done? Could that be a means of not dedicating reflexivity to the cause of neoliberal self-optimization? |
| Elaine:     | Maybe we need artistic or experimental approaches to envision alternatives? We could think of drawing, dancing, filming, writing prose or trying out quantitative tools. Though this could be criticized as being an extremely privileged position. Who, in which position, in which context, has the freedom for such creative expressions? And who is policed for not being academic enough? |
| Sarah:      | These are really interesting points, but I think we are already going to have too much content for this chapter … |

## Vignette 5

*The term 'dark side of reflexivity' was used a lot during the workshop – the idea that reflexivity should not be over-romanticized. I remember asking myself what others imagined this dark side to be. Things that make me roll my eyes in debates about reflexivity: there is an element of self-indulgence about it. It's about the research process itself and positionality and me as a researcher and me constructing my field. It's fun to deal with myself as a researcher all the time and to write down my reflections, but in the end it's also a lot … about myself. In film, you might call them auteur works. Does this mean that we always create auteur works?*

*Other things that annoy me about the debate is this turning round on oneself in the academic world and how badly we are doing. I don't want to judge whether this is really the case here, but becoming aware of other realities and breaking out of reflection can possibly be more healing than a self-reflexive research diary.*

*One last thought: Sometimes I smile when a 'method' is used to prove oneself as reflective, for example, writing about oneself. Writing about the writing process itself. Or showing yourself in the film you're making. These are useful tools – we use them here too – but also simply a way out of the responsibility of building worlds. It's just my story. And as long as I use my voice for it, there's nothing wrong with that. I can now briefly address you in this very moment as the reader of this text. Are you scared? And I've already made the reading situation itself a topic and reflected on the text, the context of the creation and the context of the reception. Job done:) These are perhaps not the darkest sides of reflexivity, but I find that these feelings awaken in me the need for a different debate on reflexivity – perhaps a more honest one, where the made nature of the text appears in the material of the text itself. That is one of our attempts here.*

## 3. Situating *Revisiting Reflexivity*

As a reminder, we are now in the third section of this introductory chapter, which is the place where we tell something about ourselves, the story of the book, and how the content in it has come together. As some of the exchanges suggest, we have found that we have more to say, at more length, in this introductory chapter than we had perhaps originally thought – but don't worry, this is the final section, and one that we aim to keep concise.

Indeed, we have already suggested many of the reasons and rationales that lie behind this volume, both the intellectual – the need to 'revisit' older STS discussions of reflexivity and to connect these to contemporary research practices – and the practical, such as an interest in reflecting on how to live and work as an academic in a particular context. In summary, our intellectual starting point is that it is timely to revisit reflexivity for a number of reasons: in order to connect older discussions of reflexivity with contemporary work on method (see section 1); because we live in a time of academic capitalism, and reflexivity may help us engage with the practical and moral questions of how to live well in academia (section 2); because we live in a hurting world, and reflexivity may help us find ways to intervene in it, for instance by drawing attention to the ontological politics of our methods (sections 1 and 2); and because exploring and promoting the connections between reflexive research practice and modes and genres of representation may aid epistemic justice within academia and beyond (section 2). In this section we will take these aims for granted, and more explicitly explain the background to this collection and some of the story – as we would tell it – of how it has come together.

Let's start by returning to the question of who 'we' are. Sarah R. Davies, Elaine Goldberg, Andrea Schikowitz and Fredy Mora-Gámez are currently writing as a collective, though – as you have seen – some of the earlier text disaggregates this collective to show some of the exchanges that we have had in developing this chapter, as well as showcasing vignettes written by particular individuals (we have kept these anonymous exactly because of the vulnerabilities they entail). We are a group who, while all are currently based at the University of Vienna, are in very different positions (PhD student, post-docs, professor) and have come to Vienna via different trajectories. Writing together flattens these differences, but also offers a level of protection. We might say that writing in this way, using the authorial 'we' and at least at times a kind of authoritative, god's-eye voice, aids the liveability of our academic worlds because it allows us to share our reflections without our vulnerabilities being individualized.

We are also writing on behalf of a larger editorial group. Esther Dessewffy, Bao-Chau Pham, Ariadne Avkıran and Kathleen Gregory have all been involved in putting this collection together, and have contributed in different ways to its production. As noted in Vignette 2, this volume has emerged out of a particular set of experiences. Coming together as a newly formed research group over the period 2020–2022, we (this editorial team) were confronted by academia as a practical problem as much as an intellectual one. How could we carry out research, and engage in collegial academic life, under pandemic conditions? What did we want collective academic life to look like, and how should this be organized? While we have documented some of these experiences elsewhere (Davies et al 2022; Pham et al 2024), negotiating these practicalities left us with an enduring interest in reflecting on the conditions of (our) academic work, and on paying attention to how knowledge production is shaped through these. In our discussions we have been interested in everything from the impacts of precarity on scholarship to what one should wear to academic conferences, how to manage and resolve conflicts, and whether it is ever possible to decolonize the university. Reflexivity, for us, has thus involved understanding the epistemic, political, social, and affective dimensions of academia as always entangled, and paying attention to the mundane aspects of academic work as connected to the concrete ways in which knowledge is produced through fieldwork, writing, co-authorship, data management, moments of creativity, and so on (Schikowitz et al 2025).

This volume has emerged out of these initial experiences and interests – though it has, importantly, expanded and exceeded them, covering topics (such as artistic research or environmental conservation) that were not part of our early conversations. This is due to the fact that it is a collective enterprise not just with regard to the group of eight editors, but to the many others who are involved in the project and who have contributed to it, through the particular chapters or contributions collected here but also via in-person conversations and activities. We have already mentioned the open panel (held at the EASST conference in Madrid in 2022, titled 'Making liveable (STS) worlds through reflexive methods') and the book development workshop (which took place in mid 2023), both of which brought together researchers whose involvement has immeasurably enriched our own thinking and this collection as a whole. Because there is not a straight line between contributions to the panel, workshop and this collection – multiple researchers were involved in the panel or workshop but not the book, while we have also gained contributors who were not involved in the earlier stages – it is important to acknowledge the role that all who participated in these various activities have played in shaping the ideas presented here, both in this introductory text and in the collection as a whole. The workshop, in particular, involved rich and collaborative discussions about the nature of reflexivity (it is from these, in particular, that we have taken the notion of the 'dark sides' of reflexivity) and about what this collection should look like ('not boring', as we have already noted). The creativity and interests of those involved, and their generosity and vulnerability in discussing both work-in-progress and experiences of academic life, have enabled this volume to become the rich and dialogic collection that it is.

*Revisiting Reflexivity* might thus be seen as a snowball: it started with just a few contributors brought together under particular circumstances, but has gathered momentum and new participants as it has travelled to different locations and involved different kinds of practices. Importantly, this snowballing process is still ongoing. One aim has always been for the physical book (the one that you are, perhaps, holding right now as you read) to be just one aspect of a wider book project, involving an online space and ongoing conversations. Several of the contributions that follow therefore offer complementary content that can be accessed online, while we hope that this collection will also enable further events and discussions that allow those of us involved in this book, but also a wider community, to continue to revisit reflexivity and to reflect on how we might nurture more liveable worlds. Our sense is that there is a hunger, in the academic communities we know and engage with, to think care-fully about mundane academic practice, the conditions of academic work, and what it means to intervene to create better worlds in academia and beyond. Our hope is that the work that follows assists in doing so.

---

### Vignette 6

We long for 'air and light and time and space,' an architecture of possibilities and pleasure; instead, we find ourselves crushed under the weight of expectations and the rubble of our fractured workdays. (Sword 2017, ix–x)

*Sword writes about 'air and light and time and space' for research. I currently have the constant feeling that this is in tension with the care relationships I enter into in my life. That the opportunity to work creatively and exploratively comes at the expense of the personal relationships I want to cultivate in my life. ... It is a well-known vicious circle, the end of which probably lies in burnout, which cuts us off from all relationships with the world for the time being. And so I find myself in a cautious act of equilibrium that sometimes tips in one direction, sometimes in the other. Right now I have air and space and time and light for my creative work. At the same time, however, I feel that I am therefore not present for people who need my presence and whose presence I need. Perhaps all we can do is be sensitive to these shifts in time and resources.*

## References

Ashmore, M. (1989) *The Reflexive Thesis: Wrighting Sociology of Scientific Knowledge*. Chicago: University of Chicago Press.

Ashmore, M., Myers, G. and Potter, J. (1994) Discourse, Rhetoric, Reflexivity: Seven Days in the Library. In S. Jasanoff, G. Markle, J. Petersen and T. Pinch (eds) *Handbook of Science and Technology Studies*. London: SAGE, pp 321–342.

Barla, J. (2023) Beyond Reflexivity and Representation: Diffraction as a Methodological Sensitivity in Science Studies. *Distinktion: Journal of Social Theory* 24(3): 444–466. https://doi.org/10.1080/1600910X.2021.1934506

Bhambra, G.K., Gebrial, D. and Nişancıoğlu, K. (eds) (2018) *Decolonising the University*. London: Pluto Press.

Bloor, D. (1991 [1976]) *Knowledge and Social Imagery*. Chicago: University of Chicago Press.

Davies, S., Pham, B.-C., Dessewffy, E., Schikowitz, A. and Gámez, F.M. (2022) Pinboarding the Pandemic: Experiments in Representing Autoethnography. *Catalyst: Feminism, Theory, Technoscience* 8(2): 1–22.

Downey, G.L. and Zuiderent-Jerak, T. (2017) Making and Doing: Engagement and Reflexive Learning in STS. In U. Felt, R. Fouché, C. Miller and L. Smith-Doerr (eds) *Handbook of Science and Technology Studies*, 4th edn. Boston: MIT Press, pp 223–250.

Downey, G.L. and Zuiderent-Jerak, T. (eds) (2021) *Making & Doing: Activating STS through Knowledge Expression and Travel*. Boston: The MIT Press.

Felt, U., Fouché, R., Miller, C.A. and Smith-Doerr, L. (eds) (2017) *The Handbook of Science and Technology Studies*, 4th edn. Boston: The MIT Press.

Fochler, M. (2016) Variants of Epistemic Capitalism: Knowledge Production and the Accumulation of Worth in Commercial Biotechnology and the Academic Life Sciences. *Science, Technology, & Human Values* 41(5): 922–948. https://doi.org/10.1177/0162243916652224

Fochler, M., Felt, U. and Müller, R. (2016) Unsustainable Growth, Hyper-Competition, and Worth in Life Science Research: Narrowing Evaluative Repertoires in Doctoral and Postdoctoral Scientists' Work and Lives. *Minerva* 54(2): 175–200. https://doi.org/10.1007/s11024-016-9292-y

Geerts, E. and van der Tuin, I. (2021) Almanac: Diffraction & Reading Diffractively. *Matter: Journal of New Materialist Research* 2(1): 173–177. https://doi.org/10.1344/jnmr.v2i1.33380

Gluzman, Y. (2021) Reflexivity Practiced Daily. In H.S. Rogers, M.K. Halpern, K. de Ridder-Vignone and D. Hannah (eds) *Routledge Handbook of Art, Science, and Technology Studies*, 1st edn. London: Routledge, pp 249–271. https://doi.org/10.4324/9780429437069-19

Goldthorpe, J. (2000) Sociological Ethnography Today: Problems and Possibilities. In J. Goldthorpe (ed) *On Sociology: Numbers, Narratives and the Integration of Research and Theory*. Oxford: Oxford University Press, pp 65–93.

Hackett, E.J. (2014) Academic Capitalism. *Science, Technology, & Human Values* 39(5): 635–638. https://doi.org/10.1177/0162243914540219

Haraway, D. (1988) Situated Knowledges: The Science Question in Feminism and the Privilege of Partial Perspective. *Feminist Studies* 14(3): 575–599. https://doi.org/10.2307/3178066

Haraway, D. (2018) *Modest_Witness@Second_Millenium. FemaleMan©_Meets_ OncoMouse™: Feminism and Technoscience*. New York: Routledge.

Jungnickel, K. (ed) (2020) *Transmissions: Critical Tactics for Making and Communicating Research*. Boston: The MIT Press.

Knuuttila, T. (2002) Signing for Reflexivity: Constructionist Rhetorics and Its Reflexive Critique in Science and Technology Studies. *Forum Qualitative Sozialforschung / Forum: Qualitative Social Research* 3(3). https://doi.org/ 10.17169/fqs-3.3.828

Law, J. (2004) *After Method: Mess in Social Science Research*. London: Routledge.

Lindén, L. and Lydahl, D. (2021) Editorial: Care in STS. *Nordic Journal of Science and Technology Studies*, 3–12. https://doi.org/10.5324/njsts. v9i1.4000

Loveday, V. (2017) Luck, Chance, and Happenstance? Perceptions of Success and Failure amongst Fixed-term Academic Staff in UK Higher Education. *The British Journal of Sociology* 69(3): 758–775. https://doi.org/10.1111/ 1468-4446.12307

Lumsden, K. (2019) *Reflexivity: Theory, Method, and Practice*. London: Routledge.

Lury, C. and Wakeford, N. (eds) (2012) *Inventive Methods: The Happening of the Social*. London: Routledge.

Lynch, M. (2000) Against Reflexivity as an Academic Virtue and Source of Privileged Knowledge. *Theory, Culture & Society* 17(3): 26–54. https:// doi.org/10.1177/02632760022051202

Martin, A., Myers, N. and Viseu, A. (2015) The Politics of Care in Technoscience. *Social Studies of Science* 45(5): 625–641. https://doi.org/ 10.1177/0306312715602073

McKittrick, K. (2021) *Dear Science and Other Stories*. Durham: Duke University Press.

Michael, M. (2021) *The Research Event: Towards Prospective Methodologies in Sociology*. London: Routledge.

Mol, A., Moser, I. and Pols, J. (eds) (2010) *Care in Practice: On Tinkering in Clinics, Homes and Farms*. Bielefeld: Transcript.

Molinari, J. (2022) *What Makes Writing Academic: Rethinking Theory for Practice*. London: Bloomsbury.

Moosavi, L. (2023) Turning the Decolonial Gaze towards Ourselves: Decolonising the Curriculum and 'Decolonial Reflexivity' in Sociology and Social Theory. *Sociology* 57(1): 137–156. https://doi.org/10.1177/0038038522109637

Müller, R. and de Rijcke, S. (2017) Thinking with Indicators: Exploring the Epistemic Impacts of Academic Performance Indicators in the Life Sciences. *Research Evaluation* 26(3): 157–168. https://doi.org/10.1093/reseval/rvx023

Pham, B.-C., Gregory, K., Davies, S., Schikowitz, A., Dessewffy, E., Goldberg, E., et al (2024) Academic Citizenship, Together: Prioritising Care and Reflexivity in Scholarly Life. *Journal of Praxis in Higher Education* 6(2): Article 2. https://doi.org/10.47989/kpdc478

Puig de la Bellacasa, M. (2011) Matters of Care in Technoscience: Assembling Neglected Things. *Social Studies of Science* 41(1): 85–106. https://doi.org/10.1177/0306312710380301

Schikowitz, A., Desssewffy, E., Davies, S.R., Pham, B.-C., Gregory, K., Avkiran, A., et al (2025) Writing Choreographies: (STS) Knowledge Production in Post-digital Academia. *Tecnoscienza*.

Sword, H. (2017) *Air & Light & Time & Space: How Successful Academics Write*. Cambridge: Harvard University Press.

Thambinathan, V. and Kinsella, E.A. (2021) Decolonizing Methodologies in Qualitative Research: Creating Spaces for Transformative Praxis. *International Journal of Qualitative Methods* 20: 16094069211014766. https://doi.org/10.1177/16094069211014766

Tronto, J. (1998) An Ethic of Care. *Generations: Journal of the American Society on Aging* 22(3): 15–20.

Woolgar, S. (ed) (1991) *Knowledge and Reflexivity: New Frontiers in the Sociology of Knowledge*. London: SAGE.

2

# A User's Guide to 'Revisiting Reflexivity'

*Andrea Schikowitz, Sarah R. Davies, Elaine Goldberg
and Fredy Mora-Gámez*

The preceding chapter introduced the aims of and background to this collection as a whole, and surveyed some of the existing Science and Technology Studies (STS) literature around the notion of reflexivity. It did not, however, realize one of the traditional tasks of an introduction to an edited volume – that is, summarizing and discussing the chapters that follow. This (much briefer) text attempts to do some of this work, though again in a rather unconventional manner (we do not, for example, try to summarize the content of the various contributions). This text comprises three sections: one that tells you something about the kinds of contributions you should expect, in terms of style and structure; one that previews the different sections into which contributions are organized; and one that offers a number of alternative (idiosyncratic) routes through the volume, based on thematic interests or other organizing logics.

## 1. What to expect

You may have noticed that we have primarily been referring to 'contributions' rather than 'chapters'. Indeed, the content that follows takes different forms with regard to format, genre, style and structure, and is not solely comprised of 'chapters' as they are generally recognized. It includes images (some standing alone, some embedded into texts), prompts and instructions for activities for you to carry out, and anecdotes and vignettes, as well as more conventional academic texts. One contribution takes the form of an email thread, another a dialogue. You should therefore expect content and arguments to be presented through a range of different formats.

This diversity relates to our understanding that reflexivity entails reflection on, and experimentation with, the forms that our knowledge is represented in. A further aspect of reflexivity is (for us) an acknowledgement of the constructedness and unfinished nature of this knowledge. In this volume we signal this through incorporating dialogue around the contributions. While each contribution is numbered sequentially, you will see that some are direct responses to those that have preceded it. This is not the case for all the content – responses or interventions have not emerged for all contributions, but they have for some. In one or two cases, we, as editors, have also written brief notes or comments on particular contributions, pulling out the themes that we see as particularly useful or important.

All of this means that the contributions that follow take different forms and are, if they involve text, of very different lengths. They are written in a variety of voices, and may be in dialogue with each other.

## 2. Mapping

What of the actual content, the themes that these contributions engage with? All of the contributions reflect, in different ways, on interlocking themes of what it means *to practice reflexivity, the forms and modes of scholarly representation, and the creation of more liveable worlds* – the three central ideas that frame the collection as a whole. As the following section emphasizes, we see a number of different ways to engage with this content, and do not think that the volume needs to be read sequentially or comprehensively. But a (physical) book demands some degree of linear organization. As well as offering different pathways through the volume, we have also chosen to organize the content within five parts, briefly previewed here.

### Part I: Navigating

The first part – which you are in the midst of – is oriented to introducing, beginning, mapping. It contains content written by us, the editors, but also other contributions that sketch out and engage with the landscape of reflexivity, academic capitalism, and liveable worlds that the volume is oriented to. One such contribution is Reuben Message, Jane Calvert and Rob Smith's email thread 'Automatic Reply: Another University is Possible' (Chapter 3), which offers an introduction to lived experiences within the contemporary (UK) university and the kinds of dynamics that drive our concern for the need for nurturing more liveable academic worlds. In Chapter 4, Anne Beaulieu offers a humorous take on reflexivity in the form of a decision tree that will also help you decide which chapters you might want to read next.

## Part II: *Affecting*

The second part includes contributions that are, in different ways, oriented to affects, bodies and interventions. These contributions take seriously the affective dimensions of reflexivity – that it is not just an intellectual or cognitive exercise, but must necessarily involve attention to embodiment and emotion.

The first section of this part focuses on *bodies*. Michael Penkler (Chapter 5), for example, describes research as 'learning to affect and be affected', using vignettes to show how he has 'become with' the phenomena he has studied, while marissa micah schut (Chapter 7) merges personal narrative with a series of prompts that support readers in engaging with the affordances and needs of their bodies.

The second section addresses experiences of *participation*. Dimas D. Laksmana (Chapter 9) and Camilo Castillo (Chapter 10) both offer detailed empirical accounts of their involvement in participatory research and how they experienced and got affected by their research partners' expectations as well as the postcolonial and hierarchical assumptions underlying transdisciplinary research by Global North institutions. While they are favourable towards their research partners' stances, Barbara Morsello (Chapter 11) reflects upon her affects towards working with vaccine-hesitant research participants during a pandemic.

As a whole the section highlights how reflexivity is always embodied, situated and experienced.


## Part III: *Experimenting*

While contributions throughout the collection experiment with form and genre, this part includes accounts that explicitly reflect on – and offer guides to – what it means to experiment as an aspect of reflexive research practice. These contributions expand what is often understood as 'research' in the social sciences, including *doing* (in the first section) and *making* (in the second) reflexivity through diverse modes, formats and practices.

Contributions focusing on *doing* insist on the validity of movement (in Ewa Łączkowska's contribution; Chapter 12) or walking (in Mirjana Mitrović's contribution; Chapter 14) as a method, while Lisa Weasel (Chapter 15) moves laboratory practices into the kitchen and invites the reader to follow suit to develop empathy for fruit flies.

Contributions that centre on *making* invite us to engage with the space created by handwritten text (Erika Szymanski's contribution; Chapter 16) or to reflect on the nature of reflexivity within artistic research (Ruth Anderwald and Leonhard Grond's text; Chapter 17).

As such the section offers inspiration for practical engagements in experimental and creative reflexive modes and practices.

## Part IV: Institutionalizing

Can reflexivity be institutionalized? How does it relate to formal organizations and infrastructures, whether universities or disciplines? How is it experienced as a practice situated not just through individual bodies and positionalities, but within geographies and institutional landscapes? This section incorporates contributions that reflect on such questions, and that ask what it might mean to formalize reflexivity.

The contributions in the first part focus on possibilities for *evaluation* of efforts to institutionalize reflexivity, for instance when Karen Kastenhofer and Doris Allhutter (Chapter 20) contemplate learning from two reflexive research projects, Katja Mayer introduces participatory evaluation methods (Chapter 21) or Annie Patrick (Chapter 22) notices the patterning of interactions and dynamics between herself as an engaged researcher and a wider institution.

The second section addresses *place* and *emplacement*, in that it considers the sites in which reflexivity is able to be realized and how these sites shape that realization. Nikolaus Poechhacker and Sarah Schönbauer reflect on the nature of 'homes' in their research experiences (Chapter 23), while Elaine Goldberg argues that the art studio should be a place for STS research (Chapter 24). In the form of a dialogue, Malcolm Ashmore and Olga Restrepo Forero (Chapter 25) ask 'Why Bogotá?', questioning the place of place in STS and reflecting on how geography comes to matter.

The part thus offers accounts of positionality beyond the personal, situating reflexive research practices within institutional landscapes and cultures.

## Part V: Revisiting Reflexivity

The final part is oriented to closing, synthesizing, reflecting and concluding. It includes short contributions by Mike Michael and Alex Wilkie (Chapter 27), Steve Woolgar (Chapter 28) and Sally Wyatt (Chapter 29), as well as some further reflections by us, the editors. While this part offers no finished answers or solutions, it includes contributions that reflect on cross-cutting themes and on the questions that we raised in Chapter 1. As a whole, the section thus draws together the ideas and experiences raised within the collection, offering a tentative place to close this iteration of revisiting reflexivity.

## 3. Choose your own adventure

The structure outlined is one way of organizing the material gathered in this collection, but it is not, as we have already noted, a final or comprehensive logic, but one that involves compromises – decisions to emphasize one aspect of a contribution over another that might be equally important to the author. To acknowledge this, and to encourage you to find your own ways to navigate the volume, we offer four alternative routes through the material, described in what follows.

If you are interested in *creative modes of representation and multimodality*, you might start by engaging with Erika Szymanski's contribution (Chapter 16), which draws attention to form by offering a handwritten essay and which forces attention to the questions of what is a research contribution and what we are doing when we write. Continuing to think about genre, you might read 'Automatic Reply: Another University is Possible' (Chapter 3) and 'Why Bogotá? The Local, the Global and the Interesting, Reflexively or STS – Here and There' (Chapter 25), both of which involve texts that use very different genres than those we are primarily used to in the academy. Finally, you might engage with 'Outrageously Open: Co-inhabiting and Expanding Knowledge-making Spaces through Somatic, Arts-based Methods' (Chapter 12), which not only describes movement-oriented research approaches but uses images to explain and illustrate these.

If you are interested in *artistic methods* … well, this is a book. And an academic one at that. And this is where we would perhaps like to make another small digression, despite all the reflections and descriptions we have already provided on forms and formats and modes of expression. In all our love for the experimental, we are nevertheless publishing an academic book. That was the plan throughout the process. And yes, we are also all academics, we need books, because to this day these are the forms of publication that make our performance as academics credible and assessable. We all want our work to be part of a book, even if our work expresses a desire to break out of these paradigms of academic research. So if you have already laughed ironically while engaging with this volume because you were hoping to receive something different, we would like to send you on the following path: Elaine Goldberg feels the need to break out of the university office and therefore writes about the art studio as a heterotopia for STS (Chapter 24). Next, we suggest an immersion into the world of artistic research with Ruth Anderwald and Leonhard Grond's 'Contemplations' (Chapter 17). This adventure ends with physical movement, either walking with Mirjana Mitrović (Chapter 14) – for those who prefer a more leisurely pace – or dancing with Ewa Łączkowska for those who still need to release some energy (Chapter 12).

If you are interested in the *care relations* we build while doing research, you can start by following the path of reflections and disturbances of ethnographic research. Michael Penkler explores how we affect and are affected within research, paying attention to how (dis)comfort with his own body relates to his research on obesity (Chapter 5). marissa micah schut is similarly interested in bodies, affects and their relation to knowledge, exploring intersectional relationships with 'nonbinary, crip, menstrual' 'bodies multiple' (Chapter 7). While in their engagement with 'in/visibilities, vulnerabilities and interdependencies' the body appears here as restrictive rather than enabling, it also gives rise to care, allowing us to imagine how academia might become more liveable for different and multiple bodies. Indeed, care is a recurrent theme in Chapters 5–11, given its entanglement or connection with embodiment and affect. Accounts of care that take a slightly different form can be found in 'Projected Reflexivity: Learnings from Two Reflexive Research Projects from-within, with-within and for-within' (Chapter 20) and 'Reflexivity in Co-Evaluation: From Challenges to Principles of Participatory Research Evaluation' (Chapter 21), which take seriously the notion that care involves tinkering with the conditions under which we live and work: both contributions describe and reflect on efforts to realize forms of caring reflexivity within particular institutional contexts.

Finally, for *the uncanny valley tour, or a visit to the 'dark side' of reflexivity*, you will take a route through discomfort, ambivalence and tensions, designed for those of you who are ready for 'staying with the trouble'. This journey will send shivers down your spine, but it will also bring to light that attending to the 'dark sides of reflexivity' might be key to overcoming them – not once and for all, but as an ongoing practice of 'becoming reflexive', as Sarah Schönbauer and Nikolaus Poechhacker argue in Chapter 23.

To get attuned to tensions and open questions in relation to reflexivity, you can start by reading Chapter 3 by Reuben Message, Jane Calvert and Rob Smith, which not only addresses many of these tensions, but does so in the form of an email exchange that breaks with the necessity to form a coherent argument or a uniform conclusion and allows for a back and forth between different positions and questions.

Now you might be ready to engage with discomfort and fear – discomfort with relations to research partners that might potentially harm them; relations to research partners who make us feel uncomfortable; and discomfort concerning your own body. Chapter 22 is a good starting point, as its author, Annie Patrick, confronts herself with her fear and horror when facing engaged research in a reflexive way, which makes her aware of the exposure and vulnerability of herself and her research partners. Chapter 9 (by Dimas D. Laksmana) foregrounds the 'productive potential of discomfort' for reflecting and acting on postcolonial power relations in transdisciplinary research. Taking his own discomfort during conducting fieldwork with Indonesian farmers in a European research project seriously, he attends to 'moments of discomfort' as potentially opening up spaces for reflexivity.

While these contributions foreground sympathy and care for research partners, in Chapter 11 Barbara Morsello reflects on being faced with research partners who make her feel uncomfortable: vaccination sceptics during a global pandemic. She elaborates how reflexivity helped her to deal with her own affects and with her research partners in an ethical and epistemically productive way, using drawings and vignettes to deal with and illustrate her anger and discomfort. Similarly, in Chapter 15 Lisa Weasel urges us to confront our own discomfort by building caring relationships with creatures that we would conventionally perceive as disgusting – fruit flies. Instead of the 'clean' and 'isolated' space of a laboratory, she experiments (and invites us to do the same in a DIY feminist science experiment) with them in her kitchen and reflects on these engagements, which give rise to affect and care.

Whichever route you choose, we hope you enjoy the adventure!

3

# Automatic Reply: Another University is Possible

Reuben Message, Jane Calvert and Rob Smith

This chapter takes the form of an email exchange among the authors between February and June 2023 – a period characterized by an unprecedented level of disruption caused by ongoing industrial action at UK universities. Tracing our attempts to discover through dialogue what our contributions to a paper on the theme of 'Making liveable (STS) worlds through reflexive methods' might be, it touches on a variety of possibilities, including: whether reflexivity gets us to politics, the affordances of the aesthetics of Dark Academia, (not) writing poetry in Madrid, and the importance of time, space and money for reflexive work. Punctuated by real life – travel, delays, family holidays, doubts, detours, culs-de-sac, unfulfilled promises, flights of fancy, jokes, conflicting priorities, strikes and out-of-office messages – it is, in its materiality, a particular outcome of the intersecting worlds in which we live. Indeed, the form itself becomes the main performer: it is the point and, in its way, a sidelong kind of answer to the question/s of reflexivity in academic Science and Technology Studies (STS) today. This decision on form emerged gradually in the course of the conversation, beginning with the inspiration of a slogan used in the automatic email reply of a striking colleague: Another University is Possible. In the process, it reflects certain verities of STS that more conventional essay forms may pass over, including the social nature of knowledge production, its messiness and its material mediation. Notably, moreover, the decision on form also precludes possibilities: we believe there are important things to say about reflexivity in the face of precarity, about learning to inhabit time and space in different ways, about solidarity and the possibility of building liveable worlds together that remain unsaid here. Such unrealized realities haunt the text – and, in so doing, we hope, also call

30

attention to the foreclosures that haunt the production of knowledge in all material systems and especially our present one. As such, for the authors at least, the optimism of the titular slogan is thus accompanied also by a sense of loss, a lament for things we could not or did not do, and a world whose possibilities we fleetingly intuit but cannot realize. This exchange can be read as presented, or by starting at the end.

**Subject:** Another university is possible
**From:** Reuben Message
**Date:** 05/05/2023 07:47
**To:** Rob Smith, Jane Calvert

```
Hello,
I've compiled a bibliography of works cited thus far
```


```
Bibliography:
Balmer, A.S. and Bulpin K.J. (2013) Left to Their Own
  Devices: Post-ELSI, Ethical Equipment and the International
  Genetically Engineered Machine (IGEM) Competition.
  BioSocieties 8(3): 311-335. https://doi.org/10.1057/bio
  soc.2013.13
Berlin, I. (1995 [1939]) Karl Marx, 4th edn. London: Fontana Press.
Fleming, P. (2021) Dark Academia: How Universities Die.
  London: Pluto Press.
Graeber, D. (2014) What's the Point if We Can't Have Fun? The
  Baffler 24. Available at: https://thebaffler.com/salvos/whats-
  the-point-if-we-cant-have-fun [Accessed 29 October 2024].
Graeber, D. (2015) The Utopia of Rules. London: Penguin
  Random House.
Hackett, E.J. (2014) Academic Capitalism. Science, Technology,
  & Human Values 39(5): 635-638.
Hebdige, D. (1979) Subculture: The Meaning of Style.
  London: Routledge.
Lerner, B. (2004) Leaving the Atocha Station. London: Granta
  Publications.
Lynch, M. (2000) Against Reflexivity as an Academic Virtue and
  Source of Privileged Knowledge. Theory, Culture & Society
  17(3): 26-54.
Lynch, M. (2009) Science as a Vacation: Deficits, Surfeits,
  PUSS, and Doing Your Own Job. Organization 16(1): 101-119.
McHardy, J. (2017) Like Cream: Valuing the Invaluable.
  Engaging Science, Technology and Society 3: 73-83.
```

Michael, M. (2012) De-signing the Object of Sociology: Toward an 'Idiotic' Methodology. *The Sociological Review* 60(S1): 166–183.

Phipps, A. and McDonnell, L. (2022) On (Not) Being the Master's Tools: Five Years of 'Changing University Cultures'. *Gender and Education* 34(5): 512–528.

Polanyi, K. (2001 [1944]) *The Great Transformation: The Political and Economic Origins of Our Time*. Boston: Beacon Press.

Stengers, I. (2005) The Cosmopolitical Proposal. In B. Latour and P. Weibel (eds) *Making Things Public*. Cambridge, MA: MIT Press, pp 994–1003.

Stengers, I. (2011) 'Another Science is Possible!': A Please for Slow Science. *Three Rotten Potatoes*. Available at: https://threerottenpotatoes.files.wordpress.com/2011/06/stengers2011_pleaslowscience.pdf [Accessed 29 October 2024].

Stengers, I. (2018) *Another Science Is Possible: A Manifesto for Slow Science*, translated by S. Muecke. Cambridge: Polity Press.

Wayne, T. and Lerner B. (2017) Interview with Ben Lerner, author of *Leaving the Atocha Station. Huffpost*, 6 December. Available at: https://www.huffpost.com/entry/interview-with-ben-lerner_b_935171 [Accessed 29 October 2024].

Whitehead, A.N. (1938) *Modes of Thought*. New York: The Free Press.

Wynne, B. (1993) Public Uptake of Science: A Case for Institutional Reflexivity. *Public Understanding of Science* 4(2): 321–337.

Wynne, B. (2007) Dazzled by the Mirage of Influence? STS-SSK in Multivalent Registers of Relevance. *Science Technology & Human Values* 32(4): 491–503.

# On 4 May 2023, Reuben Message wrote:

Hi both,

Thanks Jane, just a quick one on form and practicalities before submission re: Vienna.

I know it's crazy at the moment what with submission on the EoI for other grant due tomorrow, Rob being away, and both of you flying to the US at different times over the weekend ...♥ I'm

---

♥ Around this time, a ~£73 million funding call for projects in synthetic biology was announced. This was a major event for us as researchers studying the field, and it precipitated an intense period of work in which we were collectively involved in no fewer than five simultaneous grant applications with collaborating synthetic biologists – amongst a number of other things, including a multi-week work trip to the United States for RS and JC.

also concerned about working on Monday as the kids are off (again!) for the Coronation celebrations this time …

But:

Jane, it would be fantastic if you could pull the email chain together so we can maintain the same basic 'form' as last time out (your email software does it best!).

Rob, it would be great if you could send in something about your vignettes before D-day for this, but we of course understand given the circumstances if you can't.

I'll send the bibliography as the very last email …

R

## On 3 May 2023, Jane Calvert wrote:

Hi Reuben and Rob,

Thanks for the message Reuben. Starting with the point about the form for the draft paper, I'm thinking we should just send this email exchange as it is, ending on the references and get feedback on it. Of course, it will need some editing – cutting out some sentences like this, perhaps? (Or perhaps not?) But I think we should stick to the constraints of the email exchange form (creativity needs constraints!)

Email is not very Dark Academia[*] of course – it's too speedy and modern! Maybe we should be posting each other hand-written letters? I must admit I would struggle with that. I can barely write by hand anymore and I personally don't embrace the moleskin-notebooks-and-fountain-pens-that-leak-vibe. I only own the cheapest biros and write on random bits of paper. As you know, there's also something that irritates me about the nostalgia of Dark Academia. I realize I do work in an ancient university, but my formative years were spent in the 'modern' 1960s University of Sussex. But do I think there's something in what you said about the fountain pen as a way of literally slowing you down that might help connect Dark Academia to reflexivity.

---

[*] 'Dark Academia' is, according to Wikipedia 'an internet aesthetic and subculture concerned with higher education, the arts, and literature, or an idealised version thereof. The aesthetic centres on traditional educational clothing, interior design, activities such as writing and poetry, ancient art, classic literature, as well as classical Greek and Collegiate Gothic architecture. The trend emerged on social media site Tumblr in 2015, before being popularised by adolescents and young adults in the late 2010s and early 2020s, particularly during the COVID-19 pandemic'. See https://en.wikipedia.org/wiki/Dark_academia

It relates to Stengers' idea of the idiot, which Mike Michael (2012) has taken up in his discussions of speculative design and STS methodology. According to Stengers (2005, 994) the idiot is a figure that 'resists the consensual way in which the situation is presented' by forcing us to slow down and to take time to question our assumptions (and I think questioning our assumptions is central to reflexivity). Michael argues that speculative designers can produce 'idiotic' artefacts, material things that can make us stumble, pause and question. Perhaps the fountain pen could be thought of as idiotic in this sense? Perhaps we can draw on Dark Academia as an inspiration for introducing other idiotic 'technologies' for slowing down, like particularly cumbersome brogues that make the wearer walk more slowly, for example? This resonates with what you said about appreciating the material qualities of your notebook and pen, because idiotic design draws attention to the corporal, sensory and affective qualities of things.

I realize this is all quite playful, but I do think that play is important (and is connected to attempts to find pleasure and joy in academic work). Graeber's (2014) written a piece 'What's the Point if We Can't Have Fun?' which argues for 'a principle of ludic freedom', because he argues that play allows us to 'unthink the world around us'. This obviously connects back to the things I said in my last email about leisure and laziness, and the importance of some kind of temporary release – a 'vacation' – from the time pressures of academia. (This has now taken on an added layer of significance since I will be officially on vacation during the workshop in Vienna, so that I can get paid a full salary for some of those days while I am participating in the marking boycott.)

This is all skirting around the topic of reflexivity, which you asked about directly, so I'll try to say something coherent about that. I suppose I'd like to think that Wynne's (1993) form of reflexivity *does* lead us to the picket line, because reflexivity helps us see that those things we thought were necessary are actually contingent, and can be changed. And that this can be a motivation for action. Lynch (2000), however, in his somewhat provocatively titled paper 'Against Reflexivity as an Academic Virtue and Source of Privileged Knowledge' disagrees with this. He shows that reflexivity can be, and has been, defined in many different ways. He is suspicious of those who see it as a source of 'insight or revelation', because he thinks it is just an 'ordinary' part of everyday life. I agree with Lynch that reflexivity is everywhere. In fact I think the synthetic biologists we work with demonstrate their reflexivity on a regular basis. I also agree with Lynch that what follows from this is that we shouldn't see ourselves as the bringers of reflexive enlightenment to the poor misguided scientists. But I think if we get rid of this problematic one-sided interpretation of reflexivity and see it instead as something everyone brings (because we all challenge each other's assumptions) then it can take us in new (political?) directions.

Sorry if this is a bit gestural. This email is already longer than I intended it to be, and I also wanted to say something about the university, the future and hope. To put it too briefly, I find myself wanting to bring together the idea that 'The task of a university is the creation of the future' (Whitehead 1938) and my conviction that you don't strike without hope. This brings me back to possibility, which is a concept I keep returning to.

OK, I will leave it there for now and hope that Rob is able to reply with some semi-conclusive thoughts that will allow us to submit something coherent on Monday!

Jane

## On 25 April 2023, 09:27, Reuben Message wrote:

Hi Jane and Rob,

Thanks for your most recent Jane, it contains an awful lot. … It's hard to know where to begin!

I have an immediately relevant question connected to the coherence issue: what form do we expect our draft to take?

I do think we need to consider whether this will work for the final draft. I guess I imagined that for practical reasons we'd eventually break with the email form and divide the paper into three sections, of which we each take control of one. And then we top-and-tail these with an intro/programmatic bit and a concluding discussion. But this would efface somewhat the epistolary genesis of the paper thus far – and I don't like that!

In regard to the dilemma about action and reflexivity. How I read what you're saying Jane is that we should not be forced into a straight choice between reflexivity (defined along the lines suggested by Wynne) and the picket line. (Maybe the picket line is in some sense dependent on reflexivity, like maybe reflexivity is an essential part of deciding what is actually worth picketing about, and assessing the appropriateness of the means adopted in respect of the ends thus divined?)

Anyway, I'd be appreciative if you did write more theoretically on reflexivity for this paper since this would certainly help fix a defect in my own intended contribution, which I feel fitted well with the 'liveable worlds' theme, but without saying all that much relevant to reflexivity. I too find Wynne's definition appealing, but unclear how I'd relate it to Dark Academia!

But there was one way, which I mentioned before, in which I might consider making my discussion at least more 'personal' and reflective (if not exactly 'reflexive'). This is a vignette about stationery, specifically my fountain pen.

I've been using a fountain pen for about two or so years, since around the height of the pandemic I think. My partner bought one for me from an online, Edinburgh-based shop named *Bibliotheca & Annals*. She bought a couple for herself at the same time, as well as a range of inks and notebooks. I didn't think much of it at the time, though I've become attached to using the pen, despite running out of ink occasionally and regularly have stains on my fingers.

But one day, not long ago, I had a conversation with a research participant. In her mid-twenties, a biologist. We were busy signing a confidentiality form prior to a research interview. She commented on my using a fountain pen, and we laughed about some ink on my fingers. I joked that apparently they were fashionable again in the Dark Academia trend. She knew exactly what I was talking about and, laughing, 'oh yes, of course, they're so Dark Academia!' In saying this, she suggested I was a part of the trend.

Of course, we all a part of fashions all the time, consciously or not. And enjoyment of fountain pens long precedes the trend. This is not really the point. But the exchange got me thinking about stationery as an element in the style and experience of Dark Academia. Calligraphy certainly is a well-remarked element of the style. The deliberate anachronism of the fountain pen, the way it can literally slow you down when you write. … Combined with a high-quality notebook – a Moleskin(e)®, for instance – there is a satisfaction to this that I think many can relate to. What is the experience that this is connecting us too? In our digital world, dominated by convenience and speed, there is something stubbornly analogue about it. It cannot be easily or rapidly converted into something digital, something searchable. There are obvious disadvantages to this material system; it is differently functional. Nostalgic too perhaps, like collecting LPs or cassettes.[*]

Sure, there are elements here of 'meaningful' consumption, subcultural 'distinction' (borrowing from Hebdige's famous essay [see Hebdige 1979]), a concern with how we choose to spend communicates selected aspects of our identity to others and so on. But is there also a subjective, phenomenological experience of using these kinds of stationery solutions that is relevant here too?

So, I'm wondering whether as a way of bringing some focused kind of empirical content to my discussion of Dark Academia, I might write about this?

I also looked at the website of the shop *Bibliotheca & Annals*. It is totally Dark Academia, riding a wave, and very appropriate to literary-historical Edinburgh. It remains online only, any plans to create a physical shop shelved for now by the pandemic. Maybe it's a crazy idea, but I was thinking of reaching out to its owner for conversation about the meaning of stationery today. … Who would have a better grasp of it and its meaning for consumers? She always writes beautiful hand-written notes thanking us every time we order something from her. … This would also respond in a way to the 'data' anxiety. What do you think?

R

(RIP career I guess – he arrives intending to advance the theory and practice of RRI in relation to the development of cell and gene therapy applications, and ends up writing personal musings about stationery! How did it come to this?:):)

## On 24 April 2023, Jane Calvert wrote:

Hi Reuben and Rob,

Thanks for your thought-provoking messages! I'm sorry my message is late (again). I'm going to start with four anxieties.

Anxiety 1: Time. Obviously, time to write this paper is running out. This is a reflexive (or maybe ironic) point, since one of the things we're interested in is time in academia and

---

[*] Connections to Erika Szymanski's contribution (Chapter 16, this volume) are obvious here, especially in terms of how the different technologies that mediate our contributions embed their own temporalities. This subject may be worth further reflecting in the context of Making Liveable (STS) Worlds.

how it's necessary to make/take time to build more liveable worlds. More prosaically, it's Saturday, and because I am so late doing this I would like to send on my email as soon as I've written it, but then I would pass an obligation on to you on a weekend, which is not good collegial behaviour. (This also relates to the form we've chosen to write in, and the immediacy of receiving an email that seems to demand a response.)

Anxiety 2: Coherence. Will a paper written as a series of email exchanges come together in any coherent form? I'm not sure. But I'm also enjoying the form! Epistolary writing has its benefits. Addressing writing to a reader who will read the text soon (and is obliged to reply) is quite motivating (although I do find myself writing in a not-entirely-academic manner). I will just 'embrace the chaos' as Reuben put it in one of our chats.

Anxiety 3: 'Data' (in scare quotes). What is the data on which this paper is drawing? Do we have any data? Does it matter if we don't? Rob suggested we think in terms of vignettes (and I'll try a few of these here). Or are we writing a 'theory' paper? (I am interested in 'theoretical' questions around reflexivity and possibility, which I'll get on to in a bit.) Or are we doing something else?

Anxiety 4: Money. As you know, the current stage of industrial action of the UK's University and College Union is involved in is a marking and assessment boycott. Edinburgh University has decided that anyone who participates in the boycott will take a 50 per cent pay cut for the duration. Although it could be worse – some universities are cutting pay by 100 per cent – I'm worried about this, and I'm in a permanent professorial post. I'm even more worried about anyone who is in a less privileged position than me. Maybe it's deeply inappropriate to talk about money, but I feel it's wrapped up with our other concerns in this paper.

This leads on to my first vignette (although I must admit I'm not entirely sure what 'counts' as a vignette).

When I got the email about the 50 per cent pay deduction on Tuesday I felt like I had been hit in the chest. I was surprised that it had such a physical effect on me. I think it did because of the blatancy of being actively and disproportionately punished by my employer, who could so easily calculate the value of my work. I think that like many academics I have an affective connection to my labour, tied up with the idea of a vocation (which may be a fantasy, like Dark Academia?). This is why striking can be painful. But the point of this vignette is different. One of the interesting features of industrial action is that it crosses the whole university – the scientists and engineers I 'study' are part of it too (well, those who are in the union). This troubles further the already troubled distinction between research 'subjects' and 'objects'. When exchanging pleasantries with one of 'my' synthetic biologists after their bi-weekly seminar on Thursday I mentioned my concerns with the punitive boycott deductions. He instantly suggested we step outside the seminar room to more neutral ground outdoors in the spring sunshine where he explained to me several strategies that can be used to mitigate the impact of the pay cuts. Our collective action became far more important than our disciplinary differences.

An important thing about collective action is that it is action, not theory. Although of course the theory/action distinction is blurred – as Reuben says, Marx was a pretty influential theorist. It's significant that the call for papers for this workshop asks: 'How can reflexivity be translated into practice? How can it move beyond mere theoretical deliberations and commitments?' This brings me to an issue that I want to think about more, which is whether reflexivity can help us build better worlds. In other words, does reflexivity get us to political action? Or should we just cut to the chase and engage directly in political action (or industrial action)? (Lynch, in his paper on reflexivity argues the latter [see Lynch 2000].)

As Rob pointed out in one of our discussions, what reflexive STS methods do very well is expose assumptions. This comes out in Wynne's (1993, 324) definition of reflexivity as 'the process of identifying, and critically examining (and thus rendering open to change), the basic, pre-analytic assumptions that frame knowledge-commitments'. I like this definition and use it a lot, and I think it's the 'thus rendering open to change' part of the sentence that is really important; once we see that things can be different, we can see that they can be changed. But changed in what way?

I had dinner with Brian Wynne on Wednesday night (is this a vignette? It's definitely name-dropping), and he did maintain that reflexivity is important, and political, but he said that it is not directional. I should have asked him what he meant by 'political', because in retrospect I'm not sure. I found the Ben Lerner interview that Rob sent useful for thinking through these issues. I love what Lerner says about how poetry can 'gesture towards something beyond the tyranny of the real, our status quo'. And he does go on to say that 'I do consider this political, although not to be confused with direct political action'. He seems to be talking about the 'political' in the same way as Wynne. Perhaps this work of 'excavating alternatives' (as Rob puts it) and showing possibility can be more profound than the activist politics of the picket line? Perhaps this is what we can contribute as STS researchers? Wynne (2007, 500) says that the 'confrontation of culturally entrained taken-for-granteds' is something STS is particularly well placed to do.

This is why I think we need to think more about possibility, perhaps even instead of reflexivity. There's that David Graeber (2015, 89) quote that we keep going back to: 'The ultimate hidden truth of the world is that it is something we make. And could just as easily make differently.' I find this liberating, but as the industrial action shows, I think it is *hard* to make the world differently. Perhaps foregrounding non-obvious possibilities that are already happening, as Rob recommends, is a better starting point? Along these lines, Phipps and McDonnell (2022, 524) have an excellent paper on the difficulties of creating alternatives within the neoliberal university. They suggest 'the formation of small, self-organised groups of staff and students who imagine new ways of relating and solving problems together', which is perhaps what you were thinking of Rob? But they also stress that this requires institutional resources such as money, space and time.

This takes me back to my first anxiety, and Reuben's points about the necessity of taking time, which I completely agree with. (Apparently Wittgenstein recommended that philosophers should greet each other with the phrase 'Take your time'.) I think we need freedom from time pressures to be able to imagine how things could be different. (And maybe the escapism of Dark Academia is part of this?) This reminds me of Lynch's (2009) paper on science as a vacation, arguing that it is leisure time that 'gives rise to non-standard modes of interpretation and criticism' (Lynch 2009, 106), and McHardy's (2017, 81) point that 'any form of creative expression requires laziness'. I think your grandfather would agree with all of this Reuben! Although a danger of foregrounding leisure and laziness is that this can distract us from the point that slowing down in academia can be a political act, 'a form of resistance to extant pressures shared across the natural and social sciences' (Balmer and Bulpin's 2013, 331). I must admit I'm not entirely sure how we go about slowing down, though. Maybe a fishing trip?

Jane

# On 18 April 2023, 14:12, Reuben Message wrote:

Hi,

Rob, what you suggest about poetry and political action reminded me of Isaiah Berlin's famous remark about the irony of Marx's work (and life). 'It [his work] set out to refute the proposition that ideas decisively determine the course of history, but the very extent of its own influence on human affairs has weakened the force of its thesis' (Berlin 1995 [1939], 208) The quote goes on, but the point is that for a man who did nothing but sit in a library and write about how little ideas matter, his ideas were pretty influential!

I'm not sure that Dark Academia represents an alternative to political action and critique. For reasons we've discussed – it's escapist and elitist, and seems to call for a disengagement with the demands of society in the way it romanticizes the Ivory Tower. I think this is an unviable (and unrealistic) alternative to the temporalities demanded by the world. In this respect I think some of Stengers' (2018) critique of the Slow Science movement could be applied to Dark Academia. This said, individual works of literature that engage with tropes of the genre may well be sources of deep insight into the contemporary malaise, in the same way that science fiction, despite its obvious unreality, has often been a site of profound thinking about present-day political realities and alternatives.

So I think what we mean when we say 'Dark Academia' is no alternative is that swanning around acting out a fantasy life of a student in a 1930s Ivy League University, adopting the dress, indulging in psychologically intense quasi-intellectual inter-personal relationships and all the rest of it, as a way of life, is not an alternative, for us at least (and I suspect no one). This said, I still do not wish to snobbishly dismiss the possibility that Dark Academia practices and aesthetics could represent fleeting moments of succour that help make living an actual university life liveable for some – escapism has its place, surely? Maybe that's an empirical question though. Who wants to set themselves up as judge?

I was really intrigued to ask though what it was you thought Ben Lerner's book represented in terms of an alternative? Speculatively, is it the life choices of the protagonist? Take grant money and doing something quite different to what you promised to do with it …? I think there are really interesting questions to explore here about the conflict between the morality/moral expectations encoded into this kind of economic arrangement and the morality of slowing down and resisting the transformation of moral existence into mere reflex, mechanism, measurement and 'accountability'.

I think when we were talking I mentioned the story about my grandfather who went on sabbatical, ostensibly to perform philosophical research and write, but instead reported to his colleagues that he simply 'went fishing' that year. I'm sure he loved the shock value of this. But I'm also very sure he felt his fishing activities were philosophically meaningful, much more so than stringing words together in a text in a way that would make it likely a colleague would cite him, much more so than 'contributing to the development of the field', or any such petty thing.

I'm sure he'd say he was thinking during this time – as he was when he cooked, climbed mountains, botanized and enjoyed his garden – and who is to say where thought will take us? Was he wracked with guilt, like Lerner's protagonist? I don't know. I know that I essentially composed this email while walking to a nearby coffee shop: I took the time away from my desk and it helped to order my thoughts.

I'm concerned that I'm sounding very conventional now, but it seems to me that 'taking time' in this kind of modest way is seriously important to making a life in research not simply liveable but intellectually possible.

R

## On 17 April 2023, Rob Smith wrote:

Hola,

I'm experimenting with time-blocking to write this email. Have you heard of this? Apparently it's a thing.

As I've just come back from Uganda, I've been thinking a bit about how time there is different to time here. I guess ideal university-time wouldn't completely be Ugandan time – it's all a bit chaotic there – but they do seem to have some kind of focus on relationships and 'just talking' rather than the managerial time we seem to live in in the UK. When I was in Kampala last month, the dean of the faculty of social sciences seemed to just be walking around talking to people openly. He was just wandering around in the sun, striking up conversation with people in the faculty. I've got more quips about all that, but the thing I wanted to add to the pile is this:

A couple of weeks ago I read a book called *Leaving the Atocha Station* (Lerner 2004). It was recommended to me by a random person I met climbing. Basically the plot of the book is that a middle-class American wins a 'prestigious fellowship' to travel to Madrid, research the Civil War and write critical poetry using the archival material he finds there. Instead of doing that, he spends his time smoking weed and wandering around Madrid on his own until he finds a group of people to make friends with. A lot of the book is about how he just feels guilty, anxious and a fraud (he has panic attacks about all this). Anyway, when I read it, I couldn't help but feel like it's a better – more realistic? more STSy? – reading of time, reflexivity and liveability than Dark Academia. It's not some utopic Oxbridge pastiche being projected; it's something really conflicted but also obviously full of time (because he's got time to smoke weed and hang out for a year). Oh also it's quasi-autobiographical.

The other thing that made me think is there's this theme about critique and political action. So the book is set around the 2004(?) Atocha bombings. After the bombings there was a lot of political protest because the government tried to blame ETA for them; it turned out to be Al Qaeda. His argument for the poetry he doesn't write in the fellowship app is the classic tradition of critique one – by excavating alternatives we can imagine new worlds. But the main character wrestles with this throughout; it's the protests in response to the Atocha bombings that bring a new world into being, not his unwritten poetry.

Ok finally, I also found an interview with Ben Lerner (https://www.huffpost.com/entry/interview-with-ben-lerner_b_935171), the author, that's maybe the most useful thing (see below). Basically he seems to be saying that maybe poetry can't do the political action thing and to try and do that would always be a failing project. Instead it can do something else (show possibility). I'm not sure whether or how this applies to reflexive methods but I'm kind of drawn to it.

Anyway, I'll try and be more productive next time (and reply to the digital scab stuff) …

rob

~ ~ ~

Excerpts from interview with Ben Lerner, author of *Leaving the Atocha Station*, HuffPost Entertainment

>If I write a poem that arises out of the desire to, say, abolish our corporatist oligarchy, I know the poem is going to fail to effect that change. If the poem had the

power to achieve such a thing it would cease to be art altogether and become historical intervention (which is a traditional avant-garde fantasy). But even if the poem is doomed to stop short of achieving what it sets out to do, it can nevertheless gesture towards something beyond the tyranny of the real, our status quo. And I do consider this political, although not to be confused with direct political action.

> Poetry can make us aware of our capacity to think and feel beyond the merely actual, but it doesn't provide a blueprint for revolution or environmental stewardship or what have you. People who go around celebrating or lamenting the 'death of poetry' are often really talking about the demise of our capacity to desire alternatives in general, to imagine some other organization of our societal forces, or at least to imagine imagining it instead of just surrendering to the world we've made as if it were a natural, timeless order.

## On 14 April 2023, Jane Calvert wrote:

Just replying (late) and guiltily to this. Feel like I should include at least *some* content. Hmmm, how about: what would happen to time pressures in the ideal university?
Jane

## On 5 April 2023, 17:21, Rob Smith wrote:

Hi both,
   More serious follow up: I think that there's a university policy that we have to reply to student emails within 36–48 hours of receiving the email. Unless we have some rules we're probably not going to get to a finished paper by doing the email thing, so perhaps we should give ourselves a 48-hour turnaround rule to reply to the last email in this thread?
   Rob

## On 5 April 2023, 16:14, Rob Smith wrote:

Hiya,
Sorry I've been so terrible at replying to this. It's all been really busy since we've been off strike.
   Rob

## On 21 March 2023, Reuben Message wrote:

Hello both,

The tiler working in our bathroom accused me of 'digital scabbing' yesterday when he saw me on my computer, so I don't feel bad about writing to you guys on a strike day now because I've got nowhere lower to fall.

I'm thinking a bit about Liveable Worlds and how we need to find a way of keeping the ideas-ball rolling on it.

In terms of the Dark Academia theme, I've mulling over a few issues that it would be great to air in dialogue with you both. These involve, among other things, an empirical consideration of the consolations of stationery (Moleskine notebooks, fountain pens, etc).

For the moment I wondered if you thought it was a good idea for me to explicitly position myself/my contribution to the discourse on Dark Academia as outside of the lit. crit. universe? Sure, I will try to listen to some audio books in the genre, inc., Donna Tartt's *The Secret History* – supposedly the Bible of the genre. Plus, I'll watch some more recent things that have been absorbed into the Dark Academia standard, for example, *The Goldfinch*, Mary Shelley, Tolkien, *The Queen's Gambit* (more suggestions welcome). But the point, maybe, is the existence of the phenomena itself, not any detailed critique of the frankly bewilderingly array of texts people say exemplify it. While I'm not anti it per se, I just don't see my work here in terms of performing close readings of texts, be these books, films or internet-based fashion trends. Absent close or detailed analysis of Dark Academia texts however, I'm not yet sure what kind of material I might use to base my argument on. This is perhaps where a somewhat phenomenological account of the stationery aspect comes in … But more on that another time.

I've found it really generative to think about this stuff with you both, so please feel free to respond with your thoughts on this, or just what it sparks off for you when you're thinking about the theme of Liveable Worlds.

Best,

R


## On 20 February 2023, Jane Calvert wrote:

I think I can see how this could come together. Our paper could be an email exchange? Although the reader would have to start at the bottom of the document … maybe that would be too irritating? I'll try to reply properly soon.

Jane

## On 20 February 2023, Rob Smith wrote:

Part of me is thinking we should set a rule of writing only through email (as a way of resuscitating the joy of correspondence, which is also kind of performing Dark Academia?) on strike days …

Ha!

Rob

## On 17 February 2023, Reuben Message wrote:

Rob I rather like the focus on those personal, emotional moments … I'm sure we can dig up some literature on the 'hacks' and 'ways of coping' in academia that may be useful in terms of giving those ideas some conceptual ballast, or at least as something to bounce off?

I was thinking that perhaps my take on Dark Academia is not totally off the mark for this paper? It does have something to do with making liveable worlds.

Dark Academia is the name of a recent book that concerns the connection between changes in the higher education sector over the last two decades and the 'psychological hell endured by staff and students' today (Fleming 2021). Dark Academia is also, according to Wikipedia, an 'internet aesthetic' that has burgeoned within the last decade, and especially since COVID. Characterized by clothing styles reminiscent of the 1930s, an obsession with Gothic architecture, museums and libraries, cups of tea on rainy evenings, and an altogether brooding yet also cosy sense of melancholia. Highly Instagrammable: Dark Academia can surely be read as a response to changes in the experience and meaning of university. Emerging at a time when it is often easier for students to 'access' a 'free' mindfulness seminar than an unsupervised conversation with a professor, it idealizes a time before providing services to chronically indebted students became the core activity of university bureaucracies. It fetishizes Thinking and Learning through an historical aesthetic that pays homage to an idea of the university as the home of scholarship, precisely at a time when, many feel, the joy of discovery has been rendered unavailable as an experience. While romanticizing an experience of the university that, if it ever existed, existed only for a privileged few, Dark Academia's anachronism projects the simulacrum of another university with a different temporality. In other words, it is culturally intelligible precisely because of the stark reality of the contemporary university experience. Can we pursue an interpretation of this phenomenon as more than warped nostalgia and escapism but also as a psychologically-rooted form of 'protective response' (cf Polanyi 2001 [1944]) against the harder edges of academic capitalism (Hackett 2014)?

Let me know what you think and how we might incorporate something on DA as a section of a prospective paper? Maybe a sort of framing device?

R

## On 16 February 2023, Rob Smith wrote:

Writing this while eating a plate of kale and halloumi so it probs needs a bit more chewing …

The phrase 'another *currently problematic object* is possible' invites us to speculate, to imagine and then to build (?) a different world. But it can also be an invitation to excavate and foreground non-obvious possibilities that are already happening.

I actually think the way we've worked in our two big research projects might have some of those non-obvious possibilities in it. For example: When I think about some of the ethnographic work I've done with synthetic biologists, the things that stick out are the weirdly emotive moments — hugging an iGEM student who was stressed out because they'd been locked in a hotel room practising their presentation for two days; turning to my left and seeing Elsa crying to an indigenous speaker's keynote. I don't think this is just about me doing the emotional labour for synthetic biologists — I've got similar memories of our own interactions as a group of STS researchers … waiting upstairs at the 'End of Synthetic Biology' workshop with B, then suffering from chronic fatigue, horizontal on the top floor of a tapestry museum trying to get the energy to run the final plenary. Or I could point to the ways that we, as a group, have used small, nominally insignificant pots of money won through consultancy projects to give Siphiwe, Callum, Ann, Joe and Nina — researchers just out of their PhDs — some semblance (although maybe it's an illusion?) of job security.

I'm not really sure how to analyse these things, and to be honest I'm not sure how far ideas like reflexivity or complicity get us in doing so. The obvious way of making sense of it is probably to roll out one of those clichéd Tsing quotes – something about living in capitalist ruins? But that feels unsatisfactory too. Anyway, I think these are ways that we've tried to make universities liveable. I guess the rub is that they've depended on taking lots of money from synthetic biology grants, or ERC projects …

I'll go and update my out of office now. More ambiguity means I can pretend I'm on strike whenever I want, not that it stops us working (evidently).

Rob

## On 15 February 2023, Jane Calvert wrote:

Hi Reuben (cc Rob),

Sorry for emailing on a strike day. Just to say that Rob and I are playing around with ideas of an abstract on 'Another university is possible', or 'Making liveable worlds in the university'.

To explain: I was at a teach-out on the picket line yesterday. The familiar phrase 'another university is possible' made an appearance (someone even chalked it on the side of the building). But it only resonated (and then reverberated) with me when I got Rob's out-of-office, who ended his email with that phrase. A moment of revelation! The university is the world we are currently trying to make liveable by our action.

Can STS help us build another university? What do reflexivity and care do in this context? Is it caring to no longer teach our students? If 'reflexivity enables us to contribute to worlds we perceive as desirable' (call for papers for this workshop) how can reflexivity help us on the cold picket line? (As our local UCU branch reminded us last week 'The main risk during this strike is hypothermia…')

What happens to the relationship between research subjects and objects when we are all on strike? And how can we retain the joy and pleasure of academic work when we are resisting overwork, underpay and precarity?

I am also drawn to the idea of possibility – perhaps it's more helpful than reflexivity here? Stengers (2011) says that possibility 'calls for imaginative engagement instead of submission to the given definition of a state of affairs'. But possibility is hard. We need others to help us ask what another university would look like. (Sometimes it's a relief to be reminded of the STS point that all knowledge is social.)

Sorry this is brief. I've been writing it in guilty moments when I shouldn't have been working (although according to the employers I should!)

Jane

## On 14 February 2023, Rob Smith wrote:

Yes! See what Reuben thinks?

Rob

## On 14 February 2023, Jane Calvert wrote:

> Another university is possible …

Yes! Brainwave: this is what we should do our Vienna abstract about! Drawing on the resources of STS (reflexivity, and so on) to differentiate it from other discussions of the topic. Strong connections to Stengers of course (and the whole idea of possibility), also links to otherwising.

What do you think?

Jane

## On 14 February 2023, Rob Smith wrote:

Subject: Automatic reply

18 national strike days have been called by the Universities and Colleges Union in February and March. This is because of a long running dispute over pay, pensions and the extensive use of short, fixed term contracts in the sector.

Sorry for the resulting delay in getting back to you – I will prioritize urgent stuff. If you'd like to learn more you can do so here: https://www.ucu.org.uk/

Another university is possible …

Rob

## On 14 February 2023, Jane Calvert wrote:

Subject: Automatic reply

I am currently taking part in the University and College Union's (UCU) strike action. I am striking over pay, equality, excessive workloads and casualization, and against pension

cuts. Over 70,000 university staff at 150 universities
are participating in these strikes. For more information
see: https://www.ucu.org.uk/rising
  Best wishes,
  Jane

## Funding

This work was supported by the Biotechnology and Biological Sciences Research Council, grant number BB/W014610/1 and Economic and Social Science Research Council, grant number ES/V002600/1.

4

# Is My Work Reflexive Enough?

*Anne Beaulieu*

Source: Graphic in collaboration with https://www.irrlicht-impressions.com

PART II

# Affecting

# Bodies

5

# Learning to Affect and to be Affected: Articulating Self and World in Empirical Research

Michael Penkler

## Introduction

Sometimes, interviews get the most interesting when the interviewer has said their ritual thank you and is ready to leave. Such was the case with an interview I conducted on how the informant deals with their bodyweight (see Penkler 2016). After I had packed up my recorder and notes, poised to get up, the interviewee asked, hesitantly: 'May I ask you a question, too?' 'Of course', I said. In fact, I had already asked her, like I habitually do at the end of every interview, if she would like to know more about my research. But instead, she asked: 'Don't you think that you yourself have a problem?' I did not quite understand, or perhaps I did not want to: 'What do you mean?' 'I'll rephrase that: Are you content with your own weight?' She was speaking about my own body. The researcher, the one who posed the questions, had become the questioned. I felt uncomfortable, and stammered a bit: 'Well, yes … well, sometimes people say that I could lose weight. … Do you think I have too much?' She answered quite firmly: 'Yes, for your age, I'd say so. But one also notices that you are self-content and confident. And that's the most important thing.'[1]

My interview partner's hesitation to ask me a personal question showed her appreciation of an implicit cultural script that governs how roles and authority are distributed in interviews (Atkinson and Silverman 1997; Callon and Rabeharisoa 2004). My participant entered a situation in which it was

---

[1]   The interview has been conducted in German. Translation by the author.

legitimate for me, as the interviewer, to pose intimate questions about her body – questions I would not ask strangers in other circumstances. The interview encounter follows an implicit script of sharing information that, as opposed to therapeutic conversations that may involve the shared elaboration of a common problem, is culturally framed as one-way. The interviewee asking me to explain myself for my body shape thus posed a breach of the implicit order of the interview, which was both visible in her hesitation and my feeling of unsettlement. I felt my 'academic armor' (Lerum 2001) weaken, as my position as an outside observer became unsettled and I became affectively drawn into the situation. My bodyweight, quite suddenly, became something I had to account for.

This instance and the awkwardness I experienced became a pivotal point, a revelatory moment in my research (see Trigger et al 2012; Schmidt et al 2023): it showed me how interviews are opportunities for telling 'moral stories' about one's body and self, and how I as a researcher am not simply observing but deeply implicated in these story-making practices. I started to realize that I myself, while conducting my research but also in everyday life, have been performing 'moral stories' surrounding my bodyweight (see Penkler 2016). My own implication in my research matter taught me new ways to approach it, but also changed how I myself related to my body in everyday life.

I want to take this instance from my research as a starting point to think about empirical research as a process in which the researcher becomes a sensory instrument to perceive and construct the phenomena of interest. As we conduct research, we not only engage with the world and develop an understanding of it, but also change in the process of doing so. In other words, we are acquiring novel capacities to affect and to be affected. We form new attachments as we make ourselves available to the world, allowing us to emerge as researcher subjects that are, in the words of Gomart and Hennion (1999, 220), 'never alone, never a pristine individual, but rather always entangled with and generously gifted by a collective, by objects, techniques, constraints'. Drawing on Science and Technology Studies (STS) theories of embodiment and attachment, I aim to develop in this chapter an account of empirical research as a process in which researcher subjects reshape the world and become reshaped at the same time. Crucially, this is a process in which bodies, becomings and 'affective entanglements' (Myers and Dumit 2011, 249) play a central role and in which novel forms of caring relations (to oneself, one's research subjects and the wider world) may emerge.

I will develop this argument by drawing on empirical findings from two research studies. The first study was my doctoral research project in which I investigated how bodies and selves are performed in bodyweight narratives (Penkler 2016). I conducted 21 qualitative interviews and six focus group discussions with a total of 48 participants to investigate how people perform themselves as certain kinds of subjects while working on and speaking about their bodyweight, hoping to get insights into how bodyweight is tied to subjectivity and why it becomes such a virulent and often problematic matter of concern in many lives. The second study was a postdoctoral research project on how metabolic diseases are increasingly researched as life-course disorders, and what the implications of these changing research assemblages are for how we understand and act upon non-communicable chronic disease in clinical practice, in health policy and in everyday life (Penkler 2022). I was conducting 3.5 months of full-time and 18 months of part-time ethnographic fieldwork with two European biomedical research groups, and I accompanied the researchers to international workshops and conferences. Fieldwork consisted of shadowing researchers, participating in research meetings and conducting a total of 28 formal and numerous informal interviews.

In what follows, I will juxtapose more theoretical accounts with 'autoethnographic vignettes' (Humphreys 2005) from my research, in which I reflexively trace the different ways in which I became affectively entangled in my own research. Through revisiting my own previous research (Vaughan 2004), I aim to contribute to a reflexive theorization of how we become subjects and build worlds in and through our qualitative research practices. I start with an autoethnographic account of my growing discomfort to discuss bodyweight in my private life while researching narratives on bodyweight.

## Researching bodyweight and researcher sensitivity

The instance from my doctoral research recounted earlier was unusual in how it breached the usual cultural script of interviews and reversed the familiar distribution of roles. It also put a spotlight on my growing discomfort to discuss issues of bodyweight in my day-to-day life. Knowing that I work on bodyweight, friends regularly began to talk to me about their struggles to stay thin or lose weight. 'It's like an inner terror', a friend once told me on a beautiful summer hike, and I remember the discomfort I felt when discussing what was my academic interest on such personal terms with somebody close to me. Then again, other friends did not want to hear too much about my research or about my own half autoethnographically inspired, half serious attempts at losing weight. A roommate told me: 'If people around me start occupying themselves more with their bodies, I myself begin to do so, too…' They said that if I wanted to try losing weight, it would be stupid not to, but that it still bothered them as they felt it also affected their relations to their own bodies.

It increasingly felt viscerally uncomfortable when people close to me discussed issues of bodyweight. I remember vividly one conversation with my parents. 'I've managed to lose two kilos', my father said, 'but your mother, we have to get her on track, she's letting herself go'. 'Don't tell me such things, dad!', I remember replying and asking myself a question that echoed my research interest but felt very personal at the moment: how can you let weight become such a focus in your life? Over the course of my research, I increasingly disliked when others alluded to my body and its shape: 'That's no good', my partner said one day when we were dressing, pointing to my belly, 'you eat too much!' 'Oh, come on', I remember replying, 'I'm writing my PhD on that, how can you …'. 'I know', they said, 'but what should I do, I don't feel comfortable when you are too fat'.

During my research, I had grown sensitive towards the topic, perhaps in a way that is painfully familiar for many growing up as girls (for example, Bordo 1993), but which was new to me in this intensity. And this new sensitivity was tied to the ways in which I started to theorize and make sense of the topic, as the relation of bodyweight to our sense of self and to one's status as a worthy subject became a central concern in my research. I increasingly became entangled in my own topic of research, as personal experiences, theoretical insights and affects became inseparably intertwined. In the next sections, I aim to develop a conceptual framework to make sense of my growing sensitivity towards the topic during my research.

## Mutual becoming: a conceptual framework, part I

STS offers a rich theoretical repertoire to make sense of how subjects develop novel capacities as they engage with the world, which allows us to develop an understanding of how researchers become affectively entangled in the topics of their research. In their 'sociology of attachment', Hennion and Gomart have proposed to extend Actor-Network Theory to a description of what they term 'subject-networks' – that is, the ways in which subjects emerge while engaging with the world (Gomart and Hennion 1999; Gomart 2004; Hennion 2007). According to Hennion and Gomart, subjects and bodies have no inherent capacities, but emerge as they enter a 'dispositif', that is, the 'objects, conditions and means through which entities in networks emerge' (Gomart and Hennion 1999, 245). Based on their own empirical research with drug users and musical amateurs, Gomart and Hennion show how the practice of experiencing in these two distinct empirical settings is tied to 'making oneself available' to the agency of heterogeneous materials. Music lovers and drug users alike prepare, arrange and condition all kinds of (material and non-material) entities for these entities in turn to act on them in a way that produces the desired experience and behaviour: a process Gomart and Hennion describe as 'faire-faire', as 'being left to and made to arrive' (1999, 222).

In this perspective, practices always require a variety of contributing agencies to be accomplished. Importantly, the subject is not privileged over other agencies, as it itself emerges within the process. This is a tentative process of experimental adaptations and realignments as drug users or musical amateurs learn to produce the effects and experiences that they desire, such as the enjoyment of music or drugs:

> Sportsmen, drug addicts, music lovers, disabled people only know one manner of proceeding: an obligatory pragmatism. Unable to judge their own action but from the effects produced, they are forced to collectively depart from the present state of bodies and things, operate by trial and error to facilitate displacement and to permit not a liberation, but partial substitutions. They live not a series of mastered choices flowing out of a world of stable objects, but a trajectory made up of withdrawals and retractions of the self, crafting little by little, experience after experience, bodies that are different. (Hennion 2010, 1, quoted in Danholt 2013, 378)

According to Danholt (2013, 376), practices are best understood as 'the continuous distribution and configuration of agency. ... All the different entities and actors in the process are occupied in assigning, forming and shaping the agency of others and themselves'. Important here is the stress on the word 'continuous': establishing a dispositif that produces the desired forms of agency, embodiment and subjectivity requires the patient rearrangement of the involved elements until an arrangement that 'works' is found. This is a process in which the materialities and resistances of the world need to be considered and enrolled (Callon 1986; Law 1992) and in which one must open up towards the action of the world that surrounds us (Gomart 2004). Such a theory replaces a focus on 'action' with a concern for 'emergence' (Gomart and Hennion 1999, 225), and necessarily troubles established dichotomies like 'agent/structure, subject/object, active/passive, free/determined' (Gomart and Hennion 1999, 220).

In their study of scientists working and playing with computerized visualizing techniques, Natasha Myers and Joe Dumit (2011) have encountered similar situations in which subjects and bodies are not exterior to the practices they engage in. They propose to engage with the concept of 'middle voice', a grammatical form now lost in most living languages, to describe how actors become 'themselves at stake' (2011, 249):

> This is where the subject is interior to and affected by the action being signified by the verb. The middle voice ... is sometimes assumed to be 'in between' the active and passive voices. ... The subject of the middle voice is affected by the verb, interested or invested in the process, and often transformed in the doing of it. ... The scientist conducting an experiment becomes scientist as she is 'reshaping and being reshaped' in the experiment. (Myers and Dumit 2011, 248)

Myers and Dumit describe situations in which scientists in order to be able to learn need to let themselves be changed in the process. These are situations in which one's own body and subjectivity become a crucial means for knowing the world, like, for example, visualization practices that require scientists to 'play' with the data through deploying their own body and immersing themselves in a virtual reality. But Myers and Dumit stress that this way of proceeding has more general implications beyond the highly specific practices they study. According to them, knowledge practices in general require the capacity to be moved by the world one encounters, and hence constitute processes of mutual becoming that result in novel forms of 'affective entanglements' (2011, 249).

Many researchers, especially those trained in a qualitative paradigm, will find that these descriptions of knowledge practices as processes of mutual becoming resemble their own experiences of designing and conducting empirical research. Introductory textbooks to qualitative research tend to stress the emergent and cyclical nature of qualitative research projects (for example, Charmaz 2006; Braun and Clarke 2013). For example, Kvale (2008, 19) describes qualitative research as a 'journey', where the researcher as 'traveler' ventures out to explore the world but is changed in the process. Scholars embarking on a research process often have only a preliminary grasp of what their research project will be about, and it is standard advice to encourage qualitative researchers to be prepared that their research questions will change throughout the research process (Agee 2009). Some approaches, like grounded theory (Strauss and Corbin 1998), encourage researchers to go into a field without a preformed research question, and stress that the topic of the research and the analysis emerges throughout the research process. In such descriptions, we do not encounter a researcher who gets to better know a reality exterior to them, but a researcher that is moved by the world they encounter as they make themselves available for new experiences.

This description resembles my own experiences in my study on bodyweight practices and narratives. As my research project developed, it changed in its focus. Through preparing and leading interviews and focus groups, analysing diet magazines and advertisements, through talking with others and reading and writing I developed new ways of seeing and approaching bodyweight as a personal, embodied and cultural phenomenon. These new sensibilities were not restricted to my role as an academic researcher but encompassed how I perceived myself and my body in everyday life: in a very real sense, I changed together with the analysis I was building and describing through my research.

And I was certainly not in the driver's seat, leading the process as an active subject that gets to know a passive world. Gomart and Hennion (1999) as well as Myers and Dumit (2011) make human action describable as the arrangement of entities that in turn make the human actor act in specific ways. That means, to act, one needs to be capable of being moved or affected by other entities. This, perhaps, is best described as a process of developing new sensitivities. According to Latour, this affectivity is not given, but something that needs to be learned. Turning to his theory of articulation next will allow me to further develop a conceptual repertoire for understanding how researchers emerge as subjects in the process of conducting their research.

## Becoming articulate: a conceptual framework, part II

In a 2004 paper, Bruno Latour proposed to view the body 'as an interface that becomes more and more describable as it learns to be affected by more and more elements' (Latour 2004, 206). His arguments allow us to further conceptualize how bodies and selves acquire novel capacities as they learn to be moved by other entities through the mediation of heterogeneous materials.

To explicate processes of 'learning to be affected', Latour introduces the example of the training of professionals – so-called 'noses' – in the perfume industry (Latour 2004). Instructed by a teacher, trainees learn with the help of an odour kit, a so-called 'malette à odeur', to differentiate between ever more subtle differences of scents where they could not make out any differences before. Acquiring novel capacities to smell means to be able to be affected – moved – in different ways by situations that formerly would have elicited the same response. Crucially, Latour describes this not as a process in which a subject gets to know a pre-established world better and better. One becomes more 'articulate', able to register more differences, at the same time as the world is articulated in novel ways:

> Through the training session, she learned to have a nose that allowed her to inhabit a (richly differentiated odoriferous) world. Thus, body parts are progressively acquired at the same times as 'world counter-parts' are being registered in a new way. Acquiring a body is thus a progressive enterprise that produces at once a sensory medium and a sensitive world. (Latour 2004, 207)

Both the subject and the world the subject inhabits are composed in a new way, giving form to differences and relations that have not been there before. Taste is not the passive discovery of qualities, but an active performance (Teil and Hennion 2004). In this process, mediations play a crucial role. In order to learn to be affected by ever more subtle differences of scents, the trainee requires among other things the material arrangement of smells in the odour kit, the classifications embedded in these arrangements, the words they learn to relate to the scents, and the instructions of the teacher. It is the engagement with heterogeneous materials – both material and discursive components (like classification systems and languages) – through which humans acquire a body to be able to perceive the world in more articulate ways (Latour 2004).

According to Latour, there is no essential difference between the trainee in a one-week training session and, say, the teacher who learns how best to teach the trainees, or the chemist who works in the lab in order to develop new scents: 'Each of these actors can be defined *as bodies learning to be affected by hitherto unregistrable differences through the mediation of an artificially created set-up*' (2004, 209; emphasis in original). For Latour, this is a general feature of (human) being in the world: we only acquire the capacity to differentiate and thus be affected by the world through the mediation of other entities.

The same is true for researchers, we might add. Consider coding, a common practice for analysing qualitative data (Charmaz 2006; Braun and Clarke 2022): while being confronted with pages and pages of manuscripts often seems daunting at first glance, a set of codified procedures, a specialized computer program with distinct applications, pens, markers, papers and the developing coding scheme and categories all help the researcher to do what is sometimes described as 'breaking up' the data (Charmaz 2006, 50): that is, becoming more sensitive towards differences and relations in the data that have not been there before. Heterogeneous materials, both material and discursive, play a central role here in developing novel capacities to affect and be affected. Especially the developing coding scheme, which grows more sophisticated and differentiated during the process as codes are grouped into categories and subcategories and further differentiated, plays an important role in making the researcher be sensitive to more and more nuances: the more developed the coding system is, the more one can see in one's data. This is not a process in which preformed categories are simply 'discovered' ('themes do not just "emerge"', as Braun and Clarke [2006, 96] proclaim), but an active process of articulating one's data, that means, imbuing it with meaning.

Becoming more sensitive to one's data is not only a process that is mediated by specific material set-ups through which the researcher develops new capacities to perceive and to act. It is also a profoundly embodied experience: as researchers grow more experienced, they also become more apt to register differences – they become more articulate as they develop the 'art of hearing data' (Rubin and Rubin 2012). In a sense, the researcher themselves, their capacity to register differences, to affect and to be affected, is the central instrument in qualitative research.

Autoethnographic research and other methods for strong reflexivity are built on this assumption: that the researcher's emotions and feelings – in all their ambiguity – can give insights into the phenomena of interest (see schut, Chapter 7 in this volume). In the process of conducting research, we become more sensitive and we learn to register differences where we were not previously able to do so. We become more articulate. This certainly was the case in my research: the unease I felt when being confronted with my own body shape, the way that my perception of my body changed, led me to important insights about how bodyweight is tied to how we relate to ourselves and others, and shaped the subsequent course of my research that focused on the relation of bodyweight, subjectivity and embodiment in contemporary late capitalist societies. Similarly, the ethnographic journey is about getting to know a certain field better and becoming more articulate, seeing and perceiving things you previously were not able to perceive. This is not simply a process of 'going native', but of articulating the field in specific ways by learning to be affected by more and more differences, and of changing in the process.

For Latour, there is no endpoint to this process of subjects becoming more articulate at the same time as the world is articulated in new ways. Being interested in the epistemological implications of his propositions, he argues that there is no point in which the world is adequately represented: 'The more contrasts you add, the more differences and mediations you become sensible to' (2004, 211). Equating the body with a progressive capacity to register differences also provides Latour with a normative criterion to evaluate different states of embodiment as increasing or decreasing the ability to affect and be affected. Echoing Deleuze and Guattari's definition of health as the 'capacity to form new relations' (Buchanan 1997, 82), Latour (2004) argues that the more differences a body can register, the more it is moved by the entities it encounters, the more alive it is: 'There is nothing especially interesting, deep, profound, worthwhile in a subject "by itself" … a subject only becomes interesting, deep, profound, worthwhile when it resonates with others, is affected, moved, put into motion by new entities whose differences are registered in new and unexpected ways' (Latour 2004, 210). This vitalist conception of health and of subjectivity, while being seductive, is also problematic. For one thing, it is important to point out that not all bodies are equally capable of becoming affected in the same way: Not everybody has a body to start with that carries the possibility of becoming a nose in the perfume industry, for instance. But seeing the capacity to affect and to be affected as something inherently positive also does not resonate with my research on and personal experiences with bodyweight. Remember the friend of mine who experienced the constant urge to occupy themselves with what and how much they eat as a form of 'inner terror'? For them, the capacity to be increasingly affected by food, sensing more and more differences, that is, becoming articulate, was a terrifying, not a liberating, proposition. Similarly, my heightened experience of my body and how people around me relate to it was also an unsettling experience. This unsettling experience manifested itself in seemingly paradoxical ways. On the one hand, I became more sensitive and anxious about my and others' bodies and how they are perceived and judged, and on the other hand I found myself trying to avoid the topic in everyday life. The more I worked on the topic, the more I also wanted to repress the ways it manifested in my own life.

It does not seem then, at least to me, that being articulate is always a good thing. On the contrary, this depends on the kinds of articulations – whether they are caring and nourishing, or not. In other words: If it is true that the researcher co-emerges with the world they describe, this raises questions about mutual care, to which I turn in the next section.

## Caring in and for research

It is common to feel overwhelmed by the field and all the things one sees and learns at the beginning of one's ethnographic journey. Excitement mixes with confusion about how to make sense of all the different impressions and how to relate this to the more or less specific research interest with which the researcher has approached the field. I certainly had these feelings when I embarked on another research project of mine – an ethnographic study of two biomedical research groups in the field of Developmental Origins of Health and Disease (DOHaD).

This interdisciplinary biomedical research field is based on the hypothesis that environmental experiences during the mother's pregnancy or the first years of life can influence the developing organism in ways that make it more or less likely to develop non-communicable disease, such as cardiovascular disease, diabetes or certain psychiatric disorders, in later life (Poston et al 2022). At least in theory, DOHaD considers a wide range of environments from the intrauterine environment to nutritional, chemical and stress exposures and wider social structures, and traces how these environments influence the development of health and disease over the entire life course. Compared to the size of the field, DOHaD research has received relatively broad interest in the social sciences and humanities (Pentecost et al 2024). A major reason for this is that it seems to offer what has been termed a 'biosocial' perspective on health: a perspective that allows for a greater appreciation of how social processes and structures shape biological processes, health and disease (Müller et al 2017; Penkler et al 2019). DOHaD has been described as providing a 'social justice' lens that allows studying how social inequalities are embodied, leading to worse health outcomes among disadvantaged populations. At the same time, social scientists have often been very critical of what have been described as reductive tendencies to focus on one particular environment: the maternal body and the mother's behaviour, which is often implied to be the most relevant environment for the development of health and disease, thereby reproducing stereotypical attributions of responsibility for offspring and reproduction.

When I approached the field, I was armoured and readily outfitted with this feminist critique. I was equipped with a specific conceptual repertoire that guided my perspective on the field and how I perceived it. But stumbling into the field, I quickly realized that these preformed assumptions and perspectives did not resonate with what I experienced. I had the good luck of having kind and highly helpful gatekeepers that welcomed me and guided me into the field. As I became more engaged with my fieldwork, I became more and more concerned with many of the critiques that have been voiced towards DOHaD from other social scientists and myself in the past. Yes, it appeared certainly true that DOHaD's focus on maternal bodies and behaviours as the most relevant environments reflected deeply engrained gender stereotypes. This focus on the 'maternal environment' at the same time contributes to an environment where mothers are increasingly blamed and put under surveillance in the name of their yet unborn kids (Sharp et al 2018; Valdez 2022). This is a concern that rings particularly true given the current political climate in many places. And yet, these critiques also seemed to misrepresent DOHaD researchers' own attitudes and commitments, and how they themselves were often struggling with reductionist tendencies in their own work.

This became evident to me when I presented my work at the research seminar during the beginning of my research stay at one of the research groups (see Penkler 2022). I was nervous about how my talk, which reiterated what by then had become standard social science critiques of the field, would be received by the community that I would work with in the upcoming months. I was worried that they might be defensive, resistant or dismissive of my work. I was half expecting to find myself in a similar situation as the one described by Gusterson (1997), where he found himself ridiculed by the weapon researchers he was studying. But nothing of the sort happened. Indeed, the audience was not only generous in their praise of my talk, but also seemed genuinely interested. One member of the audience said: 'I absolutely agree with everything.' She went on to say, 'This is really, really important! At the same time, I find it really hard to integrate more complex approaches in my own work. If you read my own papers, I'm sure I myself am guilty of blaming mothers.' A lively discussion ensued on the reasons for why it is difficult to consider the complexity of social determinants of health and disease in one's work (see Penkler 2022). Researchers pointed, among other things, to structural features of the current science and public health system that they experience as driving them towards 'more simplistic approaches', as another participant said.

Like the interview in which I was asked if I felt comfortable with my own weight, this was a revelatory moment (Trigger et al 2012) in my fieldwork that made me reconsider the kind of approaches I brought towards the field. In the subsequent weeks and months, many of the researchers I worked with seemed way more open towards these kinds of critiques than I had originally anticipated. I started to ask myself, what can I contribute to this community when so many of the things I thought of as outside critique were actually voiced and shared by insiders? My academic armour started again to weaken, but in a different way than in my previous research project. It made me reconsider how I as an outsider could have the audacity to speak to these researchers about the social, political and ethical aspects of their own work. But some participants were adamant that, in the words of one of the central gatekeepers of my research, 'we need people like you in DOHaD to remind us of the complexity of our work'.

The more articulate I became, the more entangled I became in the field, and the more wrong it felt to critique the field from the outside. Critiquing the field from the outside felt like doing an injustice to how DOHaD researchers themselves are struggling with the very same issues, and to how this is an affectively charged issue for them. Moreover, on a personal level, it also felt like a form of betrayal on the side of myself as an ethnographer towards the people that so generously welcomed me, supported me in my research, collaborated with me and became my friends. It increasingly appeared to me that I, the ethnographer, and my research subjects, the biomedical researchers, were motivated by the same things: how to adequately address the social determinants of health and disease in DOHaD research, and how to make this biomedical research field and its translation into health care and health policy more responsive towards questions of social justice (see Penkler et al 2021; Penkler 2022).

My entanglement with my research field, the relationships that I built, and my changing normative commitments impacted not only how I perceived the research field and my own research, but also transformed the kind of story I wanted to tell through my research: a story that foregrounds common concerns and struggles, shared ways of caring for what motivates both DOHaD researchers and myself to do the research we do, and a collaborative way of struggling and tinkering together. This also changed me, as I increasingly got attached to my research field. This was not simply a process of going native – but a process of becoming open to both new perspectives and to new caring commitments. A process of developing new capacities, new ways of perceiving the field – which are also new ways to care about the field, to be moved by it, to be entangled in it. In this perspective, knowing and caring, knowing and relating appear as one and the same movement.

## Conclusions

As we conduct research, we not only explore the phenomena that interest us, but are also transformed in the process. We make sense of the world as we move through and engage with it. We change, we develop, we grow – and so does, at the same time, the world we are building through our research. Drawing on STS concepts of subjectivity and embodiment, I have tried to develop a conceptual toolkit that allows me to describe this as a process in which an articulate researcher and an articulated world co-emerge in a process of mutual becoming. In a very real sense, we researchers are ourselves the instruments through which we build knowledge and worlds. This implies developing novel ways of resonating, of relating to and caring for the worlds that emerge in our research.

I have used this toolkit to make sense of my research journey in two past research projects of mine. Both cases involved an affective journey in which I developed new sensibilities and novel relations to my research field and the topics that I was interested in. But the two cases also differ in how much I felt at stake, and they posed different, albeit related, questions of care. In my doctoral project on bodyweight narratives, research quickly became personal, not only for me but also for others surrounding me. I felt losing my academic armour and becoming vulnerable in ways that facilitated novel insights but also posed urgent questions of self-care. I have also experienced losing my academic armour while conducting my postdoctoral ethnographic research, but in a way that perhaps related less to my body. But losing my stance as somebody that approaches the field critically from the outside was also an embodied experience that put my subjectivity into question and opened new ways of perceiving and relating to the field. It let me reconsider what kind of stories I tell about the field and how I and my informants collectively attend to shared 'matters of care' (Puig de la Bellacasa 2011). Both cases have thus in common that they show how the researcher becomes affectively entangled with their research and how subjectivities, affects, caring relations and knowledge are co-emergent.

Understanding the researcher as the sensory medium through which we register differences and articulate the world highlights questions of self-care: becoming an articulate researcher engenders novel ways of perceiving and relating to the world, but it also may become a burden and endanger the researcher. I have argued against a vitalist understanding of becoming articulate as a necessarily positive process: we become vulnerable as we open ourselves to the world, develop novel capacities to affect and be affected, and become invested in our research. I strongly believe that shedding our academic armour and highlighting our affective entanglements can produce stronger and better accounts and foster novel caring relations with our informants and surroundings: good research should move you. But how do we engage in the necessary self-care to do so?

During my past research, discussing my feelings and changing understandings with friends and colleagues was a crucial support for me. But in retrospect, I certainly would have benefited from more institutionalized forms of (self-)care. Perhaps it is helpful to draw inspiration from other professions that foreground subjectivity and interpersonal relations for producing (actionable) knowledge, such as psychotherapy. In psychotherapy, there are institutionalized frameworks to deal with the un/intended effects of opening oneself up as part of the therapeutic process, such as regular supervision sessions or techniques for introspection and distancing. Building similar infrastructures for researchers and putting a bigger emphasis on (self-)care in training may help make more liveable worlds for researchers.

The first step every researcher can take in this direction is to regard every research project as having necessarily an autoethnographic component. Listen to your own affects and emotions, record them, reflect on them and talk to others about them. Take notes and keep a research diary. By paying close attention to how you feel in the field, by becoming vulnerable and reflecting on your experiences and feelings you might gather new insights that will guide your research in new directions. It will also help you engage in the necessary self-care during your research journey which so often has its emotional highs and lows. Also report on your experiences in your publications: it will make your study so much more interesting and engaging if you show your readers how your research has moved you. To adapt a famous quote attributed to Emma Goldman: If I can't dance, it's not my research.

## Acknowledgements

I thank Esther Dessewffy, Sarah Davies, Natalie Sontopski, marissa micah schut, Dimas D. Laksmana, Kathrin Gärtner and the editors of this collection for providing valuable and engaging feedback on different stages of the manuscript. This chapter is partly based on the PhD thesis *On Gaining and Losing: Performances of Bodies and Selves in Bodyweight Narratives* (Penkler 2016).

## References

Agee, J. (2009) Developing Qualitative Research Questions: A Reflective Process. *International Journal of Qualitative Studies in Education* 22(4): 431–447.

Atkinson, P. and Silverman, D. (1997) Kundera's Immortality: The Interview Society and the Invention of the Self. *Qualitative Inquiry* 3(3): 304–325.

Bordo, S. (1993) *Unbearable Weight: Feminism, Western Culture, and the Body.* Berkeley, CA: University of California Press.

Braun, V. and Clarke, V. (2006) Using Thematic Analysis in Psychology. *Qualitative Research in Psychology* 3(2): 77–101.

Braun, V. and Clarke, V. (2013) *Successful Qualitative Research: A Practical Guide for Beginners.* London: SAGE.

Braun, V. and Clarke, V. (2022) *Thematic Analysis: A Practical Guide.* SAGE.

Buchanan, I. (1997) The Problem of the Body in Deleuze and Guattari, or, What Can a Body Do? *Body & Society* 3(3): 73–91.

Callon, M. and Rabeharisoa, V. (2004) Gino's Lesson on Humanity: Genetics, Mutual Entanglements and the Sociologist's Role. *Economy and Society* 33(1): 1–27.

Callon, M. (1986) Some Elements of a Sociology of Translation: Domestication of the Scallops and the Fishermen of St. Brieuc Bay. In J. Law (ed) *Power, Action and Belief. A New Sociology of Knowledge?* London: Routledge & Kegan Paul, pp 196–233.

Charmaz, K. (2006) *Constructing Grounded Theory: A Practical Guide through Qualitative Analysis.* London: SAGE.

Danholt, P. (2013) Factish Relations: Affective Bodies in Diabetes Treatment. *Health: An Interdisciplinary Journal for the Socal Study of Health, Illness and Medicine* 17(4): 375–390.

Gomart, E. (2004) Surprised by Methadone: In Praise of Drug Substitution Treatment in a French Clinic. *Body & Society* 10(2–3): 85–110.

Gomart, E. and Hennion, A. (1999) A Sociology of Attachment: Music Amateurs, Drug Users. In J. Law and J. Hassard (eds) *Actor Network Theory and After.* Oxford: Blackwell, pp 220–247.

Gusterson, H. (1997) Studying Up Revisited. *PoLAR: Political and Legal Anthropology Review* 20(1): 114–119.

Hennion, A. (2007) Those Things That Hold Us Together: Taste and Sociology. *Cultural Sociology* 1(1): 97–114.

Hennion, A. (2010) Open Objects, Open Subjects? … Bodies, Things and Attachments IKKM Annual Conference 'Open Objects', 28–30 April, Weimar.

Humphreys, M. (2005) Getting Personal: Reflexivity and Autoethnographic Vignettes. *Qualitative Inquiry* 11(6): 840–860.

Kvale, S. (2008) *Doing Interviews.* London: SAGE.

Latour, B. (2004) How to Talk about the Body? The Normative Dimension of Science Studies. *Body & Society* 10(2–3): 205–229.

Law, J. (1992) Notes on the Theory of the Actor Network: Ordering, Strategy and Heterogeneity. *Systems Practice* 5: 373–393.

Lerum, K. (2001) Subjects of Desire: Academic Armor, Intimate Ethnography, and the Production of Critical Knowledge. *Qualitative Inquiry* 7(4): 466–483.

Müller, R., Hanson, C., Hanson, M., Penkler, M., Samaras, G., Chiapperino, L., et al (2017) The Biosocial Genome? Interdisciplinary Perspectives on Environmental Epigenetics, Health and Society. *EMBO Reports* 18(10): 1677–1682.

Myers, N. and Dumit, J. (2011) Haptic Creativity and the Mid-embodiments of Experimental Life. In F.E. Mascia-Lees (ed) *A Companion to the Anthropology of the Body and Embodiment.* Oxford: Wiley-Blackwell, pp 239–261.

Penkler, M. (2016) *On Gaining and Losing: Performances of Bodies and Selves in Bodyweight Narratives,* unpublished PhD thesis, University of Vienna.

Penkler, M. (2022) Caring for Biosocial Complexity: Articulations of the Environment in Research on the Developmental Origins of Health and Disease. *Studies in History and Philosophy of Science* 93: 1–10.

Penkler, M., Hanson, M., Biesma, R.G. and Müller, R. (2019) DOHaD in Science and Society: Emergent Opportunities and Novel Responsibilities. *Journal of Developmental Origins of Health and Disease* 10(3): 268–273.

Penkler, M., Jacob, C.M., Müller, R., Kenney, M., Norris, S.A., da Costa, C.P., et al (2021) Developmental Origins of Health and Disease, Resilience and Social Justice in the COVID Era. *Journal of Developmental Origins of Health and Disease* 1–4.

Pentecost, M., Keaney, J., Moll, T. and Penkler, M. (eds) (2024) *Handbook of DOHaD and Society: Past, Present and Future Directions of Biosocial Collaboration.* Cambridge: Cambridge University Press.

Poston, L., Godfrey, K.M., Gluckman, P.D. and Hanson, M.A. (eds) (2022) *Developmental Origins of Health and Disease*, 2nd edn. Cambridge: Cambridge University Press.

Puig de la Bellacasa, M. (2011) Matters of Care in Technoscience: Assembling Neglected Things. *Social Studies of Science* 41(1): 85–106.

Rubin, H.J. and Rubin, I. (2012) *Qualitative Interviewing: The Art of Hearing Data*, 3rd edn. Thousand Oaks, CA: SAGE.

Schmidt, J., van der Weele, S. and Sebrechts, M. (2023) In Praise of Awkwardness in the Field: Increasing Our Understanding of Relational Concepts by Reflecting on Researchers' Emotion Work. *Qualitative Research* 24(4): 813–831.

Sharp, G.C., Lawlor, D.A. and Richardson, S.S. (2018) It's the Mother! How Assumptions about the Causal Primacy of Maternal Effects Influence Research on the Developmental Origins of Health and Disease. *Social Science & Medicine* 213: 20–27.

Strauss, A.L. and Corbin, J.M. (1998) *Basics of Qualitative Research: Techniques and Procedures for Developing Grounded Theory*, 2nd edn. Oakland, CA: SAGE.

Teil, G. and Hennion, A. (2004) Discovering Quality or Performing Taste? A Sociology of the Amateur. In M. Harvey, A. McMeekin and A. Warde (eds) *Qualities of Food*. Manchester: Manchester University Press, pp 1–37.

Trigger, D., Forsey, M. and Meurk, C. (2012) Revelatory Moments in Fieldwork. *Qualitative Research* 12(5): 513–527.

Valdez, N. (2022) *Weighing the Future: Race, Science, and Pregnancy Trials in the Postgenomic Era*. Oakland, CA: University of California Press.

Vaughan, D. (2004) Theorizing Disaster: Analogy, Historical Ethnography, and the Challenger Accident. *Ethnography* 5(3): 315–347.

# 6

# Becoming Instrument

*Joshua D. Evans*

Dear Michael,

Before, during, and after reading your thoughtful and articulate text, I have been reflecting on the right form for offering you a response. The vulnerability and sense of care that suffuse your story, and how you connect them all to a worldliness, have led me to settle on a letter. We haven't met, but, through reading your text, I feel that, at least in some way, we now have. So I hope you'll permit me, or at least entertain, a letter's intimacy.

I'd like to share with you one of the many things I learned while reading your chapter, that I am grateful for and feel invited to think more about: that becoming articulate, learning to affect and be affected, is not always a positive experience. I was keen to read your chapter in part because I have also found this 2004 paper by Latour, 'How to Talk About the Body?', of use in my own work. It has helped me theorize and engage taste and smell as forms of expertise in culinary practice, and specifically in fermentation. Like Latour's argument, my findings in this research emphasize the pleasant, 'positive' side of these things, in which becoming more articulate draws us closer to the richness of the world as it unfolds. For my participants, this is a delicious, enticing richness, a sensory diversity that invites multispecies relationality. So I have found helpful your reminder that, while these aspects also exist, they are not the only effects of becoming articulate, of learning to be affected and to affect.

One conviction in your chapter I believe we might share was about the promise of more collaborative positions we as Science and Technology Studies (STS) researchers can take towards our scientist participants and colleagues. You so well articulate the kind of implicit, well, shall we say arrogance that can easily creep into critical STS if we assume we are more aware of the issues than our scientist participants. Sometimes this can be the case; but I have found, like you, that often it is not, and that scientists themselves can also be acutely aware of the complexities they, often for various structural reasons, are forced to gloss over in their science. They talk about them at lunch though, or after work at the bar. What might happen, I wonder, how might science itself be transformed, if we STS researchers focus our efforts on working with our scientist colleagues to change those structural conditions, or at least explore ways to negotiate and maybe subvert them, such that complexity can come back in? To me this feels of course by no means easy but ultimately a much more respectful, productive and appealing way to do STS, and indeed science. Reading your chapter, in a different empirical area from mine but with a similar theoretical and methodological orientation, I feel only more empowered and equipped to pursue this approach.

In this vein, there was a moment in this part of your discussion I had an idea about, and thought to maybe offer back to you. You describe what I sensed you might have experienced as a tension, suggested by a 'but', between being unsure you had/have the authority to speak to the researchers about their own work, and one of your gatekeepers assuring you that they need 'people like you'. I can share, for whatever it might be worth, that I have received your story as a beautiful illustration of how, with the right approach, it can become possible to speak to our scientist colleagues about their work and be received. Your central gatekeeper, along with other of your participants, insisted your presence in their world was valuable. You yourself discovered, as you describe, how maybe it was less about whether you speak with them about their work or not, and more about how. Together, these experiences of yours suggested to me a larger learning for all of us working in STS, and indeed, I might even propose, in any kind of research across disciplines and epistemic cultures: that perhaps this kind of esteem, this way of being welcomed and accepted into worlds not our own, can be enabled through a humble presence, a presence of solidarity, less being a witness than cultivating a 'withness'.[1]

These are just some of the many thoughts reading your chapter sparked for me. In the spirit of reflexivity and autoethnography that you invite us to embody and recognize in every research project, I wondered what might happen if I understood my own experience of reading your chapter in the same way. The result was feeling permitted, indeed encouraged, to notice how reading your story wove my own 'personal experiences, theoretical insights, and affects' together in new ways. I want to thank you for sharing how your own work has moved you, for in doing so it has also moved me.

---

[1] S. Atkinson, C. Brives, S. Biederman, J. Cañada, D. Chartier, A.C. Davidson et al, 'Introducing "With Microbes": From Witnessing to Withnessing', in *With Microbes*, edited by C. Brives, M. Rest and S. Sariola (Manchester: Mattering Press, 2021), 17–40, https://doi.org/10.28938/9781912729180.

And as a researcher–instrument, becoming ever more attuned to my own 'instrumentality' can only, I think, help me become attuned to everything else, for worse and for better, while learning the practices of care necessary to keep the instrument in shape, and the dance developing.

Warmly,<br>Josh

## Acknowledgements

The author is funded by the Novo Nordisk Foundation, grant number NNF20CC0035580.

# care embodied: speaking from a nonbinary, crip, menstrual body

*marissa micah schut*

**reading guide**

This chapter aims to sensitize you to the affordances, needs and multiplicities of your body, and to how these emerge together with particular environments. Throughout the chapter, prompts are offered to encourage you to engage with your own embodiment and with moments of care related to it. Autoethnographic vignettes guide the reader by pointing to particular experiences of in/visibilities, vulnerabilities and interdependencies of bodies in and beyond academic spaces. The chapter contributes to discussions of reflexivity by exploring the ways in which our various bodyminds are (not) cared for contributes to liveability, and by asking how (academic) spaces might be made more liveable for different bodies.

prompt 1:
(re-)connect with your body: close your eyes if comfortable. take three deep breaths, inhale through your nose and exhale through your mouth, sighing it out. take a minute to tune in to your body. how does it feel right now?

## letting the bodies speak

We are all made up out of a variety of different bodies which are embedded within each other, and in turn are embedded in their environments. For example, I reside in nonbinary, disabled (crip), menstrual bodies. It is from this embodiment that I make sense of the world; it is from this embodiment that I make knowledge. I am queer in multitude, not only in terms of both sexuality and gender, but also as all these embodiments are marginalized positionalities disrupting the norm that is cishet, White, male. I am crip in multitude: I am chronically ill (I have Myalgic Encephalomyelitis/Chronic Fatigue Syndrome [ME/CFS]) and I am Autistic.

To capture the multitude nature of our bodies, I adopt and adapt Annemarie Mol's term *the body multiple* throughout this chapter. These multiple bodies hold their own meanings and experiences, which intra-act and thus influence and affect each other. However, they cannot be separated from each other. They are entwined, fluid. As Mol states: 'The *body multiple* is not fragmented. Even if it is multiple, it also hangs together' (2022, 55, emphasis in original). Furthermore, my use of body includes the mind (also known as bodymind), as they are not separate entities.

---

prompt 2:
close your eyes and take a deep breath again. tune into your embodiment. which are the bodies that you inhabit? how many? how are they different from each other? in what ways are they alike?

---

This body of mine is cyclical, not only in reference to the menstrual body. Much like my gender, my body is fluid; not one day is the same. Its functions and abilities shift over time, and are often difficult to predict. Moreover, my body is White and therefore comes with a whole lot of privilege that is embedded in anything I do, write or say – including this chapter. Thus, even while speaking from my 'multiply marginalized embodiment' (Hubrig and Cedillo 2022, 1), I continue to benefit from privilege. My Whiteness speaks louder, and is more easily heard, than my nonbinary, crip, menstrual peers who are Black or people of colour. Therefore I am attentive to the racial dynamics embedded in this conversation and aim to use my voice to reimagine an equitable future (present) in which all bodies are cared for.

*This chapter looks at what it means to do research from the body multiple. Asking, how can the multilayered nature of the body be translated to reimagine – to queer – a liberating and expansive practice of care?*

There is no denying that care has been a popular topic over the last few years, making its way into all kinds of fields and practices in academia. No wonder, as we have been globally and collectively going through a pandemic unprecedented within our times. Moving through this care crisis exposed many layers of the uncaring and tough environment that is currently experienced, which in turn has left a deep need for a more caring climate. Within academic contexts, care is aimed to theorize, expand and reimagine it. Lindén and Lydahl (2021, 3) write that care promises 'caring agencies' and potentialities as well as a critical lens 'needed to interrogate and disrupt enduring and intensified injustices and damages'. What is often missing here is the engagement with disability studies, crip theory and most definitely disabled people, while, as Leah Lakshmi Piepzna-Samarasinha writes, 'we are the ones who know, more than anyone, the technology of how to actually care' (2022, 36). Therefore, I write this chapter not only from a disability-informed framework, but from my embodied plural experience and existence as a crip, nonbinary person. Thereby giving a voice to those bodies that experience (receiving and giving) care, and offering an embodied perspective of – and on – care. As it 'highlight[s] not only that things *could be* otherwise, but that they *already* are so, if we attend closely and attentively to the daily doings of care already existing alongside predominant ideals' (Lindén and Lydahl 2021, 8; emphasis in original).

Moreover, this means I am applying the body as method. Centring my body multiple as method is a way of doing strongly reflexive research. Strong reflexivity as described by Andrea Ploder (2022, 26) relies on the researcher's vulnerability as it centres their own experience, 'using their entanglements with the field as a decisive source of data and interpretation'. Because of this, Ploder argues it is an epistemological necessity in creating (academic) environments in which kindness and care is centred. Moreover, it is a queer way of doing research. As Ploder writes:

> Like queer theory and practice, strongly reflexive research blurs categories and genres, embraces art as a valuable theoretical and practical tool, resists orthodox methodologies, is inventive, creative, messy, and personal. These features, combined with the central role of the researcher's own experience, make it a valuable choice for queer social research. (Ploder 2022, 27)

Thus, it allows for the messiness of the body, the chaos of the mind, the flow of it all, and above all emphasizes the overlapping intra-action between the plethora of identities we inhabit, blurring the lines between them; merging them together.

Centring the body multiple in research environments and academia in general, offers an inevitable and necessary slow-down in a system that values productivity and capital over care and community – a system that universities and academic institutions are inherently part of, and perpetuate. Moreover, allowing somatic awareness within our practices of reflexivity extends a renewed presence for the material – not only research material but especially our corporeal materiality – which allows for a more holistic approach to practising our situationality and politics of location as researchers and academics. Thus, being with the body extends a valuable contribution to creating more liveable worlds in academia.

---

prompt 3:
tune inwards again. envision or recall an environment in which your bodies might ask for care? how do your bodies ask? do some require more care than others? what do they need today? can you take a moment to offer it?

---

## vignettes

These entries have been written in the beginning of 2023 over a time period of two months, the course of two menstrual cycles. Starting out, I had planned to write daily entries on the three aspects of my body multiple: crip, nonbinary and menstrual. However, through writing them I found it was impossible to separate them (as they, of course, are not separate in essence). It depended on the day which of my bodies/embodiments was more centred that day. Its central presence defined through the environment(s) and interactions of that day.

*Cycle day 8 – very confronted with my gender. being in an environment where i'm not 'out' as nonbinary is hard. especially when the environment is grasping on to the binary so hard. it feels like it's shouting 'you do not, cannot, exist'! my body is on edge, anxious here. waitress feeling weird about giving the pink cup to [my youngest nephew] cause he's a boy and apparently she thinks the oldest is a girl (because of his long hair?). the toilets that are unnecessarily gendered – to the extreme. 'ONLY GIRLS' (above the wheelchair accessible toilet, even); 'femme'; 'men to the left because the women are always right'. I stand out in this crowd because i am different. i am other. this crowd is my family.*

*Cycle day 1 – felt it immediately: my period would start today. it is hard to describe, but it is a specific kind of pain/ache in my lower stomach and my legs. different pain than usual. splitting headache. different than usual. my body being called back to bed, but i had plans so i took two painkillers and went on my way anyway (should not have). did not stay out long, though. did not feel any cramps, which could be because of the painkillers but my cramps are usually still felt even with painkillers, so it might be another pain-less period (not without, but less). same as last cycle. that is new. was called 'lady' today, which irritated me. just feels so unnecessary.*

*Cycle day 28 – end of my cycle. menstruation is near and its faint callings are heard throughout my body. my joints especially. shoulders are tense. energy sluggish. focus short-lived. headache loud and demanding. my body is calling for rest. i listen.*

*Cycle day 22 – in bed with my partner all day. we went dancing last night – at a queer party. never felt so free in my being, my body. visibly queer, visibly nonbinary – a sense of belonging unmatched. the prize paid for this belonging is the exhaustion and fatigue felt today (and coming days?), but i am claiming it to be worth it. i don't get that many opportunities to be out in queer spaces.*

*Cycle day 17 – outside in the park today. my body held by the grass, the trees, the sun. it is here i feel most myself; connected. whole. my body is at peace – my mind quiet.*

---

prompt 4:
envision or recall your body multiple in different (research) situations (for example, in your office, during teaching, during fieldwork, at conferences) how do your bodies feel seen (or not) in these situations? which aspects/versions/functions of your bodies are visible in these situations? how does it feel to be seen in these ways?

---

## on in/visibility

What is visible and what is invisible? Who determines what (and who, and how) is seen? In/visibility is a recurring theme in my embodiment. My crip body is invisible, most of the time. Invisible in the sense that I am not visibly disabled: I do not use a wheelchair or other mobility aids for example. Therefore my disability is/goes unseen, except for the few times I do use my walking cane. My disability, however, is visible to those who *care* to really see me as it *is* visible in the amount of times I have to sit down, slow down, for example. It is visible in my planning, my social schedule (close to non-existent), and the shortness of my days. Its in/visibility depends on how you look at it.

It leads me to Johanna Hedva's seminal essay, 'Sick Woman Theory' (2016), which is an acknowledgement to the feminization of needing (receiving) care and providing (giving) care. As they write: 'the most anti-capitalist protest is to care for another and to care for yourself. To take on the *historically feminized* and *therefore invisible* practice of nursing, nurturing, caring' (2016, part 6; my emphasis). Hedva's figuration of the Sick Woman speaks to the systemic gendering of disability, and challenges this as the Sick Woman is not just a woman; it is both a non- and multi-gendered entity. My nonbinary, crip, menstrual body is a Sick Woman. Moreover, Hedva speaks to the invisibility of disabled people as a systemic oppression: the way the system is built, disabled bodies are excluded from many places, including activism. As Hedva points out the importance of being seen in order to be seen as a political agent within the current system, they also challenge the legitimacy of this, asking: what does it mean, then, to not be seen? And, most importantly, how can we create change if/when we are not seen, or made invisible?

Same goes to my menstrual body: that, or when, I menstruate is invisible. A body's ability to menstruate is not visible, yet often assumed. The sexed and gendered aspect of menstruation means that people see my assigned female at birth (AFAB) body and assume I am woman, and therefore that I menstruate. The (social) assignment to womanhood means my queer, nonbinary body is also in/visible, which is illustrated in being referred to as 'lady'. This assumption is similar to my crip body, except that people assume I am able-bodied, thereby invisibilizing my disabled reality.

As I wrote in the entry, this period allowed me to go out (albeit with painkillers) and thus be seen. Unfortunately, that included being misgendered. My body was read, but I was not really seen. Usually, when on my period, the pain makes me unable to get out of bed. I retreat into myself, stay inside, isolate. It is confronting for the paradoxal in/visibility to be this loud in this menstrual time-space. I do not wish to be seen in this particular body.

---

prompt 5:
sense into the body that feels most vulnerable. how does this vulnerability manifest within your inner body? what happens to your breath, your heart? how does it manifest outwards? does your posture change? which environment feels most safe to your vulnerable body/bodies? offer a loving self-touch to those vulnerable parts.

---

## on vulnerability

The in/visibility of my bodies affects their vulnerability. For example, the assumption of able-bodiedness on my crip body means I am vulnerable to going over my boundaries. Sometimes by choice, sometimes by force – oftentimes a combination of both. But my boundaries – the boundaries of my bodily ability – and their permeability, is determined by accessibility (or lack thereof), and therefore much more than a topic of self-care.

'The norm of human life is to be, or to aspire to be, invulnerable' (Scully 2014, 206). Johanna Hedva also points this out and theorizes that to see illness as temporary, it also reduces care to be temporary. They write:

What is so destructive about this conception of wellness as the default, as the standard mode of existence, is that it invents illness as temporary. When being sick is an abhorrence to the norm, it allows us to conceive of care and support in the same way. Care and support, in this configuration, are only required sometimes. When sickness is temporary, care and support are not normal. (Hedva 2016, part 5)

Both my menstrual body and crip body are fluidly debilitating (from a medical perspective), however the practices of care are not limited to when they need it the most. Preventive practices of care are always present.

My menstrual body, my crip body and my nonbinary body are vulnerable in their own ways. Vulnerable as they are typically seen as unreliable, fragile, less than. Because these bodies are non-normative in our current system, they are considered to be 'specially vulnerable'. As Jackie Leach Scully writes in 'Disability and Vulnerability' (2014, 205): 'they have greater chance than others of being subject to harms. Special vulnerability can mean that people are more vulnerable to specific kinds of harm or that they are just more likely to experience harms in general'. To illustrate, the ability to menstruate has historically been presented as a reason not to let those menstrual bodies be in positions of power.[1] The crip, disabled bodymind is considered vulnerable due to 'bodily instability', its dependence on care, among many other reasons. The nonbinary, queer (all bodies under the trans★[2] umbrella) body is vulnerable to harm stemming from queerphobia, from microaggressions to verbal and/or physical violence. However, as Scully points out in her research, this assigned vulnerability is more often than not 'contingent on social or environmental factors' (2014, 208) rather than inherent, thereby engaging with vulnerability from the political/ relational model of disability.

As a nonbinary person, menstruation remains a loaded experience and topic for me, as it continues to be framed in cis-womanhood. By doing this research, I learn to care for myself. To see my menstrual body for myself; reimagining it in a frame that feels good to me. One that does not harm me, or does not cause (or at least, less) harm (dysphoria). And by doing so, I create an environment of care for other menstruating people for whom the experience, the topic, is also a vulnerable one. Speaking on, and from, my menstrual experience that is also queer and crip, allows for a more nuanced understanding of what constitutes the menstrual experience. Thus, acknowledging the cycle's debilitating potential/reality for many, without further pathologizing menstruation.

---

[1]  For years, patriarchy has labelled Woman as sick and unfit due to hormonal fluctuations. Disguised under various labels (hysteria, hormonal hostages) women were put aside because they did not fit into the normative standard of a healthy or able body.

[2]  Trans★ is used as an umbrella term to include all genders outsides of the cis-binary.

prompt 6:
how can this practice of listening, tuning in, help you build a practice of care for yourself as well as those around you? how do your bodies multiple depend on each other? does caring for one of your bodies affect (care for) the others?

# interdependency

Interdependency is an imperative aspect of care. As the Care Collective write in *The Care Manifesto* (2020, 30), 'we need to break the destructive linking of dependency with pathology and recognise that we are all formed, albeit in diverse and uneven ways, through and by our interdependencies'. Care cannot function one-sided: there needs to be a reciprocity, a mutual dependence, between those who receive care and those who give care. Moreover, these categories of receiving and giving are not fixed: every body needs to be cared for in one way or another, from time to time. Whether it is being called 'lady', being in an environment rigidly perpetuating the gender binary, or being fully acknowledged in my queerness by other queer people, these relations inform – to a certain extent – how I inhabit my body. All of them are confrontations of sorts, and affect my experience. As Stacey Alaimo writes in 'Trans-Corporeal Feminisms and the Ethical Space of Nature' (2008, 255): 'the human body is never static because its interactions with other bodies always alter it'. Not only do these interactions (including interactions with more-than-human bodies) affect the experience, they also alter the materiality of my physical body, for example, causing (or diminishing) stress and a dysregulated nervous system. This in turn also impacts on the different aspects of the bodies I inhabit: regular or chronic stress influences the menstrual cycle, my crip body gets depleted even faster.

Within the disability justice movement and community, these interdependencies are known as care webs. In their book *Care Work* (2018) Leah Lakshmi Piepzna-Samarasinha emphasizes the importance of recognizing that this form of mutual aid has long been practised and formed by Black, Indigenous and brown communities. I would argue that the relation between my nonbinary, menstrual, and crip body is another form of care web; they inform each other's caring needs. Sometimes – as in the case of going out to the queer party – my crip body takes a backseat in order to care for my nonbinary body. My menstrual body is also part of this; at the end of my cycle this would not have been possible for the fatigue (crip body) would have been amplified. Of course, it is not ideal but it is also reality, as most queer and/or night spaces are not accessible. So choices have to be made.

Part of this care web are the people around us. It is essential for me to have people with me who I feel safe with to take care of me. People who know to check in with me, to remind me to check in with myself: am I going over my boundaries and is it time to go, or can I stay a little longer? Do I need to adjust something in order to stay? And the importance of aftercare: staying in bed for at least a day (I usually need at least two days, due to post-exertional malaise) after a long night out dancing, paired with other care practices such as food and drinks or (self-)massage, for example, to replenish my bodies. The more I can practice this with the help of others, the easier it becomes to do by, and with, myself. And vice versa, it also allows me to do this for and with others. Thereby establishing a supportive and sustainable cycle of giving and receiving care.

Of course this is not limited to social gatherings or recreational activities. This can be (and perhaps should be) practised during academic gatherings, research work, and so on. How to frame your work so it does not spill out into the other parts of your day, your life? Especially when researching something close to us, or when we find ourselves more entangled with our research than expected perhaps, it is imperative to integrate care practices that work for us into our work, our relation to our research — whether we are working with other humans, the more-than-human realm, textual or otherwise — so that we may stay centred within our bodies as we are in relation with, and thus affected and altered by, our practice.

---

prompt 7:
take a moment to close your eyes again while imagining a more liveable world for your body multiple. how does it feel in your body? does your breathing change? what happens to your shoulders, your stomach? how does your body feel when you think of the current academic environment? notice any differences.

---

## reflection

Care is, in its essence, an embodied experience. Therefore, only theorizing care is not viable, as it can only do so much. As Lindén and Lydahl Mol write, 'Care is not something to be judged "in general terms and from the outside, but *something to do, in practice*"' (2021, 4; my emphasis; quoting Mol et al 2010). Thus, while doing research and thinking about care, it is crucial to centre its *experience*. Therefore, thinking with the body — doing research with/from the body — contributes to creating liveable worlds by speaking from the source; the heart of the matter. It highlights current practices of care, and it indicates how these are lived; how they are experienced, and how they affect the body — the materiality of it.

In the process of writing this chapter, I went through a period asking for a profound need for care, even more than usual. I found myself in a burnout which urged me to stop working. In spring 2023, I got diagnosed with Autism and shortly after my relationship ended. I was thrown into a grief cycle. Grieving the relationship, everything that came up from being diagnosed relatively late in life, and grieving the things I had previously 'lost' due to being chronically ill which I thought I had already processed before. I was in a state of processing so much loss that my bodymind just completely shut down. It told me to stop everything else, and focus on the recovery process.

The paradox of trying to write a chapter about care and centring the body during research, and simply not being able to write anything because my body needed to be centred, is definitely not lost on me. I had to let go of the intellectualized concept of 'this is such an interesting position to be writing from, I should write this all out', and actually let go and stop working on this chapter altogether. To give myself the permission to do so was much harder than I had thought. Many times my care-coach urged me to let the entire project go – at least until I had recovered. At first, I kept trying to find ways to continue working on this chapter, as well as another paper I was in the process of publishing – working with a reviewer and revising my original text. I asked for accommodations in both situations. And here I was confronted (once again) with the general inaccessibility of academia for divergent bodyminds. You can read my chapter in this book because the editing team behind this project met me where I needed to be. The care that we all talk about in this book, this project, was actually practised. The other paper will not be published. There, they told me it was all fine, but did nothing to change the process for me. Their actions did not meet their words, as is so often the case. After tuning into my body, I made the decision to not proceed the publishing/editing process with them. The stress it put on my bodymind was not worth the exposure of getting my paper published.

During my burnout, I got to practice and live the questions I propose in the introduction. I learned to truly prioritize the needs of my bodies by holding space to consistently check-in with them, learning to listen and translate to what they were telling me. Some of the practices that were needed for me, once I felt ready to slowly start doing some work again: work for a maximum of 30 minutes on the days I could, properly frame the periods of time I would spend doing work (through scent, taste, sound, space, and so on), practice a short guided meditation for focus before work, and a qigong somatic practice to release and re-centre afterwards. By taking all this time to reconnect with myself, I also transformed the way I was in relationship to others by not overextending my social battery, practising expressing my boundaries, and sharing somatic practices with my friends.

The fact is, and remains, that every bodymind needs care and everyone (human and more-than-human) would benefit from reframing and reimagining care – from outside of a neoliberal capitalist system which sees care as not normal, and thus temporary (see Hedva 2016). The temporality of care is accentuated in the 'post-COVID' era; how quickly we were urged (and willing) to collectively be in denial about its declining threat; how quickly masking was dropped; how quickly hybrid education and work was deemed too costly and unnecessary. Even during the pandemic, what was a perfect opportunity to prioritize and practice caring interdependency, became a polarizing event underlining the abundant carelessness embedded in our current societal structure as 'neoliberalism is uncaring by design' (The Care Collective 2020, 10). It is my hope that this iteration of my personal experience of embodying care might add to answering the questions: How can we translate the bodies' messages to create care practices that embrace and celebrate interdependencies between humans and the more-than-human? How can we reimagine those practices into a politics of care that center the embodied experience and its diversity?

---

prompt 8:

tune back into your body. notice where you may be holding tension after reading. are your shoulders and/or jaws clenched? release them. take a moment to observe how/ if these prompts offered any insights and/or energy shifts. integrate this knowledge by taking three deep breaths, in through the nose and out through the mouth.

---

## References

Alaimo, S. (2008) Trans-Corporeal Feminisms and the Ethical Space of Nature. In S. Alaimo and S. Hekman (eds) *Material Feminisms*. Bloomington: Indiana University Press, pp 237–264.

The Care Collective (2020) *The Care Manifesto: The Politics of Interdependence*. London and New York: Verso.

Hedva, J. (2016) Sick Woman Theory. *Topical Cream*. Available at: https:// topicalcream.org/features/sick-woman-theory/ [Accessed 5 May 2023].

Hubrig, A. and Cedillo, C.V. (2022) Guest Editors' Introduction. *Community Literacy Journal* 17(1): 1–8. doi: 10.25148/CLJ.17.1.010642

Lindén, L. and Lydahl, D. (2021) Editorial: Care in STS. *Nordic Journal of Science and Technology Studies* 9(1): 3–12. Available at: https://www.ntnu. no/ojs/index.php/njsts/issue/view/309 [Accessed 23 July 2023].

Mol, A. (2002) *The Body Multiple: Ontology in Medical Practice*. Durham, NC: Duke University Press.

Piepzsna-Samarasinha, L.L. (2018) *Care Work: Dreaming Disability Justice*. Vancouver: Arsenal Pulp Press.

Piepzsna-Samarasinha, L.L. (2022) *The Future is Disabled: Prophecies, Love Notes, and Mourning Songs*. Vancouver: Arsenal Pulp Press.

Ploder, A. (2022) Strong Reflexivity and Vulnerable Researchers: On the Epistemological Requirement of Academic Kindness. *Queer-Feminist Science & Technology Studies Forum* 7: 25–38. Available at: https://queersts.com/forum-queer-sts/queer-sts-forum-7-2022-towards-academic-kindness/strong-reflexivity/ [Accessed 1 May 2023].

Scully, J.L. (2014) Disability and Vulnerability: On Bodies, Dependence, and Power. In C. Mackenzie, W. Rogers and S. Dodds (eds) *Vulnerability: New Essays in Ethics and Feminist Philosophy*. Oxford: Oxford University Press, pp 204–221.

# 8

# Movement, Rest, Bodyminds

*Ekat Osipova*

marissa micah schut's piece resonated with me a lot. There were so many parts I could relate to, even if our bodyminds also diverge in different ways. Reading the piece felt soothing; it was the kind of fuzzy, joyful feeling Mia Mingus describes as access intimacy (Mingus 2011). This feeling evoked reflections on the bodyminds I inhabit and the different ways of knowing and caring enacted by those bodyminds. Produced in a time of dissociation, exhaustion and brain-fog, the result is a small compilation of textual/pictorial vignettes. Their fragmented nature reflects my neurodivergent way of making sense of things in research and beyond (akin to Kender and Spiel's found footage ethnography 2023).

There is no point ignoring your body. And yet, academia expects you to. More often than not, research is presented as disembodied. Knowing is seemingly a detached, immaterial activity. Any basic bodily need is not allowed to matter when you have to push through to make the deadline.

When my body is overwhelmed by stress and sensory overload, I cannot ignore it. My entire body starts to feel sore from within. My skin feels very sensitive, and I feel a burning tightness and tension in my chest. If I don't rest or get out of the situation causing these sensations, my body eventually shuts down. If I don't listen to my body's demands for care, I start feeling numb, my head gets clouded, and I can't speak properly. At some point I just get so tired, I can fall asleep instantly. My body takes the rest it needs (Figure 8.1).

Stimming is a recurring rhythm of the bodymind. Yergeau describes stimming as a preservation and a neuroqueer retrofit to inaccessible environments:

[W]hile stimming holds many sensory meanings, it is frequently a means of seeking sensory balance in an overwhelming, stressful, or painful situation. A neurodivergent person might rock their body hard against a wall in order to remain in a room; the rocking, in this instance, is a

**Figure 8.1:** Ekat and their cat resting in bed. Ekat's head is leaning on a Blåhaj plush toy

way to create access in an inaccessible situation, a way to relate within or around normative space. (Yergeau 2023, 41)

Stimming, thus, is a practice of care enacted by the body (Figure 8.2). When my body stims, my affects, whether tumultuous or joyful, are directed outwards. When I stim, the boundaries between my inner life and my environment blur.

## References

Kender, K. and Spiel, K. (2023) Banal Autistic Social Media: A Found Footage Autoethnography. In *Proceedings of the 25th International ACM SIGACCESS Conference on Computers and Accessibility (ASSETS ,23)*. New York: Association for Computing Machinery, Article 101, pp 1–7. https://doi.org/10.1145/3597638.3614552

**Figure 8.2:** Ekat's hands fidgeting with an infinity cube

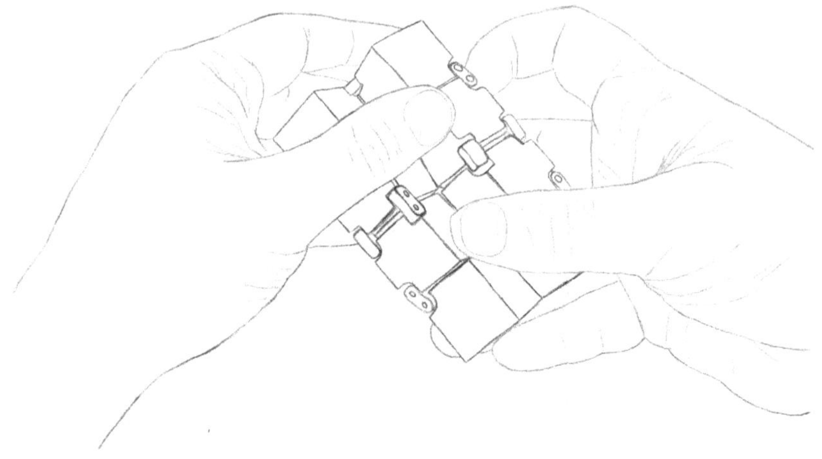

Mingus, M. (2011) Access Intimacy: The Missing Link. *Leaving Evidence*, 5 May. Available at: https://leavingevidence.wordpress.com/2011/05/05/access-intimacy-the-missing-link/ [Accessed 4 September 2024].

Yergeau, M.R. (2023) Composing Perseveration / Perseverative Composing. In M. Mills and R. Sanchez (eds) *Crip Authorship: Disability as Method*. New York: New York University Press, pp 38–47.

# Participation

9

# Epistemic Erasure
# in Participatory Research

*Dimas D. Laksmana*

## Where to begin?

In late 2017, at the beginning of my fieldwork in Pakem District, on the slopes of Merapi volcano on Java, Indonesia, I lived with a host farmer family who introduced me to several organic farmers in the area. With its fertile volcanic soil, this area to the north of Yogyakarta is the home of smallholder farmers who grow vegetables, paddy rice and fruit trees. As someone who was active in various farmer organizations in her hamlet and village of Purwobinangun, my host Risa suggested I talk to Sarto, a rice farmer and a mechanic who was also a regional organizer of a national peasant movement who trained farmers in organic agriculture.[1] My first meeting with him left me with an enduring sense of discomfort that drove me to critically reflect on my positionality as a member of an international transdisciplinary project. The following encounter is my first hint on epistemic erasure that happened in my research.

On one late morning in January 2018, I rode on my scooter along the winding roads of Pakem District, nestled between wet rice fields, to get to Sarto's repair shop. When I arrived, he was sitting on his front porch, waiting for the monsoon rain to subside. After parking my scooter by the side of the road, I greeted him and introduced myself as a researcher who currently lived with Risa and was interested in interviewing him. Once he agreed to my request, I explained that the purpose of the Indonesian–German research project, IndORGANIC, was to identify possible societal

---

[1]    All names are pseudonyms.

93

transformation pathways towards organic agriculture in Java. This aim is achieved by combining insights from sociology, development economics, anthropology and societal knowledge about the current state and visions of organic agriculture (Padmanabhan nd). Though I did not use the term transdisciplinarity, I explained that his insights could influence the questions that researchers asked and spaces of public participation in science that researchers created. This practice characterizes transdisciplinary research as a form of participatory research that aims to democratize science through knowledge co-production (Padmanabhan 2017).

I began by asking him broad questions, such as what he did, how did he do organic agriculture, how did he learn organic agriculture, and so on. At the end of the interview, I asked him to refer me to other farmers, following a typical snowball sampling method. He caught me unawares when he asked, 'So if farmer friends want to know if you are willing to cooperate with them, would you do so?' I was not sure what he meant by *kerjasama* (cooperation). So I asked, 'Cooperation in what sense?' He replied, 'Well, cooperation in planting, and then *pemasaran* (marketing), or [accessing] *modal* [capital], for example. Farmers usually have this question. ... If I bring someone from a campus or university, that question is there. If it is not asked upfront, it is asked behind their back.'

This encounter, and other similar experiences during my PhD research, left me feeling uneasy, and also puzzled and disoriented. In this chapter, inspired by the 'productive potential of discomfort' (Alburo-Cañete et al 2022), I reflect on my experiences of embodied 'transdisciplinary moments' (Laksmana 2023) over the past seven years. I argue that jointly practising reflexivity during these moments of a bodily and affective process, often expressed through the experience of discomfort, can foreground tensions arising from the hierarchical organization of different ways of knowing in a transdisciplinary context (Laksmana 2023). I consider this politics of knowledge as coloniality in a transdisciplinary approach that adopts pre-defined and fixed terms of knowledge co-production. Practising reflexive participation, thus, requires researchers to transform the unequal relations in knowledge production and reflexivity that often characterize public participation in science.

This conceptualization is inspired by the notion of reflexivity as a way of accounting for 'how participatory experiments frame and produce particular versions of the objects (issues), subjects (participants/publics) and procedures (philosophies) of participation' (Chilvers and Kearnes 2016, 267–268). As these practices are dynamic, reflexivity in participation cannot be pregiven but is continually co-constructed in situated research practices (Chilvers and Kearnes 2016). I take this approach further by arguing that the 'how' question needs to be thought of in tandem with questions on the politics of reflexivity: (1) Who reflects on whose experiences? (2) Why is reflexivity needed to transform coloniality in participatory research? Therefore, transdisciplinary moments go beyond reflexivity as an afterthought and consider it as part of a situated research practice with its embedded power dynamic (Millora et al 2020). In practice, it means reflecting on my shifting positionalities as I recently moved from Germany, where I completed my PhD, to Indonesia, where I have started to build an academic career. This reflection is important because of the geo- and body-politics of knowledge that highlight how knowledge construction is linked to the privileging of certain geographical locations, like the First World, and bodies, for example, according to racial hierarchies and patriarchal normativity (Mignolo 2009, 166, 172). This conception rejects the (often hidden) assumption of scientific knowledge as universal, and of the knowing subject as a detached and neutral observer, that marginalize other ways of knowing (Smith 1999; Mignolo 2009, 162). As I further discuss in what follows, this is the kind of coloniality in participatory research that I contest and try to delink from.

## Geo- and body-politics of knowledge in writing as usual in precarious academia

In this section, I elaborate on my shifting positionality by reflecting on writing as usual while navigating precarious academia, from Germany, where I completed my PhD, to Indonesia, where I have started to build an academic career. In both places, the neoliberalization of academia creates precarity. This reflection is important because of the previously mentioned geo- and body-politics of knowledge and the idea of reflexivity as a method of interrogating oneself in relation to a subject of enquiry (Stirling 2006). Therefore, my positionality informs and motivates my critique of participatory research in an international setting.

While writing this chapter, I returned to my hometown after being away for half of my adult life to study and work abroad. Being back with the intention of creating and finding an intellectual home, or 'epistemic living space' (Felt 2009), I realized that this process is much more challenging than I had expected – compared, for example, with continuing my previous academic trajectory and staying abroad among a more established and familiar network of scholars based in Europe. The concept of epistemic living space, that highlights 'the personal, the institutional, the epistemic, the symbolic and the political' in scholarly work, helped me to foreground my embodied experiences in navigating academia and understand the importance of 'feeling intellectually and socially "at home"' in research practice (Felt 2009, 19). Although I was mentally prepared to engage in this process, when I applied for academic jobs in Indonesia, I soon learned how the bureaucratization and neoliberalization of higher education since 1998 (in post-authoritarian Indonesia) have driven the proliferation market-oriented scholarship, at the expense of critical social science (Rakhmani 2019). While it resonates with the recent expansion of neoliberal state policies that contribute to precarious employment conditions in higher education globally (Alburo-Cañete et al 2022), entering Indonesian academia with its own particularity from a more-resourceful academia in Germany struck me with the severity of inequality in global knowledge production as my following encounter with Kartono illustrates.

A few months after returning to Indonesia in late 2023, I arranged a meeting with Kartono, a lecturer, from a leading state university to discuss my interest in working there. He explained to me about the funding of the university, that is directly linked to employment opportunities and work conditions. He said:

> Right now, this university no longer receives state funding [or the state funding has decreased – which of these is true is less important than the effects on the university's income] so we need to take more students than before. As a result, lecturers spend most of their time doing administrative tasks. We have very little time for doing research, just so you know.

On my enquiry about job opportunities, he confessed:

> We don't have any openings now and we already have a few internal candidates in case a permanent lecturer position becomes available in the future. If you want, you can apply for a casual lecturer position while waiting for a permanent position. You will be paid per teaching session [*not* per teaching hour]. The remuneration is about IDR 200,000 [around €13].

Kartono graduated from a German university. I felt our similar academic backgrounds compelled him to be upfront about the current condition of higher education, a gesture that I truly appreciated as somebody who was unfamiliar with Indonesian academia. It was 9 o'clock in the morning. The brief meeting that lasted less than an hour left me disconcerted. During my PhD in Germany, I learned the exploitative nature of academia through my experience of being hired through a *Lehrauftrag* (teaching assignment contract). On reviewing the contract that detailed my working hours, I became aware of the extent to which teaching was undervalued, as the payment was only for teaching hours, and not the preparation for each class. I also learned that it is common practice for non-permanent academic staff, like myself, to rely on *Arbeitslosengeld* (unemployment benefit) during some periods of their career.

The normalization of precarity in academia and different forms of dependency PhD researchers must navigate are issues that I criticized in my dissertation (Laksmana 2023). Critical reflection by Benedetta Zocchi (2021, 5) on the PhD as 'a site of oppression and a site of resistance' encouraged me to portray the process of reclaiming my agency in my dissertation, while still being subjected to disciplining by PhD procedures. For these reasons, highlighting different forms of marginalization that happens in and through research practice is central to my work.

As I am now trying to establish an academic career in Indonesia, I wonder whether doing writing *as usual* while continuing to navigate precarious academia, in its different manifestations across institutional and geographical locations, is a sign of commitment to scholarship or a symptom of (normalized) self-exploitation, or perhaps a combination of both?

The rest of the chapter is my attempt to respond to this reflexive question in relation to the main argument of this chapter, which is that practising reflexivity during transdisciplinary moments could potentially transform coloniality in transdisciplinary research. The following is structured as follows: I begin by situating my transdisciplinary research against the backdrop of the Green Revolution in postcolonial Indonesia to argue politics of development is inherent in transdisciplinary research. My transdisciplinary moments with farmers who requested marketing opportunities and have had extractive relationships with researchers further demonstrate this argument. Against this background I show how a 'residual realist' approach to participatory research (Chilvers and Kearnes 2016) reproduces coloniality by contributing to the ongoing marginalization and exclusion of certain knowledge production practices, or, in short, epistemic erasure (Méndez 2021). Specifically, the transdisciplinary research that I practised can be characterized by a predefined and fixed notion of participation and a 'technicalization' of societal transformation. I conclude by proposing a reflexive participatory research that is based on the geo- and body-politics of knowing. This is my proposition to enable reflexivity to contribute to more liveable worlds by potentially transforming coloniality in participatory research. I illustrate these points by drawing on my nine months of ethnographic research in the Special Region of Yogyakarta, Java, Indonesia, between 2017 and 2019, my dissertation, my current experience of returning to Indonesia to become a university lecturer, and literature that takes a critical perspective on public participation in science.

## Politics of (agricultural) development under postcolonial Indonesia

In this section, I describe how reflexive writing, which helps me to interpret my shifting positionality in precarious academia while engaging with my intersubjective experiences during fieldwork with farmers, brought me to an understanding of how the technicalization of agricultural development and postcolonial Indonesia shape farmers' interaction with my transdisciplinary research. This process is understood as 'politics of development' (Sultana 2007), which I argue is inherent in, instead of external to, knowledge co-production in my transdisciplinary research in that it shapes relations between myself, as a researcher, and organic farmers and other actors.

'Why are German researchers interested in our agriculture?' asked one farmer during my fieldwork in Indonesia. I was asked this numerous times during my fieldwork with organic farmers. Why was I, an Indonesian field researcher, part of an Indonesian–German research project (IndORGANIC nd), so puzzled by this question? I typically replied to farmers by reciting the aim of the transdisciplinary project to promote societal change towards organic agriculture at the beginning of each interview. Given that societal transformation towards organic agriculture depends not only on technical solutions, but also institutional change, I told them, the project adopts transdisciplinarity, with its problem-solving orientation (Gibbons et al 1994). However, as I elaborate in the following sections, the predetermined research design to confine knowledge co-production into discreet activities, specifically workshops, was unable to respond adequately to farmers' expectations of immediate and tangible benefits from the project, and more importantly, to the notion of participation that emerged during the research. As a result, the research project's imposition of societal transformation through state policy making remained unchecked.

Some of these expectations, I initially thought, were beyond the scope of the project, or were addressed by project activities such as organic agriculture training, workshops and joint publications. However, the question remained unanswered, and became a source of discomfort and discontent with the participatory approach that I had adopted, as I reflected on the process of writing my PhD dissertation:

> My research experience allows me to reflect on the interplay between enquiry that guides research, and on the writing that guides my response to that enquiry. ... Writing is imbued with reflexivity and empathy, allowing me to approach and get a glimpse of other people's multiplicity of experiences and to accept the possibility of these experiences changing my presumptions on what the world is and should be. (Laksmana 2023, 30)

Through reflexive writing as a mode of thinking, I further investigated the initial puzzlement and curiosity that I shared with organic farmers about German researchers' interest in organic agriculture in Indonesia. In 'Postcolonial Developments: Agriculture in the Making of Modern India', Akhil Gupta (1998) provides a similar account of his fieldwork in the 1980s, as an Indian PhD researcher from an American university. Some of his farmer interviewees in rural India were initially puzzled by his research. Gupta writes:

> When I tried to explain that I was studying agriculture, they were genuinely puzzled. Why would someone be sent from a country with such 'advanced' agriculture to a place where there was hardly any machinery? What could possibly be learned from studying agriculture in such a 'backward' place? But the elders remembered another young man who had come to 'study' there almost two decades earlier. 'He kept asking us questions—he wanted to know everything, including how many handheld hoes we had!' they recalled. 'Do you want to do the same kind of study?'. (Gupta 1998, 26)

He explains that the differentiation made by these farmers between 'developed' and 'underdeveloped' is shaped by the circulating discourses of (agricultural) development at multiple scales (Gupta 1998, 6).

I argue that, in the Indonesian context, this differentiation is the result of the 'technicalization' of development intervention (Kothari 2005) in the form of the Green Revolution since the 1960s. The intensification and industrialization of agriculture through technology transfer depended on highly specialized and institutionalized knowledge, expertise and rules. Technocratic institutions created a hierarchy of expertise by giving authority to extension workers to instruct farmers on how to synchronize their planting and harvesting using standardized and input-intensive techniques incorporating high-yielding rice varieties in combination with chemical pesticides and fertilizers (Sawit and Manwan 1991). Together with the implementation of large-scale irrigation schemes, the Green Revolution changed the ecological conditions of farming and subjected farmers to a new dependency on the technological packages that were distributed to them (Fox 1993). As a result of top-down, instead of dialogical, communication between farmers and government officials and technological-driven agricultural development, and less on education, interactions tend to be transactional and low on trust (Winarto et al 2018).

Some of these characteristics can still be observed in the current government's approach to organic agriculture, that is regulated and defined by market-driven certification schemes and centralized bureaucratic institutions that ignore other 'meanings' of organic agriculture (Schreer and Padmanabhan 2020; Laksmana and Padmanabhan 2022). This historical context motivated my research to adopt transdisciplinarity with its participatory aspect of incorporating societal knowledge in identifying societal transformation. In the broader context, the Green Revolution embodies a linear science-driven paradigm, implemented through predominantly top-down knowledge and technology transfer. This approach has, however, been critiqued for more than three decades, from the perspective of 'Farmer First' (Chambers et al 1989) and, later, 'Beyond Farmer First' (Scoones and Thompson 2009). The latter critique underlines the complexity of societal transformation in agriculture by showing the interconnections between power relations, actors and different forms of knowledge in agriculture (Scoones and Thompson 2009).

In the Indonesian context, this complexity can be understood as a feature of what Gupta (1998, 6) terms the 'postcolonial condition', which refers to situations 'in which contradictory logic and incommensurable discourses are intermingled with one another'. There are farmers who *do research* on the variability of rainfall in their fields and life cycles of pests (Winarto 2004; Winarto et al 2018), and apply a combination of local knowledge with agroecosystem analysis and meteorology to *solve* agricultural problems. The postcolonial condition of Indonesian agriculture, thus, problematizes the clear distinction between 'scientific' and 'societal' knowledge production (Pohl et al 2017) that informs my transdisciplinary project's approach to societal transformation. More importantly, in postcolonial Indonesia farmers point their analytical gaze to researchers by reflecting on their experiences of being researched. The following farmers' reflections on having their knowledge extracted by researchers and university students highlight how their situated knowledge is unsettling for my transdisciplinary approach that isolates itself from the postcolonial condition in which it operates. Understanding this encounter as a moment of joint practice of reflexivity, I began to understand the extent to which agricultural history shapes present-day dynamics between science and society, which my research was part of. Therefore, politics of development (Sultana 2007) is inherent in transdisciplinary research.

When farmers learned of the aims of my transdisciplinary research project, many shared Sarto's expectations that the project would provide support for marketing. For example, Sutar, a coconut tapper who supplies a cooperative selling organic coconut sugar for the international market, told me: '[I]f you can help us to find sales opportunities, perhaps it would help us.' As mentioned earlier, the institutionalization of organic agriculture (Laksmana and Padmanabhan 2022) often makes it difficult for smallholders to enter the niche market for organic products. These examples, and the story of Abu's laboratory, reflect the postcolonial condition, where farmers show their agency while interacting with scientists, while being subjected to a long history of agricultural development that has positioned them as objects.

When I reflect on the position of a farmer as someone who is being asked, and their reflections on this, I identify with their resentment and disappointment with this form of participation. Sutar, for example, was often visited by potential importers from Europe and university students. He candidly informed me of his disappointment at not getting anything back in return for his knowledge and experience in organic agriculture. For example, he was once visited by a filmmaker from a non-profit organization who, he explained:

> [C]ame and asked many questions. That was all. … But when we waited for the result, [the filmmaker recorded] for example the climbing, the process of making [coconut sugar]. Interview like what we are doing here. … He did not help, in the end, up to today. There was no update. Then what about us? Nothing. Only the interview – that's it. … The reality is up to now we haven't received any assistance, not even for marketing.

The issue of people, and specifically university students and researchers, only 'asking questions' and not making significant contributions to farmers in return came up numerous times during my fieldwork. The head of a farmers' association that exports organic snake fruit reflected on his interactions with university students. He explained to me:

> What I mean is, don't only come for information, but come to look, listen, [see] what can be developed at the association, that's it. For example, the cultivation method, the market, the organization, these can be good things to write about … as academics they should be able to think about the future. … So don't only come to gather information, [so you can] graduate, but also to think together.

In our transdisciplinary project, we framed agricultural history as external to our own research. For example, in our analysis the misalignment between different interests and visions of actors in organic agriculture were the result of the Green Revolution. This, we thought, could be addressed through inclusive policies that were formulated in a participatory manner (Fritz et al 2021). I further problematize this assumption in the following section. This project design, I argue, was influenced by the logic of the new public management (Felt et al 2016), prevailing in Europe, that values conventional academic outputs and efficiency, while discounting societal valuation of research. We were unable to address the form of subject positions that the state and scholars impose on farmers (see Chilvers and Kearnes 2016). In other words, we failed to appreciate how agricultural history is internal to current tensions between different forms of participation envisioned by researchers and their research subjects. Following Kothari (2005), the externalization of history in participatory research is an ordering of different forms of knowledge that follows colonial relations.

In the notion of participation as 'thinking together', or the lack of it, there is a convergence of the discomforts that I experienced throughout the transdisciplinary moments described. What kind of participation enables thinking together when the terms of participation are based on coloniality? In the following section I show the importance of being reflexive towards the implications of this messiness of knowledge co-production to understand how transdisciplinary research reproduces coloniality through 'technicalizing' societal transformation akin to the Green Revolution.

## Coloniality of societal transformation

The previous section argues farmers' engagements with research are influenced by the technicalization of agricultural development since the Green Revolution and postcolonial condition of Indonesia. Inspired by my transdisciplinary moments with Abu, a farmer who participated in my transdisciplinary workshop, I situate the discussion within the politics of knowledge in participatory research to argue that participatory research that follows 'residual realism' reproduces coloniality. The technicalization of societal transformation through policy recommendations in my transdisciplinary research demonstrates this point. By politics of knowledge, I mean what and whose forms of knowledge matter and how field research constructs them (Fabian 2012). Therefore, the transdisciplinary aim of co-producing knowledge, which becomes the basis of societal transformation, is saturated with power, affecting the selection of the research agenda, and, consequently, the validation and hierarchization of different forms of knowledge. The politics of knowledge is of course manifested in a dynamic process where not only researchers exercise power, since people can also do so by simply refusing to participate in research (see Sultana 2007). However, at a time when participatory research, including transdisciplinary approach, permeates the discourse of international cooperation agencies like the German Federal Ministry of Food and Agriculture (2022), it is important to interrogate the notion of participation itself to highlight the reproduction of coloniality in such spaces.

I consider the conception of participation that informed my transdisciplinary work corresponds to what Chilvers and Kearnes (2016, 11) call 'residual realism', whereby researchers confine participation to procedures based on a set of predefined theoretically driven assumptions. Furthermore, participation is conceived as a series of discreet events that are assumed to be appropriate across different issues and contexts (Chilvers and Kearnes 2016). Based on these assumptions my transdisciplinary research operationalized the integration of 'societal knowledge production' and 'scientific knowledge production' (Pohl et al 2017) or, in short, knowledge co-production, through multi-stakeholder workshops. This approach, thus, leaves the possibility of knowledge co-production in everyday transdisciplinary research practice unexplored (Schikowitz 2020).

This approach, I argue, contradicts the initial aim of participatory research to redistribute authority (see Cooke and Kothari 2001) and contributes to the reproduction of coloniality, by which I mean 'the logic, metaphysics, ontology, and matrix of power created by the massive processes of colonisation and decolonisation' (Maldonado-Torres 2016, 10). In other words, coloniality can be understood as the social order during colonialism. In contemporary international development, Kothari (2005) points out that coloniality is reflected in the creation of expertise that divides people according to their authority and knowledge. This is accomplished through the valuing of technical knowledge, which is considered as universal and neutral, over in-depth place-based knowledge, which is situated (Kothari 2005).

My participatory research reproduced coloniality by 'technicalising development interventions' (Kothari 2005, 437), and specifically by making policy recommendations to be implemented by the government as drivers of societal transformation. According to Kothari (2005), development interventions increasingly rely on institutionalized forms of knowledge, tools and frameworks, all of which contribute to the creation of expertise. In my research, this process took place through transdisciplinary workshops where researchers selected the agricultural problems that merit scientific investigation and transformed societal knowledge into scientific knowledge according to 'system', 'target' and 'transformation' knowledge (Hadorn et al 2008), which is then used to formulate policy recommendations (Fritz et al 2021). This is reflected in my further response to Sarto's request at the beginning of this chapter, where I explained: 'Well, we want to turn our research results into policies, so the problems and challenges that farmers face can be communicated to the government, then they can provide solutions through policies. That is why we try to analyse [organic agriculture] from multiple perspectives, multiple angles.' The universal knowledge here is 'evidence-based policy making' that is used to justify the assumption underlying our participatory research: that it was acceptable for farmers as research subjects to have to wait 'patiently' until our research started producing outputs which might benefit them, while we *immediately* collected data from them.

My transdisciplinary moments with Abu, a rice farmer, revealed how this form of coloniality led to epistemic erasure (Méndez 2021), that is the marginalization and exclusion of knowledge production practices characterized by the inseparability of bodily experience and the geographical–historical location of knowing, or in short, the geo- and body-politics of knowledge (Mignolo 2009). I argue that this approach marginalizes the situated knowledge of societal actors and their role as agents of societal transformation by excluding them in co-producing the terms of participation in transdisciplinary research. Furthermore, the transformative potential of public participation in science through state policy making is interpreted as being to reconcile contestations in Indonesian agriculture which is marked by the historically asymmetric relations between the state, public and science (Laksmana 2024).

I first met Abu in early 2017, during the first scoping mission to Yogyakarta at the beginning of my PhD project. The Department of Agriculture of Sleman Regency referred me to him as he had been practising 'environmentally friendly' agriculture with reduced use of chemical fertilizers and pesticides since 2010. During the first visit to his house in Minggir District, accompanied by my Indonesian research counterpart, I was fascinated by a laboratory where he cultivated *Beauveria baciana* and *Trichoderma*, which are fungi that can be applied to agricultural soil to control diseases.

In mid-February 2018, I visited him again to learn more about his laboratory and agricultural practices. We began our interview by recalling our shared experience of the first transdisciplinary workshop that he attended in late 2017. He felt he benefited from it since he was able to share his agricultural experience with multiple stakeholders and extend his social network, which helped him to expand his marketing channels. As the head of a farmers' group in his village, he enjoyed taking part in training sessions and meetings, where he acquired new agricultural knowledge and learned about agricultural support programmes. As a voluntary extension worker, he was often invited by government agencies to attend workshops on, for example, the System of Rice Intensification and preparing bio-based agricultural products. Through participation in these events, he was also able to obtain government support to build his laboratory. There are a few other farmers who engage in similar activities, including hosting scientists or researchers in their villages, as I discovered during my fieldwork. Through this conversation I began to understand his motivation to participate in the transdisciplinary workshop.

During the conversation, I asked him about his research on *agen hayati* (bio-based agents). His response steered the conversation in a surprising direction as it resonates with Sarto's response at the beginning of this chapter. The following extended quote illustrates his situated knowledge on the practicality of practising environmentally friendly agriculture and his vision on societal transformation:

> Then what is the follow-up on this [the first transdisciplinary workshop]? The follow-up on our gathering at Pessona Tugu Hotel [the venue of the workshop]? Can Dini [a research counterpart in Indonesia] *mengajukan* [submit] [a funding proposal to support his laboratory]? If I want to develop bio-based agents, to make them more perfect in the sense of they become more [standardized], at least they can support young farmer friends who want to switch [to more environmentally

friendly agriculture]. Is it possible? What do you think, *mas*? … If we [farmers] want to develop *pertanian ramah lingkungan* [environmentally friendly agriculture], we need to be ready so that farmers can find [bio-based inputs] easily. This is our opinion. Farmers should be able to find [bio-based agents] easily, so it shouldn't be a headache to find them. That is the challenge.

For Abu, one pathway of societal transformation towards organic agriculture is by making bio-based agents more readily accessible for young and conventional farmers. According to transdisciplinary terms, his vision is a transformation knowledge that informed the project's policy recommendations. However, I felt uneasy when he further explained, following the earlier conversation: 'So this is the problem, *mas*. In simple terms, I am searching for a donor to cooperate with. I already have this [the laboratory in his house]. … To develop these bio-based agents I need, at least according to the standard, equipment like that.' Here he is referring to equipment at typical laboratory such as he has seen at a university laboratory that analyses soil samples from his field. My discomfort is not because my project was not able to respond to such request, but because we did not try to think about our understanding of societal transformation and knowledge co-production through Abu's situated knowledge. Abu's insight was simply explained by pregiven notions of transdisciplinarity.

Interpreting this encounter with Abu, and other similar instances, as transdisciplinary moments prompted me to reflect on how the participatory research that I was engaged in contributed to the knowledge hierarchy by the adoption of a detached and neutral point of observation, from which hierarchies between knowing and known subjects are sustained (Mignolo 2009). Based on this assumption, we centred the state as the primary agent of societal transformation. Furthermore, the transdisciplinary project reproduced coloniality by pushing for societal transformation that is based on institutionalized forms of expertise, such as that of social scientists and policy makers, over those with place-based knowledge, thus disregarding the geo- and body-politics of knowing. That is, Abu's situated knowledge drew on his extensive experience as a farmer who received support and interacted with the government since 2013, developed bio-based agricultural inputs, and is familiar with farmers' attitudes. Therefore, the formulation of policy recommendations by our project failed to reflect on how our intervention was shaped by and (re)produced the science–state–society relations in postcolonial Indonesia.

On the contrary, taking situated knowledge seriously means being reflexive during these moments to consider the possibility of transforming politics of knowledge in public engagement in science. This could mean reorientation of the project's transdisciplinary approach by questioning its initial strategy for achieving societal transformation. This would have involved asking questions about the extent to which local initiatives can provide the starting point for more diverse forms of public participation that foreground power dynamics among different forms of knowledge as the driver of societal transformation. This suggestion points to a practice of reflexive participation that is responsive to diversities and uncertainties of participation and their public articulations and effects (Chilvers and Kearnes 2016). This gesture also refers to a form of reflexive scholarship that acknowledges how insights from fieldwork 'must be understood as deriving from a peculiar confluence of circumstances, relations, and consequences' (Chua 2015, 614). I conclude this chapter by discussing the potential of geo- and body-politics of knowledge for transforming hierarchical relations in knowledge production and doing reflection.

## Doing reflexive participation in a neoliberal academia

The transdisciplinary moments discussed in this chapter foreground the politics of knowledge in the practice of participatory research. On the one hand, for example, Sarto could determine the terms and conditions of farmers' participation in the project since he understood the value of their experiences and knowledge for my research. My inadequate answer in response to his request led me to seek out other farmer communities to interview. On the other hand, in my research practice, by deciding that this empirical finding was beyond the scope of my research, I disregarded the capacity of geo- and body-politics of knowing to redefine public participation in transdisciplinary research. Thus, I contributed to a hierarchy between knowledge which is situated within a particular historical–geographical condition of agricultural development in Java and the implicit universality of scientific knowledge produced by doing participatory research with agricultural communities.

Simultaneously, these transdisciplinary moments point to the possibility of redefining participation that emerged during my fieldwork in Indonesia. These moments bring forth coloniality on the ground that leads a participatory research that is unable to respond to the emerging nature of participation and that renders the politics of locations and bodies in knowing, in other words the geo- and body-politics of knowledge, invincible. I argue this conception of knowledge to be the basis of reflexive participatory research, while recognizing that the potential for reflexivity to alter the hierarchy of power is contingent on a particular situation, which often involves negotiation, with its embedded power dynamic (Millora et al 2020). This approach, thus, acknowledges the neoliberalization of academia, whereby we, as academics, are predominantly evaluated according to quantified indicators that uphold the hierarchy of ways of knowing, of technical over place-based knowledge. While I acknowledge the benefit of publications, like journal articles and policy recommendations, from the transdisciplinary project, simultaneously I am critical of how the transdisciplinary research practices reproduce coloniality, contributing to epistemic erasure in the context of societal transformation in postcolonial Indonesia.

The paradox that I face is that doing critical scholarship that contests conventional participatory research is still situated within unequal global knowledge production that explains 'the Global South' using a research apparatus comprising values, theories and resources from 'the Global North' – rather than understanding that the two are interconnected and analysis can go both ways. This is reflected in the lack of reflexivity in the participatory approach adopted by my transdisciplinary project. By making visible how knowledge construction is linked with the privileging of certain geographical locations through reflexive writing, I attempt to decentre Western scientific institutions as primary sites of knowledge production, and transform the hierarchy that acts as barrier to a more horizontal co-production of knowledge (and co-construction of participation) between scientists and local actors (Manuel-Navarrete et al 2021). In practice, I propose 'creating an environment in which we could affect and be affected by each other' (Alburo-Cañete et al 2022, 7) as a starting point for delinking participatory research from coloniality. Based on the reflections on my shifting positionalities, I contend that reflexivity as situated practice may contribute to more liveable worlds by highlighting and, potentially, transforming coloniality that contributes to epistemic erasure in participatory research.

## References

Alburo-Cañete, K.Z., Banerjee, S.A., Hak, S., Jakimow, T., Ngin, C., Sadjad, M.S.O., et al (2022) (Dis)comfort, Judgement and Solidarity: Affective Politics of Academic Publishing in Development Studies. *Third World Quarterly* 43(3): 673–683.

Chambers, R., Pacey, A. and Thrupp, L.A. (eds) (1989) *Farmer First: Farmer Innovation and Agricultural Research*. London: Intermediate Technology Publications.

Chilvers, J. and Kearnes, M. (eds) (2016) *Remaking Participation: Science, Environment and Emergent Publics*. Abingdon: Routledge.

Chua, L. (2015) Troubled Landscapes, Troubling Anthropology: Co-Presence, Necessity, and the Making of Ethnographic Knowledge. *Journal of the Royal Anthropological Institute* 21(3): 641–659.

Cooke, B. and Kothari, U. (eds) (2001) *Participation: The New Tyranny?* London: Zed Books.

Fabian, J. (2012) Cultural Anthropology and the Question of Knowledge. *Journal of the Royal Anthropological Institute* 18(2): 439–453.

Federal Ministry of Food and Agriculture (2022) Announcement No. 04/22/33 'Innovative Nachhaltige Produktionssysteme' ('Innovative Sustainable Production Systems'). Available at: https://www.ble.de/SharedDocs/Downloads/DE/Projektfoerderung/InternationaleForschungszusammenarbeit/Forschungskooperationen_International/2022_Bekanntmachung-Produktionssysteme/Bekanntmachung_Nachhaltige-Produktionssysteme_en.pdf?__blob=publicationFile&v=3 [Accessed 3 June 2024].

Felt, U. (ed) (2009) *Knowing and Living in Academic Research: Convergence and Heterogeneity in Research Cultures in the European Context*. Prague: Institute of Sociology of the Academy of Sciences of the Czech Republic.

Felt, U., Igelsböck, J., Schikowitz, A. and Völker, T. (2016) Transdisciplinary Sustainability Research in Practice. *Science, Technology, & Human Values* 41(4): 732–761.

Fox, J.J. (1993) Ecological Policies for Sustaining High Production in Rice: Observations on Rice Intensification in Indonesia. In H. Brookfield and Y. Byron (eds) *South-East Asia's Environmental Future: The Search for Sustainability*. Kuala Lumpur: Oxford University Press, pp 210–224.

Fritz, M., Grimm, M., Keilbart, P., Laksmana, D.D., Luck, N., Padmanabhan, M., et al (2021) Turning Indonesia Organic: Insights from Transdisciplinary Research on the Challenges of a Societal Transformation. *Sustainability* 13(23): 13011.

Gibbons, M., Limoges, C., Scott, P., Schwartzman, S. and Nowotny, H. (1994) *The New Production of Knowledge: The Dynamics of Science and Research in Contemporary Societies*. London: SAGE.

Gupta, A. (1998) *Postcolonial Developments: Agriculture in the Making of Modern India*. Durham: Duke University Press.

Hadorn, G.H., Hadorn, G.H., Hoffmann-Riem, H., Biber-Klemm, S., Grossenbacher-Mansuy, W., Joye, D., et al (2008) *Handbook of Transdisciplinary Research*. Dordrecht: Springer.

IndORGANIC (nd) Available at: https://www.uni-passau.de/en/indorganic [Accessed 1 January 2024].

Kothari, U. (2005) Authority and Expertise: The Professionalisation of International Development and the Ordering of Dissent. *Antipode* 37(3): 425–446.

Laksmana, D.D. (2023) *Knowledge in the Making: Embodying Transdisciplinary Moments on Organic Agriculture in Yogyakarta, Indonesia*, doctoral dissertation, Universität Passau.

Laksmana, D.D. (2024) Farmers' Creativity and Cultivated Senses: The Immediacy of Embodied Knowledge in Alternative Agriculture. *Engaging Science, Technology, and Society* 10(3): 65–89.

Laksmana, D.D. and Padmanabhan, M. (2022) Strategic Engagement in Institutions of Organic Farming in Indonesia. In V. Beckmann (ed) *Transitioning to Sustainable Life on Land*. Switzerland: MDPI, pp 373–405.

Maldonado-Torres, N. (2016) *Outline of Ten Theses on Coloniality and Decoloniality*. Frantz Fanon Foundation. Available at: http://fondation-ran tzfanon.com/wp-content/uploads/2018/10/maldonado-torres_outline_of _ten_theses-10.23.16.pdf [Accessed 14 June 2024].

Manuel-Navarrete, D., Buzinde, C.N. and Swanson, T. (2021) Fostering Horizontal Knowledge Co-Production with Indigenous People by Leveraging Researchers' Transdisciplinary Intentions. *Ecology & Society* 26(2): 1–13.

Méndez, P.T. (2021) Decolonizing Healing: Weaving the Curandera Path. *Globalizations* 20(2): 316–331.

Mignolo, W.D. (2009) Epistemic Disobedience, Independent Thought and Decolonial Freedom. *Theory, Culture & Society* 26(7–8): 159–181.

Millora, C., Maimunah, S. and Still, E. (2020) Reflecting on the Ethics of PhD Research in the Global South: Reciprocity, Reflexivity and Situatedness. *Acta Academica* 52(1): 10–30.

Padmanabhan, M. (nd) *Detailed Project Description and Work-plan. IndORGANIC The Societal Transformation of Agriculture into Bioeconomy – Turning Indonesia Organic?*

Padmanabhan, M. (ed) (2017) *Transdisciplinary Research and Sustainability*. London: Routledge.

Pohl, C., Krütli P. and Stauffacher, M. (2017) Ten Reflective Steps for Rendering Research Societally Relevant. *GAIA – Ecological Perspectives for Science and Society* 26(1): 43–51.

Rakhmani, I. (2019) Reproducing Academic Insularity in a Time of Neo-liberal Markets: The Case of Social Science Research in Indonesian State Universities. *Journal of Contemporary Asia* 51(1): 64–86.

Sawit, M.H. and Manwan, I. (1991) The Beginnings of the New Supra Insus Rice Intensification Program: The Case of the North Coast of West Java and South Sulawesi. *Bulletin of Indonesian Economic Studies* 27(1): 81–103.

Schikowitz, A. (2020) Creating Relevant Knowledge in Transdisciplinary Research Projects: Coping with Inherent Tensions. *Journal of Responsible Innovation* 7(2): 217–237.

Schreer, V. and Padmanabhan, M. (2020) The Many Meanings of Organic Farming: Framing Food Security and Food Sovereignty in Indonesia. *Organic Agriculture* 10(3): 327–338.

Scoones, I. and Thompson, J. (eds) (2009) *Farmer First Revisited: Innovation for Agricultural Research and Development*. Rugby: Practical Action Publishing.

Smith, L.T. (1999) *Decolonizing Methodologies Research and Indigenous Peoples*. London: Bloomsbury Publishing.

Stirling, A. (2006) Precaution, Foresight and Sustainability: Reflection and Reflexivity in the Governance of Science and Technology. In V. Jan-Peter, D. Bauknecht and R. Kemp (eds) *Reflexive Governance for Sustainable Development*. Cheltenham: Edward Elgar, pp 225–272.

Sultana, F. (2007) Reflexivity, Positionality and Participatory Ethics: Negotiating Fieldwork Dilemmas in International Research. *ACME: An International Journal for Critical Geographies* 6(3): 374–385.

Winarto, T.Y. (2004) *Seeds of Knowledge: The Beginning of Integrated Pest Management in Java.* New Haven: Yale University Southeast Asia Studies.

Winarto, T.Y., Ariefiansyah, R., Prihandiani, A.F. and Taqiuddin, M. (2018) Nurturance and Trust in Developing Agrometeorological Learning in a Changing Climate. *Indonesia and the Malay World* 46(136): 360–381.

Zocchi, B. (2021) Be Brave but Be Smart – Can PhD Researchers Be Epistemically Disobedient? *Decolonial Subversions* II: 1–22.

10

# Making More Liveable Worlds Beyond Academia: Reflexivity in Collaborative Research Practice

Camilo Castillo

## Introduction

On a cold Saturday morning in May 2024, together with some friends, I attended a meeting of the Sindicato de Trabajadores Agrícolas de Sumapaz (henceforth Sintrapaz), a *campesino* (smallholder farmers) organization from the Sumapaz Region, located in the Andean mountains south of Bogotá, the capital of Colombia. That day, we were returning our theses to the organization, a commitment that we had made when my friends and I began our research projects back in 2018. That day was special for us, because for the first time we could share some of our research reflections with some of the people that made it possible. In the years before, we were collaborating with *campesino* communities in Sumapaz through our research projects.

In my case, my research studied the tensions and conflicts between *campesino* communities and public authorities generated by the conservation of the Sumapaz *páramo* (Castillo 2023). Located in the high mountains of the northern Andes, *páramos* have been considered as an 'strategic ecosystem' by the Colombian government because of their role in the water cycle. For the life sciences, *páramos* are also unique places that sustain a vast biodiversity (Hofstede et al 2003; Cleef et al 2008), which makes them an important biodiversity hotspot in the world (Madriñán et al 2013). Sumapaz *páramo* is one of the more than 30 *páramos* that exist in Colombia according to the environmental authorities in the country (Morales-Rivas et al 2007; Sarmiento Pinzón et al 2013). Besides, Sumapaz was also one of the epicentres of the origins and development of the Colombian armed conflict in the 20th century (Comisión de la Verdad Colombia 2022).

But despite their undisputed importance for human and nonhuman lives, the conservation of *páramos* have proved to be a very conflictive matter for *campesino* communities. When the Colombian government decided to demarcate *páramos* through maps in order to enforce prohibitions on 'human activities' within their limits (Republic of Colombia 2010), a profound conflict with different communities inhabiting *páramos* in Colombia emerged. Previous research on *páramos* conservation in Colombia has analysed the authoritarian conservation scheme organized by the Colombian state with the demarcation of *páramos* (Ungar 2021). So, it is not surprising that the 'demarcation of *páramos*' has found resistance from diverse communities living in those places all over the country (Parra Romero 2019; Blake et al 2023).

In the case of Sumapaz, *campesino* communities sued the Colombian Ministry of Environment, since the demarcation of the *páramo* in Sumapaz did not involve any participation from them. A court decision backed the *campesino* demand and since 2019 the Colombian government is making a new demarcation of the *páramo*, which must be made with the participation of *campesino* communities (Rama Judicial de Colombia 2019). In the middle of that dispute, I was allowed by *campesino* communities in Sumapaz to conduct my research in their lands under the commitment of not only sharing my research outputs, but also of collaborating with them in defending their presence in their lands located in what the Colombian government demarcated as a *páramo* area in 2017 (Colombian Ministry of Environment and Sustainable Development 2017).

This chapter aims to analyse that collaboration process with *campesino* communities. It highlights the practical importance of reflexivity as the means to navigate the sociomaterial process that makes collaboration possible. It also shows how reflexivity allows to understand the making of collaboration as a process that reveals the dynamic multiplicity of the positions that enable researchers to act in the task of making more liveable worlds. In other words, doing research involves adopting various roles based on the relationships we establish. The way these relationships are assembled in practice, along with our participation in that process, significantly shapes how academic research transforms our positionality as researchers.

Drawing upon my experience researching *páramos* conservation in Colombia and my collaboration with *campesino* communities, the remainder of this chapter empirically explores the relationships between reflexivity, collaboration and making more liveable worlds. In the following section, I show how reflexivity helped me to understand how collaborative research involves a transformative process that reconfigures both the researcher's position and her capacities to act with others. Then, the second section examines the formation of a collective to situate reflexivity as a back-and-forth process when researchers work in collaborative relationships with collectives beyond academia. Finally, in the conclusion, I present a resituated version of reflexivity in the context of collaborative research where the question of making more liveable worlds becomes central for researchers.

## Collaborative research and shifting positions

The conservation of a place like the *páramo*, which supports the vital processes of multiple forms of life, seems in principle a desirable plan for building more liveable worlds. However, the presence of *campesinos* in *páramos* made visible for environmentalists, public officers and local authorities the contradictions of conservation when it does not address the presence of people.

For *campesino* communities in Sumapaz, the recognition of their presence in the *páramo* by the Colombian government was necessary for defending their lands and their modes of living. That was the expectation that Sintrapaz, the *campesino* organization mentioned at the beginning of this chapter, had when accepting researchers in their lands back in 2020:

> I met the president of Sintrapaz in the same restaurant where I had lunch the first day I arrived in San Juan de Sumapaz. When I told him that I was planning to conduct a research about the conservation of the *páramo* and its consequences to the *campesino* lives, he told me that this was a topic that could help them [*campesinos* and Sintrapaz], because the current situation in Sumapaz was going to 'deepen the environmental conflicts in the region'. (Field journal)

This brief encounter with the Sintrapaz president preceded my first meeting with the assembly the day after. In the same schoolroom where years later I returned my thesis, I presented the project. There, one of the attendees remarked again how 'conflictive' was the conservation of the *páramo* in Sumapaz. This problematization of *páramos* conservation by *campesinos* was crucial for getting the approval from Sintrapaz to conduct my research there. That day I reached an agreement with Sintrapaz, which consisted of working with them to critically study the conservation of the *páramo*.

A first mechanism to do it was by attending the meetings organized by the 'Research Commission', which was the commission from Sintrapaz responsible for ensuring that researchers like me kept in touch with the organization. These meetings were held from June to August 2020 and, together with other researchers and members of Sintrapaz, we had the chance to discuss the consequences of future policies designed for Sumapaz by the municipal and national authorities.

Since the first meeting, my role as researcher began a transformation. Now, I was mobilized by Sintrapaz representatives as a potential ally that could redescribe topics of relevance for *campesinos* such as, for example, the conservation of *páramos*. Besides, the meeting was also the occasion for

Sintrapaz to highlight our political role as researchers, because according to Sintrapaz members, we as researchers had the potential to articulate our projects to the 'political processes' happening in the region. These processes referred to the different activities through which *campesinos* in Sumapaz were strengthening their organizations so they could defend themselves collectively in matters such as the conservation of the *páramo*.

These first steps in engaging with *campesino* organizations from Sumapaz offer an opportunity to think about how reflexivity helped me to navigate across the shifting positions of my role as researcher. First, reflexivity is what enabled me as researcher to recognize key moments in research where other actors, like *campesinos* in this case, were also participating in shaping the concerns of my project. Second, reflexivity made me realize that collaboration is a process where the role and positionality of the researcher is socially negotiated with those with whom we work in our research. Third, reflexivity was the way to be attentive that in order to collaborate with communities like *campesinos* from Sumapaz, it was necessary to 'articulate' new relationships so a research project could align with collective concerns such as those of *campesinos* in the Sumapaz *páramo*. Overall, reflexivity became in this project a sensitivity to navigate the relationships and conditions that shaped the relationships I formed with *campesinos* and their organizations. As I will later show, that opens the way for reflexivity to engage with the task of making more liveable worlds.

The conditions for researchers like me to collaborate with *campesinos* were then paved by the situations, like, for example, those meetings, where the

**Figure 10.1:** *Campesino* house in the *páramo*

attributes and potential actions of us as 'researchers' were configured. In this way, the normativity of my collaboration with *campesinos* depended more on those practical circumstances establishing the conditions for collaboration and my role on it, rather than on abstract and idealized notions of collaboration distant from its practical making or from fixed positionalities.

Here, I coincide with Penkler (Chapter 5, this volume) when he argues that through research, we make novel forms of attachments that we make available to the world, which allows us to emerge as researcher subjects. I would add that when those attachments take the form of 'collaboration', we become part of relationships where the multiple positions of the researcher subject are more evident. In my case, by establishing a collaboration with Sintrapaz, my position as researcher was also defined by being a 'potential ally' and by the expectation from *campesinos* of contributing to the 'political processes' taking place in Sumapaz.

When reflexivity attends to the conditions through which we sustain the relationships that make research possible, it becomes more evident that as researchers we do not occupy a single position. In fact, positionality reveals itself as mobile and fluid (Mol and Law 1994), instead of static and fixed. This means that 'positionality' is not, at least in collaborative projects, the source for reflexivity, because 'positions' are not immediate and given. Positions then, are reflexively achieved, that is, through the relationships that make possible a research project. This consideration invites us to think of reflexivity as mediated by the negotiations and commitments reached with the communities that we work with.

This consideration makes it necessary to respecify previous questions around reflexivity as the active concern with one's own production of knowledge (Ashmore 1994), because in collaborative research, exploring the consequences of challenging the assumption of the analyst's (privileged) position (Woolgar 1991) has renewed implications. In the scenario of collaborative research with communities like *campesinos* in Sumapaz, reflexivity works as a sensitivity to understand what happens with our research practices (and ourselves) when engaging in collaborative relationships. For example, collaboration was a condition for making possible my research with *campesinos*, so it emerged as part of my fieldwork configuration. It would not have been possible for me to learn from *campesinos'* worlds in the *páramo* without the commitment to help them in their struggle with conservation. In that way, becoming a collaborator for *campesinos* was the condition for me to become a researcher of *páramos* conservation.

However, that involved a negotiation in which I was expected by *campesino* organizations to attend political meetings, be part of *campesino* discussions about the conservation of the *páramo* and participate in dialogues with public authorities. This created a discontinuity between my research project and my research role with *campesinos*. By this, I mean that, for *campesinos*, my collaborative role was restricted to be present in already-made places, rather than creating new ones where my research could contribute to collaboratively find new understandings that *campesino* organizations could appropriate and mobilize in their discussions with public authorities. In other words, although *campesinos* knew that I was doing academic research, for them my position as a collaborator was more important. But it is important to clarify that both positions were not necessarily separated in the view of *campesinos*. They often introduced me to other people or in meetings as a 'researcher', however, that position depended on being a collaborator. This could suggest that reflexivity is a way to disentangle the multiple positions that coexist in a collaborative project. Most importantly, reflexivity helps to situate the occasions when certain positions gain more importance than others, without implying that they are fractured or separated.

In that way, my position(s) as researcher were shaped by the collaborative relationships that allowed me to work and think about the conservation of the *páramo* with *campesinos* in Sumapaz. But calling these relationships 'collaboration' is not necessarily done with representational purposes or with the aim to describe my particular experience as pertaining to the genre of ethnographic collaboration (Rappaport 2008). Collaboration, here, was more a way to negotiate and build relationships and the researcher's positions with *campesinos* through my research.

So, reflexivity in collaborative research is important for researchers to trace the connections and new possibilities of action with others beyond academia. In the case of *campesino* organizations in Sumapaz, collaboration with researchers was crucial for them to find new allies that could work with them in their struggle regarding conservation. Here, reflexivity worked in my research to respecify the task of creating more liveable worlds. Because when that task is resituated through collaborative work with communities like *campesinos*, then making more liveable worlds becomes a collective activity that happens beyond academia. For that reason, the activities involved in the formation of the collectives where the task of making liveable worlds is assembled are particularly interesting. They provide the opportunity to situate how research roles and positions are shaped as collectives are formed. In the following section, I spell out how reflexivity helps to navigate the formation of a collective so research positions can be connected with making more liveable worlds.

## Reflexivity as a back-and-forth process within collectives

In 2019, after several meetings, *campesinos* from Sumapaz decided to create the 'Coordinadora Campesina Regional of Sumapaz' (henceforth Coordinadora Campesina), a regional organization that reunited 48 *campesino* organizations from Sumapaz and other allied organizations from Bogotá (Coordinadora Campesina de Sumapaz 2019). Its aim was to create a meeting place where organizations that were previously dispersed could now act together against the Colombian Ministry of Environment in their struggle with the conservation of the Sumapaz *páramo*. It was from the Coordinadora Campesina that the assembling of a new *páramo* and conservation in Sumapaz began.

Such a task involved the creation of a collective, that is, the project of assembling new entities and forms of sociality not yet gathered (Latour 2005). It is worth nothing that these collectives are more than social, in the sense that they engage both with the human and nonhuman world to generate new spaces of alternative and autonomous existence (Papadopoulos 2018). This is important to take into account, because creating more liveable worlds is a very practical and material activity. Throughout the Coordinadora Campesina, *campesinos* were able, together with other allies including researchers like me, to intervene in the politics of *páramos* conservation in Sumapaz (Castillo 2023).

The main meeting scenarios for the Coordinadora Campesina were the assemblies. They are collective events and occasions where people meet in the same place to discuss and decide over a variety of matters of collective concern. One of the organizations participating in the Coordinadora Campesina was the Research Group on Agrarian and Campesino Studies from Sumapaz (henceforth Research Group). Despite its apparently academic name, the Research Group was not affiliated with any university or educational institution. On the contrary, it was an initiative led by independent researchers and militants from different political organizations. Its aim was to support *campesino* organizations in Sumapaz through the production of knowledge with the expectation of fuelling future debates and the decision-making processes that were taking place within the Coordinadora Campesina.

I mention this organization because, in October 2020, I was invited to be part of it by one of its founders, who was also a member of Sintrapaz. This invitation did not come as a surprise to me, as I was already actively working with Sintrapaz in the meetings mentioned in the previous section. Besides, I was also a regular attendant of the meetings of the Coordinadora Campesina, so I was already familiar with its decision-making process. I wrote the following in my field journal after the first assembly that I attended as a member of the Research Group:

> We were in front of an audience of at least 70 *campesinos*, on the previous days we had already arranged our participation in the assembly with the Coordinadora Campesina's Secretary. When it was my turn to introduce myself, I said that I was a member of the Research Group

and that our commitment with the Coordinadora Campesina was to support its discussions and debates from our academic experience. Besides, we also mentioned that our research would be informed by *campesinos'* concerns and preoccupations, so we were basically willing to collaborate with anything that we might help the Coordinadora Campesina. (Coordinadora Campesina Assembly, 28 November 2020, field journal)

That was one of the moments that crystallized the 'we' that my other friends from the Research Group and I were constituting together with the Coordinadora Campesina. From there, my research began to take place in the activities and spaces where collective issues were raised and decisions made (Rappaport 2020). This involved the process of helping in the organization of meetings, writing reports, discussing with public authorities along with *campesinos* and more. My position as researcher also changed for *campesinos* and the Coordinadora Campesina. It became more flexible, since now I was giving reports in the meetings, partaking in discussions and having responsibilities more related to the Coordinadora Campesina than with my research project. Those activities of course shaped my research concerns, but how that happened is a topic that exceeds the purpose of this chapter.

Here, again, reflexivity invites us to think about and navigate the multiple positions that researchers generate in collaborative projects. In the first place, I was producing research about the ontological politics of conservation in Sumapaz. Second, I was a member of the Research Group and, third, I was collaborating with the Coordinadora Campesina. These three positions had different concerns, which of course were not in opposite directions. However, they were not identical, and they were not at play simultaneously everywhere. For example, within the Research Group we had our own views that some *campesinos* and other organizations did not share in the same way. In the Research Group we believed that most of the environmental policy designed for Sumapaz was bad for *campesinos*, whereas other organizations had fewer reservations about environmental policies.

At that point, I realized that becoming a collaborator and member of the Research Group made me also part of the politics of *campesino* organizations in Sumapaz. That meant, to me, that I could no longer work with some organizations in Sumapaz because their members knew that I was part of one organization, so my interests were not perceived as exclusively academic. My collaboration with the Research Group positioned me in a wider arena of political differences and made me more aware of them. In the long term, that limited my ability to learn from other organizations that did not necessarily coincide with the same views that the Research Group had. But at the same time, that created more affinity between me and other *campesinos* and organizations that shared similar views with the Research Group.

So, being a collaborator established a more fluid set of positions and priorities as researcher. There were periods in which I was more active discussing with my friends from the Research Group about an upcoming Coordinadora Campesina meeting, which meant that I was not dedicated in the same way to analysing data or reviewing literature. There were moments, in turn, when I was so absorbed in my thesis writing that I could not join very interesting meetings of the Coordinadora Campesina. Collaboration, then, did not follow a singular trajectory in which all my research positions could be harmonized and accommodated. Sometimes collaboration meant making huge efforts to support the Research Group or the Coordinadora and, sometimes, it meant spending less time with my collaborators to turn those experiences into academic knowledge such as this book chapter.

Coming back to the Coordinadora Campesina, I mentioned earlier that as a collective it was engaged in the project of assembling a different conservation of *páramos* in Sumapaz. So the collective, rather than being devoted to producing more 'accurate' representations of the *páramo* and conservation, was engaged with a movement of ontology (Papadopoulos 2018) to reconfigure conservation and the *páramo* altogether. Such an effort could be only sustained by the formation of a collective where this ontological move could be put into practice. For doing so, material activities such as planning legal actions, designing flyers, writing reports, discussing issues, keeping communication with public authorities and others were necessary for the Coordinadora Campesina to maintain the existence of the collective (examples can be found on the website).

The traditional problems addressed by reflexivity were quite different when engaging in collaborations with a collective such as the Coordinadora Campesina. Here, reflexivity was not a matter that emerged with the tensions associated with the representation of 'objects' (Woolgar 1991). That was a secondary problem, because in my case, reflexivity was more present in the situations where research did not necessarily involve the representation of phenomena. By this I mean that the Coordinadora Campesina was rather producing and sustaining different subjects and positions, such as activists, researchers, *campesinos* and so on that were necessary for the collective itself. In other words, those who were participating in materializing the Coordinadora were also emerging as new subjects.

In previous paragraphs, I presented an implicit view of reflexivity as a collective achievement, that is, as an outcome of establishing relationships with *campesinos*. I also showed that reflexivity helped to shape my interactions and contributed to orient collaborative research. This back-and-forth of reflexivity will be developed better in the coming paragraphs, but for now, it suggests that reflexivity is not singular. It can be a tool to orient action and on other occasions a collective achievement resulting from working together with other people and expanding our positions as researchers.

To illustrated better this back-and-forth process, my experience working with the collective that *campesinos* were forming is particularly relevant. Mainly because a collective is dealing with shaping its aims and who can partake of it. That creates a situation where attachments are sorted (Bruun Jensen 2007) in a collective, so researchers and other participants can engage in a variegated set of activities like meetings, decision making and, of course, researching. But as I mentioned before, not everybody in the Coordinadora Campesina had to necessarily agree on the same.

In 2021 there were profound differences between *campesino* organizations regarding the negotiations with the Ministry of Environment about the conservation and demarcation of the *páramo*. Those differences could be summarized in positions ranging from rejecting the demarcation policy as the way to conserve the *páramo* and others accepting the demarcation but only if it there were guarantees to include the active role of *campesino* communities. However, those differences did not represent any fragmentation of the Coordinadora Campesina, they were not an obstacle to continue the formation of the collective. In fact, the differences were the reason for the collective to seek coordination (Mol 2002) strategies to hang together the heterogeneous coalition that the Coordinadora was in practice.

So, how on earth could a collective with so many differences be sustained? How could *campesinos* and their allies maintain the Coordinadora Campesina? A reflexive approach to that question made me pay special attention to the material organization of the Coordinadora Campesina. Because if there was something called Coordinadora Campesina, where different positions, subjectivities and differences emerged, then there should certainly be practical occasions where all those elements were arranged. That became clearer to me in the meetings held after the COVID-19 lockdown in 2021. One of those took place on 6 June 2021, when the Coordinadora Campesina organized a meeting in the rural area of Pandi, a municipality from the Sumapaz region.

The photo in Figure 10.2 exemplifies this; it shows a scene from the meeting in Pandi. The *campesino* wearing the blue face mask on the right side of the picture is telling the audience that they needed a set of 'minimum demands' to negotiate with the Ministry of Environment. Some of the attendees at the meeting can be seen around him, but in the middle, there is a table with a black device on it. It is a projector, which is connected to a laptop. Both are plugged into the socket next to the red window through a cable extension. Near to the window, hanging on the wall, there is a router providing an internet connection to the laptop, so the projector can display the videocall on the white blanket hanging on the wall for attendees that were virtually attending the meeting.

The course of practical action that allowed us to meet that day was possible due to the gathering of all those elements. This arrangement of people, laptop, projector, chair, router, cables and even a white blanket hanging on

**Figure 10.2:** Hybrid meeting in Pandi, June 2021. People attending remotely and in person

a wall all participated in the making of the Coordinadora Campesina that day. If there was a collective that was able to meet, discuss, negotiate and make decisions it was as an outcome of the heterogeneous association of the elements at play in the meeting. This materiality was constitutive of the collective, which means that all these elements were not passive mediums, but the very condition for the composition of the collective and its capacity to act (Rodríguez-Giralt 2011). It should be noted that this coherence of the collective should be understood as a temporal, contingent and precarious effect of the collective capacity of organizing itself in practical action.

Reflexivity was here the means to align my shifting research positions with the task of making more liveable worlds. Being a researcher here meant as well trying with other people (and nonhumans) to compose a collective. That of course was not an objective of my research, but as a collaborator I could not simply distance myself from responsibilities and commitments that arise from organizing a Coordinadora Campesina meeting and the subsequent tasks that emerge from it. It was from occasions like that meeting, where we could make come into being the Coordinadora Campesina as a collective, that the roles, attributes and subjectivities of all of those participating in it were shaped. So, composing a collective was the way for *campesinos* to make more liveable worlds. Within the collective, that task meant the possibility of creating alternative spaces, where the *páramo* and its conservation could be reconfigured to allow the relationships that maintain the existence of *campesinos* in their lands.

Reflexivity, then, helped me to understand the task of making more liveable worlds as both practical and multiple. Practical, because as I showed in the previous paragraphs, the material associations that allowed the Coordinadora Campesina to act, like for example through a meeting, are the means through which more liveable worlds can be created. And multiple, in the sense that participants that contribute to the formation of a collective are differently shaped when they are engaged in the creation of more liveable worlds. In my case as researcher, this was translated into collaborative activities to support the maintaining of the Coordinadora Campesina. They included writing reports of meetings, helping with the moderation of discussions, making presentations, and more. In short, making more liveable worlds as a collaborator involved an expansion of the kind of activities, positions and places that made possible my research. For *campesino* communities participating in the collective, making more liveable worlds was similarly a task that depended on the permanent collaboration with actors beyond their communities. However, for *campesinos*, making more liveable worlds involved a more immediate and urgent concern to defend themselves and their lands in the middle of the negotiations with the Ministry of Environment around the conservation of the *páramo*.

## Conclusions

Back in the 1980s, when reflexivity was in vogue among Science and Technology Studies scholars (Ashmore 1989; Woolgar 1991), it served as a tool to interfere with the conventions of realist representation practices. Now, in an academic world where collaborative projects seem more necessary and common to attune our research work with the task of creating more liveable worlds, reflexivity becomes again an important companion to understand the effects of our research practices. This is crucial for researchers whose work involves close relationships with collectives or communities beyond academia. As I have been arguing in this chapter, reflexivity becomes relevant for researchers seeking ways to account for the conditions that shape the different positions that enable them to establish collaborative relationships in research projects.

When we can reflexively unpack collaboration, we as researchers can be more committed with performative ways of making knowledges, such as those present in collectives like social movements, political organizations, grassroots organizations and so on (Escobar 2008; Rappaport 2020). What this means is that reflexivity reminds us that conducting research for making more liveable worlds does not translate automatically into a set of fixed positions, let alone singular political goals. As the topics we research, and the research work itself, collaboration is uncertain and involves translation and coordination work between diverse world–making practices.

In my case with Sintrapaz, the Research Group and the Coordinadora Campesina, reflexivity served as a compass to understand how my research relations enacted different research positions in my work. In this collaboration, I engaged with *campesinos* not with the aim of making 'better' or more 'accurate' representations of them and the *páramo*. Our collaboration involved the very task of working towards the possibility of assembling a different *páramo* conservation where *campesinos* could be a constitutive part of it. For doing so, the material organization of meetings and other activities that I had the chance to support along with more people, whose aim was to intervene (Hacking 1983; Zuiderent-Jerak 2016) into the politics of *páramos* conservation in Sumapaz, were necessary. These activities were the entry point to reflexively understand how research and collaboration could be connected with the creation of more liveable worlds for *campesino* communities in Sumapaz. As I analysed in the chapter, that was a task that required the material composition of a collective and the occasions where it could reach its temporal coherence to hang together despite its internal differences.

This insistence on performativity, that is, the work involved in making both collaborations happen and those involved in it, is perhaps one of the main lessons of reflexivity for the creation of more liveable worlds with(in) collectives. This means that collaborations are necessarily mediated, so they require constant building, supporting and renovating. In that work, researchers involved in collaborative projects are always negotiating with their collaborators their positions and what their collaborations consist of. This basically means that collaboration is not a shortcut to fixed positions, positions cannot be known and established either in advance or once and for all. A reflexive take on collaboration and our shifting research positions is a tool for situating (Haraway 1988) the creation of more liveable worlds.

In this context, reflexivity emerges from *resisting and helps to resist* taken-for-granted notions of collaboration and normativity. In that way reflexivity occurs in a back-and-forth process where it operates to orient action and as a collective achievement. Regarding the former, reflexivity can potentially orient researchers about the multiple positions that they engage in when working in collaborative projects. That can help researchers to better realize the affordances, limitations and challenges of the different concerns and commitments that each position entails. Regarding reflexivity as a collective achievement, the chapter showed that reflexivity is also realized through the relationships that we as researchers create with counterparts in tasks such as making more liveable worlds.

Attending to the activities that form collectives is a reminder that the creation of more liveable worlds must be literally made with others, with whom we can collaborate beyond academia. That is why the invitation for researchers engaged with the creation of more liveable worlds is to cultivate reflexivity, so we can attend to the work that could make worlds more liveable not only for us as academics, but also liveable for more, including all of those involved in the collectives that we help to shape and sustain.

## References

Ashmore, M. (1989) *The Reflexive Thesis: Writing Sociology of Scientific Knowledge*. Chicago: University of Chicago Press.

Ashmore, M. (1994) Social Epistemology and Reflexivity: Two Versions of How to Be Really Useful. *Argumentation* 8(2): 157–161. https://doi.org/10.1007/BF00733367

Blake, L.J., Chohan, J.K. and Escobar, M.P. (2023) Agro-extractivism and Neoliberal Conservation: Campesino Abandonment in the Boyacá Páramos, Colombia. *Journal of Rural Studies* 102: 103071. https://doi.org/10.1016/j.jrurstud.2023.103071

Bruun Jensen, C. (2007) Sorting Attachments: Usefulness of STS in Healthcare Practice and Policy. *Science as Culture* 16(3): 237–251. https://doi.org/10.1080/09505430701568636

Castillo, C. (2023) *Reconfiguring Conservation and Ontological Politics*, PhD thesis, Linköping University.

Cleef, A.M., Rangel, J.O. and Arellano, P.H. (2008) The Paramo Vegetation of the Sumapaz Massif (Eastern Cordillera, Colombia) of the Sumapaz (Massif Cordillera Oriental, Colombia). In T. van der Hammen, J.O. Rangel and A.M. Cleef (eds) *La Cordillera Oriental Colombiana, Transecto Sumapaz*. Berlin-Stuttgart: Verlag J. Cramer, pp 799–914.

Colombian Ministry of Environment and Sustainable Development (2017) *Delimitación del Páramo Cruz-Verde Sumapaz a Escala 1:25.000*. Bogotá.

Comisión de la Verdad Colombia (2022) *Caso: Estigmatización y violencia política en Sumapaz*. Capítulo Territorios. Comisión para el Esclarecimiento de la Verdad, la Convivencia y la No Repetición.

Coordinadora Campesina de Sumapaz (2019) Acción de Tutela Delimitación Páramo de Sumapaz-Cruz Verde. Archive Coordinadora Campesina Sumapaz-Cruz Verde.

Escobar, A. (2008) *Territories of Difference: Place, Movements, Life, Redes*. Durham, NC: Duke University Press.

Hacking, I. (1983) *Representing and Intervening: Introductory Topics in the Philosophy of Natural Science*. Cambridge and New York: Cambridge University Press.

Haraway, D. (1988) Situated Knowledges: The Science Question in Feminism and the Privilege of Partial Perspective. *Feminist Studies* 14(3). https://doi.org/10.2307/3178066

Hofstede, R., Segarra, P. and Mena, V.P. (eds) (2003) *Los páramos del mundo. Proyecto atlas mundial de páramos*. Quito: NC-UICN/Global Peatland Initiative/EcoCiencia.

Latour, B. (2005) *Reassembling the Social: An Introduction to Actor Network Theory*. Oxford: Oxford University Press.

Madriñán, S., Cortés, A.J. and Richardson, J.E. (2013) Páramo is the World's Fastest Evolving and Coolest Biodiversity Hotspot. *Frontiers in Genetics* 4. https://doi.org/10.3389/fgene.2013.00192

Mol, A. (2002) *The Body Multiple: Ontology in Medical Practice*. Durham, NC and London: Duke University Press.

Mol, A. and Law, J. (1994) Regions, Networks and Fluids: Anaemia and Social Topology. *Social Studies of Science* 24(4): 641–671. https://doi.org/10.1177/030631279402400402

Morales-Rivas, M., J.O. García, T. van der Hammen, A.T. Perdigón, C.E. Cadena Vargas, C.A. Pedraza Peñaloza, N. Rodríguez Eraso, C.A. Franco Aguilera, J.C. Betancourth Suárez, É. Olaya Ospina, E. Posada Gilede and L. Cárdenas Valencia (2007) *Atlas de páramos de Colombia*. Bogotá: Instituto de Investigación de Recursos Biológicos Alexander von Humboldt.

Papadopoulos, D. (2018) *Experimental Practice: Technoscience, Alterontologies, and More-Than-Social Movements*. Durham, NC: Duke University Press.

Parra Romero, A. (2019) *Producción y movilización de conocimiento en conflictos socioambientales estudio de caso del conflicto por minería a gran escala y defensa del agua en el páramo de Santurbán – Colombia*, PhD thesis, Universidade Estadual de Campinas. https://doi.org/10.47749/T/UNICAMP.2019.1096003

Rama Judicial de Colombia (2019) *Expediente 11001-33-37-040-2019-00257-00*. Juzgado 40 Administrativo de Oralidad del Circuito de Bogotá, Sección Cuarta.

Rappaport, J. (2008) Beyond Participant Observation: Collaborative Ethnography as Theoretical Innovation. *Collaborative Anthropologies* 1(1): 1–31. https://doi.org/10.1353/cla.0.0014

Rappaport, J. (2020) *Cowards Don't Make History: Orlando Fals Borda and the Origins of Participatory Action Research*. New York: Duke University Press.

Republic of Colombia (2010) *Mining Code: Law 1382, 2010*. Bogotá.

Rodríguez-Giralt, I. (2011) Social Movements as Actor-Networks: Prospects for a Symmetrical Approach to Doñana's Environmentalist Protests. *Convergencia Revista de Ciencias Sociales* 18(56): 13–35.

Sarmiento Pinzón, C.E., C.E. Cadena Vargas, M.V. Sarmiento Giraldo and J.A. Zapata Jiménez (2013) *Aportes a la conservación estratégica de los páramos de Colombia actualización de la cartografía de los complejos de páramo a escala 1:100.000*. Bogota: Instituto de Investigación de Recursos Biológicos Alexander von Humboldt.

Ungar, P. (2021) Assembling an Ecosystem: The Making of State Páramos in Colombia. *Conservation and Society* 19(2): 119–129.

Woolgar, S. (ed) (1991) *Knowledge and Reflexivity: New Frontiers in the Sociology of Knowledge*. London: SAGE.

Zuiderent-Jerak, T. (2016) If Intervention Is Method, What Are We Learning? *Engaging Science, Technology, and Society* 2: 73–82. https://doi.org/10.17351/ests2016.90

11

# Reflecting on Discomfort: Fieldwork with Vaccine-Hesitant Participants During the COVID-19 Pandemic

Barbara Morsello

In 2020, I participated in a research project focused on studying Refused Knowledge Communities, which are diverse groups that endorse knowledge refused by public health institutions and mainstream science (Neresini et al 2024). My role involved conducting qualitative research, including interviews and observations, with vaccine-hesitant individuals. In the meantime, in March 2020, the Italian president announced a national warning about COVID-19, and Italy soon became the first European epicentre of the pandemic, surpassing China in deaths (Alberti et al 2020). Social tensions were high, and a decree was issued restricting regional travel and enforcing a strict lockdown, which was initially criticized by other countries (Viola 2022).

However, my research team and I viewed the pandemic as an opportunity to study the decision-making processes of vaccine-hesitant individuals, as mass vaccination campaigns began in late 2020. I was enthusiastic about exploring this controversy during such a pivotal time but apprehensive about potential resistance from participants, given the polarized views on vaccination exacerbated by the pandemic (Figure 11.1).

Listening to participants discuss government conspiracies and deny the benefits of vaccination, especially amid widespread death, quickly became exhausting as I underestimated the physical and emotional toll of engaging with vaccine-hesitant individuals during the COVID-19 pandemic. Indeed, on one hand, I experienced discomfort because I did not share their beliefs about alleged vaccine damage, particularly when adherence

**Figure 11.1:** Dealing with tensions during the COVID-19 pandemic

to COVID-19 guidelines was crucial for public health. They held an individualized perspective on health management, whereas I believed in a more collective approach to public well-being. It was challenging for both the participants and me to overlook these differences, especially since we were all deeply affected by the pandemic, albeit in varying ways. I was deeply concerned about my health and that of my loved ones, burdened by remote work and lockdown measures. They, on the other hand, were unable to work and often isolated from their social circles, particularly those who did not share their views. During the interviews, participants often displayed hostility, perceiving me as embodying the epistemic authority of mainstream science and as a representative of institutions that dismissed their knowledge and practices (Morsello 2024). On numerous occasions, they refused to sign the informed consent form or suspected I was there as a government representative to gather information about their views on vaccination, prompting them to leave the interview settings or suspend the interview. In other instances, some ceased responding to my calls or withdrew their consent after the interview.

I felt frustrated by the many obstacles I faced in interviewing them and uncomfortable with being continually framed as an enemy or impostor.

**Figure 11.2:** Doing research with challenging participants

This situation made it difficult to empathize with them. Considering that empathy is an epistemic resource that allows researchers to understand the perspective of respondents and move beyond normative biases (Davies and Spencer 2010), these challenges posed severe obstacles to the success of my fieldwork (Figure 11.2).

I realized that I needed to carefully reflect on my methodological stance.

As a Science and Technology Studies scholar, I was aware that to deeply examine a controversy, I needed to adopt the principle of symmetry (Bloor 1976; Lynch 2017), which dictates that truth is a matter of perspective, requiring equal consideration of all sides in a controversy. In line with scholars like Sismondo (2017) and Jasanoff and Simmet (2017), I believe we are not in a post-truth world; rather, what counts as 'facts' are contextually rooted, subjectively experienced, and acquire social meaning in relation to the social worlds in which they are co-produced according to the desires, practices and worldviews of the actors involved (Jasanoff 2004; Latour 2005). Despite this, a binary framing of the pandemic – science/experts/evidence versus conspiracy theories/fake news – created a sort of 'epistemic competition' (Sismondo 2017) that unconsciously influenced my approach to fieldwork (Figure 11.3).

**Figure 11.3:** Looking for a symmetric perspective

Reflecting on this and discussing it with my research team, I realized that symmetry alone was inadequate for building trust with my subjects and overcoming my personal and emotional limitations. While the principle of symmetry is useful for treating science and non-science equally in terms of truth claims, it did not help in deconstructing my position as a researcher in the field. What helped was reflecting on the concept of agnosticism, as described by Jaron Harambam (2020) in his book on fieldwork with conspiracy theorists. Being agnostic did not mean adopting an unrealistic stance of neutrality, which qualitative researchers know is impossible (Gouldner 1968; Haraway 1988; Scott et al 1990). Instead, it entailed studying vaccine hesitancy during the pandemic from the perspective of my research subject without questioning the validity of their claims.

Adopting this perspective required significant effort. I engaged deeply with participants views on alleged vaccine damage participating in long discussions where we exchanged and debated our perspectives. I tried to build relationships by spending time with them in non-traditional settings – during walks, meals or leisure activities. I opened my home to them, and they did the same for me. This immersion allowed me to see that, despite our different worldviews, we were all navigating a process of sense-making amid uncertainty and fear.

As suggested by Rossella Ghigi, during the presentation of our research book *Manufacturing Refused Knowledge in the Age of Epistemic Pluralism* (Neresini et al 2024), fear can become a tool for accommodating the perspective of the participants and restoring their epistemic dignity by acknowledging the value of their marginalized viewpoint (Figure 11.4). Participants compel us to re-evaluate our positioning, addressing potential clashes of worldviews that can arise during fieldwork. In this regard,

**Figure 11.4:** We are all in fear

reflexivity allowed me to consider my biases, experiences, assumptions and the social context of interactions with participants (Denzin and Lincoln 1994; Maynard and Purvis 1994; Watt 2007; Cunliffe and Karunanayake 2013; Hammersley 2019), leading to more accurate data interpretation (Gouldner 1971). It enabled me to start viewing the pandemic from the perspective of vaccine-hesitant individuals, helping me build fruitful relationships with them. Reflexivity became an ongoing process, extending beyond the completion of my fieldwork (Figure 11.5).

Today, conducting a meta-reflection years after fieldwork is made possible through various methods, such as diaries, audiovisual recordings and drawing, which centre the subjective experience and enable a return to research data (Moretti 2023). The illustrations presented here serve a purpose beyond mere depiction: drawing has helped me revisit memories (Figure 11.6) and articulate my feelings and emotions, allowing me to retrace the fieldwork and identify gaps in my relationship with participants. Drawing is integral to my reflexive approach, aimed at acknowledging that participants possess a privileged viewpoint in the epistemic construction of knowledge.

**Figure 11.5:** Reflexivity as an ongoing process

**Figure 11.6:** Retracing fieldwork experience

Through this reflexive exercise, I came to recognize my limitations and reframed vaccine-hesitant individuals as marginalized subjects in the pandemic controversy. Their claims were frequently dismissed by institutions, which heightened their hostilities. Reflecting on my own discomfort and that experienced by the participants entails acknowledging our unique perspectives on power dynamics in society, especially since vaccine-hesitant individuals lack influence in epistemic debates surrounding vaccination, unlike academic researchers.

This awareness does not imply alignment with their views but rather aims to comprehend their standpoint. It underscores the importance of incorporating discomforting positions into research narratives, even those that may be difficult to fully grasp or accurately represent.

## References


Alberti, M., Ruotolo, N., Di Donato, V. and John, T. (2020) Italy Surpasses China in Number of Coronavirus Deaths. *CNN*. Available at: https://edition.cnn.com/2020/03/19/europe/italy-death-toll-intl/index.html [Accessed 17 April 2025].

Bloor, D. (1976) *Knowledge and Social Imagery*. London: Routledge & Kegan Paul.

Cunliffe, A.L. and Karunanayake, G. (2013) Working within Hyphen-spaces in Ethnographic Research: Implications for Research Identities and Practice. *Organizational Research Methods* 16(3): 364–392.

Davies, J. and Spencer, D. (eds) (2010) *Emotions in the Field: The Psychology and Anthropology of Fieldwork Experience*. Stanford: Stanford University Press.

Denzin, N.K. and Lincoln, Y.S. (1994) *Handbook of Qualitative Research*. Thousand Oaks: SAGE.

Gouldner, A.W. (1968) The Sociologist as Partisan: Sociology and the Welfare State. *The American Sociologist* 3(2): 103–116.

Gouldner, A.W. (1971) *The Coming Crisis in Western Sociology*. London and New Delhi: Heinemann.

Hammersley, M. (2019) The Radical Reflexivity of Contemporary Qualitative Research. *Sociology* 53(4): 679–693.

Harambam, J. (2020) *Contemporary Conspiracy Culture: Truth and Knowledge in an Era of Epistemic Instability*. Oxon: Routledge.

Haraway, D. (1988) Situated Knowledges: The Science Question in Feminism and the Privilege of Partial Perspective. *Feminist Studies* 14(3): 575–599.

Jasanoff, S. (ed) (2004) *States of Knowledge: The Co-Production of Science and Social Order*. London: Routledge.

Jasanoff, S. and Simmet, H.R. (2017) No Funeral Bells: Public Reason in a 'Post-truth' Age. *Social Studies of Science* 47(5): 751–770.

Latour, B. (2005) *Reassembling the Social: An Introduction to Actor-Network Theory*. New York: Oxford University Press.

Lynch, M. (2017) STS, Symmetry and Post-truth. *Social Studies of Science* 47(4): 593–599.

Maynard, M. and Purvis, J. (eds) (1994) *Researching Women's Lives from a Feminist Perspective* (1st edn). Routledge. https://doi.org/10.4324/978131 5041025

Moretti, V. (2023) *Understanding Comics-Based Research: A Practical Guide for Social Scientists*. Leeds: Emerald.

Morsello, B. (2024) Respecifying Fieldwork: Refused Knowledge Communities Explored Through the Reflexive Lens. In F. Neresini, M.C. Agodi, S. Crabu and S. Tosoni (eds) *Manufacturing Refused Knowledge in the Age of Epistemic Pluralism*. Singapore: Palgrave Macmillan, pp 257–284.

Neresini, F., Agodi, M.C., Crabu, S. and Tosoni, S. (eds) (2024) *Manufacturing Refused Knowledge in the Age of Epistemic Pluralism*. Singapore: Palgrave Macmillan.

Scott, P., Richards, E. and Martin, B. (1990) Captives of Controversy: The Myth of the Neutral Social Researcher in Contemporary Scientific Controversies. *Science, Technology, & Human Values* 15(4): 474–494.

Sismondo, S. (2017) Post-truth? *Social Studies of Science* 47(1): 3–6.

Viola, L. (2022) 'Italy, for Example, Is Just Incredibly Stupid Now': European Crisis Narrations in Relation to Italy's Response to COVID-19. *Frontiers in Communication* 7: 757847.

Watt, D. (2007) On Becoming a Qualitative Researcher: The Value of Reflexivity. *The Qualitative Report* 12(1): 82–101.

PART III

# Experimenting

# Doing

12

# Outrageously Open: Co-inhabiting and Expanding Knowledge-making Spaces through Somatic, Arts-based Methods

Ewa Łączkowska

An accompanying short film on somatic research process through dance can be found at https://www.youtube.com/watch?v=7VGMrh8Th68.

## Introduction

Imagine a social science conference without PowerPoint. Instead, you are invited to experience the gathered knowledge with your senses. You move through an art installation showing research results, to a workshop in methods taught through dance theatre, and then to a storytelling event by the fire. Academics and non-academics intermingle in a way that makes our childlike curiosity about the world sparkle. We acknowledge our somatic, relational embeddedness as both knowledge makers and receivers. We allow every *body* to partake. There, multiple realities coexist, interact with one another, and create inferences. This would be a space where the undone aesthetics of all of our translations of the world is laid bare. Would we dare to dance? Would we dare to enter a space where we do not know with clarity? One thing is sure: we would need much more sense of humour about our academic work to do that.

Opening to this kind of space means questioning what counts as 'knowledge'. And this is risky. The boundaries between 'knowledge' and the things that do not earn that status define our being in the world and

139

the framework of our understanding. Stabilizing them is our daily bread as human beings: the boundaries serve as a way to make our world small enough for us to feel safe. Questioning them in a radical manner means questioning our subsistence.

The risk increases if you find yourself in a knowledge-making profession. Here, the question of 'knowledge' becomes the question of legitimation. Because of this, especially in an academic context, we tend to talk about 'knowledge' in a very neat, comfortable manner: manoeuvring between concepts and categories, arranging them in new ways, but never leaping too far out of familiar, established ways of doing. This is knowledge we can control. But is control a meaningful goal for knowledge-making? To assume that our concepts describe reality adequately is to mistake the stars reflected in a pond at night for those in the sky.[1]

I feel that the simplest way to go beyond control is to make knowledge into a verb. An activity. A process. An experience. A *knowing*. The point of this chapter is to invite academic knowledge-making into the intuitive space of somatic and artistic knowing – where boundaries are everything but clear. It is to relate scientific research to a mode of inquiry where translations are many; where they are allowed to coexist, collaborate, and multiply. By making room for this kind of sensitivity, we open towards a deeper relationship with the world and others inhabiting the inquiry space. Then, we can let ourselves be led by what wants to be known.

Here, I tell my story of a collaboration between sociology, dance pedagogy and arts. I invite you to reflect with me on what this kind of collaboration can teach us – experimenting with inquiry spaces outrageously open for knowing our world in a multiple, incomplete, but abundant and vibrant way. You might notice performative echoes of these qualities in the text. This is because these spaces invite disruptions and collaborations that – if taken seriously – *prevent me from being in charge*. My writing has been derailed by the outrageous openness I write about. This kind of chaos, while time-consuming and inherently turbulent, has a potential to immensely expand any inquiry. Evoking sensual knowledge-making spaces we can share, this chapter is a call on bravery in research – beyond the safety of clear-cut concepts. Because I agree with John Law that 'if we want to think about the messes of reality at all then we're going to have to teach ourselves to think, to practice, to relate, and to know in new ways'.[2] And for me, all this begins with *practice*.

Will you dive with me?

---

[1]    As far as I know, this metaphor was most recently used by Andrzej Sapkowski in his book series 'The Witcher' (published originally 1992–1999).

[2]    A main point of his book, *After Method* (Law 2004, 2), which has been the first signpost on my journey towards what I present here.

# In the beginning, there was movement

Every representation of the world is a *translation* that arises from our perception of the world. To translate means to *displace*: to remove from one place and carry elsewhere. It's an impactful process. Displacement and its hardships change the displaced. They also transform known arrangements: creating absences where people and things used to be and out-of-place manifestations somewhere new, where they engage with a new environment, eventually unwittingly ingraining into it. This seems to be something implicitly understood throughout different cultures. Take the Māori word for 'representation' – *whakaahuahanga* – which has its root in the verb *whakaahua* – to transform; to change and acquire new form or shape. And while the etymological roots of English *-form* has been lost to time; the *trans-* part of the word points towards Proto-Indo-European *tere-*: to cross over, to pass through – that is, beyond the point of origin. *No translation is without consequence.*

In the beginning of what you're reading right now, there was movement. There was learning, feeling, listening, watching, talking, thinking, painting. Then, they were transformed into field notes, recordings, pictures, texts. Now, I displace again – I cut my experience into pieces to arrange it into a new, smaller constellation. In the end, the smell of the freshly oiled hardwood floor of the studio, the feeling of my aching body after four hours of movement, the music that still lives in my bones, the relations we have built there over time – they all have been displaced to the point of unrecognizability. A linear, written text is especially hard on the sensual travellers.

Every translation is a *betrayal:*[3] it delimits the messy multiplicity of the world into a singular reality. Some of our translations may be able to let the chaos of reality shine or echo through. However, science and its tools aim at producing *clarity*. They tend to reject anything that cannot be squeezed into a concept. Through that, we displace with a special kind of violence. In our singularities, we might be able to talk about the world with some kind of authority – in contrast to, let's say, poets – but in doing that, we strip our research subjects of any life. We withdraw from any kind of relationship we had with them.[4] And while in the past decades many have already called

---

[3] It is a betrayal because each representation leaves the object of it behind. It makes it *absent* in order to give presence to the translation. There is no judgement involved in using this word; just an emphasis on certain effects. Let's look at etymology again: *betray* is closely related to *deceive*, *delude* and *mislead*. Originally, it comes from Latin *tradere* that means nothing more than *hand over* or *hand down (to posterity)*. And we land by translation again. John Law (2006) was the first to equate translation and betrayal in the Science and Technology Studies context.

[4] *Dead sociology*, made of *fossil facts* and *zombie concepts*, is how Les Back (2012) describes it in the context of social science.

out science on this, I feel that this critique has rarely been *practised*. In that, it has rarely been truly reflective.

There are different ways of approaching translative transformations. For Māori, *whakaahua* does not only mean transforming our world into representations; it is primarily about striving to transform *oneself*: to align with the natural world and dissolve the separation between humans and the environment. Through ritual, storytelling and performance, Māori believe to be able to embody the landscape and allow its energy to be expressed through dancing bodies.[5] This framing of translation puts explicit emphasis on the fact that is not solely us who displace – we ourselves are a part of what's being displaced in the process. It's about moving beyond individual identity as a 'knowledge-maker' and becoming *part of the knowing* – one with the landscape, channelling it through the body.

This kind of sensual relationship with the world is a one that exists beyond any static representation. It incorporates the ever-changing nature of everything. It also emphasizes our interactive relationship with the world and the need to nurture this connection in its dynamic interplay. It requires us to let the perceived world be as alive as it is and to let it *take possession* of our perception. In that way, perception is an inherently participative experience: it involves an intimate coupling between the animate, living *sensible* and our sensing body.[6] On a somatic level, this relationship never ceases – our bodies physically cannot survive without it. It is a reciprocity operating on a level completely beyond our control. But on a mental level, *we can withdraw from it*. Way too often, we readily do.[7] We repress our sensual involvement and deny – whether consciously or not – our own displaceability. Through that, we restrict ourselves to a small habitat of detached, fixed concepts that we can manipulate easily; seemingly without being touched by the world ourselves. This denial impacts the way we see and describe our reality. And since our reality is not independent from our translation tools, the withdrawal impacts our reality. We enact a world deprived of embodied reciprocity. We objectify it into submission.

So, for me, reflexivity in Science and Technology Studies *must begin with facing our individual fears* about our utterly personal, intimate relationship with the world. This is why both indigenous and phenomenological points

---

[5]   This account is based on Ojeya Cruz Banks' (2017) story of *whare tapere*, Māori community houses and Māori contemporary dance incorporated by Atamira Dance Company (2015; 2021).

[6]   Perspective based on the phenomenology of Maurice Merlau-Ponty (1962). A fascinating integration of both indigenous and phenomenological perspectives on that matter (in a unwittingly Science and Technology Studies way) is presented by David Abram in his book *Spell of the Sensuous (2017)*.

[7]   I dive deep into what this means in my artistic research on distance (Łączkowska 2023).

are so important here. This is also why embodiment and returning to our individual entanglement with the world play an essential role in dealing with the effects of our representations on our realities. My writing might give some direction; but ultimately, the way towards outrageous openness is *out there* – beyond the pages of this book. As William Blake says, experience is the only thing that has the power to transform people. Experience will change us – *if we let it displace us.*

We need to reflect on the violence of the methods, representations and realities we produce. In the following, I invite you to a world of knowledge-making that supports translational reflexivity rooted in embodied experience.

## Let's dance: crafting imaginaries open for multiplicity

The research project this chapter originates from grappled with tacit knowing as a phenomenon and the challenge it presents to the established ways of doing sociological research.[8] Tacit knowing is knowing that cannot be put into words. It is essential for making sense of our world and acting within it. It is also the ground of all cognitive understanding and communication. At the same time, tacit knowing is neither conceptual nor rational: it comes out of somatic, multimodal sensing of ourselves and our intersubjective experience of the world.[9] That is why studying, transferring and representing tacit knowing is something science has not been very good at – seemingly blind to the ways it exiles the tacit dimension from its findings by insisting on linear clarity. We have been in urgent need of a better scientific approach to understanding tacit knowing – independent of the specific context. This called for new practices – ones that would not regard the conceptual elusiveness of tacit knowing as a problem, but as a gateway to completely new modes of inquiry, reflexivity, and sensitivity towards our scientific translation processes.

I set out to search for practices that could bring social science closer to the boundlessness of knowing that lies beyond concepts. I did so by diving into other ontologies, unrestricted by scientific rationales. I looked for translation repertoires that could accommodate the aliveness of tacit knowing; ones equipped to communicate between different modes of knowing. Because in the chaos of everyday life, all displacements are temporary. No element can be enclosed in a stable relationship or a role for good: the dynamic nature of everything resists stagnation. The translations are multiple and overlapping.

---

[8] The original thesis (in German) is available upon request (email at ewa.laczkowska@ pm.me). A following publication in English (aimed at practitioners, teachers and researchers) is being published in form of a blog/podcast at https://wildgrowingsky. substack.com/s/entangled-translations.

[9] A useful introduction into the tacit nature of knowing is offered by Polanyi (2009).

They are not coherent, and not always compatible with each other – still, they coexist and are capable of situative negotiating with one another. And while our conceptual minds may have trouble wrapping around that exploding incoherency, it's not a problem for our somatic, tacit awareness: it is used to operating complexity.

I have aimed at situating myself in an imaginary attuned to tacit knowing; open for multiplicity and inferences – one that is able to mediate between translations. Using my personal experience, I drew on contemporary dance, arts, somatic work, and dance pedagogy as a rich creative environment that puts embodied knowing at the core of its work. Contemporary dance[10] is inherently defined by ambivalence and constant evolution of forms of moving and knowing. It regularly questions established rules and orders, seeking for new ways of artistic storytelling and human expression. Its pedagogical approach has always been a somatic research practice that is focused on producing new knowing, rather than just learning new steps.

This is especially the case with *Axis Syllabus dance pedagogy*, which I chose for my research context.[11] Axis Syllabus is a 'living information archive' that explicitly connects many different ontologies in its study of the human body in motion, reaching from anatomy, biomechanics, medicine and physics to anthropology and dance practice. This multimodal approach aims at a comprehensive, embodied understanding of the anatomic functionality of the human body in movement. As children, we all possess an innate ability of moving within the natural constitution of the body. With socialization, as we gradually get lost in our concepts and ideas, our connection to what is natural for the body is mostly lost – as is our relationship with the sensual world beyond us. Axis Syllabus pedagogy seeks to facilitate individual, situational rediscovery of that practical sense for movement in line with natural predispositions of the body. Through that, it supports expanding the individual playroom for creative expression and somatic inquiry – whether in dance, arts, sciences, or while cutting vegetables for dinner. On a meta-level, *Axis Syllabus sensitizes for noticing functional connections in entangled systems in an embodied way.*

People that take part in the classes are invited to explore the functional principles of movement: through theoretical knowledge, visual and spatial models of human anatomy, and above all somatic experience: working with one's own body or with the body of a partner. In this context, the inquiry

---

[10]  To get an idea of the versatile field of contemporary dance, see, for example, wild growing sky (2017).

[11]  My research was done in collaboration with *dieSynapse* (https://www.instagram.com/diesynapse), a dance and research studio in Düsseldorf, Germany. To learn more about Axis Syllabus, see Axis Syllabus Research Meshwork (2011; 2020).

and the learning process happens primarily not in the *ex-post* analysis of the movement, but *in the movement itself*: through doing and witnessing. These modes of inquiry operate mostly beyond conceptual representations, on a somatic level that activates knowing without having to resolve to linear, rational thinking.

A dance class is a communicative situation: as such, it must still resolve to translations in order to evoke knowing. But it does so in a very different way from what we are familiar with in science. Its foundation always lies in the direct experience of the body. This has an impact on the emerging translations. They dwell in the liminal space between soma, arts, poetical language and anatomy – thinking in terms of what is *useful*, rather than what is 'reliable' or 'unreliable' information. The primary inspiration of my research was to understand the translational effects of the Axis Syllabus learning environment and simultaneously integrate its practices into my own methodology. I was counting on it to displace me and the sociology I dragged there (albeit kicking and screaming) with me.

I grounded my research in a multisensory autoethnographic framework. This means that my inquiry was rooted in tapping into my own somatic experience of dance to better understand the effects of different tools on translating and communicating tacit knowing.[12] This also means that I have documented my inquiry primarily *in my body and the movement itself*. I had to be mindful about the consequences of translating it into tangible form. So, naturally, I set out to voyage beyond the written field notes to include experimental and intuitive formats: watercolour paintings, sketches, snippets of music, photos, and videos. This allowed me to try out different translations of my somatic experience. In addition, I decided to write my textual fieldnotes by hand – to retain more freedom in the form and make the writing process more somatic. I wanted to explore the performativity of my method and the performativity of tacit knowing itself.

Rather than following a pre-conceptualized design, I used fieldwork as a learning process and improvised according to the situative experience of studying tacit knowing through dance. I followed my embodied knowing, the human and nonhuman actors I encountered in the process, as well as the moments of translation at hand. I also invited participating dance teachers and students (and, inadvertently, a cat) to enter my inquiry and collectively reflect on knowledge-making through creative reflection sessions – not as research

---

[12] It is beyond the scope of this chapter to explain the method in detail. Concerning autoethnography, good food for thought is the discussion by Carloyn Ellis and Arthur Bochner (2006). I also learned a lot from Tim Ingold's (2000; 2011; 2014) approach to ethnography. As for the sensory part, in retrospect, I learned more about it through working with the body than through methods texts – with also goes for arts-based methods. You can read up on it (for example, Neilsen 2004), but better just go and do some art.

*subjects* but as transdisciplinary research *partners* that bring equally valuable knowledge, practice and experience. This collaboration was probably the most fruitful part of the research.

Although I have worked in an explicitly somatic context, this kind of strategy can just as well be used in other, not so obvious, settings. Because whatever we do – the body is there. Breathing. Receiving. Experiencing. Learning. It just needs to be allowed to speak and be heard. Through tapping into its boundless knowing, we can work towards receiving the world more fully – in our personal lives *and* in our research. And the personal does matter. The translations utilized here were necessarily centred around my own experience – which reaches beyond just sociology. My ontological beliefs and filters have been shaped by various contexts: my decade-long experience with dance and life-long occupation with the body; my passion for arts and my fascination with indigenous and Buddhist ontologies. I live in multiple realities, and – through my migration experiences – in multiple cultural and linguistical spaces. All that affects what I register as presence and what I blend

**Figure 12.1:** Fieldnotes: the flow of movement. Watercolours on paper

out as background noise. But maybe, just maybe, multiple experiences allow me to see the negotiating potentials of different realities better. Maybe we need more of what Gloria Anzaldúa (2002) calls *nepantleras* – the threshold people. I have tried to use all my resources to stay as close as possible to the multiplicity and contingency of translation. I aimed to stick to the call '[t]hat we refuse the distinction between the literal and the metaphorical … that we refuse the dualism between the real and the unreal, between realities and fictions, thinking, instead, in terms of *degrees* of enacted reality, or more reals and less reals. That we imagine coherence without consistency' (Law 2004, 139, emphasis in original).

How can dance pedagogy imaginary help us do that? Let me tell you a story of my dance through the webs spun by the learning spaces of Axis Syllabus. I evoke this story as a parable of sorts. I hope it will convey the importance of sensitivity towards the usefulness of inviting many translations and the delicate balance they dance within. The imperative of dropping the need for control in the process will lead our way. Ultimately, I aspire to encourage an outrageous openness towards embodied entanglements with the world in any art of inquiry. I hope this story will inspire you to explore further, *in practice*, beyond the literal. I hope it will awaken a longing to learn by being displaced. It will be an incomplete story – but aren't they all?

## Co-inhabiting somatic knowledge-making spaces

> Teaching is like digging a riverbed for the knowledge to flow. And I don't want to funnel with cement. … I like to dig, but to do that … I first need to see the landscape and decide where it makes sense to dig. And then, the water comes. And the water is not only the people in the class, but everything that happens there.[13]

The water opened the way for us. I hadn't thought about it consciously; it was more of an intuitive decision to always have watercolours within the reach of a hand – both for me and my research partners. The fluid nature of water seemed an adequate metaphor for thinking about movement. And so, through painting, liquid metaphors of Axis Syllabus came to life. A flowing river. Teachers' goal: to steer the flow in a certain direction. But just like a river remaining at the mercy of natural forces, Axis Syllabus class is an inherently unstable situation. Whirlpools and floodings emerge. The flow of water affects the environment and shapes the banks, which in turn manipulate the stream. Let's see where the current takes us.

---

[13] From the conversations in dance studio.

The nature of a river manifests in its flow and direction that affects the landscape it moves through. Axis Syllabus' river carries sediment that nourishes the ground for *sensory experience*. It invites somatic awareness: it provokes self-inquiry of the moving body through information, imagination, sound, and physical impulses. What does this experience contain? We sense ourselves from the inside: tension, pain, emotions. We sense ourselves through contact with the outside: temperature changes, pressure, pull. We can explore our world and our bodies through haptic and tactile sense perceptions: touching and being touched. Through proprioception we know where and how our body is positioned – if it sits, stands, runs, or falls. We know up from down by tracing the constellations of our head, torso, and extremities in relation to space. Changing sensations show us what we are doing. But it's not something we can easily talk about. The complexity and multiplicity of it all makes an accurate literal description almost impossible. And that's exactly the point: sensing transports us on a tacit level of understanding that allows us to inquiry into our experience and know things *without having to think about them*. We enter a relationship with our soma. Staying with it deepens our knowing. And if we take it seriously, it also pushes us to find translations of our experience that help us understand it without alienating it.

> Many things we can sense have no names. Still, they can be felt very clearly. Try it out. You may want to close your eyes for this exercise. Breathe deeply a few times; in and out, through your belly. Settle.
>
> Where are you?
>
> How are you?
>
> Where are your legs? Are you touching the ground, and if so, can you sense it under your feet?
>
> How is your body keeping you in balance right now? Can you feel the sitting bones that support your position and the subtle dance of your spinal structure that keeps you upright?
>
> Can you feel any tension in your body? Are you discovering, maybe just now, how your back cramps after a long reading time? Try to touch the tension with your breath, feel its structure. Let it dissolve and drip down to the earth you're sitting on. Then, slowly, try changing your position, moving your arms and spine a bit. Maybe try getting up and walking some steps. Can you feel how your body orients itself in space?
>
> What is it doing to you, to feel all that? Or maybe, to feel nothing like that?[14]

---

[14] This exercise is inspired by somatic meditation practices as taught by Reginald A. Ray (2016; see also Dharma Ocean 2023).

**Figure 12.2:** Sensing and translations at work. Photo: Stephan Thomsen; artwork: watercolours on paper

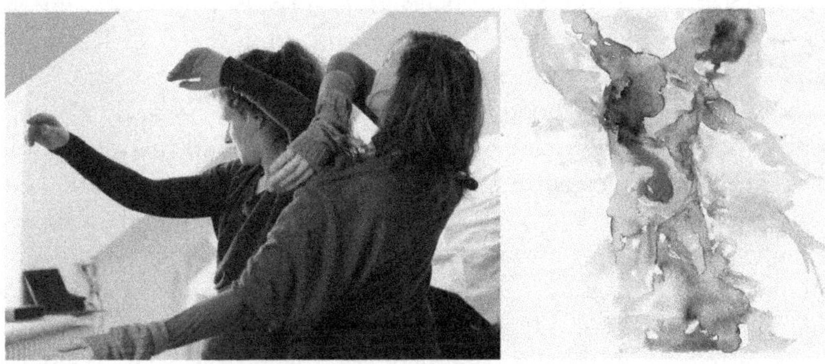

Opening to the sensing quality of our soma sharpens our awareness of what's happening inside the boundary of our body. But we do not sense in separation. Returning to the experience of the body also heightens the tacit understanding of what is happening around us and how the entanglements of our environment touch us. Beyond that, as we start to feel the effects of our translations from the perspective of the wordless knowing of the body, we can see the developing processes of translation more clearly.

In the embodied inquiry, I could feel – *not because I read it in a book, but from my sensual involvement in the practice* – that the flow of sensory experience is not completely free: it is shaped by the material-semiotic networks present. Some of them are introduced consciously – like the impulses brought into dance by Axis Syllabus teachers: models, exercises, stories told. Others manifest themselves spontaneously. Bodies move in space, anatomical concepts delimit the movement, music breaks through everything. Unintentional effects arise, spontaneous reactions to what is happening occur. All that affects what is there and how we perceive it. Through that, they build up the riverbed of inquiry – the corridor in which we experience. Axis Syllabus teachers evoke many translations of the somatic knowing to steer the learning: anatomical two- and three-dimensional models; symbolical models that emphasize the principles of the motion; linguistic metaphors that speak to the quality of the movement; music, rhythm and evoked space. The bodies present in the room become living models as well: they accentuate the knowing through their expression in space.[15] Since each translation can only make an excerpt of the knowing present, Axis Syllabus opens the space for concurrent existence of multiple

---

[15]  A detailed description of all these models and the effects they produce is beyond the scope of this chapter.

representations. It invites a relationship with *abundance* – even when, inevitably, the models and their effects contradict each other in their multidirectionality.

The translations are simultaneously *results of*, and *actors in* the communication of tacit knowing. The material used for regulating the river has its own quality – it escapes the control of the human agents trying to teach. This can easily disrupt the planned structure of a class. Scientific thoroughness squabbles with the poetics of sensing; anatomical explanations displace bodies into concepts of bodies. A moment later, sensing – with the aid of music – takes over and derails the diligence of trying to name all the muscles, inviting us instead to just move and know them by moving.

All of that is seen as part of the learning situation: an inquiry in itself. An invitation to dance with everything that is there. And like in dance, one movement invites another, every loss of control and every fall to the floor offers opportunities to use the momentum and move further. This is what I have found most extraordinary about Axis Syllabus: the improvisatory character and the elasticity of its pedagogical structure. *The teachers do not claim dominance in the network*. They do not insist on coherence and linearity. They do not try to control the situation at all costs but follow the effects unfolding and improvise with them. This have turned out to be remarkably efficient – *as long as no translation dominated the situation*. If that happened, collaboration was over, and the facilitating space fell apart.

Incoherence needs balance. And this balance needs to be dynamic – like a skilled mover, always adjusting their presence in space to appear in equilibrium. The integrity of Axis Syllabus inquiry space depends on *elasticity*: that is, the ability to recoil to the centre after being stretched. This is where our metaphor of a river falls apart and the chaos enters. The linearity of a riverbed and the illusion of control it gives is not here anymore. It has been displaced by my story. Now it must give way to different translations – ones that have been improvised rather than anticipated.

Last collaborative inquiry session. And I forgot to bring watercolours. 'Wait, I want to use wool yarn' said my research partner out of the blue. Five minutes later, she was spinning the yarn around the room, from column to column, from a chair to a box, creating a more and more complex web. Emma the cat, who was with us in the studio, became suddenly interested in what we're doing. Paper was boring, but yarn! She now felt inclined to enter the inquiry – and it didn't occur to her to ask us if she may. Again and again, she hunted the yarn, manipulating the already spun web or partially tearing it apart. She was insistent on reminding us we are not in control. I didn't have to do anything – other researchers were already on to something. The knowing was emerging. All I did was give room for the collaborative creativity to happen.

As the cat, worn out by all the impressions, fell asleep in the corner and the spun web took shape and gained robustness, we started to move between

**Figure 12.3:** Unexpected research partners

the threads while talking to each other. We tried out different possibilities of affecting the web – leaning with our weight into it and letting its integrity carry us; pulling on individual threads and letting go to observe its elasticity. Without really thinking about it, we created a perfect metaphor for Axis Syllabus learning space: the web has materialized as a framework structuring the learning space. We were suddenly restricted in our mobility: the threads and their presence were forcing us to move in a certain manner. At the same time, the web remained elastic and dynamic in its constant negotiation with all present actors. The many threads expressed the multiplicity of translations at hand: multidirectional and constantly interfering with each other. There was no leading thread – and no linearity. The network was being brought to life by the cooperation of all elements.

The web remained open in its structure: like Axis Syllabus translations and models, the threads were not fixed. Nor did they cover the whole learning space. They allowed room for other actors to move in. Their elasticity could integrate the emerging vibrations – unless worked upon with brute force of domination to the point of breaking. But as long as the threads were held in

**Figure 12.4:** Spatial reflection through working with the web

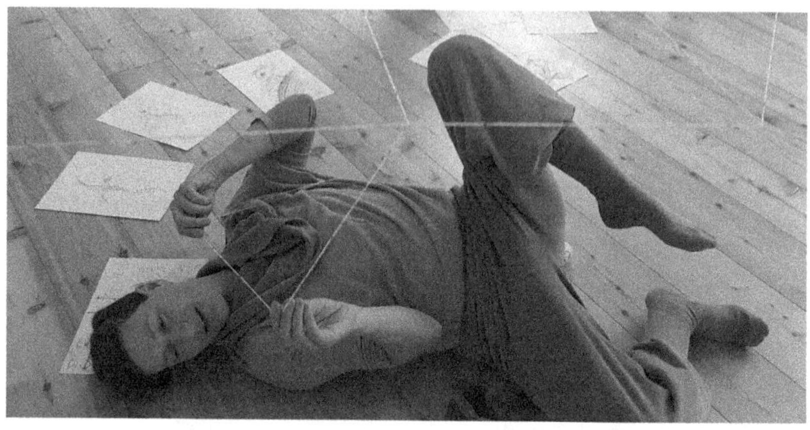

cooperative balance, the web gave space and opportunity for development and movement of all actors. It also allowed room for our tacit reflection to travel into words. As my research partner expressed:

> Now the threads are entangled. I have entangled the threads. We entangle ourselves in the threads. And through that, possibilities emerge. Look, behind you, there is a thread. … You can let yourself be moved by it or you can move it. What's the difference anyway? Are you being moved or do you move? And can you tell them apart at all, or is it the same, or maybe I am doing it, here?

*Knowing manifests in interspaces.* It is not told in a single story but arises from the performative entanglements of multiple translations. It calls upon us to give up control and enter an unstable, risky, always changing relationship, granting space for the bodies to experience. Attuned to the somatic multiplicity of sensing, we begin to understand in a multiple way. Our rootedness in experience helps us to imagine translations that do not alienate.

The story of my research and of Axis Syllabus imaginary is the story of relationship and co-inhabiting inquiry spaces. Our knowing is inherently sympoetic[16] – it emerges in company; in touch and in relationship with the world. In the space of knowing, everybody is a researcher – even a cat. As my research partner reflected:

> The knowing I embody is not independent of you. And it's not independent of the threads. It's always in becoming through our

---

[16]   A term coined by Donna Haraway (2016).

interplay. … When I move the threads, I don't speak directly to you. I speak to something else. But it affects you. And you affect it; you decide whether you hold your position or let yourself be led by the threads. And whether we want to arrange this web together.

A good translation of the world dwells in multiplicity, and we cannot find it alone. We cannot find it withdrawn from our basic relationships with the world and its companions. And we need to become more than just allies – it's important to recognize that we are involved in one another's entangled knowing. In the following, I reflect on how art helps us get there.

## The invitation of somatic, arts-based methods

For me, doing arts is primarily about getting back to the personal relationship with what's going on. You breathe, you feel, and from that, you express. You go back to the ground of your experience and become a conduit for the situation. It's not something that can happen if you try to control it. Instead, you get yourself in a certain zone and start resonating with the world. The dramaturg Matthew Goulish puts it well into words:

> A work [of art] is an object overflowing its frame. Work is an event in which the human participates; the human is an organism that works. A work works when it becomes an event of work. A work works when it becomes human. This becoming occurs when we realize it. Specifically it occurs when we realize it where it occurs. It occurs inside. We do not need to find a way into a work, since the work is already inside. Instead we realize a work and its harmony with our point of view. Then it and we begin to work, and the play of work begins. (Goulish 2000, 102)

And so, it's not a matter of pointing our attention towards an external thing and describing this supposed stranger as if it wasn't interwoven with our perception of it. It's a matter of finding this stranger inside of us and realizing our unspoken connection with what's around us. It's a practice of paying attention to the tacit understanding of the world we embody – to what is there before we start moulding it into coherence of thoughts.

Therefore, arts-based research defines itself through its performativity. By doing that, it lays bare the hidden nature of our translations of the world. The focus on *aesthetics* (meaning the sensual effects of our translations) reveals not only what we want to know but also the process of *how we get to know it*. At the same time, it expresses a yearning for an inquiry rooted in personal, embodied experience.

Our arts-based inquiry allowed us to constantly reflect on the problem of translation of tacit knowing. *What gets lost in the process? How are translations*

**Figure 12.5:** Translations of dance. Coloured pencils on paper

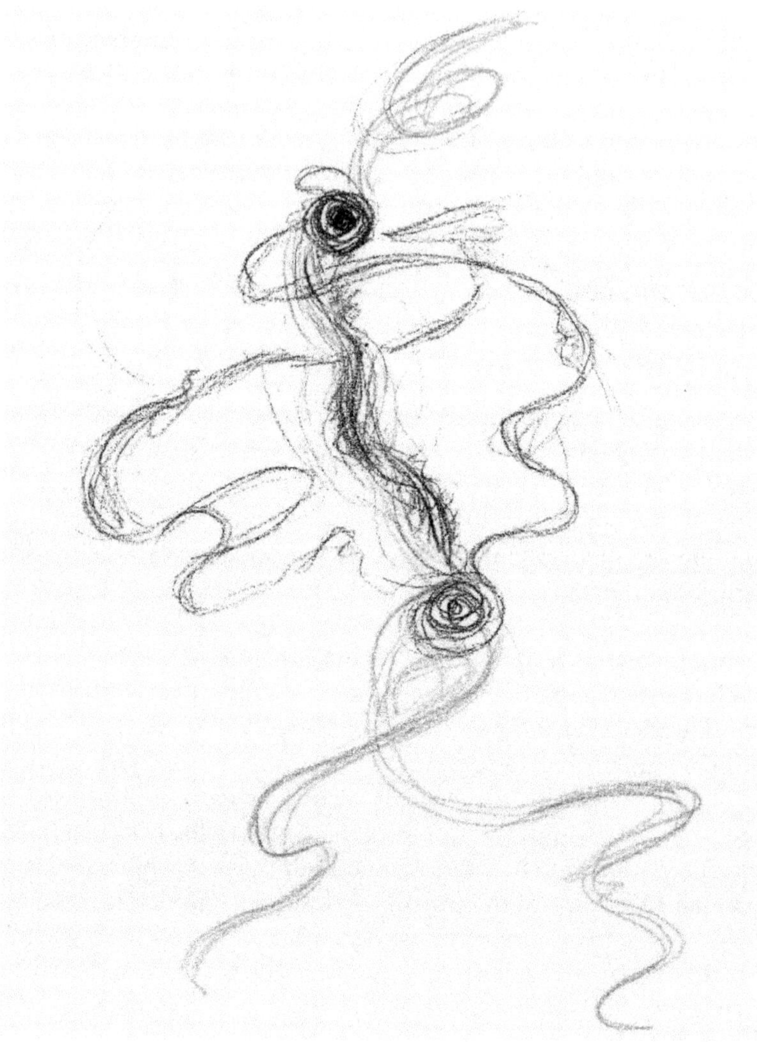

*created and at what cost?* The performative, nonconceptual work of dancing and painting together granted us artistic 'thinking mediums' that helped us to reflect on our translations in a very precise way – *not despite their ambiguity, but because of it.* The aesthetic explications allowed us to understand and document what we have learned beyond the linearity of rational thinking. And yet, we could never content ourselves with our translations. They all seemed undone. The constant dissatisfaction with the result, which could never measure up to the knowing we embodied, pushed us further. It sensitized us in our search for metaphors. It changed my own research process as it evolved: by deepening my reflection on what I was trying to do, it inspired me to stray further beyond the 'legitimate' scientific boundaries. Of course, I could not do it alone. I looked for accomplices. And where I found them was far away from the established understanding of social sciences: in sociological liminal spaces, at collaborative public art installations, and especially in the *sociological underground*, where artists – poets, dancers, musicians, visual artists – do sociological work without asking us for permission. Sociology evolved to happen in unexpected places and in unexpected ways.[17]

Sociologists, too, move through artistic peripheries. For example, John Law and Evelyn Ruppert (2016) evoke baroque as a resource for studying and knowing the complex world. Baroque could accommodate things usually othered by science: passion, bodies, heterogeneity, excess. It *knew* things differently. In its self-aware theatricality, it held different kinds of realities simultaneously and refused to be contained inside defined boundaries. It evoked the bravery needed for knowing. In that way, baroque

> does not offer the satisfaction of a sense of mastery or being in control. It seeks to make the lack that is at the heart of all world-making 'experienceable' … [I]t does not seek to make up for the tensions it produces. It does not shy away from the discomfort it gives rise to – to a sense of non-accomplishment, unfulfillment and impotence – but seeks to add such affects to its palette. (van de Port 2016, 185f)

To know the world is to enter uncharted territory – one that is more abundant and more wondrous than the maps we make of it.

Your turn. Find a blank piece of paper and some coloured pencils, or a brush and paints. Close your eyes for a moment in front of it and find your way back to your body. Breathe through every cell of your body. Settle. Feel the weight of your body, how it is planted on the earth. Feel the tension in your body again and try to release it down with the breath.

Then, focus on your sense perceptions. Listen to the world around you, feel it, without naming what you perceive. Feel the space around you and the air, slightly cool, as it enters your nostrils.

Now move your attention to the centre of your chest. You can place your hands gently at the level of your heart. Feel what's going on in there and the quality of your

---

17 If you want to dive into the peripheries, liminal spaces and undergrounds, here is a list of a few people that can show you the way: Nirmal Puwar (2011, Puwar and Sharma 2012), Peter Cole (2002), Huw Wahl (2014), Agnes Chavez (2016), Akram Khan (Khan and English National Ballet 2021), Ólafur Arnalds (Arnalds and Zophoníasson 2017; Arnalds and Moon 2021).

> presence. Feel back to the story I told you and how did it make you feel. Breathe into that feeling in the centre of your chest for a moment, to get to its core. Look for it as it were a wild animal in its habitat – you don't want to scare it away. Let it approach you instead of reaching for it with force.
>
> When you're ready, open your eyes, take a pencil or a brush, and bring that feeling onto paper.[18]

Knowing manifests in practice. An accurate translation of knowing requires enactment of a space in which we can experience it, and *not just think about it*. In that space, knowing can emerge and be received. Then, we can produce translations that do not dominate the experience but rather refine our attention and our ability to understand and reflect.[19] To work in this way means to expand our knowledge-making spaces in a twofold way: by letting ourselves know *in touch with our embodied experience and via many translations*, and by allowing ourselves to know *in relationship with and the company of the others*. In that way, we can enact inquiry as a shared, experiential activity, in which there are no fixed definitions of knowledge and knowing. And if that is the case, there is no control. There is only the primordial space of not-knowing.

Expanding our inquiry in that way would give us the possibility to discover the research process anew – not only as its dominant enactors but also as the audience and participants of the performed knowledge-making space that starts to live its own life. Reflexivity in these very much alive knowledge-making spaces would be akin to how Tim Ingold describes knowing, as

> moving about in it, exploring it, attending to it, ever alert to the signs by which it is revealed. Learning to see, then, is a matter not of acquiring schemata for mentally constructing the environment but of acquiring the skills for direct perceptual engagement with its constituents, human and non-human, animate and inanimate. (Ingold 2000, 55)

Reflexivity blooms if we allow it to unfold beyond the conceptual regime and enter the world in its sensuality. And I think the motivation for enacting this kind of reflexivity should not just come out of a wish to do better 'science', but out of desire to know the world in a more complete way. To get back to the childlike wonder about the world that pulled us towards being researchers.

---

[18]  This practice is partly based on *felt sense* exercises by David I. Rome (2014).

[19]  Tim Ingold (2000) calls this art of inquiry the *education of attention*.

## Outrageously open: an invitation

'It matters what thoughts think thoughts. It matters what knowledges know knowledges. It matters what relations relate relations. It matters what worlds world worlds', writes Donna Haraway (2016, 12), and she's right. Linear, controlled ways of doing knowledge cannot breed liveable worlds for us to inhabit.

Enacting such worlds needs time: it's a dish cooked over many hours, which are scarce in current ways of doing academia. It may be outrageous to take time for inquiry practices that the body and the arts invite us into. It may be even more outrageous to give up the authority of being a 'researcher' and enter the horizontal, multidirectional underground mycelium of creative shared knowing, where we are a feeling body entangled in relations with other bodies and with the world. This will be risky and uncomfortable. It will require a lot of courage. But through each act of doing that, we enact a different knowledge-making reality: one that is open for the actual world. One that is alive, rooted in experience, and willing to dance with us. I still agree with the appeal of an unknown Roma girl to a famous dancer that refused to dance: '*dance, dance, otherwise we are lost.*'

It matters, if we dare to dance.


## References

Abram, D. (2017) *The Spell of the Sensuous: Perception and Language in a More-Than-Human World*, 20th anniversary edn. New York: Vintage Books.

Anzaldúa, G. (2002) Now Let Us Shift … the Path of Conocimiento … Inner Work, Public Acts. In G. Anzaldúa and A. Keating (eds) *This Bridge We Call Home: Radical Visions for Transformation*. New York: Routledge, pp 540–574.

Arnalds, Ó. and Zophoníasson, B. (2017) *Island Songs*. Available at: https://www.islandsongs.is [Accessed 8 December 2024].

Arnalds, Ó. and Moon, V. (2021) *When We Are Born*. Available at: https://youtu.be/ZKz8J3Xi9oA [Accessed 8 December 2024].

Atamira Dance Company (2015) *Mitimiti: Episode 3, Finding the Language*. Available at: https://youtu.be/gIypBmZ4Xw0 [Accessed 8 December 2024].

Atamira Dance Company (2021) *ATAMIRA*. Available at: https://youtu.be/LZdeVuacmcQ [Accessed 8 December 2024].

Axis Syllabus Research Meshwork (2011) *The Axis Syllabus*. Available at: https://youtu.be/c0Jy-UcRGh4 [Accessed 8 December 2024].

Axis Syllabus Research Meshwork (2020) *Axis Syllabus Forum*. Available at: https://www.axissyllabusforum.org [Accessed 8 December 2024].

Back, L. (2012) Live Sociology: Social Research and Its Futures. *The Sociological Review* 60(S1): 18–39.

Chavez, A. (2016) *(X)Trees Installation at ISEA2012 Machine Wilderness*. Available at: https://youtu.be/_vvaqa3115E [Accessed 8 December 2024].

Cole, P. (2002) Aboriginalizing Methodology: Considering the Canoe. *Qualitative Studies in Education* 15(4): 447–459.

Cruz Banks, O. (2017) Haka on the Horizon: Māori Contemporary Dance and Whare Tapere. *Mai Journal* 6(1): 61–73.

Dharma Ocean (2023) *What Is Somatic Meditation?* Available at: https://www.dharmaocean.org/what-is-somatic-meditation/ [Accessed 8 December 2024].

Ellis, C.S. and Bochner, A.P. (2006) Analyzing Analytical Autoethnography. *Journal of Contemporary Ethnography* 35(4): 429–449.

Goulish, M. (2000) *39 Microlectures: In Proximity of Performance*. New York: Routledge.

Haraway, D.J. (2016) *Staying with the Trouble: Making Kin in the Chthulucene*. Durham, NC: Duke University Press.

Ingold, T. (2000) *The Perception of the Environment: Essays on Livelihood, Dwelling and Skill*. London and New York: Routledge.

Ingold, T. (2011) *Being Alive: Essays on Movement, Knowledge and Description*. New York: Routledge.

Ingold, T. (2014) That's Enough About Ethnography! *HAU: Journal of Ethnographic Theory* 4(1): 383–395.

Khan, A. and English National Ballet (2021) *Creature by Akram Khan: Unearthing the Story*. Available at: https://youtu.be/WUNrHTVqb8g [Accessed 8 December 2024].

Law, J. (2004) *After Method: Mess in Social Science Research*. Abingdon and New York: Routledge.

Law, J. (2006) Traduction / Trahison: Notes on ANT. *Convergencia. Revista de Ciencias Sociales* 13(42): 47–72.

Law, J. and Ruppert, E. (eds) (2016) *Modes of Knowing: Resources from the Baroque*. Manchester: Mattering Press.

Łączkowska, E. (2023) THE [W A L L S] WE CREATE. on distance in research practice. *Research Catalogue*. http://dx.doi.org/10.22501/rc.2260209

Merlau-Ponty, M. (1962) *Phenomenology of Perception*. London: Routledge and Kegan Paul.

Neilsen, L. (2004) Aesthetics and Knowing: Ephemeral Principles for a Groundless Theory. In A.L. Cole (ed) *Provoked by Art: Theorizing Arts-Informed Research*. Halifax: Backalong Books, pp 44–49.

Polanyi, M. (2009) *The Tacit Dimension*. Chicago and London: University of Chicago Press.

Puwar, N. (2011) Noise of the Past: Spacial Interruptions of War, Nation, and Memory. *Senses and Society* 6(3): 325–345.

Puwar, N. and Sharma, S. (2012) Curating Sociology. *The Sociological Review* 60(S1): 40–63.

Ray, R.A. (2016) *The Awakening Body: Somatic Meditation for Discovering Our Deepest Life*. Boulder: Shambhala Publications.

Rome, D.I. (2014) *Your Body Knows the Answer: Using Your Felt Sense to Solve Problems, Effect Change, and Liberate Creativity*. Boulder: Shambhala Publications.

van de Port, M. (2016) Baroque as Tension: Introducing Turmoil and Turbulence in the Academic Text. In J. Law and E. Ruppert (eds) *Modes of Knowing: Resources from the Baroque*. Manchester: Mattering Press, pp 165–196.

Wahl, H. (2014) Negotiating Representation in Israel and Palestine. *Visual Studies* 29(1): 1–12.

wild growing sky (2017) *What Is Contemporary Dance?* Available at: https://vimeo.com/236827661 [Accessed 8 December 2024].

13

# An Invitation to Who?

*Maria Vlachou*

You asked me my dear Ewa; you asked me as your reader: 'Will you dive with me?'

I am impatiently accepting the invitation my dear friend – as a 'trickster' myself, as a 'borderland' or as a smuggler as you nicely put it in your chapter, I cannot but accept your invitation (Tlostanova 2013). But, I must admit, my heart is full of burning questions. Please tell me which sea are we swimming in? Which part of the world does it belong to? On which side of the colonial difference are 'we' standing?

Who is this 'we' you invite to take up the challenge of disrupting, betraying, ideally destroying epistemological hierarchies and the consequent plethora of epistemological and ontological violence, abuse and hijacking?

Your intuition is right, the antidote to coloniality is indeed delinking from the modern/colonial taxonomical system of knowledge, perception and being. Coloniality refers to the fact that we are still witnessing the full dependence of models of thinking, interpreting and taxonomizing the world on the norms and the geopolitical agendas created and imposed by/in the Western modernity (Quijano 2007; Tlostanova and Mignolo 2012). One of the main facets of coloniality is its mechanism of dividing the Earth population into fully human and not-quite-human, which stems from the basic modern/colonial binary opposition of nature and culture, the soul/later mind and the body, human and animal (Tlostanova 2017). But let's say it as it is: Academia is a colonial/modern institution. It feeds on the disqualification of Other(ed) forms of knowing, of Other(ed) world makings: its very existence depends on it. I mean, look at us! Two dancers/ movers, two migrants, two women, squeezing our connection into an academic book, concepts, the English language …

If you are inviting us to merge worlds, to bridge worlds, what kind of building materials and what kind of tools should be used? I have been dwelling in and curving liminal spaces for most of my life, and I keep coming back to this, in my view, ethico-political question.

So, let's dance together! Please, my dear dance companion, tell me which music are we dancing to? Whose singing voices make our bodies vibrate? Where do we stand ethico-politically? Whose knowledges are 'we' citing in our academic papers and with which intention? Who is our audience? Let's work on weaving worlds together but which threads are we following, which ones are we entangling our bodies with and which kind of yarn are we using? Who made it?

Is dance enough to mess with the coloniality of knowledge? Which kind of dance is allowed to contaminate the academic rigour? The problem with the Western-modern dance canon is that contemporary dance exists in its opposition, exclusion and negation of 'other(ed)' dances – the ones 'assigned to an outside of the genealogy of contemporaneity, as an object of classification and exhibition for the ethnographic or the folkloric, or as a commodity for touristic consumption' (Vázquez 2024, 59). Shall academics then expand their knowledge-making experimentations beyond the Western/modern dance canon, beyond the Western/modern art aesthetics? Would this be an option, and more importantly, would it be an ethical proposition? I need to apologize, for I sound like a pessimist, but the colonial neoliberal academia has mastered the art of extractivism and co-option, so we cannot afford any amount of naivety.

Please, my dear friend, don't take my questions as your own burden. I am struggling with them almost daily. So, it's my turn to invite you to dive with me into the complexity and the ethics of merging worlds, of bridging, of research as non-colonial 'coalitional building' (Lugones 2003). Let's *sentipensar* together.

> Why does one write, if not put one's pieces together? From the moment we enter school or church, education chops us into pieces: it teaches us to divorce soul from body and mind from heart. The fishermen of the Colombian coast must be learned doctors of ethics and morality, for they invented the word *sentipensar*, feeling-thinking, to define language that speaks the truth. (Galeano 1991, 89)

You so accurately sensed, my dear dance companion, that academia strips us from the multisensorial knowledge-making process, it strips us from our human complexity and our connection to the more-than-human world. This is exactly what these fishermen already so beautifully articulated by this mixed word they invented and that is brought in vignettes by Eduardo Galeano in his book *El libro de los abrazos*, originally published in 1989! Instead of thinking exclusively with those who have already memorized and performed all the colonial steps towards secure, permanent White ableist male positions, why don't we look together into these marginalized and neglected writings and so many others and let's *sentipensar* together in a dance, a collective improvisation to the rhythm of merciless drumming led by 'token', ticking the diversity box, 'space invaders' kind of bodies (Puwar 2004).

Which academics and more-than-academics would want to join this dance ceremony?

## References


Galeano, E.H. (1991) *The Book of Embraces*. New York: W.W. Norton.

Lugones, M. (2003) *Pilgrimages/Peregrinajes: Theorizing Coalition Against Multiple Oppressions*. Lanham: Rowman & Littlefield.

Puwar, N. (2004) *Space Invaders: Race, Gender and Bodies Out of Place*. New York: Berg.

Quijano, A. (2007) Coloniality and Modernity/Rationality. *Cultural Studies* 21(2–3): 168–178.

Tlostanova, M. (2013) *Transcultural Tricksters beyond Times and Spaces: Decolonial Chronotopes and Border Selves*. Язык. Словесность. Культура (2–3), pp 9–31.

Tlostanova, M. (2017) Transcending the Human/Non-Human Divide: The Geo-Politics and Body-Politics of Being and Perception, and Decolonial Art. *Angelaki* 22(2): 25–37.

Tlostanova, M. and Mignolo, W. (2012) *Learning to Unlearn: Decolonial Reflections from Eurasia and the Americas*. Columbus: The Ohio State University Press.

Vázquez, R. (2024) *Vistas of Modernity: Decolonial Aesthesis and the End of the Contemporary*. Zwaag, NL: Pumbo.nl.

# 14

# The Third Space Walk:
# An Approach to Understanding
# ~~Analogue-digital~~ Urban Spaces

*Mirjana Mitrović*

## 1. Current ~~analogue-digital~~ urban spaces

Today in a lot of cities all over the world digital technologies have become a constant companion of their inhabitants. The smartphone is often the first thing people look at in the morning and the last thing they put away at night. But it also accompanies its owners throughout the day as they move around the city: routes are followed live on the screen as they are walked, tickets purchased for public transport through applications, appointments and reminders are noted and managed in the digital calendar, finances and even data about their own body are digitally recorded, processed, monitored and reacted to if necessary. Also communication with colleagues, friends, lovers and relatives in other places – nearby or far away – takes place via text messages, pictures or video calls while sitting in the metro or walking the streets. It turns out that not only some but almost all areas of life are influenced by digital technologies. At the same time, the infrastructures behind – as cables under the streets – seem invisible and the rhythmic switching of traffic lights, monitoring by surveillance cameras or advertisements on large displays are rarely consciously noticed as part of the digitalization of the urban space, though they are a crucial part of today's cities. As a result, the question arises: what kind of space do we currently live in? How can this interweaving of analogue and digital spaces, which takes place in parallel on so many levels, be perceived, analysed and shaped in a fair and inclusive way?

In this chapter I present the method of the Third Space Walk, which I developed to better research and understand contemporary cities as a hybrid between analogue and digital worlds. It is based on an understanding of urban space as a third space, while the walking practice itself is inspired by flânerie. In the following, I first present five steps of the method to give an impression of what the Third Space Walk is. These steps serve as a basic framework and invite the reader to make their own modifications. Building on this short overview of the method, two main aspects of the Third Space Walk will be explored in more depth. The first is to reflect on the terms that are used to describe the mixing of analogue and digital spaces and to problematize how often these descriptions are trapped in Western binary thinking. Visualizing this problem by crossing out the words (see Derrida 1997) ~~analogue-digital~~ can only be a short-term solution while a closer look on the potential of hybridity concepts such as the third space can be enriching. The second is a brief insight into how walking is used both in art and increasingly in science as a reflexive method to better understand spaces and societies and why flânerie is especially helpful for researching in-between spaces in cities.

## 2. Development and five possible steps for the Third Space Walk

The Third Space Walk has developed in several stages.[1] Since 2020 I have given seminars at Berlin University of the Arts where we read and discussed queer, feminist, de- and postcolonial concepts of hybridity and flânerie, and at the same time we tried out different walking exercises. The experiences from the seminars helped me to design workshops for women★[2] in Mexico City and Berlin, which took place in early 2022. Then, workshop participants and artists from both cities were invited through an open call to participate in an exhibition. A selection of works curated together with Valentina Sarmiento Cruz, independent writer and researcher based in Mexico City, and Anna-Lena Panter, editor and programme coordinator of a media art festival based in Berlin, was presented in August 2022 in the exhibition *Third Space Walk. Flâneuses★ between virtual and material urban spaces*. It was shown

---

[1]   I presented different states of my work on the Third Space Walk at various conferences and talks. In that context, I published a visual patch about my method (Mitrović 2022a) and a short summary of a talk I gave at a conference organized by the AK Feministische Geographie in Berlin, Germany (Mitrović 2022b).

[2]   The ★ after the word women and flâneuses was used in the invitation to the workshops and the open call for the exhibition as well as in the title of the exhibition to welcome all people who identify as women to participate. Even though I am aware that this spelling is controversial for some, from my point of view it questions the construction of binary gender concepts and has been used in books such as *Flexen. Flâneusen★ schreiben Städte* (Flexen. Flâneuses★ write cities) by Dündar et al (2019).

**Figure 14.1:** Exhibition opening

in Berlin (Figure 14.1) and online (it can still be visited at https://thirdsp acewalk.mirjana-mitrovic.de). Without the students, workshop participants, artists, curators and many more people this research would not have been possible – a big thank you to all of you!

The Third Space Walk has gone through a number of stages in over two years. For most of the future applicants it will be difficult to have the time to repeat all these formats (seminars, workshops, exhibition, webspace). Nevertheless, in the following I present a short version of five important aspects that stood out for me during the process. These are intended to serve as inspiration and to be open to further development. Therefore, I propose a structure, but one that is flexible enough to be adjusted, as it can – and should – be adapted to different needs depending on the research focus. In the following, only the most necessary cornerstones are pointed out, which should be considered a prerequisite for being able to use the Third Space Walk as a reflexive method that connects individual as well as collective experiences and opens a space for discussion and exchange on today's ~~analogue-digital~~ urban spaces.

## General conditions

The Third Space Walk should be applied in a group with participants who live in the city, where the workshop takes place. From my experience between three and 15 people is a manageable size. It should take a minimum of three hours, but can be longer or even last various days. The workshop should take place in a room or a comfortable space outside that is quiet enough for conversations, equipped with tables and chairs and/or other additional seating possibilities, some drinks and snacks. DIN-A1 posters, DIN-A4 sheets of paper, pens, Post-Its, tape and copies of the chapter 'M [The Flâneur]' from the *Arcades Project* (1999) by Walter Benjamin are also required. The room should preferably be in the city centre, so leaving it the participants find themselves in a crowded space.

*The first step* is the introduction to the workshop and the main topics. We start with a warm welcome and a short self-introduction by everyone. Thereby, it is great to already get an impression who knows or associates what about hybridity and flânerie. It is not essential that all participants possess identical prior knowledge; however, they will inevitably form an initial impression of the subject matter and may potentially gain new insights from one another. In accordance with this approach, I typically commence with an examination of flânerie. I give every participant some pages of Benjamin's text and let them read and cut it on their own. Afterwards they come together in groups and put their citations on a poster with keywords like space, gender, time or whatever else comes to their mind. A joint playful work with Benjamin's *Arcades Project* has proven to be fruitful, as it allows participants to work first alone and then together on characteristics of the practice such as walking very slowly, walking alone, trying to get lost, perceiving the overlaps between history and everyday life with all our senses, but also the not-always-clear line between reality and fiction. Inspired by Benjamin's understanding of flânerie, this method takes place in a city and not in the countryside and it makes sense to walk in a city where you live. This gives the possibility of exploring details you were not aware of, but perhaps would also not catch your attention as if everything is new to you in an unknown city. At the end we also take a closer look at things we can criticize and often non-White, non-male persons quickly share reflections on their walking experiences and how they differ from what Benjamin writes. At this point I introduce authors like Lauren Elkin and Garnette Cadogan, who write about these other experiences and how for some walking is a vulnerable everyday exercise and takes a lot of courage. Refusing to be driven out of public space and appropriating urban space with the help of flânerie can therefore be understood as a practice of resistance.

Afterwards a short examination of the concept of hybridity follows. We discuss how already in Benjamin's text different spaces and times overlap and have a closer look at the postcolonial concept of third space by Homi K. Bhabha. From this point on we ask ourselves what it means when analogue and digital spaces interweave and how we can understand what happens when these processes interact. How can we perceive that kind of hybridity in our everyday life and what kind of role plays a hybrid figure like the cyborg by Donna Haraway? This is important, as in order to be able to perceive the urban space as a third space, a shared basis must first be created that everyone will enter the urban space with in the next step.

*The second step* is the walk itself, which is practised alone. In contrast to the previous step, everyone now tries to have the previous discussions in the back of their mind but at the same time to clear their head as much as possible in order to allow for all kinds of sensory impressions. This moment is about opening up and perceiving what is happening inside and outside of your body, trying to listen to the rhythm of your slow movement, to your surroundings as well as to your thoughts as they come and go. It is not about catching ideas, more about noting them and letting them go for the moment: getting lost in your mind and on your way and thereby get access to third spaces between analogue and digital worlds in the city.

When doing this exercise for the first time, it is helpful if everyone leaves the workshop room more or less at the same time – but on their own. A fruitful task is for all participants to set an alarm for about 60 minutes (depending on the workshop schedule), mute their phones and put them in a bag (rather than a pocket on their body) so as not to be distracted by a call, a message or the desire to take a photo or audio. Even if this sounds simple, it is a magical moment for most of the participants, how differently they can perceive the walk in the urban space. When the alarm goes off, everyone should come back by the quickest route – and as one of the characteristics of flânerie is to walk very slowly, they should normally be back quite quickly.

*The third step* is when everyone comes back to the room and collect their impressions. There are many different possibilities of how to do so. One is, to invite them to use *écriture automatique* to bring their impressions of the walk to paper (Figure 14.2).

Automatic writing is a method in which participants are invited to write down all their thoughts in a flow that is as uncensored as possible. On the one hand, this initiates movement: if possible, pauses should be avoided. On the other hand, it is about accessing the subconscious and letting the writer's associations run free. This method was popular in surrealist circles, for example (cf Nagel 2007), and has been used by artists interested in creating a different kind of knowledge.

I always prepared the participants before the walk so that they knew that when they came back to the workshop room I would give them a blank piece of paper and a pen. This was done to ensure that, while their physical movements ceased, their thoughts would gradually slow down. The objective was to simply record, in a spontaneous and uninhibited manner, whatever thoughts and ideas came to mind. This could include written text, drawings, or any other form of expression. When no thoughts or ideas emerged, the participants were instructed to write 'nothing comes to my mind' until something new arose. It was made clear that the papers would not be collected afterwards. The purpose of this was to ensure that the

**Figure 14.2:** *Écriture automatique* exercise during a workshop in Mexico City in 2022

participants could write freely, without concern for the opinions of others. Subsequently, these notes facilitated discussion about the events of the walk and any matters that had aroused curiosity.

*The fourth step* is to reflect on the impressions of the walk and use these thoughts for an in-depth study. The objective is to identify an observation, perception or experience that illustrates the intertwining of analogue and digital realities in urban environments. The following research on the topic will enable the participants to integrate their observations from the micro level into a broader context, thereby facilitating an understanding of the potential issues and solutions at the macro level. This process entails a shift in perspective from the local, everyday aspects of life to the global systems that shape them.

Given the constraints of a three-hour workshop, it is often not feasible to complete this step (and the subsequent one) within the allotted time. Consequently, it is frequently a voluntary take-home exercise. The workshop may be concluded with a designated period during which participants engage in a collaborative review of their notes from the walk and the automatic writing exercise, conducted in pairs. It is therefore not only of interest to consider what has been noticed, but also what has been unnoticed and remained invisible. Normally, at this juncture, associations arise with ease, rendering it unnecessary to rely on the initial notes and preliminary thoughts. Alternatively, one may choose to build upon questions that emerge subsequently. It is imperative that the individual experience be transformed into a more general concept, based on a profound level of investigation. The research may be conducted in an artistic, scientific or combined manner. This decision merely alters the format of the research process, influencing the format of the findings' presentation.

*The fifth step* is to present and communicate what you have found out. At this juncture, it is necessary to consider the most suitable format for conveying both questions and results to other parties, the opportunity to create a space in which others may engage in collective or individual reflection on the topic at hand. It is possible to present the results in isolation; however, I found it more beneficial to present them as individual works in a collective format. This could take the form of an exhibition featuring works from students, workshop participants and artists or a zine. The Third Space Walk's principal strength lies in its capacity to unite disparate works, thereby creating and presenting a mosaic or collage of the urban space as a third space. This process allows for the emergence of new insights into the intertwining of analogue and digital realms.

Concluding, I thus understand the Third Space Walk not only as walking, but as a processual practice that involves the acquisition of prior knowledge, sensitive and emphatic perception while walking and getting lost in the city, the ability to wonder and reflect, and finally the processing and presentation of the knowledge and/or questions that arise.

## 3. Getting out of the binary trap: hybridity and the third space

As described in the first step, for practicing the Third Space Walk it is essential to enter the streets with a specific understanding of space. I propose to use the postcolonial concept *third space* by Homi K. Bhabha (1994) in combination with other concepts of hybridity to understand the analogue-digital space in current cities. In 2017 and 2018 I conducted research into cyberfeminist movements in Mexico City (and beyond) (cf Mitrović 2024). Throughout this period, I encountered a persistent question regarding the precise nature of the 'cyber' element within the context of cyberfeminism. It quickly became clear that since the 1990s activists have been organizing themselves online but also on the streets – fighting against patriarchal structures in both spaces. The advent of the internet, however, led to a shift in the conceptualization of analogue and digital spaces, resulting in a proliferation of new interpretations. With the spread of the internet, the understanding of analogue and digital spaces changed and multiplied, making it difficult to separate the spaces both linguistically and socially. In the exhibition *Enlaces | Links* about cyberfeminism in

Mexico and Germany, which I realized together with the filmmaker Jan-Holger Hennies, the questions arose: 'Can "virtual" and "real" space still be separated? How are they connected?' (cf Mitrović and Hennies 2017, translation by the author). These questions were essential, for example, to understand hashtag actions like #Aufschrei [Outcry] (2013) in Germany or #MiPrimerAcoso [MyFirstHarassment] (2016) in various countries in Latin America. These hashtags became relevant because of the number of participants sharing their experiences online, and the subsequent attention in media, press and politics for harassment and violence in the analogue space. In 2019 – without anticipating at all that the interaction of these worlds would be more present than ever during and after the COVID-19 pandemic one year later – I started researching the questions: How has the current urban space been changed by digitalization and how is this process linguistically described? Why are the terms mostly linked to dichotomies and what kind of imaginaries about the space have thereby been created?

I therefore started to take a closer look at associated terms and concepts. It is impressive, how many already have been proposed to describe the interwovenness of analogue and digital spaces, but at the same time it seems none describe the big picture and researchers in that field keep criticizing that none are completely satisfactory (for example, Grammatikopoulou 2020; Voigt 2021, 2023). Still, until today there are new ones popping up. One popular example is *phygital* that is most often seen in business and marketing (Grammatikopoulou 2020, 90), as by the fashion label LUKSO at Fashion Week 2022 in Berlin, Germany (Vogelsteller in Wagenknecht 2020). In an interview, Fabian Vogelsteller, one of the founders of LUKSO, defines it as followed: 'We use phygital to describe the mix of digital and physical. This shows us what will happen in the next few years, namely the transition to virtual reality and virtual experience' (Wagenknecht 2020). This illustrates how the term is based on other terms like virtual reality and virtual experience – which are quite different and for specific areas of the digitalization process – and at the same time tries to describe something more general and a space in-between. Yet it remains trapped in a binary framework. In contrast, de Souza e Silva, for example, uses the term *hybrid space* and distinguishes it from these and other concepts: 'A hybrid space is conceptually different from what has been termed mixed reality, augmented reality, augmented virtuality, or virtual reality' (de Souza e Silva 2006, 262). This seems essential to me because terms such as augmented reality and virtual reality work for a much smaller defined space where digital technologies play a role: They only work with a specialized technical device, and if it is not accessible also the hybrid world is not accessible. In Pokemon Go, for instance, one uses a smartphone to view game characters on the screen that at the same time overlap with the live camera view. In contrast, in virtual reality special glasses have to be worn in order to dive into a different visual and auditory world. In other words, these terms only describe the conscious use of technological devices for the temporary consumption of certain experiences, but not the everyday and all-encompassing changes shaping urban space. As myself, also de Souza e Silva focuses in her research on a wider understanding of the current ~~analogue–digital~~ space and takes a look at movement and mobile digital technical devices that connect users via the internet: 'By walking around connected to the Internet (and consequently to other geolocated users) we could experience both digital and physical spaces simultaneously, and for this reason, it was pointless to address physical and digital as two (often disconnected) spaces' (de Souza e Silva 2023, 59).

Still, similarly as in the term *phygital*, the quote shows how de Souza e Silva also references a dichotomy between 'physical and digital spaces' (de Souza e Silva 2006; 2023). Concurrently, the term *phygital* but also the definition of the hybrid space by de Souza e Silva implies that digital and physical are dichotomous, thereby opposing each other. Consequently, the digital is not physical. However, this idea that the digital is immaterial and hovering invisibly above us – evoked by terms such as 'cloud storage' – is no longer tenable today (Voigt 2021, 161; Suárez Estrada and Lehuedé 2022, 3). The (often violent) sourcing of materials for devices such as smartphones, the effects of server farms on the climate, and the tearing up of asphalt in order to lay internet cables make the physical aspects of digital all too visible.

Other concepts like *expanded space* by Grammatikopoulou (2020) or *interspace* (also sometimes written as *Inter_Space*) by Voigt (2021; 2023) have trouble – like this research, too – with avoiding these traps and dichotomies but try to describe in a more precise and complex way the phenomenon of the dissolving border between the analogue and digital in urban spaces:

> The everyday experience of most people now takes place within this continuum of online and offline spaces, whereby the digital networked space, experienced through the permanent use of computers and mobile communication tools, constantly transforms the experience of physical space. The understanding of space that goes along with this implies not starting from two separate poles of connectivity, not thinking in categories of online and offline, but understanding space as a sum of all possibilities: physical, expanded, virtual, mixed, and hybrid. (Grammatikopoulou 2020: 90)

A sum of possible levels and spaces was already part of cities with extremely complex structures before digitalization: 'the urban is itself an extremely heterogeneous and dense structure, in which different actors act locally and globally as well as materially and immaterially with each other, and both analogue and digitalized communications take place permanently' (Weber and Ziemer 2022, 38f, translation by the author). But now 'cities are dynamic hybrids of digital and analog practices' (Weber and Ziemer 2022, 38f, translation by the author). Voigt therefore uses the term *interspace*: 'Cities have long become interspaces, entangled in materialities and virtual worlds' (Voigt 2023, 1). For Voigt, the 'Inter_Space is a constant spatial continuum between online and offland,[3] expanding the dimensions of analog with digitality and vice versa. Binary categorized boundaries are blurred in it' (Voigt 2021, 159, translation by the author). It becomes clear to me that the dissolution of dichotomies is decisive to understanding contemporary urban space between analogue and digital worlds and that hybridity is one of the core concepts that is present in all these (de Souza e Silva 2006; 2023; Grammatikopoulou 2020; Voigt 2021; 2023; Weber and Ziemer 2022) and other attempts (for example, Zook and Graham 2018, 391; Lettkemann and Schulz-Schaeffer 2021) to approach the ~~analogue-digital~~ urban space.

In order to move away from a purely descriptive term, and to see the hybrid space between analogue and digital as an emerging possibility with critical potential, I refer to Homi K. Bhabha's theory of cultural hybridity: '[t]he process of cultural hybridity gives rise to something different, something new and unrecognisable, a new area of negotiation of meaning and representation' (in Rutherford 1990, 211). This understanding makes it possible to understand interwovenness as a process, and at the same time to focus on what is emerging instead of clinging to dichotomies:

> [F]or me the importance of hybridity is not to be able to trace two original moments from which the third emerges, rather hybridity to me is the 'third space' which enables other positions to emerge. This third space displaces the histories that constitute it, and sets up new structures of authority, new political initiatives, which are inadequately understood through received wisdom. (Bhabha in Rutherford 1990, 211)

From my point of view this idea of the third space is an opportunity to again reflect on – and thereby better understand – urban space. In doing so it is important to extend the concept of hybridity from the space to the bodies that are closely linked to technology within it, drawing from (queer) feminist figures such as Gloria Anzaldúa's mestiza (Anzaldúa 1999) which deal with cultural hybridity or Donna Haraway's cyborg (Haraway 1985) that is already focused on bodies and technology.

---

[3]  Maja-Lee Voigt uses the term offland and explains it as follows: 'In this composition of words, emphasizing the territorial, what constitutes an urban materiality' (Voigt 2021, 157, translation by the author).

At the same time the concept of hybridity is important not only for the first step of the Third Space Walk, but for all the steps. It is important to have this complex understanding of hybridity in mind while walking and reflecting, that hybridity is not about only one dichotomy but always several components that come together. The concepts of the third space combined with others can help us to try to observe ourself when we get trapped by the binary thinking that we learned, but it is also fruitful to have it in mind when thinking of the research and how to present knowledge. How can we show a hybrid process, something not binary and not finished, but still transmitting knowledge and inviting others to think about the results and questions raised during the Third Space Walk? Therefore, inspirational works from various authors and artists should just quickly be mentioned: The *Bilderatlas Mnemosyne* by Aby Warburg or the *Psychogeographic Guide of Paris* by Guy Debord. Also the *Arcades Project* by Walter Benjamin, that invites through collected short paragraphs and hypertext – a kind of analogue system of hyperlinks (cf Hartmann 2006, 305) – to get lost and explore unexpected connections between thoughts of Benjamin himself and citations of others he collected. Current works like *Permanente Obra Negra* (2019) by the Mexican author Vivian Abenshushan inspire by multiplying these possibilities of connecting different elements by presenting her work in four versions: As a classic paperback; as a hardcover book in which all the pages have been cut horizontally into three parts and can therefore be combined into individual sections; as an index card box; and as a website (www.perm anenteobranegra.cc).

Including the concepts of the third space in a wider sense allows to reflect on one's own binary thinking about ~~analogue-digital~~ spaces, current cities, but also academic thinking and writing. By being open about crossing borders also in the context of how knowledge has to be created and (re)presented, I see the opportunity not only to be able to understand urban space better theoretically, but also to be able to encounter it with a different approach, in a manner that allows new insights.

## 4. Flânerie: understanding urban space by walking through it

Beside the concept of the third space, of course, also walking as a research method is an essential part of the Third Space Walk. Walking has proven to be an enriching research method in arts, activism and academic research that incorporates reflexivity. Art exhibitions like *Walk!*, presented in 2022 at the Schirn Kunsthalle in Frankfurt am Main, Germany, provide a good overview of various forms of walking and their diverse application in artistic works: from artists like Francis Alÿs (Ulrich et al 2022, 24–27) to Milica Tomić (Ulrich et al 2022, 228–235). The museum director Philipp Demandt mentions: 'Artistic practices that involve walking mark social spaces in various ways. The known appears unknown while the unknown seems familiar. The visible becomes invisible while the invisible is made visible' (Demandt 2022, 33). Additionally, Demandt argues that walking offers a special means of questioning existing concepts in relation to the current urban space, while at the same time creating space for other concepts (cf Demandt 2022, 33). Being able to open up third spaces between binaries by walking is therefore fruitful for my Third Space Walk.

The *Walk!* catalogue also refers to traditional walking practices, mentioning flânerie, dérive – also known as psychogeography – and promenadology (Ulrich et al 2022). In such contexts, reference is almost always made to the same authors: flânerie is connected with Charles Baudelaire and Walter Benjamin and psychogeography with Guy Debord, while promenadology can be traced to Lucius and Annemarie Burckhardt[4] (Lubkowitz 2020; Rohde and Wildner 2020; Ulrich et al 2022). Often these and other practices of walking get mixed up, though taking a closer look shows that some differences are notable. While flânerie is something that someone practices on his/her own, dérive should preferably be done in a group (Debord 2006), while strollology has also often been carried out in groups. Flânerie was practiced in the context of art and literature; however, for psychogeography and strollology, the artistic aspect is essential, though with a focus on urban policy and often with direct interventions into urban space. In the case of strollology, its academic context, that it is often focused on traffic politics in cities, and its interest in urban but also rural landscapes distinguish it even further from the other two. And, last but not least, flânerie is practised in big cities which are generally well known by the person, as opposed to walking through unknown spaces. Nevertheless, all of these practices include the body, with observations based on sensory perceptions emerging from movement being included in one way or the other in the presentation of the results.

In academic scholarship contributions such as the chapter 'Walking in the City' (1984) by Michel de Certeau or *Ways of Walking: Ethnography and Practice on Foot* (2008) by Tim Ingold and Jo Lee Vergunst justify the use of this seemingly banal and everyday practice also as an academic research tool. Scientists use walking in a wide variety of contexts and forms: Some practice it in the countryside, others in the city; some focus on what they see, while others try to involve all of their senses. It is notable that some scholars create their own methodology, while others base their approach on existing practices. In academic realms, artistic practices are often used and

---

[4] Lucius Burckhardt invented promenadology (cf Burckhardt 2015) together with Annemarie Burckhardt, an artist and Lucius' wife, but quite often she is not mentioned.

translated into artistic research, or directly framed as a form of ethnography (Pink 2009, 22). Other scholars base their method on existing walking practices. For example, Aldo Legnaro invites us to use flânerie as a method for social research. He speaks of a reflexive art of flânerie (Legnaro 2010, 282) and describes how a flâneur or flâneuse exposes themselves to the dynamics of the masses in urban spaces, trying to consciously perceive the space and what is happening in it while at the same time seeking to react to it rather unconsciously (Legnaro 2010, 282). A challenging but thoroughly productive dilemma.

The Third Space Walk is mostly inspired by Flânerie, a practice that can be seen as one of the first that understood walking as an aesthetic practice (Rohde and Wildner 2020, 242). To fully benefit of this practice and to use it as a reflexive method in academic research, I examined the characteristics of the flâneur by Benjamin – walking alone and slow in a known city, trying to get lost and opening all senses, like mentioned in step three – and updated it with current queer, feminist and postcolonial forms of flânerie. In the last years the practice of flânerie has been de- and reconstructed: Books concerned with flânerie have been published with feminist, queer and (post)migrant perspectives (Elkin 2017; Dündar et al 2019; Iglesia 2019), articles by Black female and male authors have highlighted walking from their point of view (Cadogan 2016; Forna 2018), and there have even been festivals like *Nocturnal Unrest: A Feminist Festival for Theory, Performance and Radical Flâneuserie* in 2021 in Frankfurt am Main, Germany. Today an elementary aspect becomes clear that was not as present in the texts by flâneurs around the 19th century: it makes a difference who practices it when, where and how. Reference is often made to the problems of sexual harassment on the street that women experience and being afraid of walking in the dark, to racism and prejudice that Black people experience, to people with prams or older people who encounter other limitations (Kern 2020). Flâneuses★ thereby produce glitches in today's technourban cities by walking the streets (Mitrović and Voigt 2025). The glitch is 'an error, a mistake, a failure to function. Within techno culture, a glitch is part of machinic anxiety, an indicator of something having gone wrong' (Russell 2020, 7) and critical geographers like Leszczynski and Elwood follow Russell and include the glitch as a concept to the discourse on platform cities (Leszczynski and Elwood 2022a; 2022b). Flâneuses★ practising the Third Space Walk in Berlin and Mexico City created glitches by refusing to be excluded from the urban space, ignoring the borders of ~~analogue-digital~~ urban spaces and thereby opening up third spaces.

Finally, it is important that even if the experience of flâneuses★ walking the technourban space csan be hurtful and the classic figure of the flâneur is often criticized, the last decades show that practising flânerie has lost none of its relevance for reflecting on and at the same time occupying contemporary urban space. It becomes clear that, when mobilized from these marginalized perspectives, flânerie offers the opportunity to make more perspectives visible with regard to urban space, as well as to draw attention to social grievances and thus, in the best case, to change them.

## 5. Conclusion

Both the postcolonial concept of the third space according to Bhabha and the practice of flânerie – from Benjamin's flâneur to the current flâneuse* – break down existing dichotomies and thus open up potential spaces outside of them. This combination makes the Third Space Walk so fruitful to question the current state of ~~analogue-digital~~ urban spaces. Discussing and practising the Third Space Walk in groups was so valuable, because it gave me and the participants time and space – that we often do not have and/ or take – to reflect on our own as well as together on questions like: How and why do I, we or others behave in public space? What kind of social dynamics can be perceived? What kind of role does digitalization play and on how many layers does it impact our everyday life? The invitation to think outside of the classic dichotomies and instead to see potential in the hybrid and combine it with the technique of free association made it possible to highlight a much wider range of topics that concern women* than usually found in social and academic discourses. At the beginning of the seminars and workshops, the focus of the participants was mostly on smartphones and certain apps but the works that emerged after the Third Space Walk showed a much greater variety of topics and aspects that were relevant to the women*. At the same time they found other creative and artistic ways of expressing themselves in order to transform their experiences and the questions that arose during the Third Space Walk into a published work and thus address a wider audience in a stimulating way and invite them to reflect on topics they care for.

The Third Space Walk is a method that makes it possible to examine contemporary public urban space understood as ~~analogue-digital~~ spaces and finally as a third space. With the premise of understanding the urban space as a third space and then entering it with a practice based on flânerie, it makes it possible to focus on the interweaving between analogue and digital spaces. In this chapter I have presented the theoretical development and practical application of the Third Space Walk as a means of better understanding urban space. It became clear how confusingly used terms make such understanding difficult. However, instead of getting lost in definitions of dichotomies, by using the concept of the third space I strive for the possibility of detaching oneself from the respective origins of the emerging space, and instead concentrating on what has been created.

The Third Space Walk method has proven to be very fruitful on various levels. Based on the concept of the third space and the practice of flânerie, this method allows for opening up in-between spaces, and making them visible and experienced. The concept of third space itself encourages us to break away from dichotomies, which is quite a challenge. Flânerie, on the other hand, seeks to enable different kinds of observations and insights by changing perception and sensual access to urban space and the social structures articulated in it. All this became visible in various research steps, and had a direct effect on the people who contributed across the different phases. During exercises in the seminars and workshops walking in urban space led to a change of perception: on the one hand, in relation to one's own body to the urban space, and, on the other, to the space itself, which one tried to perceive with all of the senses. Further, the exhibition showed how we as curators – an interdisciplinary team aiming to provide a platform for multi-perspective artistic explorations of ~~analogue-digital~~ urban space – were able to create a third space between three languages, two cities, numerous video calls, and the exhibition venue in Berlin.

All of these steps were also about engaging with urban space in order to gain a better understanding of technological developments and their effects, and ultimately to be able to keep up with them. There was thus a constant appropriation of the space; even during the seminars and workshops. When people were out and about in the city, they occupied the space through performative walking and thus changed it, even if perhaps only for the moment. The exhibition was also about creating a space in which perspectives become visible that have been historically suppressed. Dialogue was always invited, because in addition to showing the works, it was also about motivating visitors to think about contemporary urban space and, in the best case, to themselves get involved in order to shape it and make it accessible to more people. I understand it as a great advantage that this method is practised as a group, while at the same time individual subjective experiences are made and then shared with others. This makes it possible to gain a different insight into other experiences. Finally, it helps to recognize other perspectives, to look beyond one's own nose, and at the same time to position oneself in society in a reflective way, so as to be able to exchange ideas and act together.

## References

Abenshushan, V. (2019) *Permanente Obra Negra*. Mexico City: Sexto Piso. Available at: www.permanenteobranegra.cc [Accessed 10 December 2024].

Anzaldúa, G. (1999) *Borderlands/La Frontera: The New Mestiza*. San Francisco: Aunt Lute Books.

Benjamin, W. (1999) M [The Flâneur]. In *The Arcades Project*. Cambridge, MA: Harvard University Press, pp 416–455.

Bhabha, H.K. (1994) *The Location of Culture*. London: Routledge.

Burckhardt, L. (2015) *Why Is Landscape Beautiful? The Science of Strollology*. Basel: Birkhäuser.

Cadogan, G. (2016) Walking While Black. *Literary Hub*, 8 July. Available at: https://lithub.com/walking-while-black/ [Accessed 30 October 2022].

de Certeau, M. (1984) *The Practice of Everyday Life*. Berkeley: University of California Press.

Demandt, P. (2022) Foreword. In M. Ulrich, F. Hesse and M. Oucherif (eds) *Walk! Schirn Kunsthalle Frankfurt*. Wien: Verlag für moderne Kunst, pp 32–35.

Derrida, J. (1997) *Of Grammatology*. 3. korrigierte Auflage. Baltimore: Johns Hopkins University.

de Souza e Silva, A. (2006) From Cyber to Hybrid: Mobile Technologies as Interfaces of Hybrid Spaces. *Space and Culture* 9(3): 261–278.

de Souza e Silva, A. (2023) Hybrid Spaces 2.0: Connecting Networked Urbanism, Uneven Mobilities, and Creativity, in a (Post) Pandemic World. *Mobile Media & Communication* 11(1): 59–65.

Dündar, Ö.Ö., Othmann, R., Göhring, M. and Sauer, L. (2019) *Flexen. Flâneusen* schreiben Städte*. Berlin: Verbrecherverlag.

Debord, Guy (2006) Theory of the Dérive. In: Knabb, Ken (Hg.): Situationist International Anthology. Revised and Expanded. Berkeley: Bureau of Public Secrets.

Elkin, L. (2017) *Flâneuse. Women Walk the City in Paris, New York, Tokyo, Venice and London*. London: Vintage.

Forna, A. (2018) Power Walking. Aminatta Forna on the Streets of London, Freetown, and NYC. *Literary Hub*, 19 September. Available at: https://lithub.com/power-walking/ [Accessed 30 October 2022].

Grammatikopoulou, C. (2020) Viral Gender-performance. In C. Sollfrank (ed) *The Beautiful Warriors. Technofeminist Praxis in the Twenty-First Century*. New York: Autonomedia, pp 89–109.

Haraway, D. (1985) Manifesto for Cyborgs: Science, Technology, and Socialist Feminism in the 1980s. *Socialist Review* 80: 65–108.

Hartmann, M. (2006) Der Kulturkritiker als Flaneur. Walter Benjamin, die Passage und die neuen (Medien-)Technologien. *Medien & Kommunikationswissenschaft* 54(2): 288–307.

Iglesia, A.M. (2019) *La revolución de la las flâneuses*, 2nd edn. Terrades: Wunderkammer.

Ingold, T. and Vergunst, J.L. (2008) *Ways of Walking: Ethnography and Practice on Foot*. Hampshire: Ashgate.

Kern, L. (2020) *Feminist City. Claiming Space in a Man-made World*. London: Verso.

Legnaro, A. (2010) Über das Flanieren als eine Methode der empirischen Sozialforschung. Gehen – Spazieren – Flanieren. *Sozialer Sinn*, 02/2010, S. 275–288.

Leszczynski, A. and Elwood, S. (2022a) Glitch Cities. *Dialogues in Human Geography* 12(3): 401–405. https://doi.org/10.1177/20438206221129208

Leszczynski, A. and Elwood, S. (2022b) Glitch Epistemologies for Computational Cities. *Dialogues in Human Geography* 12(3): 361–378. https://doi.org/10.1177/20438206221075714

Lettkemann, E. and Schulz-Schaeffer, I. (2021) Das CAMPP-Modell des Zusammenhangs von Bedeutung und Zugänglichkeit öffentlicher Orte und seine Anwendung auf lokative Medien. In M. Löw, V. Sayman, J. Schwerer and H. Wolf (eds) *Am Ende der Globalisierung. Über die Refiguration von Räumen.* Bielefeld: Transcipt, pp 257–280.

Lubkowitz, A. (ed) (2020) *Psychogeografie.* Berlin: Matthes & Seitz.

Mitrović, M. (2022a) Third Space Walk. *Feministische Geo-RundMail 'Stories of Mapping within Feminist Geography'*, 89, 2 May. Available at: https://ak-feministische-geographien.org/rundmail/ [Accessed 1 May 2024].

Mitrović, M. (2022b) Hybrid Spaces: Walking between Analog and Digital Worlds. *Feministische Geo-RundMail 'Shocks, Turmoil and Transformation: Symposium Feminist Geography'*, 91, 26 October. Available at: https://ak- feministische-geographien.org/rundmail/ [Accessed 1 May 2024].

Mitrović, M. (2024) 'Cyberfeminists in Mexico City. Discourses and Tactics'. In P. Birle and A. Windus (eds) *Conocimiento, poder y transformación digital en América Latina.* Frankfurt am Main / Madrid: Vervuert / Iberoamericana, pp 171–184.

Mitrović, M. and Hennies, J.-H. (2017) Enlaces | Links. Available at: https://enlaces-links.net/ [Accessed 10 December 2024].

Mitrović, M. and Voigt, M.-L. (2025) Glitch(ing)! A Refusal and Gateway to More Caring Techno-urban Worlds? *Digital Geography and Society.* https://doi.org/10.1016/j.diggeo.2025.100115

Nagel, J. (2007) *Die Kunst des Surrealismus. Wie erkenne ich?* Stuttgart: Belser.

Nocturnal Unrest (2021) *NOCTURNAL UNREST. Ein feministisches Festival für Performance, Theorie und radikale Flâneuserie.* Available at: https:// nocturnal-unrest.de/ [Accessed 10 December 2024].

Pink, S. (2009) *Doing Sensory Ethnography.* London: Thousand Oaks.

Rohde, K. and Wildner, K. (2020) Urban Citizen Walkers. *Methodologische Reflexionen zum kollaborativen Gehen in der Stadt. sub\urban. zeitschrift für kritische stadtforschung* 8(3): 241–256.

Russell, L. (2020) *Glitch Feminism: A Manifesto.* London: Verso.

Rutherford, J. (1990) The Third Space. Interview with Homi Bhabha. In J. Rutherford (ed) *Identity: Community, Culture, Difference.* London: Lawrence & Wishart, pp 207–221.

Suárez Estrada, M. and Lehuedé, S. (2022) Towards a Terrestrial Internet: Re-imagining Digital Networks from the Ground Up. *Tapuya: Latin American Science, Technology and Society* 5(1). https://doi.org/10.1080/ 25729861.2022.2139913

Third Space Walk (2022) *Third Space Walk. Flâneuses★ between Virtual and Material Urban Spaces*. Available at: https:// thirdspacewalk.mirjana-mitrovic.de/ [Accessed 10 December 2024].

Ulrich, M., Hesse, F. and Oucherif, M. (eds) (2022) *Walk! Schirn Kunsthalle Frankfurt*. Wien: Verlag für moderne Kunst.

Voigt, M.-L. (2021) *Cyber Feminist City: Stadtschaffende Praktiken Zwischen Artificial Intelligence, Algorithmen und Asphalt*, Master's thesis, HafenCity Universität Hamburg.

Voigt, M.-L. (2023) We Build this City on Rocks and (Feminist) Code: Hacking Corporate Computational Designs of Cities to Come. *Digital Creativity* 34(2): 162–177. https://doi.org/10.1080/14626268.2023.2205406

Wagenknecht, S. (2020) Wie das Unternehmen LUKSO phygitale T-Shirts auf die Blockchain bringt. *BTC Echo*, 16 January. Available at: https://www.btc-echo.de/news/wie-das-unternehmen-lukso-phygitale-t-shirts-auf-die-blockchain-bringt-83430/ [Accessed 1 May 2024].

Weber, V. and Ziemer, G. (eds) (2022) *Die Digitale Stadt*. Bielefeld: transcript Verlag. https://doi.org/10.14361/9783839464748

Zook, M. and Graham, M. (2018) Hacking Code/Space: Confounding the Code of Global Capitalism. *Transactions of the Institute of British Geographers* 43(3): 390–404.

# 15

# From Model Organism to Companion Species: A Laboratory Guide to Feminist Reflexivity in Experimental Biology Research

*Lisa Weasel*

## Introduction: Reflexive methodologies and a feminist practice of science

The concept of reflexivity has been both foundational and contested in feminist science studies. At its most basic, reflexivity necessitates the inclusion of the researcher themself within the research frame. Feminist reflexivity, in turn, further requires an analysis of power within the relationship between knower and known (Dottolo and Tillery 2015). Feminist science studies scholars such as Donna Haraway and Karen Barad have pushed the boundaries of feminist reflexivity in science further, interrogating the binary that remains in such conceptions between knower and known, subject and object, and proposing instead constructs of diffraction as differential entanglement (Campbell 2004; Barad 2007). Incorporating reflexivity, and specifically feminist conceptions of reflexivity, into the practice of science can serve as an important tool for developing liveable worlds through a care-based approach that blurs boundaries between researchers and subjects.

As a feminist cell and molecular biologist trained to work with *Drosophila* fruit flies, bringing a reflexive feminist practice into the laboratory has been a lifelong project of mine. Ironically, within this rich scholarly field, such an endeavour has sometimes felt like an exercise in isolation. While theories of feminist reflexivity have been well developed, examples of how these can be directly applied and integrated methodologically into conventional everyday laboratory practices have been fewer and further between. Reflexivity has yet to be recognized or embraced within conventional practice in fields such as molecular biology, while laboratory science is still uncommon within academic feminist departments.

One exception to this is the work of Deboleena Roy, who over the course of her career as a feminist reproductive neuroendocrinologist has developed feminist models directly applicable to laboratory practice (2004; 2008). I draw on her work as well as the work of Sara Giordano (2018) here as I attempt to explore and share what a feminist reflexive practice in experimental biology might look and feel like, and indeed, might do within the world.

In this chapter, I intertwine my own positionality and experience as a laboratory scientist with feminist theoretical work on reflexivity in science, and include instructions for the reader to actively participate in a DIY feminist science experiment alongside this reading, to create an experimental reflexive feminist laboratory manual of sorts. It is my hope that readers can use this situated interactive laboratory manual to experiment with reflexivity in science directly while reading and reflecting on the chapter.

In structuring the chapter in this way, I aim to expand the boundaries of science and extend them into the home, where from a feminist perspective they have lived all along (Jen 2015). I also extend the boundaries of my own practice as a natural scientist back to my early childhood years, where my fascination and interactions with the natural world began. Reflexive relationships with what eventually become the subject of science (moss, mud, rocks, the stars in the night sky) are often seen as more acceptable in the childhood years, where expressions of emotional connection and keeping oneself in the frame, rather than severing connection as a detached observer, are not discouraged or scorned as much as they are in later years in the practice of professional science.

My quest for an expanded model of experimental biology research stretches back to my first laboratory, a four foot high alcove under the steps of my childhood home, where my sister and I earnestly incubated bits of moss, sticks and pebbles in discarded plastic pill bottles. Periodically we would pry off the caps to assess the brewing results. Our assay was smell, and our data was recorded in familiar childhood terms like 'old broccoli' or 'dirty socks'. Growing up with the luxury of safe and welcoming access to the outdoors, a privilege accorded by my middle-class White upbringing, shaped my early encounters with the subject of science.

These early forays into the 'experimental of the everyday' convinced me that I wanted to be a biologist. However, an early experience in a laboratory course in which a white rat with beady red eyes was hastily thrust under a guillotine by an instructor and I was handed its still-warm liver to homogenize, shattered any illusion that this path would unproblematically bring me closer to the world I wished to understand. To know something is to kill it, was one of the earliest epistemological lessons I learned in the lab. Was this, I wondered, the price one must pay to participate in biology, a 'life science' that had always been presented on its face as in service to a 'better world' through knowledge-based cures and forward progress, yet now seemed at odds with the very life it purported to improve?

As I continued down the by now rather bumpy path to become a scientist (the numbers of women dwindling with each step of my educational ladder), I never felt at home within the constraints of the laboratory that forced a severance between observer and observed, that mandated that values and emotions be checked at the laboratory door. As a graduate student, I would bring my *Drosophila* fruit fly cultures home, keeping them in the laundry drying cabinet above the water heater at night so that I could gather the newly eclosed virgin females in the morning before work. Years later, the COVID-19 quarantine period once again allowed me to blur the home/laboratory boundaries, as I captured fruit flies in my kitchen and cultivated them in my makeshift workspace in the attic. It is out of this latter experience that this feminist reflexive laboratory manual was born.

## *Drosophila* as companion species at home and in the lab

During the summer and early fall, kitchens around the world play host to tiny winged guests, hovering around the fruit bowl, landing and alighting wherever scraps of fruit and vegetable matter accumulate, the riper and more fetid the better. Left long enough, bruised or blemished fruit will soon show signs of decay, followed by masses of tiny writhing larvae. These household invaders, most commonly belonging to the species *Drosophila melanogaster* (translated from Latin as black bellied dew lover), are one of the few species of fruit fly that readily and willingly enter human abodes and happily remain there. Found on every continent other than Antarctica, *D. melanogaster* has evolved in tandem with human habits and migration (Keller 2007).

Like humans, it is thought that the earliest ancestors of *Drosophila melanogaster* arose in sub-Saharan Africa (Lachaise et al 1988) where they thrived on fruits, especially banana. *Drosophila melanogaster* (along with the closely related *Drosophila simulans*) evolved into a 'cosmopolitan' species, largely through their adaptation to human food and activity, such as their willingness to enter human homes (Watanabe and Kawanishi 1976). By the late 1800s *Drosophila melanogaster* was identified in both Europe, in association with port cities suggesting arrival on ships (Keller 2007) and in the United States, where *Drosophila melanogaster* was 'bred from a jar of pickled plums' in New York in September of 1875 (Linter 1882). Other common food sources for *Drosophila melanogaster* include 'canned fruits and pickles, decaying apples, cider mill refuse, fermenting vats of grape pomace, and raspberry vinegar' as well as stale beer; as Keller (2007) points out, 'all these food sources are domesticated fruits or other products of human activity'.

Today, *Drosophila melanogaster* can be found on every continent other than Antarctica (Markow and O'Grady 2005). As Robert Kohler writes in 'Lord of the flies: *Drosophila* genetics and the experimental life':

> [W]ho has not seen fruit flies congregating about decaying vegetables and fruits in gardens, or around garbage bins in public parks? Who has not kept banana or cantaloupes too long in hot weather and wondered at the sudden appearance in the kitchen of a swarm of the little flies, seemingly by spontaneous generation? Who has not had drosophila share a glass of beer or cider, or had a microscopic view of them in a high school or college biology class. … No wild creature, except perhaps the cockroach, is a more familiar companion of humankind. (Kohler 1994, 19)

This dual role as kitchen invader and laboratory workhorse make *Drosophila* ideal subjects for exploring a feminist ethico-reflexive practice of science. At once intimate in our homes and exalted under the microscope, fruit flies are easily accessible co-conspirators in a quest to engage directly in reflexive questions, while living side-by-side with us as research subjects.

This chapter invites you as the reader to capture and cultivate *Drosophila* as you explore the theoretical framings and empirical questions that arise through developing a relationship with them. The structure of the chapter is necessarily porous, intertwining methods with theory, reflection (on the part of the reader) with response (on my part as author). This playfulness with structure and form is in direct contrast to conventional scientific writing, which is written in third person as if the researcher did not exist, often using the past tense. The hybrid form of this chapter toggles between lab versus kitchen, us versus them, and reader versus author, with the goal of offering an immersive reflexive experience rather than a disembodied reading.

## Cultivating relationships with fruit flies: capture and containment

Because *Drosophila melanogaster* is a human commensal, flies are often easy to capture in kitchens and around compost piles when the season allows. Fruit flies reproduce most prolifically in summer and fall, when temperatures are between 18 and 30 degrees Celsius. When fruit flies are not active in your immediate environment, *Drosophila melanogaster* cultures are also readily available from science education suppliers, local genetic or agricultural researchers at universities, or reptile supply stores (*Drosophila* can be used as foodstuff for reptile pets).

*Fruit flies can be captured using readily available and recycled household items. Even if you do not see fruit flies in your kitchen, compost, or rubbish area, by setting a trap you may be able to capture them to observe. To prepare the trap, gather the following items:*

1. *a clean recycled clear plastic cold drink cup with lid that fits tightly (such as from take-out coffee or drink shops);*
2. *tape sufficient to seal any holes for straws or sips in the cup;*
3. *a ripe banana, and if available, a tiny amount of baking yeast (grains or paste);*
4. *a lighter, candle, or other small source of flame;*
5. *a large wire paperclip (or a piece of 40 gauge wire);*
6. *a jeweler's loupe or other handheld magnifying lens such as used to examine photos, stamps or gemstones (can be purchased online).*

*To prepare the trap, place the lid tightly on the cup, and use tape to seal up any holes or access for straws or sips.*

*Next, unwind the paperclip and use the flame to heat the end of the paperclip. Use caution not to overheat, and be sure to use a plain wire clip that is not coated with paint or other flammable substance. After a few seconds in the flame, use the paperclip to poke five holes on the sides of the cup just under where the lid attaches. The hot clip will melt the plastic to make the hole. Ensure that the clip goes easily back and forth in the hole and the melted plastic does not accidentally reseal the hole.*

*Remove the lid, and place an approximately 1 inch piece of banana in the cup. If you have baking yeast available, sprinkle a very small number (~10) of yeast grains, or a tiny dollop of yeast paste, onto the banana.*

*Then place the cup with the banana (and yeast if available) in a warm location close to a source of food, such as in a kitchen, next to a compost pile, or close to a rubbish bin where food is disposed of. Places with proximity to fruit, vegetable, or food waste scraps will attract* Drosophila. *(If you need to place your trap in public, you can make a note on it explaining it is part of an experiment.) Flies develop best if exposed to day/night light cycles, so avoid keeping your flies intentionally in the dark such as in a closet or cupboard, for long periods.*

*Watch for small flies to accumulate in the cup over the next few days.*[1]

---

[1]    If it is out of season or if your attempts to capture wild fruit flies are unsuccessful, you can obtain a culture of *Drosophila* through the mail by ordering online from a pet supply store (*Drosophila* are frequently cultured as reptile food) or through a university fly facility,

This act of capture provides an entry into reflexive questions regarding power. According to Deboleena Roy, 'although the methods used in a feminist inquiry will not be different than a conventional scientific inquiry, the relationship between the scientists and the subject of examination must be recognized and articulated' (2004, 273). In capturing and containing flies, an obvious power relationship is constructed. This power relationship is in turn shaped by our social conception of fruit flies, and the relationships that already exist between flies and humans. Recognizing these relationships, whether founded upon respect or disgust (or any other emotion), is a necessary step towards building a science that undergirds a more liveable world. Organisms that on the surface appear as wildly different as a human and a fruit fly do not exist in isolation from one another, and foregrounding such relationships in scientific practice can lead to knowledge supporting more liveable worlds.

Based on its seeming dependence on human food and activity, in biological terms, *Drosophila* is considered a human commensal. Commensalism by definition is a relationship in which one organism (the fly) benefits, while the other (the human) is unaffected. Yet through the lens of companion specie-ship as articulated by Haraway, it is clear that humans have benefited greatly, as well as been shaped through and by, the human–fly relationship as well.

Haraway distinguishes between companion animals and companion species: '"companion species" is a bigger and more heterogeneous category than companion animal, and not just because one must include such organic beings as rice, bees, tulips and intestinal flora' (Haraway 2003, 15). In Haraway's construct, '[c]ompanion species differs from companion animals (such as guide dogs for the blind) in this crucial respect: it implies a two-way dependency. Haraway argues that neither human animals nor non-human animals pre-exist their relationship to one another. This is because the relationship is productive or co-constitutive' (Buchanan 2018). While Haraway's work focuses primarily on dogs, the productive and co-constitutive nature of human–*Drosophila* relationships is no less richly substantiated.

*Drosophila* entered the laboratory at the turn of the 20th century and quickly became a prototypical 'model organism'. They have been participants in six Nobel prizes (beginning in 1933 and as recently as 2017) and are often celebrated for their genetic similarity to humans, sharing nucleotide sequences of approximately two-thirds of important human disease genes (Chien et al 2002). Their sex lives have been fastidiously scrutinized and

such as the University of Cambridge in the UK, The National Drosophila Species Stock Center at Cornell University in the United States, or a science education supplier such as Carolina Biological or Ward's.

applied to humans, as in an article from the Harvard Medical School that purported to explain how the 'neurobiology of fruit fly courtship helps illuminate human disorders of motivation' thusly: 'Two fruit flies meet in an acrylic mating chamber and check each other out. It's the insect version of speed dating for science' (Brownlee 2018). In these, as well as a plethora of other genetic, behavioural and neuroscience research, definitions and distinctions of what it means to be 'human' are tightly tethered to and refracted through interaction with the material compositions and agency of other organisms. As Kohler observes of laboratory fruit flies:

> Once in the lab, they were physically reconstructed and adapted to experimental uses. They were, however, active players in the relationship with experimental biologists, capable of unexpectedly changing the rules of experimental practice. Fruit flies were not just molded like putty by geneticists and put through their paces. Even as the standardized instrument of genetics they had the capacity to change and frustrate drosophilist's plans and change the purposes for which they had originally been brought into the lab … we need to see the relation between *Drosophila* and drosophilists as an interactive and evolving symbiosis with the special ecological spaces of experimental laboratories. (Kohler 1994, 19)

Here, in acknowledging the material agency of fruit flies as active participants in the experiments, Kohler leans towards Karen Barad's conception of agential realism and intra-action:

> The notion of intra-action recognizes that distinct agencies do not precede, but rather emerge through, their intra-action. It is important to note that the 'distinct' agencies are only distinct in a relational, not an absolute, sense that is, *agencies are only distinct in relation to their mutual entanglement; they don't exist as individual elements.* (Barad 2007, 33, emphasis in original)

Kohler's reference to 'an interactive and evolving symbiosis' hints at Barad's emphasis on the mutual dependence and fundamental inseparability of an independent 'observer' and 'observed' in this relationship. Barad introduces the idea of 'agential cuts' to describe the boundary-making processes enacted by apparatuses, reconceived of as entanglements of contingent relations. Apparatuses include not only what we conventionally think of in a Cartesian model as observers and observed, as well as any measuring devices, but the entire context and construction of the laboratory condition – all co-constituted and defined through relationship. 'Apparatuses enact agential cuts that produce determinate boundaries and properties of "entities" within phenomena, where "phenomena" are the ontological inseparability of agentially intra-acting components' (Barad 2007, 148).

Working with *Drosophila* in the laboratory constitutes one such apparatus, in which particular agential cuts enact boundaries that precipitate meanings and knowledge. *Drosophila* in kitchens, gardens and agricultural fields are enmeshed in other apparatuses, with the possibility of different agential cuts and thus different sedimentary meanings. Analogously as light can be both particle and wave, depending on the constitution of the apparatus, *Drosophila* as a companion species can enact the double identity of both model organism and pest, with the possibilities for different agential cuts and thus different knowledges and response-abilities. These multiple and overlapping identities and relationships are a feature of liveable worlds – worlds in which life is malleable, responsive, and imbedded and imbued with multiple agential potentials.

## Getting lost in the attic with *Drosophila*

My entanglement with *Drosophila* in the laboratory led to agential cuts that produced visualizations of genetic interactions during morphogenesis, the shape-shifting process through which chemical information and matter transform into bodily shape. In this context, a particular and consequential force in that apparatus included my own feminist orientation to the research. As molecular endocrinologist Deboleena Roy observes, 'when a feminist scientist actually finds herself in front of a lab bench, she may be motivated to ask difficult questions that typically would not have been raised in her traditional scientific training' (Roy 2018, 71). Ultimately, these questions led me for a time outside of the laboratory, as I followed a not-unfamiliar path into more theoretical engagements with feminism and science. But this did not mean that my relationship with *Drosophila* had ended. Fruit flies continued to flutter and sometimes even swarm through my life, hovering over the fruit bowl in my kitchen, infesting my garden compost pile in the spring.

In the spring of 2020, the disruption of the COVID-19 pandemic interrupted business as usual, and I found myself relegated to my attic, rather than venturing to my university office each day. With my material connections to other humans reduced, and confined to my small living space as the warmth of summer dawned, I decided to see if I could culture some of the fruit flies that shared my kitchen, to get to know these nonhuman others again, albeit on different terms.

The fruit flies in my kitchen enthusiastically welcomed the opportunity to fly around in and lay their eggs in a recycled plastic cup baited with banana and a sprinkling of baker's yeast. Over the next week, I watched as the larvae morphed through their different instars, first digging deep into the decaying banana, and then crawling up and out on their path towards pupation. Sequestered at home, I had to adapt and devise my methodologies to the technology on hand. Without the laboratory luxuries of incubators, dedicated carbon dioxide anaesthetizing setups or a microscope for closer inspection, I found that a few minutes in the freezer would put the flies into a chill coma, during which I could examine them with a handheld loupe magnifier.

Initially, I did not understand myself to be conducting science. But as the summer wore on and I continued to examine more closely my tiny winged attic companions, and to pass generations of flies into new cups and jars from around the house, I found myself eager to follow their progress, marking my time by their stage of development, watching closely to see if there were differences between each successive generation. But at the same time, I chastised myself that this wasn't 'real science'. Not only was I lacking the conventional tools of any self-respecting fly lab, I didn't even have a fixed research question.

In this way, without really meaning to, I had veered towards what Deboleena Roy (drawing on Patti Lather), in her articulation of a 'microphysiology of desire', refers to as 'getting lost in the lab'. Roy states, 'at first glance, "getting lost" may be disorienting to the feminist scientist. We are used to following clearly labeled flow charts and neatly organized protocols. Getting lost may seem counterintuitive, but it does address the question, What can we do?' (Roy 2018, 82).

As if the ravages of the COVID-19 pandemic were not enough, at the end of that summer, unprecedented wildfires raged close to my home, and my living space was inundated with thick, acrid smoke and air quality readings ranging into the danger level and beyond. I retreated downstairs to cleaner air, but my flies remained in the attic. I wondered how they were experiencing this change in our surroundings, with their very different chemosensory system primed to distinguish so many volatile hydrocarbon cues. Did this interrupt their ability to recognize one another? Did they struggle with their confinement in the cup, wishing to be able to fly away, as I had when I descended in search of cleaner air below?

Through the next fall and winter, I struggled to keep my 'kitchen strains' going on a warm windowsill, not really knowing where this was heading. The next summer, more striking climatic conditions arrived. By June, a heat dome had settled over the Pacific Northwest, and the temperature rose to 116 degrees Fahrenheit. It was even hotter in my attic, and I thought the flies would certainly succumb. But they survived, although I noticed them change as the summer wore on. The flies had become lighter, with less pigment in their cuticular stripes. In adapting to the multitude of geographic locations that they now inhabit, *Drosophila* have evolved the ability to rapidly moderate their pigmentation in response to temperature and other climatic cues (David et al 1990). This phenotypic plasticity enables them to lighten or darken their cuticular pigment, consistent with the thermal melanism hypothesis – as ectothermic creatures with an exoskeleton, darker pigmentation allows them to absorb more heat in a cold setting, while lighter pigmentation reflects better under hot conditions (Freoa et al 2022). Pigmentation of the *Drosophila melanogaster* cuticle also shows differences based on sexual dimorphism, with males having more darkly pigmented abdominal stripes, and females with less pigment in their body stripes.

My home-based fruit fly culture veered dramatically away from the conventional approach to research on the relationship between pigmentation and climate in *Drosophila*. My flies were subject to wildly vacillating conditions – the same dramatic smoke and temperature extremes that increasingly plague us as humans – in stark contrast to the controlled conditions required in conventional *Drosophila* research. In releasing so many of the controlled laboratory restraints, more space opened up for the flies' own agency. Recognizing the more macroscopic link between climate fluctuation and human activity that played a role in the conditions both I and the flies were experiencing re-positioned human agency on a different plane as well – in acknowledging the active human role in the indeterminacy of climate, rather than assuming absolute control as in conventional laboratory settings. Roy encourages us not to necessarily turn away from such indeterminacy, but rather pursue and engage it: 'Barad would have us orient ourselves to an ontological and ethical framework that assumes indeterminacy and asks that we as scientists become accountable to "the material nature of practices and how they come to matter"' (Roy 2018, 74).

For me, the material nature of my practice meant living with my subjects, sharing the same climate and space while understanding that our coexistence was both mutually constitutive and wholly unique, in constant flux with the context and conditions. We shared an atmosphere thick with not only benzopyrenes and other polycyclic aromatic hydrocarbons commonly occurring in smoke and pollution, but also pheromones like cys-vaccenal acetate and androstenone, setting off reverberating signals in the many olfactory bulbs and neurons contained within the walls of the attic that blurred the line between home and lab, inside and outside. Olfaction is considered to be one of the most ancient sensory systems, so the history of this human and *Drosophila* chemical entanglement reaches far back in time. Our mutual entanglement under these harsh conditions was an exercise in inhabiting liveable worlds under unliveable conditions.

## Hatching a plan: immersing in the *Drosophila* life cycle

*By now, perhaps there is some activity inside of your cup. If you see tiny flies in the cup, it should not take long before larvae hatch and begin burrowing in the food. Each female can lay approximately 100 eggs per day. While Drosophila eggs are too small to observe with a handheld magnifier, after roughly one day spent as an embryo, eggs will hatch into the first larval stage (called instars) and larvae will begin feeding on the banana surface. Drosophila are holometabolous insects, which means that the larvael body and the adult body are of totally different form. The cells and tissues that will develop into the adult are carried around internally by the larva in the form of undifferentiated imaginal discs, small sacs of simple cells that are fed and divide and grow during larvael development. Roughly a day later, the larvae will molt and the pale, wiggling second instar larvae should be visible burrowing just below the surface of the banana, which will have decomposed and settled on the bottom of the cup. Finally, when the third larval instar nears its end, after roughly one more day, the larvae will begin migrating up the side of the cup, in search of a drier spot away from the food to begin to pupate. The ambient temperature will have a strong impact on how long it takes the larvae to hatch, and how long they spend in each of their larval stages.*

*During pupariation, you will first see the larva encased within a tan case affixed to the side of the cup. The early pupa will appear undifferentiated, like a pale sausage inside the pupal case. Over the next four days or so (at temperatures of 25 degrees Celsius), the larvael bodily structures will begin to disintegrate, while the sacs of undifferentiated cells called imaginal discs that will form the adult structures will begin to take shape. Using a handheld magnifier, you will begin to see two large red dots on one end, which are the pigmented eyes forming. A little later, darkened folded wings will be apparent tucked along the sides of the pupal case. In some instances, and depending on the magnification of your handheld lens, you may be able to see a couple of legs pointing downward towards the base of the pupal case.*

*Depending on the ambient temperature, somewhere between ten days (25 degrees Celsius) to three weeks (at 18 degrees Celsius) flies will begin to hatch and you will see empty pupal cases still affixed to the edge of the cup, and adult flies flying about inside the cup. As more flies hatch, the population inside the cup will begin to get crowded.*

## Questions to ask

How is it possible to 'get lost' with the flies? What is needed, what stands in the way? What affective relationships, or not, is it possible to develop with the flies through their life cycle? How does the apparatus impact what is knowable here? How can we know more and differently through interrogating the positionality of human/fly dis/connection? How have you become 'fly-sensitized' (Mehrabi 2018)? What did it take to habituate yourself to the flies' life cycle? In what ways does living with the flies lead to consideration of liveable worlds?

## Making flies killable: embodied intimacy with unloved insect others

I had chosen *Drosophila* as a model organism for my doctoral research in developmental biology, reasoning that despite its fancy laboratory nomenclature, it was the same fruit fly species that I encountered regularly with irritation in my kitchen, where I uncritically lured them away from my fruit bowl to a self-inflicted death through a funnel inserted into a glass jar filled with vinegar. In contrast to my early encounter of 'sacrifice' with a white lab rat, these were pests, not potential pets, I reasoned when I first met the flies in the lab, and for a time that logic worked as I embarked on my research, passing generation upon generation of flies into fresh vials full of laboratory-concocted fly food, and discarding the remainder in the morbidly titled 'morgue', an Ehrlenmeyer flask filled with ethanol.

But immersion in the life cycle of my fruit flies that the project demanded crept up on me, as I carefully observed under magnification their progression from larvae foraging around in food, to tiny pupae with wings tucked and red eyes bulging as they prepared to burst from their chitinous pupal casks. When it came time for me to conduct a large-scale genetic screen, as tens of thousands of tiny, anesthetized flies swept across the magnification field of my stereoscope, I searched for the rare fly that possessed the wing mutation I was looking for. If I moved my brush or forceps a little too brusquely, a leg, a wing, even a fragile neck, would sever in the pile of sleeping flies that flew by my field of vision as if on a conveyor belt. The pang of remorse that I felt in the magnified contradictions of first generating and then tossing away so many tiny lives stemmed from my discomfort with what Donna Haraway would later refer to as 'making killable' a species even as tiny and pest-worthy as a fruit fly. As Haraway writes, 'I suggest that it is a misstep to separate the world's beings into when sp. ... It is not killing that gets us into exterminism, but making beings killable' (Haraway 2008, 79).

'Making beings killable' as a cornerstone of scientific practice seems blatantly at odds with the purported benevolence of science. To uncritically accept the death of the subject as inherent in scientific practice seems to fly in the face of liveable worlds. This does not necessarily mean that one has to feel any type of affinity or affection for their subject. In contrast to the feelings of connection I developed with my flies, Tera Mehrabi describes feelings of disgust for the flies they worked with in a *Drosophila* laboratory. This disgust did not preclude becoming what Mehrabi describes as 'fly sensitized' and deeply interrogating a feminist ethics of practice with the flies by developing an embodied intimacy. Mehrabi reflects, 'to work through the embodied intimacy and situatedness of scientific practices in a fly lab underlines the importance of feminist modes of doing science and care ... disgust was ethically important to me because it communicated my anxieties to me about science, laboratory, death, disease, waste and flies' (Mehrabi 2018, 77).

Like Mehrabi, we can take this common kitchen and agricultural insect pest (albeit one that lives a double identity as a model experimental laboratory organism) as an entry point for considering a feminist ethico-reflexive praxis of science that might contribute to more liveable worlds. It is not only in the laboratory that invertebrates proffer a fruitful site of engagement in such matters. In her study of affective, sensorial interactions between invertebrates and humans in an urban community garden, Teresa Lori-Bidart observes that 'indeed, typical garden or soil invertebrates are generally "unloved others" (Beisel et al 2013; Rose and Van Dooren 2011), unless deemed "useful" for human endeavors' (Lloro-Bidart 2018, 23). Yet like Haraway, Lloro-Bidart rejects drawing an ethical line between certain classes of organisms, or relying on external criteria to assert which kinds or species deserve ethical respect. Lloro-Bidart's

> feminist poshumanist approach, in contrast, asks what it might mean to give ethical consideration to garden invertebrates not because of their sentience, ability to have subjective experiences, or capacities to suffer, but simply because human beings not only share our food production spaces with them, but also because in the mundane routine of daily life, we are affected by them and in turn affect them. (Lloro-Bidart 2018, 28)

Recognizing the mutualism inherent between vastly different orders of beings can provide the grounding for a science of a liveable world.

## Chilling out with flies: response–ability and agential cuts

How has your observation and interaction with the larvae in the cup impacted you? In conventional scientific research, we tend to ask only how we impact the organisms that we work with through our experimental manipulations, rather than how they also reflexively alter us. Did you have a visceral reaction of disgust or loathing as you watched the pulsating larvae gyrate beneath the surface of the food? Were you drawn in with fascination?

Perhaps by now, you can see for yourself some of the wings, eyes and even legs folded like a neat insect origami inside the pupal cases on the side of your cup. How do you feel as you approach the emergence of the flies? Is it with dread, curiosity or mere passivity?

As the flies emerge, you will need to decide what to do with this next generation that you have bred inside the cup. Here, in the service of experimenting with a practice consistent with liveable worlds, we return to the feminist mandate to acknowledge and address the power inherent in the research relationship (Dottolo and Tillery 2015), whether conducted in the laboratory or, as in this case, at home. You may desire a closer look at the flies that you have hatched, or you may wish to be done with them. If you wish to explore further the adult flies, *Drosophila* can be temporarily anaesthetized by short bouts of exposure to cold temperatures, during which they enter a state known as a chill coma. If you have access to a refrigerator or freezer, you can easily chill your flies so that you can more closely observe them. If left too long at a low temperature they will die, but for short periods of observation, you can take advantage of this to stop them from moving so that you can look at them with your handheld lens.

*To coerce your flies into a chill coma, gather the following materials:*

1. *an additional recycled and washed clear plastic cup with lid (does not need holes punched; but do seal up any large openings as before);*
2. *a refrigerator or freezer;*
3. *ice: several cups of crushed, chopped or cubed ice, and a container to put the ice in, such as a bowl, plate, or small recycled plastic tub;*
4. *a recycled plastic or metal jar lid of light colour, placed on ice to chill down (can be in the same or different container as the chilled cup);*
5. *to move the flies around with: a children's paintbrush (can be cheap with plastic bristles); a toothpick, sewing pin or needle, and your handheld magnifying loupe as used earlier.*

*To anesthetize your flies in a refrigerator, place your cup on its side in the refrigerator and check on their activity after five minutes and then again at two-minute intervals. Depending on the temperature of the refrigerator, it may take in the range of 10–12 minutes for the flies to lose consciousness. (Placing the cup on its side prevents the comatose flies from getting lodged and stuck in the food on the bottom of the cup.)*

*Freezer method: You can more quickly anesthetize the flies in the freezer using the same method. In this case, check them after four minutes and thereafter in 1–2 minute increments. Remove them right away once they have stopped flying around in the cup.*

*Ice method: You can directly anesthetize the flies on ice. However, they will be easier to work with if you can use a fridge or freezer. Even if you anesthetized them in a freezer, you will need to keep them chilled on ice while you look at them.*

*If you have not already anesthetized them in the fridge or freezer, you can chill down another plastic cup by immersing it in ice for five minutes. Make sure that the majority of the cup is in contact with the ice, and keep it immersed in ice during this procedure.*

*Place the plastic funnel into the empty chilled cup, wide side facing up and tube of funnel pointing down into the empty chilled cup.*

*Hold your cup of hatched flies upright on a solid surface like a table or counter. Bang the cup down quickly and firmly; this will stun the flies and cause most of them to fall to the bottom of the cup. (Make sure to hold the lid on so it does not pop off.)*

*Quickly take the top off the cup of flies and turn it upside down and tap it onto the wide mouth of the funnel. Some flies should fall through the funnel into the empty chilled cup – you don't need a lot of flies, just enough to look at. It is also possible that some of the banana food runs down the side, or the card piece also falls into the funnel, that is OK but try to avoid all the contents dumping into the funnel. Within seconds, the flies that have fallen into the chilled cup should be immobilized. Quickly right the cup of cultured flies and replace the lid, setting it aside. Keep the collection cup immersed in ice with the flies, which should be immobile in the bottom of the cup. If they are not immobilized and are escaping, quickly put the lid over the cup, and tap it firmly into the ice to stun the flies and collect them at the bottom. Upon contact with the ice-cold surface of the cup, the flies should quickly be immobilized.*

*Whether you have anaesthetized your flies in the fridge/freezer or using the ice method, you can use the following procedure to visualize them. If kept too long on ice, flies will die, so conduct your examination quickly.*

*Chill a pale-coloured metal or plastic jar lid on ice for at least five minutes. Condensation may collect on the lid during this time, so wipe it with a paper towel just before you want to use it.*

*Tap your anaesthetized flies onto the chilled jar lid. They should stay unconscious as long as the lid has good contact with the ice. You can use the handheld loupe to magnify the flies, and you can move the flies around with the paintbrush, toothpick or sewing pins to compare and sort them. Flies can usually be kept chilled for several hours at zero degrees Celsius without serious harm, but if left at low temperatures for a long period, they will succumb and die.*

*Questions to ask*

What agential cuts can be made, and what knowledge might emerge from them? How do we see ourselves refracted through fly life cycles? How does the apparatus limit or expand the nature of the agential cuts available to us? What does it mean to control the consciousness of other beings? How does language serve to facilitate or close off particular agential cuts?

Eventually, you will need to decide how and when you wish to continue or end your relationship with the flies that you have captured. It is possible to maintain *Drosophila* for many generations, although this will depend on the conditions in which they are cultured, the ambient temperature and humidity, light/dark cycles, and infection with bacteria, fungi or parasites. Should you wish to carry on your fly culture, after hatching you can set up a new cup as you did initially, and using either the chill method or tapping and funnel to transfer some (but not all!) of the flies in your culture cup into the new cup with banana food. Since each female fly can lay up to 400 eggs, you do not need to transfer a large number of flies to the new cup! In any case, you will likely have a large number of flies for which you are responsible.

When it comes time to end your relationship with your flies, you will need to decide on a course of action, either killing them directly; letting their population in the cup die out due to lack of food or disease (flies are susceptible to fungi, mites and other forms of dis-ease); or opening the cup and releasing them. Laboratory protocols guard against release of flies, especially transgenic flies. However, the capture of flies in human homes or the environment is not usually governed by external rules or constraints. (*Drosophila suzukii*, the spotted wing *Drosophila* causes economic damage to small fruit farms and industries, so that should be considered if any of your flies appear to have the tell-tale spotted wings of this species.)

Questions to ask: how will you be response-able to these companions you are entangled with? What kind of questions will you ask, which actions will you choose to be accountable to and for?

How have you created, or interfered with, a model of a liveable world in each step of the experiment? How and for whom and what is such a liveable world defined?

*If you choose to kill and preserve individual flies for later comparison and visualization, the simplest way to kill the flies is to place them back into the freezer for 24 hours or more. From an ethical standpoint, this is similar to the conditions that flies can experience due to seasonal weather perturbations, at the end of the warm season in temperate climates with the onset of winter.*

*You can also kill the flies after they have been cold-anaesthetized by placing them into a container or jar lid with rubbing alcohol, or an alcohol-based hand sanitizer. Flies gravitate to alcohol, so this can also be done with living flies, although for ethical reasons you may wish to transfer flies already anaesthetized by chilling.*

*If you wish to preserve the flies, you can either keep them in a small container of rubbing alcohol or hand sanitizer; or you can preserve them in a drop of clear nail polish affixed to a card or a recycled jar lid. Use the magnifying loupe and a toothpick or pin to move the fly around so that it is mounted in a way that you can easily see it.*

Questions to ask: What are the feminist ethics of killing flies? Where does such 'killing' begin and end – is it at the beginning of the initial capture, or when the flies cease to display certain qualities and characteristics we define as 'life'? What value is afforded to each individual life that is terminated? How does the apparatus (such as the kitchen, the laboratory, and so on) effect the killing cuts that can be made, and what meanings are ascribed to such cuts? Is killing more or less ethical if it is carried out in a laboratory, or in a kitchen? (Donna Haraway's chapter in the book *When Species Meet*, titled 'Sharing Suffering: Instrumental Relations between Laboratory Animals and Their People' 2008 may be helpful here.)

## Conclusion: 'Feeling around' with flies: tinkering with the home/laboratory boundary

In intertwining experimental methods, feminist theoretical engagement and personal reflections, all the while living with one's research companions and within the home/laboratory itself, without a predestined research question or imposing the control required of conventional science, this chapter has attempted to develop a laboratory manual for the practice of what Roy refers to as ' "feeling around" for the organism'. Roy writes:

> Feeling around for the organism serves as an applied ethics of matter that brings together the qualities of changefulness and nonhuman becomings, kinship and hylozoism, and univocally and immanence. As a microphysiology of desire, 'feeling around' resembles a stolonic searching in motion, a reaching toward and touching of an always unfixed and incompletely knowable other, in search of a response – any response. (Roy 2018, 88)

If such practices represent one avenue towards a feminist practice of science, how can we bring such 'feeling around' to a broader audience, helping more to 'get lost' in and with a broadened conception of scientific practice? How can the methodologies proposed by feminist science scholars be experienced and operationalized in ways that combine both theory and practice? And can these methodologies lead to more liveable worlds? Here, Sara Giordano's application of 'tinkering' as a feminist avenue into experimental praxis can be helpful (2018). Giordano writes:

> [W]e can take tinkering as a form of playfulness that can be used to learn more about our worlds, ourselves, and others. This could be an orientation to the process of knowledge production. This playfulness then always has to do with how we are situated in relation to the world or 'subjects' that we are learning about and learning to identify with. (Giordano 2018, 225)

Giordano stresses the importance of 'a hands–on praxis rooted in feminist pedagogy' as a critical element of feminist tinkering practice. Fruit flies invite us into such playfulness, in their multiple intersecting identities as pests, model organisms, and companion species in our homes and labs. Indeed, at many times of year, many of us are already 'tinkering' with fruit flies, and they with us, as we share our kitchens, gardens and lab benches with them. Perhaps the liveable worlds that we strive for as feminist scientists are already those that we inhabit.

Here, I return to some of the themes with which this chapter began. *Drosophila* offer us multiple, overlapping relationships, as household pests, as laboratory models, and in many more relationships that can be experienced by living in entanglement with them. They are 'made killable' in different ways, in the kitchen and in the lab, for example. In tinkering with flies, feeling around and getting lost with them, new agential cuts are possible. However, it is necessary to confront the cut of death and the ethics of what to do with the flies, living or dead, at some point.

Mehrabi suggests that focusing on the death of flies and their transformation into 'waste' in laboratory practice and safety protocols can be a fruitful location in which to 'challenge the ways in which we think about nature and the laboratory environment as detached and separated from one another through dead matter'. She asks, 'How can we reimagine nature, life and death from the position of the exploited, the disposed, the contaminated, the toxic, and in terms of webs of interconnectedness that are always already contaminated by toxicity and waste?' (Mehrabi 2020, 141). We can ask similar, simultaneous questions about such reimaginings from the vantage of our entanglement with fruit flies as household pests as well, as we strive for a science compatible with liveable worlds.

But it is not only with fruit flies that we can tinker. Many other organisms live in our midst, and through both physical tinkering and metaphorical feeling around, we can reflexively reach out to them, asking how they re/shape us as we encounter and interact with them. It is my hope, and my invitation, that by following the protocols here and living in the always already-hybrid space that cuts between kitchen and laboratory, we may collectively ask new questions, and participate in new configurations, in the continuum of life and death, of theory and praxis, of fly and human, in our pursuit of more liveable worlds.

## References


Barad, K. (2007) *Meeting the Universe Halfway: Quantum Physics and the Entanglement of Matter and Meaning*. Durham, NC: Duke University Press.

Brownlee, C. (2018) The love lives of fruit flies. *Harvard Medical School News and Research*, 13 July. Available at: https://hms.harvard.edu/news/love-lives-fruit-flies [Accessed 18 March 2025].

Buchanan, I. (2018) *A Dictionary of Critical Theory*. Oxford University Press. Available at: https://www.oxfordreference.com/view/10.1093/acref/9780198794790.001.0001/acref-9780198794790- e- 765?rskey=RR7DwV&result=141 [Accessed 18 March 2025].

Campbell, K. (2004) The Promise of Feminist Reflexivities: Developing Donna Haraway's Project for Feminist Science Studies. *Hypatia* 19(1): 162–182.

Chien, S., Reiter, L.T., Bier, E. and Gribskov, M. (2002) Homophila: Human Disease Gene Cognates in Drosophila. *Nucleic Acids Research* 30(1): 149–151.

David, J.R., Capy, P. and Gauthier, J.P. (1990) Abdomen Pigmentation and Growth Temperature in *Drosophila melanogaster*: Similarities and Differences in the Norms of Reaction of Successive Segments. *Journal of Evolutionary Biology* 3: 429–445.

Dottolo, A.L. and Tillery, S.M. (2015) Reflexivity and Research: Feminist Interventions and Their Practical Implications. In Jack L. Amoureux and Brent J. Steele (eds) *Reflexivity and International Relations: Positionality, Critique, and Practice*. London: Routledge, pp 123–141.

Freoa, L., Chevin, L.M., Christol, P., Méléard, S., Rera, M., Véber, A., et al (2022) Drosophilid Cuticle Pigmentation Impacts Body Temperature. *bioRxiv*, 2022-12. doi: https://doi.org/10.1101/2022.12.03.518031

Giordano, S. (2018) Theorizing Feminist Tinkering with Science Methodologies. *Canadian Journal of Science, Mathematics and Technology Education* 18: 222–231.

Haraway, D.J. (2003) *The Companion Species Manifesto: Dogs, People, and Significant Otherness*. Chicago: Prickly Paradigm Press.

Haraway, D.J. (2008) *When Species Meet*. Minneapolis: University of Minnesota Press.

Jen, C. (2015) Do-It-Yourself Biology, Garage Biology, and Kitchen Science. In Matthias Weinroth and Eugenia Rodrigues (eds) *Knowing New Biotechnologies: Social Aspects of Technological Convergence*. London: Routledge, pp 125–141.

Keller, A. (2007) Drosophila Melanogaster: A History as a Human Commensal. *Current Biology* 17(3): R77–R81.

Kohler, R.E. (1994) *Lords of the Fly: Drosophila Genetics and the Experimental Life*. Chicago: University of Chicago Press.

Lachaise, D., Cariou, M.L., David, J.R., Lemeunier, F., Tsacas, L. and Ashburner, M. (1988) Historical biogeography of the Drosophila melanogaster species subgroup. *Evolutionary Biology* 22: 159–225.

Linter, J.A. (1882) *First Annual Report on the Injurious and Other Insects of the State of New York*. Albany: Weed, Parsons and Co.

Lloro-Bidart, T. (2018) Cultivating Affects: A Feminist Posthumanist Analysis of Invertebrate and Human Performativity in an Urban Community Garden. *Emotion, Space and Society* 27: 23–30.

Markow, T.A. and O'Grady, P. (2005) *Drosophila: A Guide to Species Identification and Use*. Elsevier.

Mehrabi, T. (2018) Being Intimate with Flies: On Affective Methodologies and Laboratory Work. *Kvinder, Køn & Forskning* 1: 73–80.

Mehrabi, T. (2020) Queer Ecologies of Death in the Lab: Rethinking Waste, Decomposition and Death through a Queerfeminist Lens. *Australian Feminist Studies* 35(104): 138–154.

Roy, D. (2004) Feminist Theory in Science: Working Toward a Practical Transformation. *Hypatia* 19(1): 255–279.

Roy, D. (2008) Asking Different Questions: Feminist Practices for the Natural Sciences. *Hypatia* 23(4): 134–157.

Roy, D. (2018) *Molecular Feminisms: Biology, Becomings, and Life in the Lab.* University of Washington Press.

Watanabe, T.K. and Kawanishi, M. (1976) *Colonization of Drosophila simulans in Japan. Proceedings of the Japan Academy* 52(4): 191–194.

# Making

# 16

# An Invitation to Help Redecorate a Corner of Discursive Space

*Erika Szymanski*

The following chapter is a handwritten text, presented in this format for reasons discussed in the first several paragraphs. To view higher-resolution images online, please visit: https://bristoluniversitypress.co.uk/revisiting-reflexivity/additional-content

An Invitation to (help) Redecorate a Corner of Discursive Space

From Erika Szymanski, green eng, office floor, Rm 345, Eddy (Hall), Colorado State University, Fort Collins, Colorado, USA

This is an essay about attending to writing as a mode, about writing as a mode that may encompass multiple modes, and about written scholarship as a major contribution to the worldbuilding that we do as (STS and other) scholars. I want to help make a space for questions about what sorts of reflexive writing practices might make these worlds more liveable, lively, playful, response-able, fitting for the kind of work that we (as individuals and communities) might be trying to do now, and to the worlds we want to help create/grow. I want to think about what constitutes livable textual worlds that don't just rest in the residues of genres and other institutions that may be logically inconsistent with at least some of the work that I and other STS scholars need to use this writing to do.

The essential social constructivist discourse theory starting point: Worldbuilding through text-building is not a metaphor. Texts are social spaces wherein at least some people (certainly me, probably you) do at least some of their living. (This idea is central to Critical Discourse Theory, which is old and solid enough to have earned capitalization, even if it's more an orientation or approach than a method.) Textual spaces concatenate with other social spaces, which is to say that the worlds we enact are shaped as much through the language practices that we use to handle them as through the physical practices that we employ. Nor are those two separate sets, even if analyzing one dimension or aspect characterizing any given practice can be an useful convention. As Annemarie Mol and John Law and others who taught me to think material-semiotically have shown, humans (and other creatures and entities, though that's a different paper and not my point here) do work, individually, to assemble things through diverse practices, all of which can be described in both material and semiotic dimensions.

Exactly how the material and the semiotic relate has been a subject of much STS discussion/debate, but here's my understanding: Everything that might be heuristically constituted as a thing for the sake of making sense of lived experience — can be equally described in material terms, semiotic terms, and energetic terms — because all things are always moving, in motion, and thus able to bump into and alter the course and/or composition of other things-trajectories. (It's important not to neglect the energetic dimension, I think, not only to account for how all things are always changing and extend the potential to change one another, but also to remember that holding together takes energy — that work and force are also energetic terms.) So, when I think about livable worlds, I think about how I configure textual spaces, because my own primary form of construction work (other than cooking, maybe) involves building sentences.

A tension at least potentially exists between the idea of scholarly discursive spaces being built to contain valid knowledge and the idea of those spaces as living rooms, in which social relations are played out worlding. (Gary Downey and

Team Zuiderent-Jerak wrote in the introduction to their recent edited collection on _Making and Doing_ that while their contributors were understandably inclined to incorporate much of themselves into writing about their exercises/experiments in making/doing STS, as editors, they were wary that too much of that positionality/personality ending up in the text and so exceeding the boundary of what "counts" as scholarship. I can see their point in at least two ways:

1. Scholarship is about building systematic knowledge among a community of would-be knowers who subscribe to a more or less common set of institutions/conventions for knowledge.

2. Academia is about building communities to build knowledge. We must/can should/go bring ourselves — problems/personal — into that work, but the community work, the communal work, is not about our selves as individuals. Academic workshops ≠ therapy sessions.

As the STS community has collectively articulated, building such community knowledge/infrastructure entails that members of such communities need to be able to evaluate each other's work, to use it in ways that account for how it was made, where it comes from, and therefore how it might be used elsewhere.

Consequently, part of what constitutes such a community is the set of implicit/explicit rules for what bit of epistemic provence are epistemically valuable/relevant, what bits of context count as part of academic work rather than beside the point.

Yes to other scholars' work on whom I'm drawing. No to the music I'm listening to as I compose this essay … unless, maybe, you happen to be Thomas Richet, who has theorized "ambient chiceries" through ambient music, and for whom listening to the music of Brian Eno is method. *

This, right here, is at least 45% of why the notion of writing reflexively challenges me. What do I include? Standard-issue genre conventions make most of those decisions for me most of the time, but the genre conventions of the academic article with which I (and maybe you) grew up with/received have exclusionary positivisms and cultural hierarchies embedded in their base layers — a tacit assumption that the contents being offered up for community consumption are independent of the observer's perspective and travel freely. Reflexivity.

*I wrote the first draft of this piece to a playlist that cookie egret, a collaborator of mine, wrote/composed for a workshop that we organized on multispecies response-able research. I mostly wrote the second draft to Olafur Arnalds' "Living Room Songs". The third happened alongside folk tune arrangements by the Danish String Quartet. I don't expect this to be important to you.

I'm writing this flopped on the green rug that kind of looks like moss and that lays adjacent to the bookshelves in my office on campus. This positionality — prone — is where a lot of my writing begins, though this may be the first piece I've written that also ends here. The thing is, being reflexive, thinking about what I'm building as an dwelling-space based on grammar of an argument, is easier when I'm splayed out and slowed down in the way handwriting demands. I'm comfortable. I'm also uncomfortable. This posture makes my jaw hurt after a while, but more importantly (for you, at least) I'm uncomfortable with the burden that I'm placing on you, dear reader, to try to decipher my idiosyncratic writing in this undeniably — if purposefully — different format. I'm doing it anyway because:

- I want to invite you to splay out and slow down with me.
- All texts obligate readers and construct social spaces. I want to dwell in this point.
- I think that reflexive spaces — or spaces designed to encourage reflexivity within them, more precisely — probably always need to be comfortable and uncomfortable. More on that later.
- Figuring out how to convince word-processing software to do what I can so very easily do with pen and paper felt improbable, and maybe obstructive or inconsistent.

in STS is at least (partially) about acknowledging that perspective does matter, and that capacities to travel (without being changed in the process) can't simply be assumed, so that writers and readers must work to make visible / bring forth something of how and where they're coming from. ←

I have to invent what counts as scholarly text / scholarship, because form and content are never separate / separable. I can make sentences that relate my positionality and process (ethnographers are very skilled at this. for me, originally trained in molecular biology it remains hard) ... and yet I see so many of my comrades-in-STS rushing away from textual — with-a-big-T spaces — i.e., the academic article in its various forms — to video and image and performance, and to a sometimes notion of materiality that renders the discursive inadequate.

As a writer (my positionality in this communal space), I think that we-the-collective-STS might be giving up too readily on text, giving it over to "the standard academic article" when that form has been constrained to only one corner of what writing reads / what can be done with writing. Many forms of multimodality are important AND plain old boring alphabetic writing is valuable in modes. So I have to invent my text.

I also have to invent my readers — the companions whom I'm inviting in to share this space, and whom I expect to be in the spaces I'm trying to enter. (There is no entering a space without changing it, and no constructing a space de novo from the other?.) ←

To the extent that I'm trying to redecorate my own discursive living room here, I can only draw on conventions about who might continue to use my work and what matters to them — not least because, if I begin by acknowledging my positionality with respect to the text, I have to acknowledge that my writing is as much about me trying to figure something out for myself as conveying or enabling that which I'm working out for others. In at least some senses, I'm a primary user of / audience for the text.

I also don't want to extend hospitality to everyone everywhere

← Charles Bazerman's book on *Shaping Written Knowledge* and the history it describes of the (scientific) research article has been foundational to how I've come to think about the work those articles have done. They began as letters — letters to other members of the (British) Royal Society, in Bazerman's story, or to the editor of that society's proceedings — to announce / share findings, to people whom the man holding the pen might well be able to name. Communities eventually grew too big for that. Too rather & unwieldy glosses over a bunch of details about the interrelation of epistemology and discourse communities and writing conventions: the contextual details that appeared irrelevant to the fact (or the argument about what the facts might be) of the matter of community / common interest came to be swapped all of forms oriented around the efficient production of objectivity ... making sense of many complex phenomena, writing is already a mode of many.

← Walter Ong has much to say about how this is always the case, but again, some writing exigencies are more implied than others, in ways that delegate or proformulate or standardize that inventive work so that the writer herself need not think much actively about it. (Habits are useful for freeing attention for other purposes.)

at the same time everywhere. Spaces designed through the hope of being comfortable to everyone ignore important differences in cultures of comfort. They also limit the kind of work that can be done in them.

All of my writing about writing seems to come back to Composition 101: audience and purpose.

Audience: no doubt quite small in this instance — some small, perfect fraction of other STS scholars (and folks who say "I'm not really an STS scholar, but…", maybe) who are also rethinking how (discursive) reflexivity contributes to the work our scholarly exchanges contribute to building / occupying. I can also say that, because I've made this text algorithmically inaccessible, Google is not the audience.

Purpose: I've already stated this, like a good student who leads with her thesis: "This chapter is about writing as a mode…" But what does that entail / mean? I'm certainly not writing a manual on how to write a reflexive essay; I'm writing an experiment. I'm writing an invitation. (I said so right in the title.) I'm inviting the "us" brought into being through the process of you reading this chapter — I'm inviting this temporary version of "us" to recognize that we can redecorate our shared discursive space, and to try out unexpected floorplans and furnishings with me. I'm following Malcolm Ashmore in writing about decisions that need to be made about what merits / warrants inclusion in an STS article about reconfiguring scholarly spaces, by writing about / through decisions that need to be made in what merits inclusion in an STS article about reconfiguring scholarly spaces.

Other scholars about whose discursive conventions work I'm thinking as I write:
Max Liboiron
Annemarie Mol
Bruno Latour
Malcolm Ashmore
Robin Wall Kimmerer
Maria Turner } who have worked with
cookie agar } me, and
good old } inspired by
Steve } work
Dodger

And in making this text impossible by word-processing software, I'm arguing that I don't want the academic world to be endlessly reconfigured for optimal efficiency through the capacities of computers through which — "meaningful work" is hegemonically redefined, nor academic contribution endlessly redefined through the (invisible) work (of analysis) that algorithmic activities constitute as meaningful.

Consequent decisions: I'm writing this out longhand as a lasting trace of how I found that I could only think about the kinds of (writing) spaces I want to build when I left my laptop and found a pen. …and asked readers to … and thought in less and slowed down, more multiple … and physically avoided setting read more slowly, too / lines, more … such is revision



207

So I'm going to leave some of my ambiguities [multiplicities] on the page. I'm going to include some of the introspective uncertainties and asides that would have been deleted had deleting been an option (even through what is now the third draft), as a bit of protective equipment against sounding too sure of myself, to offer more capacious room to think with [in] rather than presenting answers — or necessarily even better questions.

One thing that some of my collaborators and I ← [Jane Calvert, Koichi Mikami, Rod Smith, and others whom we've enrolled in thinking with us about "alternative practices" for RRI. We — a whole group of primarily Japan- and UK-based collaborators — have a special issue of _East Asian Science and Technology Studies_ coming out on this soon.] have learned about reflexivity in the context of Responsible Research and Innovation (RRI) is that it's most likely to happen in the absence of a script for how people are supposed to behave and for what differences are acceptable to externalize [entertain]. We were thinking about this before thinking about Madeleine Akrich's work on a script, but we think that her theorization of how artifacts embed such expectations and constraints works well for how we're thinking about spaces in place of artifacts.

The editors of _Science, Technology, and Human Values_ tell us, in a lovely editorial about what an "STS contribution" is and, that scripts are important for ensuring that authors have "expectations and guidelines" that "orient" writers [readers] toward "original material" that is "sufficiently interesting and important to warrant publication in ST&HV." They also say that peer-reviews should "iteratively revisit and renovate what science and technology studies was, is, and can be." They acknowledge how they are reflexive that they themselves are remaking STS through their roles in leading the journal, which brings them back to the question: "what counts as a contribution?"

Their answer pretty much boils down to this: contributions change something about a conversation and are clear about what they're changing. The challenge, they say, is in being _clear_ while also being surprising and maybe ambiguous — because the latter, they think, is involved in how such contributions may be "interesting, relevant, and politically engaged." This text leaves different [more] ambiguities than it would if coaxed [shoved] into computerized text (how to interpret words stacked on top of each other? In which order to read when words don't simply proceed [appear] in straight lines? To what elements of the text to attend or attribute meaning? (I had to eliminate variations in color for the sake of accommodating publishers' constraints, though I remain grateful that they were so accommodating otherwise.) Or, is there less ambiguity here because I employ a [can]

[Probably not this right here? The worth-whileness of its contents, aside (less refined than anything I could word-process, if I imagine form and content as separate, which I'm clearly choosing not to do). I wonder whether I'm making a contribution — a text that stands opposed to how in breadth that configure academic writing produce what counts? But it's not a contra(band)bution. No one is _disallowing_ me from constructing a provocation, in this sharing some thoughts way. Though, were I not a tenured associate professor, someone might be? I have a privilege to use my time contra norms that I didn't have in the same way on the other side of that bright line called tenure.]

expanded set / wider range of that which writing can do to make my point? & Or, more realist-ically, to poke at you to try to prompt you to think, because my point here isn't point at all; it's about trying to make a space to reflect on how expectations about writing configure lived realities and room for living (and thinking, and conversing, and...) Soft furnishings, rather than sharp argumentative tools? As the host of this gathering, I decided to leave raw edges exposed, to invite you in to my lived-in thinking space without tidying everything up, in the interest of discussing what a "contribution" looks like and how we can inhabit the discursive spaces through which they're made.

Those ST&V editors say nothing about genre conventions beyond that point about clarity... until the second half of the editorial, concerning "some other questions", including some questions (and concerns) about what seems to be a stylistic closing-down in the field. Or, in their words: "Where are we with method?"

Their answer is that method [scholars] should be situated and reflexive, "reliable, comparable, and transferrable." And then they leave it to the rest of us to imagine what they mean by those adjectives?

As a writer, that (productive?) ambiguity leaves me feeling uncomfortable about whether what I might be doing fits into the vision of scholarship they're inscribing / describing. This guidance seems to leave plenty of room for authors to go off-script. IF they recognize that that space exists AND reviewers and editors make good on the invitation to explore the boundaries and affordances of ambiguity and clarity, the variety in how interventions / offerings might change the conversation. Those conditions also seem to invite privilege to play a (big?) role in who can experiment while publishing.

My collaborators-in-RME and I have found that spaces for reflexivity / response-ability need to be uncomfortable. More on that point later.

& As someone who still has to prove herself, and who teaches writing, I worry / am skeptical that potentially open discursive spaces close down in practice:

1. Because of the reasonable fear that an experiment won't be published or received well.
↑ Constraints on finding / making space for voice?

2. Because writers routinely learn to write by mimicking what they see others do, without necessarily recognizing why particular choices might be made, and perhaps without seeing choices as choices that could be made differently.
( Voice

3. Because making active, deliberate choices outside the norm takes time, and who has that?
↑ Space

SPACE: Jane Calvert and Koichi Mikami and Rob Smith and I have been thinking for awhile now about enabling RRI by making (or finding and making use of) spaces wherein no one knows what they're supposed to say, do, think – so that everyone is forced/prompted to actively think about what they choose to do – and so that choices can be made that are disallowed or discouraged in more typical work environments. This, we think, cultivates reflexivity in the sense of occupants/participants in those spaces needing to decide who/how they're going to be, and being enabled to make choices that aren't possible elsewhere in ways that highlight how they aren't possible elsewhere. (We've written about this with Ken Kawamura and Ryuma Shineha in that special issue of EASTS that I mentioned.) I'm writing this chapter now in this way because I suspect/hope that the same principle applies to reflexivity in writing.

Corollary: if livable worlds are constructed through practicing reflexivity (a conclusion with which this edited collection began and which it endorses), then those worlds are always a bit uncomfortable (a point that many other chapters exemplify, I think.) Complacency, or committed combat on the part of some seem bound to make the lives of others less livable and insofar as we are all social and necessarily interdependent creatures living in some kind of (multispecies) community. Livable worlds must be collective/shared. von Uexküll's umwelt theory can be useful here for envisioning creatures as enacting/inhabiting their own individuated worlds of experience and effect while also relying on the overlaps – the shared "workspaces", the capacity for communication – with others.

VOICE in writing is a metaphor (and maybe it is: can you hear me now?) that has been interpreted in multiple ways. In the early 20th c., voice was about verb tense, so I'm told by a 1995 article by Darsie Bowden in Rhetoric Review. In the 1970s, textbooks began encouraging students to find the right kind of voice for a particular writing exigency, like choosing an appropriate outfit for an occasion. [Who/whatever gets to decide what "appropriate" means? Bowden doesn't emphasize how this pedagogical move is all too likely to be racist, but many writing studies scholars working in this century do.] And textbooks encouraging writers to "discover" an authentic voice, whatever that means? (Still likely to be racist…) From a posthumanist perspective, these two suggestions seem somewhat different, because I'm not "the author" with just one unitary self and just one way of enacting that durable and coherent self on a page. I speak differently across occasions and purposes and conversations. I'm different people on different days, and on the same day in different rooms. This all feels obvious. Yet stating it boldly like this also makes me think about how situated, reflexive writing practices might make space for both me-as-writer and you-as-reader to be not only diverse people, but diverse versions of diverse people. This notion/suggestion presumes that professional identities aren't fixed appendages or cloaks that we button up on top of our more-or-less concealed personal selves. This is certainly not the case for me? I do live my work. My personal and professional commitments aren't separate, and it's difficult to imagine a university paying me enough to compensate for the work of detaching them.

Communities - creatures who communicate - are inevitable, and lovable. And worlds that make space for both communication and difference involve imperfect communication. Anything else - or, rather, the imaginary of anything else - is simultaneously a fiction and a tool of domination, as (Haraway) lays out in The Cyborg Manifesto.

Therefore, a response-able communicator must actively watch out for what they cannot predict and allow [make space] for what they can't understand.

And Bethany Eveleth, whose MA in English Ed → I recently helped with, has been reminding me of it and helping me to better account for it in my teaching and thinking about metaphors.

My professional work [stems from & produces] a normativity that imbues [informed by] everything I do, as I imagine is true for many STS people.

So, it clearly doesn't work to try to shove STS scholarship into "an academic voice" (whatever that may mean to those who deploy the term) in ways that reinforce the wounded arguments that the idea of such a voice is unjust and exclusionary in any case.

[↑ Victor Villanueva, a now-emeritus English professor, is probably the first person to have taught me to see this lesson.]

Continuing on VOICE: Nor does separating [style/voice] from content make sense, a big lot of rhetorical theory, alongside the material-semiotic point (that might be more familiar across STS) that writing is always about making things - that we-writers are building text-objects that contribute one set of the social gathering spaces of academia. And/yet...

So many of the STS writing-experiments that I love, that involve [playing with] bending forms to an author's meta/reflective-purposes, that purposefully enlist readers in co-constituting the experiment [exploring how knowledge/writing works] are written in relatively similar voices by people who have, per the cliché, learned (even mastered?) the rules and are therefore now licensed [permitted] to break them. It's one thing to say that experiments in form must be constructed [purposefully] content-mindfully with clarity about why choices are made - which is at least one form of knowing the rules. It's another to say that only those who have proven themselves have earned the right to experiment.

I do see creative, provoking, demanding books that remodel the expected [conventional] architectures of academic publishing. Katherine McKittrick's Dear Science is on the bookshelf next to my right ear at this very moment, and was published quite recently (2021, I just checked). Yet I also see loads of colleagues - especially early-career folk (including some contributors to this volume?) rejecting "writing" - and especially the standard academic article, where experimentation feels less possible than in books - in favor of multimodal [outputs] undertakings. (At the same time, those articles remain the gold-standard currency of the academic job economy, of course, adding an additional layer of power hierarchy and risk to what they're innovating and to what I'm about to say.) Returning to those STS editors' point about closing down, I wonder whether creative and critically minded STS scholars are giving up too readily on journal articles as highly routinized spaces that they can't remodel, as routinized "contributions" that can only contain so much risk, and that therefore compel them to evacuate out into less [tightly scripted] generalized forms - at least once they've paid their dues or when they have personally interesting work to do.

On the one hand, we can [see] say that different kinds of activity are happening in different venues or formats. But I also think that we might be asking articles to do too little, that some combination of the disciplining of STS and the ever-increasing [pressure] absurdity of academic hiring and the lack of time that experimentation can take (or the understandable choice to publish as efficiently as possible) in addition to the availability of other modalities [for] those who do have the resources [+ will] to experiment, contribute to the decline of experimental writing in STS. I don't want to live in an academic world in which articles are boring? Nor one which systematically excludes [marginalized] multiple ways of being [knowing] from central conversational venues [spaces]. Maybe as a community we're becoming too comfortable with writing conventions that make journal articles uncomfortable spaces for unconventional contributions.

Following from how Jane + Rob + Koichi and I have thought about spaces for responsible research, writers [readers] probably need to be comfortable enough in discursive spaces to dwell in them, to hang out while thinking about something other than an overwhelming desire to leave, yet uncomfortable enough that writers [readers] need to keep thinking rather than falling into established scripts that disenable making choices (e.g. about how to construct and occupy a text) that differ from established norms.

I read Max Liboiron's chapter in Transmissions, an edited collection that Kat Jungnickel led on experimental methods, as an excellent example of writing that makes me uncomfortable (yet also comfortable enough to want to dwell there). Among other things, it demands that I stop mid-chapter to write something in response, and to stop reading if I refuse to accept the transactional exchange being offered. I'm then asked to consider myself as a co-author and to list the chapter on my CV - which I didn't do, even though this proposition is theoretically in line with my own thinking about how texts function. (But not in line with how I think about CVs; that was the sticking point.) But I'm uncomfortable with this. I respect and admire Liboiron, and I've violated some kind of relationship here; I've failed to hold up my end of an arrangement - even if perhaps the arrangement was unclear, maybe coercive, in how I began reading and became interested before understanding what was on the table. I don't know whether Liboiron felt uncomfortable writing it. From where I sit, their authorial voice feels

(I mean, I'm writing this as a chapter in an explicitly experimental edited volume. No way would I have considered submitting anything remotely like this chapter to ST(+V?))

+ I'm wary that, in attending so much to comfort and discomfort I'm not adequately attending to boredom. Some discursive spaces aren't so much characterised by (dis)comfort as by interest or boredom, by whether I want to stay in terms of whether I'm [being] invited to make connections. Josh Evans, who works at the Danish Technical University these days, has taught me to think about interest as a technical term, including as an alternative to configuring multispecies relations around the assumption of control. But where he starts with the term is in the rarified world of new Nordic cuisine, wherein the failure to be interesting may be the worst kind - to be boring, to be much, is to invite no confident and assured. I think that's a big part of why I feel comfortable enough to keep reading, because at least one of us knows what we're doing here. I don't necessarily know what to do with the text, but Liboiron has invited/convinced me that I can/should do something with it. So here I am, still chewing it over. I've been interested? I've been caught up. I fell into, I've been pulled aside into a conversational space in which I don't just know what to do.

My participation in Liboiron's text highlights how, in a sense, this whole chapter (the one I'm writing; the one you're reading) is about the words "with" and "we." Authors and readers coproduce texts, with each other (as mediated by and manifested through the text; "author" & "reader" are roles that come into being only in the process of relating, through their encounter with the text). Readers have roles in enacting texts as hospitable, in co-constructing the discursive space as capacious enough for surprise and multiplicity and non-ambiguity. That's probably more likely with reading slowly with an eye for why it might be interesting, and less so with reading rapidly with an [sensory organ] out for slotting some citable unit of the text into a particular predefined purpose.

Liboiron is doing several things, but one of them is arguing against extractivist reading practices, drawing on their own experience of being interested in a Twitter thread by Eve Tuck on how extractivist reading—i.e., the thing most academics are taught to do—reproduces colonial violences. Their challenge is to slow down, to read deeply and generously. It's a genuine challenge for me. I have indeed been taught to read efficiently, to extract what I need for my own constructive purposes, and to critically question (and judge) arguments rather than choosing to accept them and see where an author wants to take me, and to follow their invitation to go there with them. I know that Tuck and Liboiron are writing about me.

I paused for a long time before writing this next line. I'd thought that I was going to write about how I was unsure about whether the kind of reading Tuck and Liboiron hold up—positive, generous, accountable to the whole of a text—

response at all because I find nothing here worth responding to, because I don't recognize anything here as an invitation to any kind of action. Thinking interest in terms of invitation helps me remember how interesting is the property of a relationship, not a thing. I don't read Korean. A book in Korean doesn't interest me because I cannot respond to/recognise its invitation. It is not an imperfect communication device; when I'm the reader, it's no communication device at all.

Interest, as Josh presents it, is not in opposition to boredom, but to eat. (He's writing about culinary fermentation, in which interesting toes the line between raw and rotten. Josh explores that boundary in a vignette about tasting a (stomach-churning, to some) condiment-experiment that, in his polite analysis, was "barely structured" and "very ambiguous." (There's that word again?)

Writing and eating here feel analogous. When I read, I eat texts. I consume and chew over and metabolise them. They fuel/sustain my creative work and become part of me. Following that analogy, writing that is very ambiguous and barely structured might be rotten and thus indigestible, not nourishing, not interesting.

Rotten writing: all mixed up, barely structured, only partially metabolised by others, not good to eat.

was sufficient as well as necessary. But the longer I sit with my discomfort, the more certain I've come to feel that a more challenging synthesis is necessary for me, at least, to respond. I want to believe and figure out how to put into practice that being a generous reader doesn't exclude being a critical reader, in that dissent and critique can be offered generously with an effort to nourish the collective scholarly assemblage — contributing to the potluck rather than pissing on it. And there's no question in my mind that generosity toward what a writer might try to offer should mean tracing ideas across a text rather than text-mining for juicy bits. But the idea of the "whole" text and being responsible to the whole also runs counter with the poststructuralist and posthumanist ways of thinking that I typically find productive, and that emphasize partiality, relationality, challenging the self-evidence of inherited units of analysis. I also suspect that this analytic lens is misdirected; the point isn't the integrity of the text but the relationships constructed through it. Extractivist reading, maybe, is about taking to construct value for an I without contributing to anything of ongoing value for a we. It's also how I've been taught to survive in academia — a lesson to unlearn.

So Liboiron's chapter is simultaneously an example of a comfortable discursive space that makes me feel productively uncomfortable and a lesson/exercise in how discursive spaces are/should be co-produced among readers and writers with different orientations to that relationship. I struggle to identify a cognate example of written scholarship in which the author seems transparently uncomfortable. Maybe I'm reading the wrong things, or maybe this is a form of generosity I tend to extend to those texts. Maybe academic writing conventions tend to push us into sounding self-assured. Maybe sounding assured is essential to making a contribution?

Printed text, formatted into an article shape with a journal's and publisher's marks at the top, do a lot of work to make something look cohesive to me. The notion of hospitality in writing seems to present authors as hosts who not only might well be expected to be at home in their discursive domiciles but who need to be at home, and comfortable, to be good hosts. But, researchers dwell in texts communally? I've been writing for some time now about texts as spaces, but the article/text as an independent/individual thing is the wrong unit of analysis. Writers and readers don't meet in individual texts, in isolation, having

(Half-baked writing: in development, on a trajectory toward being nourishing, but not yet gelled or solidified enough to hold a structure that can invite a reader interact eater

(Continuing to chew on rotten writing will not make it half-baked?)

Composted writing: so thoroughly digested that it becomes part of the grounds adds nutrients to the grounds for growing new ideas without necessarily being seen as distinct.

Interesting writing: an invitation to make a connection and reciprocate a response.

Interesting writing should, then, be a mechanism for/mediator of response-ability, for cultivating capacities for response across a discourse community.

Another reason for handwriting this chapter: to disrupt the typical reading conventions that help make contributions settled. (That help settle the contradictions?)

having never met before and in the absence of additional companions. In writing-studies terms, I'm a relationist who draws on → Stanley Fish, who points to how meanings don't inhere in texts, but are produced between texts and readers in context. But Fish's way of putting things still suggests that authors, readers, & texts are discrete.

And Flusser who goes even further in deconstructing the notion of texts as singular and isolable. For him, we're not writing but curating: picking out "words and phrases" from the milieu like chickens pecking out grain.

Barthes, who, in asserting that the reader is born from the author's death, describes "the text" as a "tissue of quotations drawn from the innumerable centers of culture."

Numerous posthumanist thinkers have built on those constructivist foundations to articulate how authors, readers, and texts are themselves relational functions — not pre-existing but constituted through their interaction in the text. In this light, discursive spaces are very clearly both communally constructed and communally occupied, and constantly in being occupied. But living rooms that enable living well exit be (co-)occupied? We have to be post-Pasteurian about discursive relations, not just eating anything indiscriminately even as we discard any notions about the purity of a text and appeal of avoiding cross-contamination.

Indiscriminately: DeAnna Beasley, who now runs her own lab at the Univ. of Tennessee Chattanooga, did some work in Rob Dunn's lab at North Carolina State that demonstrated a relationship between stomach pH and how permissive or restrictive a critter's stomach might need to be to incoming environmental microbes or the denizens of its diet. Vultures who eat carrion have more acidic stomachs than mammals who mostly live on fruit and veg. Babies have less acidic stomachs than adults.

Post-Pasteurian: a phrase and theory introduced by Heather Paxson and now widely used in multispecies studies to characterize microbial — an attitude toward microbial life that accounts for Pasteur's (and innumerable others') teachings about the value of sanitation and what is now known about the benignness and beneficialness of most microbial life. Yes to sanitation; no to rampant disinfection.

Babies are actively building their gut microbiome, whereas adults are primarily in a phase of maintaining established communities. If I continue to extend this possibly unwise analogy, when people are in early active development as scholars, perhaps they have a permissive stomach for eating lots of texts and assembling companions to carry along as part of the selves that they're becoming. Once established, maybe they stop recruiting so actively in favor of stricter gatekeeping. But being an open-minded (open-stomached?) interdisciplinary person might mean being more open to taking in new companions, to environmental change — or does our more varied diet mean that we need to be more judicious about what we integrate?

Jamie Lorimer, characterizing "Rot" for Environmental Humanities' "living lexicon", describes eating windfall apples in a graveyard while placing nesting boxes for England's largest insect (the remarks that "both the stag beetle and I were zombies: well-fed forms of the dead made living." Eating and reading remediate the dead in the living; voices of dead authors (in the conventional and the Barthesian sense) speak through texts and traces of texts. Living readers eat dead peoples' words and so reanimate them; texts become alive in being eaten. Texts are creatures like tapeworms whose reproduction absolutely depends on being eaten by others – an obligate parasite of zombies who live with them in some kind of indigenous symbiosis.

So, the discursive space that we – community of scholars enlivens is itself also alive, like houses that are grown rather than built in Octavia Butler's Dawn trilogy or China Miéville's Embassytown – houses that are a living part of the community. In this sense, we readers/writers are ourselves not only zombies but ourselves parasites who must be eaten to live.

Only maybe not parasites but commensals? Because eating and digesting texts, and being eaten and digested, enables us to create newly nourishing texts for others, feeding (back into) the discursive space and refreshing/remodelling/reburnishing it. [Not everything is nourishing. Post-Pasteurian reading/eating is not indiscriminate. But surely judgements about what is good to eat must be made in context and appropriately for the eater. If humans generally have some innate sense of what should(n't) be ingested, does the scholarly version of a critical taste need to be cultivated?]

Burke suggested envisioning scholarly literature as a "parlour" (or salon, or living room) full of people having an animated conversation. As a newcomer, you don't know what's been said before you arrived, or the broader context for what's being said now. You're probably confused, maybe overwhelmed. You need to take time to listen, to suss out how individuals are contributing, to build a sense of what kinds of contributions might fit or be out of place. Only after some listening will you become equipped to speak. (Hang out for a while and you may become part of the furniture – enmeshed in the conversation, inseparable from the room.) Newcomers will admit to being eaten by choosing to hang out and so forth. Jamie Lorimer, eating apples in a graveyard, calls this – the cycle of eating and being eaten, attentive to nourishment but broad-minded about sustaining and being sustained – becoming "responsible zombies."

If writing/reading is a mode of world-making, and if doing so reflexively entails attending to what kind of world one is trying to make, then it follows that readers/writers need to be able to leave the room, to stop participating. If we're responsible zombies, though, leaving can be as simple as walking out. Someone can die to the conversation by removing themselves or being removed, but those are hardly free choices in the way that those verbs might suggest. A living person making ongoing decisions/actions might try to extricate themselves and be unable because others keep their prior work alive. Some discussants might try and fail/struggle to extricate someone else, because they have become inextricable from the furnishings of the room — they have been digested and remediated. This is one way that I understand Barthes' assertion that the author is dead; they have become nourishing zombies, eating and being eaten, that can't simply be vomited up and that certainly don't have control (what a silly word) over what those who have dined do with the metabolic energy they have derived. Acknowledging this point also does nothing to change conversationalist-companions' responsibilities — or, better, response-abilities to each other (and the room?), to offer up good food for/to this word-potluck-salon-hangout.

A final note on hospitality: As Jane + Rod + Koichi and our collaborators and I have been exploring spaces for RRI, we've recognized that they need to be going somewhere. They need to build into longer-term relationships. And they need to have a future that enables locating any given present moment with respect to something else/elsewhere, that gives it durable meaning beyond its present outlines. In other words, spaces for RRI need to be hospitable in the sense of not being organized around a host's immediate needs, but around keeping a conversation going, maintaining good relations. This is a typical expectation of academic discourse community participation. So why do I feel so uncomfortable, so called out, when Lidoiron's chapter (the one I mentioned a few pages ago) explicitly demands that I respond before being allowed — any more of their text? Am I attached to the illusion of — given access to — proceeding on "my own terms?" participating

(Here are my provisional conclusions about writing as a mode of making discursive room for reflexivity in STS, toward more 'livable' academic worlds:

1. Discursive spaces should be both comfortable and uncomfortable. They're also probably not hospitable when authors accept the burden of at least pretending to know what they're doing, or at least to feel at home doing it.

2. They need to be alive, to be well fed, and to have lives that (can be seen to) extend and ramify beyond the present.

3. They need to be composts. They need to be nutritious (and also delicious, one hopes) zombies that invite others to continue to eat and digest and remediate them.

As I've been writing this — the first draft in April 2023, the second draft in September, and now the third and final draft in December 2024 — the academic and wider worlds around me seem to be rotting. Existing, taken-for-granted structures seem to be falling apart and not in ways oriented toward a collectively nourishing remediated future. My colleagues — and me — are chronically not responding to each other, to requests that were easier to satisfy ← Rot versus compost is a human distinction predicated on culturally situated aesthetics and notions of utility, and care for some forms of life over others. This is fine. We're humans who care — understandably — about human things, including the health a few years ago ("before the pandemic," as we've all become accustomed to saying, as though the pandemic was the only culprit and an isolatable event that had an end), even regarding things that everyone involved might agree are valorous and worthwhile. Too many things are trying to interest us. We can't keep up appearances in so many rooms. Students aren't showing up because they can't assemble (or can't see the point in exerting the necessary effort to assemble) versions of themselves that can carry on as though everything is okay. Students aren't showing up because they can't find parking, because the university has increased enrollment to increase revenue, and then sold too many parking permits, because we're evidently a business that sells very expensive food and housing and parking and then educates people (and does some research) on the side... or because the bus that's supposed to bring them from their premium student apartments to campus is broken and the chronically underfunded public busses only run once an hour. and feeding of our kin. "Let it all rot" may well be a justifiable response to the present moment, but it's not the one I'm trying to make here.

A few of my colleagues seem to be composting rather than rotting. Some are only replying to emails on alternate workdays and don't mind not replying to everything. Some are trying assessment schemes that ask students to focus on community learning over individual grades. Some – like some of my colleague-contributors to this volume – are experimenting with forms of academic production that resist the equation of productivity to easily commodified contributions to one's worth as a researcher (with different stakes across our career stages, but I hope, collective benefit in providing examples of the possible). And here I am, settled down on my green rug that looks a bit like moss, taking an unreasonable chunk of time to work through some thoughts about making and finding space for reflexivity in writing, and to invite you to join me in asking what kinds of worlds might be made and might be desirable to make in this mode. The usual personal and institutional scripts that structure my typical workdays all say that this is a poor use of time, and writing this out longhand for the third time, maybe I agree. Then again, I'm the one who put the rug here.

With thanks for writing/readings with me,

Erika Szymanski

14 December 2024

* This chapter has been informed by research funded by the US National Science Foundation and the UK Economic and Social Research Council under a lead-agency award, # 2114750.

I'm grateful to the editors of this collection and at Bristol UP for being willing to figure out the logistics of a handwritten chapter.

# 17

# Contemplations: A Perspective on Reflexivity Out of the 'Brackish Waters' of Artistic Research

*Ruth Anderwald and Leonhard Grond*

What is the artist-researcher doing, looking out the window of their studio? As artist-researchers, often working with a film camera, we take its frame and the technique of montage as the starting point of our contemplation. What is visually represented, and what is reflected? Specifically, this chapter attempts to look at what reflections become perceptible on the brackish waters[1] of artistic research. How can we reflect on the work between sensory input, artistic processing and output? How could we think about the circular relation of agency, perception and epistemic processing from and within this discipline? Exemplified by our own artistic research on states of dizziness, as states of uncertainty, unpredictability and confusion, we look for the spaces that open on the liminalities of reflexivity and experience. Separating and reconnecting experience and reflection in the vestibule of their convergence, the compossible space of con-fusion allows for a rethinking of the given and wont. Therefore, it is important for the artist-researcher to simultaneously get lost in thought and stay on track.

In other words, you don't become part of thought and get swept away in it, like in a boat. You get out of the boat and examine the nature of thought itself, and that I suppose is true epistemology ... for I would

---

[1] The beautiful metaphor of the 'brackish waters' is owed to the 2023 Symposium of the Vilnius Academy of Arts Doctoral Programme, titled *Not Quite King, Not Quite Fish. In and Out of the Brackish Waters of Artmaking as Research*. https://sodas2123.lt/en/not-quite/ (Accessed 11 November 2024).

**Figure 17.1:** View of the Donaukanal

Source: Anderwald, R. and Grond, L. (2011) *Contemplations*, filmstill, 16 mm film, Cinédoc Paris Films Coop, Paris

imagine real knowledge begins with examining the nature or stuff of thought about knowledge, examining the ground in which thoughts take place. (Ginsberg 1974, 31)

The authors' film *Contemplations* (2011) ponders exactly that: can we stay on track and get swept away at the same time? And if so, what would we see? The images of Figures 17.1, 17.2, 17.6, 17.7, and 17.10–17.12 that accompany this chapter are film stills exploring the view from the artists' studio.

## 1. Artistic research and reflexivity

In an online conversation about artistic and creative practices of research with scholars and PhD candidates from Flinders University Adelaide in April 2024, contemplating together the many approaches, methodologies, prejudices and ideologies surrounding the contested field of artistic research in academia, we could all agree on one point: The quality of reflexivity differentiates artistic research from other fields of artistic (and even certain scientific) practices. Defining and explaining artistic research, nevertheless, is mainly conferred through emphasizing its diversity in methodology. As a hybrid field bringing together artistic and scientific research and their practices in its brackish waters, artistic research is commonly considered through this prism in an attempt to differentiate and organize the field of artistic research within academic practices. Having worked as experimental filmmakers for 25 years, we see similarities in the ongoing discussion on experimental (or independent) film in relation to other film genres and the discussion about artistic research in relation to academia. Experimental film emerged as a field only through a differentiation in length. Every film that was neither feature nor short film length was subsumed under 'experimental' by film festivals, thus compounding and entangling documentary, fiction and art film practices, bringing about the highly diverse field of independent or experimental film. Artistic research relates to experimental film, as, in both fields, practitioners develop a heightened awareness of context, process, methods, materiality, and impact of their work and field, as emphasized by French filmmaker Nicolas Rey. Connecting it to the political, he holds that the term 'experimental cinema' is a tautology, like 'organic agriculture' or 'participatory democracy': we only need the adjective because there's something wrong with the noun (Cohn 2014).

In like manner, we must assume that there is something amiss with the term 'research' if it were to exclude any association to creative, artistic and arts-based practices; vice versa, we can assume the expectations towards art go amiss if they were to exclude any (practices related to) research. The distinguishing principle between artistic work and artistic research work, however, is the level and quality of reflexivity and the practitioner's ensuing openness to communication, learning and accountability. Thus, the artistic process can be distinguished from the artistic-research process, not merely by the introduction of methods ascribed to other (scientific) disciplines, but rather in terms of the reflexivity concerning the actions and decision-making during the working process. While the artist can claim to simply follow a sudden inspiration and never argue or question their decision, the artist-researcher will (*a priori, a posteriori*) question and reflect on their acting on impulse, bringing each of their decisions and processing into the foreground and argue them in the larger context of their work, methodology, progress, outcome, and in relation to their chosen field and current focus of work.

In the 1990s, in fine art studies, a popular model to explain the ideal construction of an artwork in relation to an audience used a pyramid shape: On its broad basis, the artwork invites its viewers to a sensory experience and immersion. The second layer allows for connections to be discovered to other artworks throughout art history, whereas the small peak on the top invites the appreciation of scientific, theoretical and conceptual aspects of research and thought. After this model, we could conceive of artistic research turning the layers of this pyramid upside down or even into different shapes: ellipses, quadrats, diamonds, and so on. With this example, we would like to show that reflexivity is key to both practices, but the quality and conditions of its application are different, forming expectations and thus allowing a disciplining of artistic research and artistic practices. There are, of course, exceptions. Certain artistic practices, such as concept art or experimental filmmaking, may also demand 'a meticulous evaluation of the medial context and a conscious choice of terms' (Blos-Jáni 2021, 307). The rigour and importance of reflexivity in artistic research and the engagement in the communication, learning and sharing of the process and its findings, can be clarified by introducing Claire Pentecost's concept of the artist-researcher as the 'public amateur' 'who consents to learn in public so that the very conditions of knowledge production can be interrogated' (Pentecost 2010, np). Her 'public amateur' learns in the public, for and with the public, in an emancipatory act, engaging and empowering both the artist-researcher and their audience. With Pentecost, we would argue that the main distinguishing principle of artistic research from 'purely' artistic output that also may be informed by research, as in research-based art, is the reflexivity that brings about emancipation and hence opens up new possibilities.

Both a great work of art as well as a great artistic research work offer an appreciation of the level of reflexivity and conceptual grounding alongside immersive or experiential elements, even if the proportions may be different. Reflecting on artistic and artistic-research decisions is diligent, exhaustive work which grows slowly and over time. Different layers of reflexivity are added as the experience, methodology, epistemology and the project's overall trajectory progresses and transforms. In this process, it is not only the whole that becomes more than its parts, but also the parts can become more than the whole, start a life of their own, as a new idea or project. The development of the methodology, certain skills or techniques, or quite generally, the development of artistic or research practice or a specific contribution to a topic or practice, can become the leading focus. The initial spore, which sparked the project, however, will be found in every part of the work, even if the anticipated path of research and the initial project design may change in an unforeseeable manner, an occurrence which is to be found in most basic research and many PhD projects. Artistic working and thinking grow in surprising mycelia forms, as do basic and artistic research. Contemplation and observation are integral parts. Our 16 mm film *Contemplations* aims to reflect the phase in the artistic-epistemic process where observations, emergent thoughts and connections initiate, crystallize or dissolve (Figure 17.2).

## 2. Co-creation in progress

This leads us to our own artistic and artistic-research work, which we always fashion co-creatively, in changing teams or as a duo. Our own process of creating a new work, such as the case with the film *Contemplations*, involves a lot of research and discussion about the possible topic and focus of the artwork. As we have cultivated a co-creative practice for over 25 years, verbally expressing, arguing and reflecting on what we would like to engage in starts the process after the initial idea has appeared in either one of our team members. In these

**Figure 17.2:** View of the Donaukanal overlayed with historical drawing

Source: Anderwald, R. and Grond, L. (2011) *Contemplations*, filmstill, 16 mm film, Cinédoc Paris Films Coop, Paris

negotiations and expositions of an idea, turning it eventually into a topic of collective creative interest, the initial spark, fragmentary as any inspiration, is changed, challenged and enriched by the other person(s)'s input. In co-creative processes, it is never the one idea that forms the work but the in-between of ideas and perspectives, even if they will eventually fall into place as one collective focus. Along with the discussions, the process of research involves artistic as well as scientific sources to create a collective entry point. The team will consider the topic from different disciplinary scientific angles, as well as artistic work with the same or comparable interest. Only after this phase of preparatory work will we start the process of practical experimentation and creating artistic work. Filming, however, is a practice we mostly do as a duo. Enriched by the research and conversations beforehand, the process of filming is usually swift and done with very little talking. The cameras we use are 16mm or 8mm analogue cameras that pass hands between us during filming. The sound these cameras make when rolling is very informative. The person operating the camera informs the other by pointing and focusing the objective, but additionally through the mechanic sound that changes when the recording is paused or the recording speed altered, creating accelerated or slow-motion imagery. In this phase, embodied knowledge, sensory cognition, and related experiences and practices are essential. The camera, like a brush, captures and records the movements of our bodies, moving along with and between them, calibrating and recording the traces that are drawn along our movement through space on the linear strip of celluloid, which will then represent the time the viewer will be able to watch. Movement through space is converted into time, in a tribute to spacetime, that we believe only celluloid film can provide. However, even though its material may be linear, the actual experience of the viewer can be that of non-linear time, an effect realized through in-camera cuts, tempo-manipulation, montage in the editing process and, as in *Contemplations* plainly obvious, double exposure while filming. Many parts of *Contemplations* are superimposed in the camera, which means the time and exposure along the length of the film strip were planned and sectioned into different phases before filming; once exposed, the film was rewound to be exposed a second time.

After filming, the artistic work rests again; additional research adds to its reflection. As we work on analogue film, we need to send it to the lab for development and digitization. This creates a fertile distance between the moment of recording and its memorization, and the observing and contemplation of the filmed material. It is important to forget much of the sensory and epistemic processing from the moment of filming to be able to see the filmed material for what it is – and what it could become – and to distinguish it from the personal or collective memories or desires of the moment of filming.

The editing process starts with viewing the material, weighing options of adding a soundscape, if and what to cut, where to bring in more focus, and where to insert breaks or disturbances. Even though recording and speed are uttered through the sound of its mechanics, our analogue cameras are not fitted with sound recording units. The consideration of silence, sound and potential collaborations for a soundtrack is the focus of this next phase. Eventually, the way in which the process of cinematic organization models the visible then fades into the background, and the cinematic experience encourages the audience to surrender to the flow of images (Schrödl 2004).

## 3. Creation and research in-between

In terms of inspiration and research material for the film *Contemplations*, we can name Margret Mead's poetic reflection of her garden and everyday surroundings – her main inspiration and topic, or Bruce Nauman's continuous exploration of himself as the artist in his studio. Clearly, the history of what seeing means, historical illustrations of perspective, and specifically Hans Belting's book *Florenz und Bagdad. Eine westöstliche Geschichte des Blicks*[2] were an important resource; but also potentially less obvious sources had a great influence – namely a pdf of Hannah Arendt's copy of Heidegger's *Was heisst Denken?*. At one point in the process of creating *Contemplations*, we experimented with using excerpts of the book as a possible soundtrack.

---

[2]  English edition: *Florence and Baghdad: Renaissance Art and Arab Science.*

**Figures 17.3, 17.4 and 17.5:** Scans of Hannah Arendt's copy of *Was heisst Denken?* dedicated to her by Martin Heidegger, pdf, Hannah Arendt Archive, Bard College

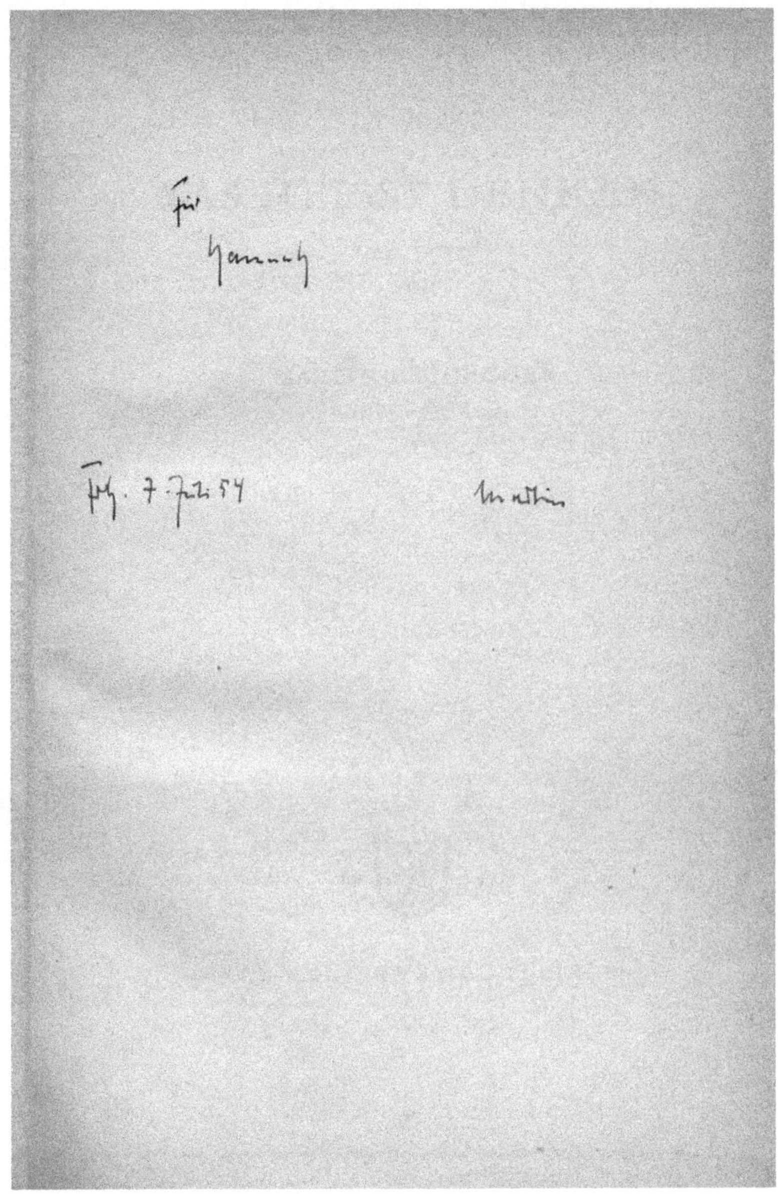

Source: Martin Heidegger, *Was heisst Denken?*, Hannah Arendt Personal Library, https://blogs.bard.edu/arendtcollection/heidegger-martin-was-heisst-denken/

(continued)

**Figures 17.3, 17.4 and 17.5:** Scans of Hannah Arendt's copy of *Was heisst Denken?* dedicated to her by Martin Heidegger, pdf, Hannah Arendt Archive, Bard College (continued)

## Erster Teil

### I

In das, was Denken heißt, gelangen wir, wenn wir selber denken. Damit ein solcher Versuch glückt, müssen wir bereit sein, das Denken zu lernen.

Sobald wir uns auf dieses Lernen einlassen, haben wir auch schon zugestanden, daß wir das Denken noch nicht vermögen.

Aber der Mensch heißt doch der, der denken kann – und das mit Recht. Denn er ist das vernünftige Lebewesen. Die Vernunft, die ratio, entfaltet sich im Denken. Als das vernünftige Lebewesen muß der Mensch denken können, wenn er nur will. Indes will der Mensch vielleicht denken und kann es doch nicht. Am Ende will er bei diesem Denkenwollen zu viel und kann deshalb zu wenig. Der Mensch kann denken, insofern er die Möglichkeit dazu hat. Allein dieses Mögliche verbürgt uns noch nicht, daß wir es vermögen. Denn wir vermögen nur das, was wir mögen. Aber wir mögen wiederum wahrhaft nur Jenes, was seinerseits uns selber und zwar uns in unserem Wesen mag, indem es sich unserem Wesen als das zuspricht, was uns im Wesen hält. Halten heißt eigentlich hüten, auf dem Weideland weiden lassen. Was uns in unserem Wesen hält, hält uns jedoch nur so lange, als wir selber von uns her das Haltende be-halten. Wir be-halten es, wenn wir es nicht aus dem Gedächtnis lassen. Das Gedächtnis ist die Versammlung des Denkens. Worauf? Auf das, was uns hält, insofern es bei uns bedacht ist, bedacht nämlich deshalb, weil Es das zu-Bedenkende bleibt. Das Bedachte ist das mit einem Andenken Beschenkte, beschenkt, weil wir es mögen. Nur wenn wir das mögen, was in sich das zu-Bedenkende ist, vermögen wir das Denken.

Um das Denken zu vermögen, müssen wir es lernen. Was ist Lernen? Der Mensch lernt, insofern er sein Tun und Lassen zu dem in die Entsprechung bringt, was ihm jeweils an Wesenhaftem zugesprochen wird. Das Denken lernen wir, indem wir auf das achten, was es zu bedenken gibt.

Heidegger, Denken

I

**Figures 17.3, 17.4 and 17.5:** Scans of Hannah Arendt's copy of *Was heisst Denken?* dedicated to her by Martin Heidegger, pdf, Hannah Arendt Archive, Bard College (continued)

Unsere Sprache nennt z. B. das, was zum Wesen des Freundes gehört, das Freundliche. Dementsprechend nennen wir jetzt das, was in sich das zu-Bedenkende ist: das Bedenkliche. Alles Bedenkliche *gibt* zu denken. Aber es gibt diese Gabe immer nur insoweit, als das Bedenkliche von sich her schon das zu-Bedenkende *ist*. Wir nennen jetzt und in der Folge dasjenige, was stets, weil einsther und allem voraus, zu bedenken bleibt: das Bedenklichste. Was ist das Bedenklichste? Wie zeigt es sich in unserer bedenklichen Zeit?

*Das Bedenklichste ist, daß wir noch nicht denken;* immer noch nicht, obgleich der Weltzustand fortgesetzt bedenklicher wird. Dieser Vorgang scheint freilich eher zu fordern, daß der Mensch handelt und zwar ohne Verzug, statt in Konferenzen und auf Kongressen zu reden und sich im bloßen Vorstellen dessen zu bewegen, was sein sollte und wie es gemacht werden müßte. Somit fehlt es am Handeln und keineswegs am Denken.

Und dennoch – vielleicht hat der bisherige Mensch seit Jahrhunderten bereits zu viel gehandelt und zu wenig gedacht. Aber wie kann heute jemand behaupten, daß wir noch nicht denken, wo doch überall das Interesse für die Philosophie rege ist und immer lauter wird, wo beinahe jedermann wissen will, was es denn mit der Philosophie auf sich hat. Die Philosophen sind »die« Denker. So heißen sie, weil sich das Denken eigentlich in der Philosophie abspielt.

Niemand wird bestreiten wollen, daß heute ein Interesse für die Philosophie besteht. Doch gibt es heute noch etwas, wofür der Mensch sich nicht interessiert, in der Weise nämlich, wie er das »interessieren« versteht?

Inter-esse heißt: unter und zwischen den Sachen sein, mitten in einer Sache stehen und bei ihr bleiben. Allein für das heutige Interesse gilt nur das Interessante. Das ist solches, was erlaubt, im nächsten Augenblick schon gleichgültig zu sein und durch anderes abgelöst zu werden, was einen dann ebensowenig angeht wie das Vorige. Man meint heute oft, etwas dadurch besonders zu würdigen, daß man es interessant findet. In Wahrheit hat man durch dieses Urteil das Interessante bereits in das Gleichgültige und alsbald Langweilige abgeschoben.

Daß man für die Philosophie ein Interesse zeigt, bezeugt noch keine Bereitschaft zum Denken. Gewiß gibt es allenthalben eine ernsthafte Beschäftigung mit der Philosophie und ihren Fragen. Es gibt einen rühmenswerten Aufwand von Gelehrsamkeit zur Erforschung ihrer Geschichte. Hier bestehen nützliche und löbliche Aufgaben, zu deren Erfüllung nur die besten Kräfte gut genug sind, zumal dann,

2

In an online resource provided by Bard College, we can see how Arendt underlined part of a sentence in a way that it became deeply impressed in the soft paper and is thus clearly visible on the reverse side of the page, even in the scan. The underlined sentence presses the question if humans, for centuries, have acted too much and thought too little about it – 'zu viel gehandelt und zu wenig gedacht' (Heidegger 1954, 2) (see Figures 17.3, 17.4 and 17.5).

These scanned pages impressed us deeply, and as if they were an artwork, we not only read their content but also their material aspects and aesthetic form – such as the transparency and colour of the paper that superimposes the dedication 'Für Hannah' (For Hannah) with the title 'Was heisst Denken?' (What is thinking?) – and the book's preservation, including light and humidity marking the paper. In addition to the marks left by Heidegger's pen and Arendt's pencil, Heidegger's words, printed and handwritten, and Arendt's lines, both denote the in-between of their thought, gender, ethnicity, attention and contemporaneity. To us, the material imprints of her visceral reaction to his propositions indicate the narrative of their fraught relationship.

After this heavily underlined sentence on acting too much and thinking too little, Heidegger explains his understanding of the term interest, again underlined by Arendt. Interest, from the Latin *inter-esse*, literally means being in-between. In the following, we will observe different manifestations of *inter-esse* through the prism of our artistic research on dizziness and how it becomes fertile regarding reflexivity. Heidegger emphasizes that rather than diminishing something by calling it interesting, we should consider that which is of inter-est is the in-betweenness, the being in the middle and between something and staying with it, 'unter und zwischen den Sachen sein, mitten in einer Sache stehen und bei ihr bleiben'. To us, being in the middle of and between something and staying with it, is exactly what reflexivity means as a practice. Being in the middle of something unfinished and staying with it furthermore reflects the work in the studio; the location and spacetime of thinking, making, explaining and discussing – inviting experimentation and reflexivity to take up shape and materiality and create momentum and energy in a circular process. We theorize this *inter-esse* as the 'compossible space' within our artistic research on dizziness and then will further connect it to the site of the studio.

## 4. The compossible space

The long-term focus of our artistic and research *inter-esse* revolves around a phenomenon we call dizziness (Anderwald et al 2019). It is essential to note that we understand dizziness as a dynamic that unbalances, unhinges and even suspends certainty, reflection, equilibrium and knowing, bringing us to a place of confusion, uncertainty, unpredictability and disequilibrium. It opens an in-between. Dizziness occurs in different contexts and on different scales: from the personal to the societal to bringing whole systems out of kilter. Becoming dizzy and unstable is a somatic and mental phenomenon that we humans know well, but it can still leave us petrified, disoriented and vulnerable. Nonetheless, our research explores dizziness through the prism that it can become a resource; we regard dizziness as an unpredictable, dynamic state that can develop into the generative and the destructive. With Søren Kierkegaard, we acknowledge that dizziness creates the 'possibility of possibility' (Kierkegaard 1980, 51), meaning that even though this state may have a petrifying effect, it also signals an alteration or multiplication of possibilities and the freedom and possibility to choose leaves us dizzy (Kierkegaard 1980). A state that suspends what we perceive as given and stable, dizziness opens spaces of encounter and transformation, with François Jullien: 'it's the grey, the intermediary, the in-between, that is interesting – it's ambiguity that makes us go back to the in-between of the non-separation of two opposites and that cracks our reflection and allows for new possibilities to unfold' (Feyertag and Jullien 2019, 58).

Together with philosophers François Jullien and Karoline Feyertag, we came to describe these heterotopic spaces of encounter and in-betweenness as the 'compossible space'. The compossible space conceptualizes a spacetime of (con-)fusing and conflating, potentially allowing new formations to emerge from its indistinctness (Anderwald et al 2018). Therefore, we understand the compossible space in two dimensions: as a theoretical and actual spacetime dynamized through states of dizziness created by the meeting of diverse and contradictory elements, atmospheres, dynamics and matter. The compossible space has become of methodological, practice-based and theoretical essence to our artistic research work. Where Heidegger's *inter-esse* seems closer to contemplation, a way to be and spend time with or between something, the compossible space is dynamic, filled with, and actualized by, dizzying motion and changing possibilities. It is more difficult to come to a space of contemplation when possibilities suddenly multiply or dissolve, as excitement or fear may set in. Building on the concepts of dizziness and the compossible space, the tides of confusion, action, experience, reasoning, contemplation and reflexivity are all needed to play out and scale the multiplicity of possibilities we may find ourselves in, and their convergence makes the case 'to release reason and subjectivity from negative typecasting, and to endow art with much needed and stronger epistemic credentials' (Beech 2021, np). As there are different modes of considering reflexivity in artistic practice and research, the term reflexivity is here introduced as a dynamic movement to a more profound awareness, understanding and critical reflection of personal, interpersonal, structural, methodological and epistemological biases and basic assumptions, as part of the 'unthought' (Jullien 2006, 15). The 'unthought' constitutes the basis of our thinking, that which we cannot think simultaneously when thinking about something as in the direction of something. As such, the 'unthought' roots and nurtures our thinking, shapes the perspectives, agencies and capacity to reflexivity, but cannot be reflected when our thinking is directed towards *something*, even though it shapes how and what we are able to consider in relation to this *something* (Jullien 2006). As Ginsberg holds, we need to get out of that boat to examine the moving ground 'in which thoughts take place' (Ginsberg 1974, 31).

## 5. Embedded observation and contemplation

Our film *Contemplations* aims to create a visual abstraction or representation of the compossible space by showing an observing view and, at times, overlaying (moving) visual planes and fusing imagery of the outside and the inside, perspectives from the studio's window, and insights from within the studio. The effect of finding outside connections to what preoccupies us is well documented in psychology. Reflecting on how these fusions play out visually and what creative impact these contemplations may have on artistic decisions was the speculative aim. More specifically, we reflect on the (visual) impact of our surroundings, conflating thought, sources and sites with sight and insight. The historical background of the geographical location we live and work in is a constant source of inspiration and is reflected in different artistic-research work, such as the performative *Mis/Guided Tours through the Neighbourhood* (2018–ongoing), which take participants on walks to specific sites of historical and/or artistic value around our studio's location, or the two EU-funded projects on resistance we initiated: *Arts of Resistance* (2024–2025) and *ART WORKS! A European Culture of Resistance and Liberation* (2019–2022) are both directly inspired by our late neighbour, Irma Schwager, who had been a well-known Austrian resistance fighter during the Nazi regime and lived upstairs from our studio. The compossibility of historical, geographical, political, or other facts and occurrences, such as personal relations, emotions, insights and attitudes, all influence the (co-creative) work in the studio. The studio work allows for confusion and vagueness. It is a spacetime for the fusion, coexistence and transformation of mutually exclusive elements. Complex and potentially new relationships of aesthetics, inner imagery, materials, skills and outside reality merge and transform here. Thus, the studio becomes the de facto space of the compossible space and its dynamic processes (see Figures 17.6 and 17.7). Moreover, and beyond the practical, the studio can serve as a metaphor for the space of materialization of transformative compossibility through the artist-researcher's work and artistic output.

## 6. The studio as the locus of *inter-esse*

The artist-researcher is a hybrid being with diverse needs, existing within different disciplines, conditions and demands related to their practice – their

**Figures 17.6 and 17.7:** View of trees overlayed with print, and of the Donaukanal overlayed with historical drawing

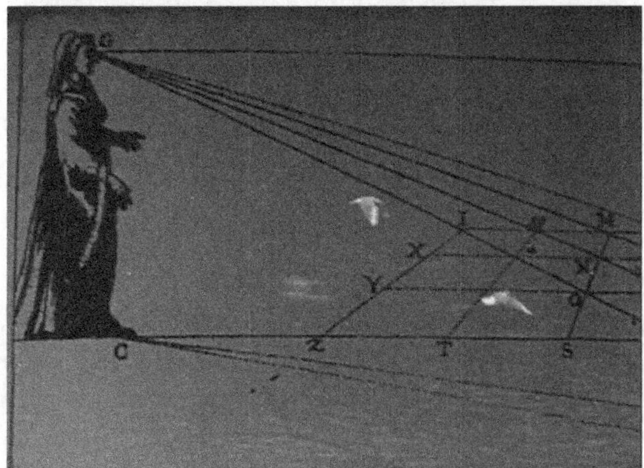

Source: Anderwald, R. and Grond, L. (2011) *Contemplations*, filmstill, 16 mm film, Cinédoc Paris Films Coop, Paris

studio, thus, necessarily a heterotopia. Be it discussion and critique or solitary contemplation, the needs of the artistic-research practice will evolve along the work's trajectory; they transform and change with the process. We can thus imagine their studio as a lab, library, stage, scriptorium, workshop, forum, cutting room, public space, or any other space predefined by technical and social possibilities supportive of their practice in the momentary stage of artistic research. This practice involves monitoring the development of artistic work, tracking the progress and outcomes of research, noting the influence of environmental factors such as changes in light, humidity and temperature, as well as social dynamics as invited participants engage with the work. Moreover, it includes listening for critical moments in a composition, reflecting on selected techniques and possible approaches to apply, and considering emerging questions and changes. This list aims to show that the studio serves as a spacetime for learning and understanding, a place for experimentation and organization. In its essence, it is fertile ground 'under the sign of process' (O'Doherty 2008, 18), making it indispensable to artistic research as a process-driven practice. Also, in terms of artistic practice, the studio can be viewed as a space for *inter-esse*, as it finds itself removed from an outside world that may be regarded as the work's inspiration and it will be again the destination of the finished work when it leaves the studio to be exhibited, stored or mounted in a home or office. The studio itself, therefore, becomes the in-between space of processing, a valuable metaphor as much as a resourceful spacetime. Its conditions become the subject of scrutiny as they impact the artist(-researcher)'s reflexivity.

Part of the treasures of the collection of Belvedere Museum in Vienna are Caspar David Friedrich's drawings showing the view from his studio's two windows to the river Elbe (see Figures 17.8, 17.9 and 17.10). The contemplative and concentrated working processes of the studio, symbolized by the scissors and frames of the right window, the key, note and broom of the left, reminding us of enclosure and the necessities of daily chores, are contrasted with the atmosphere in front of the studio: a riverbank in the sunshine, passing boats, waves and wind. It is easy to imagine voices, the murmur of water and wind to accompany the rhythm of Friedrich's artistic work. The artist visible partly in the mirror above the scissors, as he offers this perspective from the inside to the outside, the two windows, their sills and open sashes, the thick walls – the windows are the membrane to the outside, shielding the artist from, as much as connecting him with, the external world. Metaphorically, we can locate reflexivity exactly as this locus: at the window – it is the membrane, the in-between zone of two spaces with different conditions, functions, atmospheres and elements which are coinciding, opposing and merging in this sluice chamber of compossibility. Compossibility is different to coexistence. After Jullien, it describes the difference in possibility through the meeting and merging of elements, conditions and matter. Reflexivity is considered the transformation happening through, with and at this membrane, inserted between, staying with it, and instrumental to the processes of artmaking, researching and to any epistemic processing. It is the sluice chamber of the window, where the atmospheres of two spaces, their inside and outside conditions such as temperature, humidity, smells, sounds and air movements, meet.

Contemplation is a process we find very fruitful to reflexivity, the fertilization of thought through imagination processes, inviting reflexivity to settle. What can be said about artist-researchers' contemplation? Certainly,

**Figures 17.8 and 17.9:** These drawings provide a view through the windows of Friedrich's studio to the outside

Source: Friedrich, C.D. (1805–1806) *Blick aus dem Atelier des Kunstlers in Dresden*, drawings, Collection Museum Belvedere, Wien

generalizations on artists and artist-researchers' processes are not expedient. We know from experience and research that creative processes develop with individual and conditional differences and can progress quite unexpected, even for the creatives themselves (Benedek et al 2017).

Asking what the artist-researcher is observing when looking out the window of their studio, we consider our own practice, as well as that of our friends, with whom we have long and recurring conversations on the topic. Most artists and artist-researchers experience phases, when the work needs to rest, meaning that no changes are made to it in material form, but it is considered and thought about from different perspectives. This is the phase when (consciously and unconsciously) looking out of the window and

**Figures 17.8 and 17.9:** These drawings provide a view through the windows of Friedrich's studio to the outside (continued)

Source: Friedrich, C.D. (1805–1806) *Blick aus dem Atelier des Künstlers in Dresden*, drawings, Collection Museum Belvedere, Wien

contemplating happens more often. In our work, we call these recurring phases 'contemplation' rather than observation, thus the homonymous film work. From many colleagues, we hear how germane this phase of invisible work is in their practice. New approaches, less obvious connections and further experimentation can emerge from it, at times, only to start the circular process of reflection anew. The essayist and novelist Anna Kim speaks about sitting on the sofa contemplating in order to let the novel, its characters, atmospheres and environments take shape inside her, as she feels compelled to make room in herself to allow for the forming of the plot. However, when she actually writes, she is adamant about her empty white cube studio providing the needed visual and auditory quietness, taking her away from any

**Figure 17.10:** View of the skyline overlayed with historical drawing

Source: Anderwald, R. and Grond, L. (2011) *Contemplations*, filmstill, 16 mm film, Cinédoc Paris Films Coop, Paris

further inspiration, which at this point would be a distraction (Anderwald et al 2023). In his *A Lover's Discourse*, philosopher Roland Barthes (2001) explains his intermittent work process quoting Flaubert's customs:

> When his sentences ran dry, Flaubert flung himself on his divan: he called this his 'marinade.' If the thing reverberates too powerfully, it makes such a din in my body that I must halt any occupation; I stretch out on my bed and give in without a struggle to the 'inner storm'. (Barthes 2001, 201)

The film *Contemplations* reflects on this terrain: When it is storming inside, what of the outside finds its sensory entrance to the awareness of the artist? For Barthes, it is again a matter of location: 'The bed (by day) is the site of the Image-repertoire; the desk is once again, and whatever one does there, reality' (Barthes 2001, 201). As visual artists and visual thinkers, we are interested in what happens visually when 'marinading', contemplating and surrendering to the tempest of our inner life against the outside reality. What imagery penetrates our awareness and is thus observed? Is it the surroundings, or is it rather the observation of the images that arise from the imagination? Do they overlap and fuse? For the film *Contemplations*, we wanted to artistically explore and merge the different planes of visuality to offer ambiguity on a membrane, an in-between space of mental and outside perception of visual imagery; the actual surroundings and their fusing with the inner images conjured through the artistic practice, research, conversations, observation and thought. In *Contemplations*, we point the camera to the window and let it watch the outside, as we would standing by the window, then overlying its imagery with perspectival drawings that aim to understand the optical workings, geometry and physical conception of a three-dimensional space on a two-dimensional plane. By letting the camera eye contemplate what can be seen outside, we propose not only a view but indicate that the imagery is not simply there but also marks a beyond of the studio space. First, a beyond of the enclosed, concentrated space dedicated to open questions, unfinished works and scattered, fragmentary matters; second, the elements depicted are only a part of what makes the film. The black and white film material creates an abstraction, as it has a graphic quality reminiscent of a graphite drawing. This impression is further intensified by superimposed historical drawings. The title *Contemplations* indicates that these images are only the entry point to an ongoing inner monologue, an invisible or barely visible encounter of inner imagery, wandering thoughts and views of the outside world. The term hallucination, originally, was used to describe a wandering mind.

## 7. Observing art, an encounter in an *'agréable moment'*

As described, artistic research work needs time and space for contemplation. The studio's inspiration, the library's resources, or encounters with others (artworks, people, daily occurrences and surroundings) leave impressions in the mind, thus on the creative process that are transferred to paper, celluloid and other materials. To contemplate derives from Latin *contemplatus*, 'to gaze attentively, observe; consider, contemplate', but also 'to mark out a space for observation (as an augur does)'[3] and indicates deep and quiet thought and reflection over a temporal extension, the gazing in a specific direction, and spiritual modes of mediation and thought (-templum, Latin temple). It shares a closeness to Greek philosophy's understanding of theory, which needs the insertion of distance via time and space, a travel, to account for something that one experienced on a different territory and brings back to a community (Figure 17.11).

Experience is made blindly, as philosopher Marcus Steinweg (2013) writes. The insertion of spatial or temporal distance is, therefore, important to understanding and reflexivity. The blindness of experiences applies to many activities, not only to being immersed in thought and creative practice but also to perceiving art. The in-between or *inter-esse* of the artistic research practice is mirrored in the space opening between the artist(-researcher)'s intention and the reception and understanding of the recipient or audience. When visiting a cinema in France, the following announcement will be made: 'Nous vous souhaitons un agréable moment.' This sentence doesn't

---

[3] https://www.etymonline.com/search?q=contemplation

**Figure 17.11:** View of trees overlayed with historical drawing

Source: Anderwald, R. and Grond, L. (2011) *Contemplations*, filmstill, 16 mm film, Cinédoc Paris Films Coop, Paris

express the wish that you might enjoy the film; rather, it wishes for you to enjoy the moment, the temporary meeting with the artwork. This can be read as a recognition of what happens between the artwork and its participant or audience; it transgresses the film work and takes into account what an encounter between an audience and a work does. The artwork constitutes the framework for this encounter that immerses the participant in all their thoughts, emotions and knowledges. The audience spends time with the work, experiences it, and might also enjoy it. Under those circumstances, what is observed in this *agréable moment*? If we turn to the work of psychoanalyst Esther Bick, we realize that observation is an experience where we learn as much about the observed as about our own emotional, cognitive, organizational, and somatic processes and attitudes, as these are evoked during the observation. Bick argues that 'thinking and observing are almost inseparable', which constitutes 'an important lesson, for it teaches caution and reliance on consecutive observations for confirmation of any hypotheses made' (Bick 1964, 565). But it also teaches that the blindness of experience still enables *inter-esse*, as different processes play out simultaneously, actively and passively, in the tension of observation and immersion, encouraging processes of criticality and reflexivity.

## 8. Consolidating contemplations

Reflexivity is not a conscious process only but is also informed by subconscious and visceral ways of processing information and findings (Figure 17.12).

**Figure 17.12:** View of trees overlayed with historical drawing

Source: Anderwald, R. and Grond, L. (2011) *Contemplations*, filmstill, 16 mm film, Cinédoc Paris Films Coop, Paris

Enriching the term reflexivity with contemplation, observation, Flaubert's 'marinade', and the *inter-esse* of the compossible space of the studio as well as the encounter with the artwork in a cinema, we aim to draw attention to the manyfold processes impacting reflexivity in artistic research, practice and appreciation. Although we often employ the capacity for reflexivity to engage in reflection or deliberation, dizzying, non-deliberative, embedded, social, immersive and somatic experiences may constitute a generative factor for enhancing reflexivity. This is precisely why we need others as sources of knowledge, to build on their work and thinking or to enrich, criticize and question our work through their presence and attention. Reflexivity becomes the turning back of experience on itself and instigates learning and sense-making processes. George Herbert Mead strengthens the social function of reflexivity:

It is by means of reflexiveness – the turning back of the experience of the individual upon himself – that the whole social process is thus brought into the experience of the individuals involved in it; it is by such means, which enable the individual to take the attitude of the other toward himself, that the individual is able consciously to adjust himself to that process, and to modify the resultant of that process in any given social act in terms of his adjustment to it. Reflexiveness, then, is the essential condition, within the social process, for the development of mind. (Mead 1934, 134)

Artistic research progresses on different degrees of active and passive engagement of the artist-researcher themselves, their team and their audiences. These phases of engagement may challenge the perceived borders between art, research and life, between experience and reflexivity, as they, in a circular and at times unpredictable manner, transgress and enter each other; they dissolve and metamorphose in the compossible space energized by dynamics that can become dizzying and transformative. However, it is exactly the experience of dizziness that incites a rethinking of the given, thus potentially making our being with the world more generative and allowing for the discovery of unexpected relations between elements, topics, individuals and their surroundings. Dizziness involves uncertainty, unexpectedness and vulnerability that need observation and mitigation in creative as well as social processes, and in thought. To us, this is what the *inter-esse* of artistic research holds; it invites reflexivity for a more autonomous and empowered thinking and being with the world.

## References


Anderwald, R. and Grond, L. (2011) *Contemplations*, 16mm film. Cinédoc Paris Films Coop.

Anderwald, R. and Grond, L. (2023) *Dizziness, Anxiety, and Climate Action. Reflecting the Possibilities of Artistic Research from the Viewpoint of the Compossible Space*, SAR23 Conference Proceedings. Weimar: Bauhaus University.

Anderwald, R., Feyertag, K. and Grond, L. (2018) The Concepts of Dizziness and the Compossible Space in Research-Creation. *Emotion, Space and Society* 28: 122–130.

Anderwald, R., Feyertag, K. and Grond, L. (eds) (2019) *Dizziness: A Resource*. Berlin: Sternberg Press. Available at: https://repository.akbild. ac.at/de/alle_inhalte/query/23693 [Accessed 11 November 2024].

Anderwald, R., Edelsztein, S. and Grond, L. (2023) *On Certain Groundlessness*. Vienna: OH WOW Podcasts. Available at: https://www.on-dizziness.com/ resources-overview/podcast [Accessed 11 November 2024].

Barthes, R. (2001) *A Lover's Discourse*. New York: Hill & Wang.

Beech, A. (2021) *Art's Intolerable Knowledge*. Keynote for EARN European Artistic Research Network, Utrecht.

Belting, H. (2011) *Florence and Baghdad: Renaissance Art and Arab Science*. Cambridge, MA: Belknap Press of Harvard University Press.

Benedek, M., Jauck, E., Kerschenbauer, K., Anderwald, R. and Grond, L. (2017) Creating Art: An Experience Sampling Study in the Domain of Moving Image Art. *American Psychological Association* 11(1). http://dx.doi. org/10.1037/aca000010

Bick, E. (1964) Notes on Infant Observation in Psycho-Analytic Training. *The International Journal of Psychoanalysis* 45: 558–565.

Blos-Jáni, M. (2021) Uncovering In-betweens: On Photochemical Practices and Handmade Cinema. *NECSUS Journal* 45: 307–316. Available at: https://necsus-ejms.org/uncovering-in-betweens-on-photochemical-practices-and-handmade-cinema/ [Accessed 11 November 2024].

Cohn, P. (2014) Interview with Peter Snowdown. *Bomb Magazine*. Available at: https://bombmagazine.org/articles/2014/02/20/peter-snowdon/ [Accessed 11 November 2024].

Feyertag, K. and Jullien, F. (2019) On the Philosophical Potential of Dizziness and Compossible Space. In R. Anderwald, L. Grond and K. Feyertag (eds) *Dizziness: A Resource*. Berlin: Sternberg Press, pp 54–65.

Friedrich, C.D. (1805–1806) *Blick aus dem Atelier der Künstlers in Desden, Blick aus dem Atelier der Künstlers in Desden (linkes Fenster)*, drawing. Available at: https://sammlung.belvedere.at/objects/870/blick-aus-dem-atelier-des-kunstlers-in-dresden-auf-die-elbe?# [Accessed 11 November 2024].

Ginsberg, A. (1974) *Allen Verbatim: Lectures on Poetry, Politics, Consciousness*. New York: McGraw-Hill.

Heidegger, M. (1954) *Was heisst Denken?* Tübingen: Max Niemayer Verlag. Available at: https://www.bard.edu/library/arendt/pdfs/Heidegger-WasHeisstDenken.pdf [Accessed 11 November 2024].

Jullien, F. (2006) *Vortrag vor Managern über Wirksamkeit und Effizienz in China und im Westen*. Berlin: Merve Verlag.

Kierkegaard, Søren (1980) *The Concept of Anxiety*. Princeton: Princeton University Press.

Mead, H. (1934) *Mind, Self, and Society*. Chicago: University of Chicago Press.

O'Doherty, B. (2008) *Studio and Cube: On the Relationship between Where Art is Made and Where Art is Displayed*. New York: A Buell Center / FORuM Project Publication.

Pentecost, C. (2010) Critical Strategies in Art and Media: Introductory Statement 04. *FUTURE NON STOP, A Living Archive for Digital Culture in Theory and Practice*. Available at: http://future-nonstop.org/c/ca69656ff f0a0fb28ee6f3ab64c2e6c8 [Accessed 11 November 2024].

Schrödl, B. (2004) Ein filmischer Atelierbesuch und ein Maler im Filmstudio. Zeitlichkeit zwischen Produktions- und Rezeptionsprozessen. In K. Gludovatz and M. Peschken (eds) *Momente im Prozess. Zeitlichkeit künstlerischer Produktion*. Berlin: Reimer, pp 91–100.

Steinweg, M. (2013) *Philosophie der Überstürzung*. Berlin: Merve.

# 18

# Reflexivity in Artistic Research and Visual Anthropology: Response to 'Contemplations: A Perspective on Reflexivity Out of the "Brackish Waters" of Artistic Research' by Ruth Anderwald and Leonhard Grond

*Sanderien Verstappen*

Visual anthropology students often ask me what the difference is between anthropological films vis-à-vis the films made in other realms, such as art or journalism. My reply is that this question cannot easily be answered in terms of what the films look like, what technologies are used or what topics they cover. Rather, it is the filmmakers' embeddedness in their specific disciplines, each with their own traditions of thought, practice and institutionalization, that influence their entire orientation towards the medium. My experience of reading the chapter 'Contemplations' by Ruth Anderwald and Leonhard Grond (Chapter 17, this volume) illustrates this. Both these authors and I centralize reflexivity in our film-based research. But the different realms in which we work produce different frames for understanding reflexivity.

Anderwald and Grond are filmmakers in the realm of art, and artist-researchers. Their chapter asks: what differentiates art from artistic research? Their answer is: reflexivity. The 'distinguishing principle between artistic work and artistic research work', they argue, 'is the level and quality of reflexivity and the practitioner's ensuing openness to communication, learning and accountability'. They explain that reflexivity is a 'critical reflection of personal, interpersonal, structural, methodological and epistemological biases and basic assumptions' and is 'a dynamic motion to a more profound awareness, understanding'. Building on the work of French philosopher François Jullien (2006), they describe reflexivity as a self-awareness of the direction in which a researcher thinks and their consideration of other possible directions. While artists 'can claim to simply follow a sudden inspiration', they suggest, artistic researchers will question their own decisions and argue for them in an explicit way.

I was invited to respond to their text because I also make films and do research – albeit in a different realm; that of visual anthropology, a subfield of social and cultural anthropology, which is a discipline of the social sciences. The concept of reflexivity is just as crucial to anthropological research as it is to artistic research. When I teach filmmaking to anthropology students, I often use Sarah Pink's handbook *Doing Visual Ethnography* (2016), which explains that 'it is by now generally accepted that reflexivity forms an important part of scientific practice'. Pink defines reflexivity as an approach that lets go of the ambition to produce objective knowledge and instead recognizes the centrality of the subjectivity of the researcher to the production and presentation of knowledge. Being a reflexive anthropologist involves acknowledging and interrogating how the anthropologist is situated in a research setting; for example, in terms of gender, age, nationality, language and proximity to certain interlocutors, as well as the use of certain technologies, methods, processes and forms. In anthropological films, reflexivity is often made visible for the audience; for example, by showing the anthropologist's interactions with the protagonist in the film (as Willy Sier and I have done in our film *Empty Home* [2016]) instead of pretending that the anthropologist was not present by editing out the interview questions. The research processes can be explained in more detail in an accompanying text (Sier and Verstappen 2023). If reflexivity is not visualized explicitly within the film, such an accompanying methodological text becomes the main venue through which reflexivity is realized, for example, by explaining the social relations and discussions through which the film came about (as Isabelle Makay, Mario Rutten and I have done in a chapter [Verstappen et al 2021] about our film *Living Like a Common Man* [2011]).

The two descriptions of reflexivity – the artistic one and the anthropological one – overlap in their stress on the careful consideration of the factors that shape the working process and its outcomes. The difference seems to lie in the aim of the researchers and their networks, which are shaped by the institutions they work in. While artistic researchers use the term reflexivity to capture how their work differs from that of other artists, anthropologists use it to highlight the partiality of their accounts and thereby differentiate their work from that of positivistic scientists, including other social scientists who aspire to produce objective knowledge. Both framings are shaped by the researchers' orientation to the institutions in which they work and the significant others with whom they collaborate within these institutions.

## References

Jullien, F. (2006) *Vortrag vor Managern über Wirksamkeit und Effizienz in China und im Westen*, translated by R. Voullié. Berlin: Merve Verlag.

Pink, S. (2016) Ways of Seeing, Knowing and Showing. In S. Pink (ed) *Doing Visual Ethnography*. London: SAGE, pp 33–48.

Sier, W. and Verstappen, S. (2023) Empty Homes: Filming Homeownership in Rapidly Urbanising China. *Visual Studies* 39(1–2): 24–32.

Verstappen, S. and Sier, W. (2016) *Empty Home*. University of Amsterdam, 17 minutes.

Verstappen, S., Rutten, M. and Makay, I. (2011) *Living Like a Common Man*. University of Amsterdam, 65 minutes.

Verstappen, S. in conversation with I. Makay and M. Rutten (2021) Ethnocinematographic Theory: How to Develop Migration Theory through Ethnographic Filmmaking. In K. Nikielska-Sekula and A. Desille (eds) *Visual Methodology in Migration Studies: New Possibilities, Theoretical Implications, and Ethical Questions*. Cham: Springer, pp 99–116.

PART IV

# Institutionalizing

19

# On Institutions and Institutionalizing

*Andrea Schikowitz, Sarah R. Davies, Elaine Goldberg
and Fredy Mora-Gámez*

Inconsistency is useful: it keeps a reader (or recipient of communication) on their toes. We therefore do not regard it as a shortcoming that, for this section but not for most others, we offer a short introduction – a map to some of the issues and questions that will arise in it. We do this partly because it seems to us to be particularly valuable to pull out and make more explicit some of the connections between the different contributions included in this section, but also because those contributions speak to some of the fundamental challenges and tensions of reflexivity that we raised in the introduction. Institutions, and institutionalizing, are central to the ambivalences of reflexivity, in that they reflect tensions between individual and collective responsibility. The contributions that follow explore quite different spaces, experiences and sites, but all somehow speak to the question of how reflexivity can be *stabilized* – rendered available and valuable to different actors.

However, we should start by acknowledging one central question: should we even talk about institutionalizing reflexivity? Isn't this a contradiction in itself, given that earlier contributions to this volume have emphasized the necessity of affect, creativity, freedom, fluidity, intimacy and breaking with convention as prerequisites for reflexivity? How can we think about institutionalizing such properties – and should we even try to do so? Associations we might have with (our) institutions include routines and formalities, categorization and standardization, rule-following, detachment, and rationality. At the same time, however, institutionalizing might also mean assigning value and legitimacy, providing room and resources, and collectivizing responsibility. This relates to reflections raised in Chapter 3 (by Reuben Message, Jane Calvert and Rob Smith) around whether reflexivity is a 'luxury' in current academia, something that only some can afford without destroying career trajectories that require them to accelerate rather than slowing down, and to produce and perform rather than questioning their position and assumptions. Institutionalizing reflexivity might be a way to relieve individual researchers from yet another demand that they have to fulfil on top of so many others (Demeritt 2000; Sigl et al 2020; Falkenberg 2021): innovation, excellence, productivity, responsibility, relevance, and so on. In this light, perhaps it is still worthwhile reflecting on the institutionalization of reflexivity – if it should be done, how it might be done, which tensions are involved, and what questions arise from it. The contributions in this section do exactly this.

However, one observation from the contributions is that they rarely address institutionalization in a narrow sense, signalling that formal institutions might not be best suited to providing appropriate spaces and opportunities for reflexivity. Karen Kastenhofer and Doris Allhutter (Chapter 20), for instance, outline the tensions and challenges of 'projected reflexivity', showing that while formalized reflexive projects within a particular institution offered the possibility for reflection and learning, those projects were not straightforward to implement. At the same time, this and other contributions express the desire for some kind of anchoring or stabilizing of reflexivity in institutional contexts – something that goes beyond stating it as an abstract virtue or an individual duty. How, then, to create more permanent spaces that allow for ambivalence as a basis for reflexivity? Rather than formal institutionalization of reflexivity, we might think of 'institutionalizing' as an ongoing process (Meyer 2008), as understood in the tradition of the sociology of knowledge (Berger and Luckmann 1991 [1966]). In this broader understanding, institutionalizing is about collective sense-making and about the construction of a common world that facilitates social coordination. Yet it also means to fix certain relations, to routinize them and create a taken-for-granted reality. How then to facilitate reflexivity as collective sense-making that is ready to question taken-for-granted routines while staying flexible enough to accommodate change and development?

One possible way forward might be to imagine spaces for reflexivity – spaces that are collective but that allow for ambivalence, fluidity and multiplicity; spaces that provide space, time and resources for reflexivity but do not strive for specific outcomes or increasing productivity; spaces that enable intimacy and discomfort but do not expose those who engage in them. In her plea for alternative places for Science and Technology Studies (STS) reflexivity, Elaine Goldberg writes that 'it should be possible to have such a space, where paradoxical, contradictory and incompatible things and thoughts are allowed to coexist' (Chapter 24). In a similar vein, Nikolaus Poechhacker and Sarah Schönbauer explore how liminality as a basis for reflexivity manifests through a constant back-and-forth between multiple 'homes' in STS research and beyond, arguing that 'in order to become productive, liminal positions demand spaces in which tensions between different positions can exist and are valued' (Chapter 23). The latter points to another aspect: these should exactly be *spaces* of reflexivity, in the plural, as any space is exclusive and ambivalent in itself and will never fit for all purposes, needs and actors. Alternating between different spaces could be a way to prevent reflexivity from being reduced to a mere buzzword. In that sense, some spaces of reflexivity could be more closely embedded in institutions, while others would be more independent; some would be rather formal and structured and others more open, fluid and temporal; and different spaces would be open or secluded for different collectives and groups. Such a multiplicity of spaces of reflexivity could help to prevent an essentialization or reduction of what reflexivity means or how it can be practised.

As Malcolm Ashmore and Olga Restrepo Forero argue (Chapter 25), place matters for how we think, in STS and beyond. As a tentative conclusion to this section (with which you may agree, or disagree, once you have engaged with the different contributions), we might therefore suggest that only ongoing experimentation with diverse spaces of and for reflexivity can enable reflexivity ('tinkering', to draw a parallel with discussions of care; see Mol et al 2010). If reflexivity in research work is to be institutionalized – stabilized – then academic institutions must be ready to provide time, space and resources to enable such an ongoing experimentation – without asking for outcomes.

## References


Berger, P.L. and Luckmann, T. (1991 [1966]) *The Social Construction of Reality*. Harmondsworth: Penguin Books.

Demeritt, D. (2000) The New Social Contract for Science: Accountability, Relevance, and Value in US and UK Science and Research Policy. *Antipode* 32(3): 308–329. doi:10.1111/1467-8330.00137

Falkenberg, R.I. (2021) Re-invent Yourself! How Demands for Innovativeness Reshape Epistemic Practices. *Minerva* 59(4): 423–444. doi:10.1007/s11024-021-09447-4

Meyer, R.E. (2008) New Sociology of Knowledge: Historical Legacy and Contributions to Current Debates in Institutional Research. In R. Greenwood, C. Oliver, T.B. Lawrence and R.E. Meyer (eds) *The SAGE Handbook of Organizational Institutionalism*. London: SAGE, pp 519–538.

Mol, A.M., Moser, I. and Pols, J. (2010) *Care in Practice: On Tinkering in Clinics, Homes and Farms*. Bielefeld/Germany: Transcript Verlag.

Sigl, L., Felt, U. and Fochler, M. (2020) 'I am Primarily Paid for Publishing…': The Narrative Framing of Societal Responsibilities in Academic Life Science Research. *Science and Engineering Ethics* 26(3): 1569–1593. doi:10.1007/s11948-020-00191-8

# Evaluating

# 20

# Projected Reflexivity: Learnings from Two Reflexive Research Projects from–within, with–within and for–within

*Karen Kastenhofer and Doris Allhutter*

## 1. Introduction: Embarking on projected reflexivity

Between 2016 and 2020, the Institute of Technology Assessment (ITA) at the Austrian Academy of Sciences embarked on two internal, 'reflexive' projects: one addressing our own practices of policy advice, the other zooming in on the normative dimension of our epistemic as well as advisory work. *Policy Advice at ITA* (Pol[ITA] 2016–2018) was to be the first of a series of internal projects of an explicitly reflexive character. It was (at least, partly) triggered by an expansion of the institute's advisory remit, resulting from a new contract with the Austrian Parliament from 2017 onwards that added to ITA's research and advisory portfolio[1] and a perceived need to scrutinize past and future advisory practices, appropriate quality criteria and practical guidelines. This first internal reflexive project was planned and coordinated by Karen, steered by a core team of five institute members and realized with contributions of the whole scientific staff of 20, including two series of in-depth interviews (with all technology assessment [TA] practitioners at ITA

---

[1]   ITA combines basic research and mission–oriented research, participatory, communicative and advisory activities. ITA staff thus holds a hybrid identity as academic scholars and technology assessment (TA) practitioners. In this text, we will refer to ITA scientific staff as TA practitioners, thereby referring to a broad range of epistemic, collaborative, advisory and other practices.

and some external project partners and clients) and joint internal workshops to discuss and further develop the project's findings.

Launched by another colleague and steered by a core team of eight ITA members the project, *Technology Assessment and Normativity* (TAN, 2018–2020) was dedicated to the role of norms and values in ITA's research and advisory activities. Methodologically, this second internal project integrated documentary research, memory work via mind-scripting workshops with all ITA practitioners (with Doris taking the lead of the related work package), and interviews with senior TA practitioners at other European TA institutes. At that time, yet another reflexive activity fed into these projects: on the occasion of the Austrian Academy of Sciences' 175th anniversary, the institute's history was reconstructed based on archive research and interviews with founding members and central actors, delineating several distinct phases in ITA's history.

The two projects we are focusing on in this chapter, Pol[ITA] and TAN, came with an ambition to further professionalize aspects that escaped more traditional scientific quality control as established in 'normal', 'Mode I' or 'academic' science. Direct outputs of our efforts included internal project reports, published scholarly papers as well as a heightened awareness within our team of various positions held, practices performed and ramifications to be expected. Moreover, we gathered experience in performing reflexivity together in a project-based and institutionalized mode. We started to grasp the variety of practical options and ambitions that the terms 'reflection' and 'reflexivity' relate to. Inspired by discussions during a workshop organized for this book, we further developed these experiences into learnings. In this spirit, today, we can look back at the projects' lasting impact on the institute, its members and the TA community more broadly. We address the question of what it means to perform reflexivity together at an academic institute in a project-based form. What expectations and goals can this mode of reflexivity pursue? What kind of change does it contribute to? How do power dynamics frame the way reflexivity can be performed and, finally, how can we ensure that relevant learnings last beyond the project?

We embed our learnings in scholarly discussions of reflexivity as well as in existing scholarly work on 'research-from-within' and 'insider research' to discuss research from within that is simultaneously 'research-with-within' and 'research-for-within'. Moreover, we combine (more or less) linear, rather abstract argumentation with more positional, memory-based vignettes that give flesh to the more-than-epistemological ramifications of our practical choices and point to interrelations between the individual, collective and organizational level. We thus hope to outline a web of potential issues pertaining to internal reflexive projects, to illustrate how these issues might play out in distinct constellations, and to inform similar activities at other scholarly institutions and in kindred communities like that of Science and Technology Studies (STS).

## 2. What's in a name and what's in naming: 'remarkable' reflexivity

Various versions of reflexivity are certainly part of the standardized repertoires of practice in any scholarly culture.[2] Reflexivity, for example, targets methods in the form of methodological considerations, or concepts by mode of theoretical discussion. Reflexivity is also part of ordinary organizational cultures, realized in informal shop-talk situated in the in-betweens (during lunch breaks, in hallways) as well as in formal settings, like jour fixes or recesses. Still, STS – as the scientific study of scientific study (Knuuttila 2002) – has a distinct role to play in this context. STS is widely understood as a reflexive programme, providing reflexive accounts beyond the standard repertoire of scientists and of scientific organizations. Early STS scholars even adopted reflexivity as one of four basic principles (besides causality, impartiality and symmetry) of a 'strong program' of a sociology of scientific knowledge (Hess 2001). Others have contested such an interpretation, stressing that reflexivity was neither remarkable, nor a virtue nor specific to STS, seeking to 'deflate the "epistemological" hubris' of such a postulate (Lynch 2000, 47).

But if reflexivity is ubiquitous and unremarkable, why then label certain activities as reflexive at all? There is probably no general answer to this question. But our context-specific answer might be all the more important to better understand our own commitments: ITA's 'internal projects' were labelled as 'reflexive projects' so as to denote an ambition to perform reflexivity beyond the standard repertoire of routines at our institute (and beyond). Moreover, their framing as 'reflexive projects' hinted at a transformative ambition, that we considered potentially changing our self-perception and/or our practices based on insights resulting from our reflexive activities. Eventually, our internal reflexive projects were tied to the hope that our practices would consequently become more robust or that, on a meta-level, a more robust understanding of our practices would result in institutional professionalization. Our decision to organize reflexivity in a project-mode finally pointed to the temporal character of this endeavour, with a distinct beginning and a distinct end. It entailed that this kind of reflexivity would represent a special effort we would be able to organize for, engage in and shoulder for a predefined amount of time.

---

[2]   For a list of variants of reflexivity, see Lynch (2000); for the notion that academic fields come with distinct reflexivities, see, for example, Kastenhofer (2004).

That we opted for a 'remarkable' (in the double meaning of interpreted as notable and denoted as such) and projected mode of reflexive activities, also came with the possibility (or necessity) to explicitly discuss and decide about concrete modes and terms of these activities. It made us grasp the variety of practical options and ambitions that the terms 'reflection' and 'reflexivity' might relate to. 'Remarkable' reflexivity, we keep experiencing, can denote so many things, because reflexivity comes in many forms and (non-)standards vary across fields and organizations. There are strands of reflexive writing, for example, in feminist scholarship (Allhutter et al 2024). In this tradition, reflexivity is inscribed in the style of presentation and mode of communication. Reflexivity can be tied to an emancipatory programme, to organizational learning or to practical professionalization. Announced reflexivity can mean that we think about aspects of our work that we would normally take for granted, that we open distinct black-boxes of everyday practice. It is all the more important to excavate the distinct understandings, visions and ambitions that come with projected reflexivity (see section 4 on managing expectations).

## 3. Making sense of and making sense in research-from-within

To specify our methodological and theoretical approach, we situate our projects within the relevant scholarly literature and highlight three closely related aspects, that warrant consideration: the dimension of 'internality', ethico-onto-epistemological considerations, and how epistemic, interventionist and transformative ambitions are entangled.

The notion of 'internal research' can relate to two overlapping, but still *different kinds of 'internality'*: some authors focus on doing research from within an organization (most notably: organizational researchers), while others focus on doing research from within a community and culture (most notably: cultural anthropologists). Depending on which take one aligns with, for example, different methodological considerations will come up. A focus on organizations, often running under the label of 'research-from-within', will result in concentrating on issues of organizational hierarchies (for example, Coghlan and Brannick 2005; Sikes and Potts 2008). A focus on communities and cultures is often, but not consistently, labelled as 'insider research' and results in concentrating on issues of being an 'insider' or an 'outsider' (or any combination of both, for example, Collins 1986; Banks 1998). A focus on institutions is labelled, for example, as institutional autoethnography (for example, Jubas and Seidel 2016; Fujiwara 2020) or 'endogenous research' (Trowler 2011). In our case,[3] we conducted our

---

[3] It has to be noted that, to some extent, STS also engages in research-from-within as members of the scientific community study science (albeit often belonging to different

research from within a substructure of an organization (an institute of a national academy) among members of multiple scholarly communities (like STS, sociology, ecological economics and, of course, TA), all of which shared a commitment to the institution of TA, rendering all three dimensions relevant.

This constellation comes with methodological, ethical, political and existential considerations which are heavily influenced by the *ethico-onto-epistemological paradigm* one subscribes to (as this choice of elements and wording already illustrates). Anderson (2006) draws our attention to two contrasting traditions of 'realistic' or 'analytic ethnography' and 'evocative ethnography' that come with very different writing styles and roles of the written ethnographies. Brannick and Coghlan (2007) provide us with a systematic comparison of three paradigmatic ways of how to make sense of insider research or research-from-within. They scrutinize the distinct takes of positivist, hermeneutic or postmodern and critical realistic or action research on this theme. Scholarly discussions of the insider/outsider ontology and epistemology resonate with this differentiation.[4] They relate not only to purely methodological and epistemological questions, but also to political ones, like 'whose knowledge is authentic, who can know what, and who speaks for whom?' (Banks 1998; see section 4).

Closely linked to these considerations, when publishing our work in scholarly outlets, we had to position our methodology within a landscape of methodological labels that have emerged throughout the past 30 years' growth of autoethnography as a genre. As (yet again) not all scholars pack the same methodology under the same label, we had to make do with select definitions. Delamont (2009, 58), for example, introduces the terms 'reflexive ethnography' or 'reflexive autobiographical writing on ethnography' as 'a reflexive account of doing research in a subculture to which one has previous links of ethnicity, language or biography'. As a special variant of a 'traditional' or 'peopled' ethnography she contrasts this approach with 'autoethnography' as an ethnography 'where there is no object except the author herself to study'. Both these approaches apply self-observational techniques, but only the former does so with interests beyond the self.

Alvesson (2003, 174) defines 'self-ethnography' as 'a study and a text in which the researcher-author describes a cultural setting to which s/he has a "natural access," is an active participant, more or less on equal terms with

---

scholarly fields) and as they are mostly members of the same (Western) culture and innovation regime.

[4] They stretch from Merton's (1972) discussion of insider/outsider research, Maruyama's (1978) 'polyocular research' and Coghlan and Brannick's (2005) 'insider/outsider team research' to Collins' (1986) 'outsider within', Banks' (1998) 'indigenous-insider', 'indigenous-outsider', 'external-insider' and 'external outsider' (see Acker 2000).

other participants'. The researcher takes the role of observing participant and the research interest again goes beyond the self. As synonymous terms, he introduces 'home-culture-ethnography' or 'insider-ethnography'. For memory work within feminist research, Alvesson (2003, 175) notes a focus on strongly personal experiences in 'autobiographical texts', but yet again, with 'an aim to carry out cultural analysis and not introspection, although … one's own feelings, thoughts and experiences may offer valuable material'. Sharing an interest in the everyday with this research, Dorothy Smith's (2005) 'institutional ethnography' explores how social relations structure people's everyday lives. By looking at the ways that people interact in and enact social institutions such as school, marriage or work, she focuses on how these interactions are institutionalized.

For analysing the trans-individual 'modes of how subjects and institutions are affectively invested with power relations' (Allhutter 2021, 447), the method of mind scripting – an adaptation of memory work – suggests a collective process for epistemic communities and communities-of-practice to deconstruct their self-representations, embodied experiences and affective involvements in autobiographical vignettes. For the classic school of action research, Brannick and Coghlan (2007, 66) note that the researcher '[is bifurcated] into two separate parts: the participant role that interacts with members and forms relations and the research role that gathers data [...] suppress[ing] the membership role by analyzing the material from the outsider perspective and emphasizing detachment'. Within our own activities, we applied reflexive techniques, but also modes of distinctly collaborative work like team interviews, mind scripting, joint interpretive sessions, collective discussions and feedback cycles. While we followed a self-ethnography or insider-ethnography approach as defined by Alvesson (2003), we did in many instances also split into two role sets as described by Brannick and Coghlan (2007) for action research.

Eventually, there is the need to position our activities as to their multifold, epistemic, interventionist and transformative ambitions, to clarify potential prioritizations, and to further specify what the ambitions of all participants were, how they fed into the process and how they played out (see Vignette 1). Our own research clearly represented research-from-within; but it was also *research-with-within* as members of the institute not only figured as primary investigators, research team members, research participants and research addressees and *research-for-within* as the project had been initiated by the institute itself and formally commissioned by the institute's directorate. In designing and conducting the projects, epistemic goals as well as practical considerations of organizational and institutional professionalization and identity work weighed substantially. But at the same time, they were not explicated and discussed in full detail from the very beginning (see section 4). In hindsight and in light of the existing literature, it is safe to say that there was a general motive to gain a better understanding of and inform our advisory practices, but we did certainly not apply a full change management or action research programmatic, neither did we explicitly and collectively aim at questioning the organizational fundaments of our practices. It was, after all, also a research-with-within and research-for-within, that did not seek to jeopardize the very basis of the 'within'.

## 4. Managing expectations in research-for-within

Vignette 1
Doris on TAN (around 2006, spring 2019, winter 2023)

Many years ago, I had used mind scripting with a team of software developers of a small company. I remember how researching collective patterns of meaning-making in an organization also pointed to issues of in/formal hierarchies and differing standpoints. I felt that presenting results of this nature also came with the responsibility to not leave the research field in ruins. Well, back then, the bosses had been quick to reconstitute their viewpoint and to silence discussions that could have had a potential for change. Nothing had been ruined, but probably not much won for them either. Hopefully, it just took time to unfold.

Then, years later, I used mind scripting for the first time in my own work context and I started to think about it in terms of institutional (self-)ethnography. Given the power-critical trajectory of mind scripting, how could I define and communicate the objectives of such a reflexive process in the context of my own work environment? What kind of reflection would a deconstruction of our collective, team-based or individual work practices get rolling? If our reflections also included the objective of change, how big were the nuts and bolts that we wanted to loosen and turn? And who would be in charge after the analytical process had been finished? It was probably something that could not be defined or planned for, but the process would show, I thought. And I introduced the method as an experimental process with an open outcome – an intervention that could inspire learning.

Looking back, I feel that deconstructing memories with colleagues that I had known for many years, and with colleagues that I got to know better during this process, came with some peculiarities. On the one hand, I knew that I was working with people who generally respected each other's boundaries. On the other hand, I wanted to get to exactly the issues that prior conflicts had been based on: how to navigate differing approaches to research and TA practice and how this was implicitly a form of boundary work that created hegemonies or informal hierarchies? How did seniority define what TA was and could be and how could young researchers appropriate the field and make it theirs? In some sense, much seemed at stake for researchers whose work practices were collectively deconstructed by their colleagues.

Reporting on the results of the three collective deconstruction workshops was not an easy process, either. My initial question on how critical or change-oriented the results should be framed gained traction once more. I decided to specify that my report was a reconstruction of the deconstruction process. I focused on describing our discussions and drawing conclusions from our negotiations of meaning. I decided not to go as far as to dive into a deeper analysis of the power-critical layers that I had usually been aiming for.

My chapters became part of the full report on the TAN project. Long periods of COVID-19 lockdowns and home office followed the end of the project and prevented corridor conversations in which the effects of this experiment could have unfolded. Were they collective or individual and dispersed, gradually different for each person, or altogether non-existent? Therefore, what stayed with me was the question how the learnings of institutional (self-)ethnography could (be helped to) unfold in collective practices.

---

Planning and coordinating a project is substantially about managing expectations. This applies to state-of-the-art research projects and the relating epistemic expectations and it applies all the more to the hybrid kind of research our internal projects can be categorized under. Part of managing epistemic expectations is to position them in distinct research schools and methodological traditions, as done earlier here. Epistemic expectations of research-from-within pertain to positive aspects such as easier and better access, better preunderstanding, more profound analyses and the higher ability to produce 'emic' accounts that are meaningful to the field under study (Alvesson 2003; Anderson 2006; Brannick and Coghlan 2007; Trowler 2011). They pertain to potential limitations, for example, when the insider-researcher is 'too steeped in the organization's culture to adequately or objectively describe it' (Dutton et al 2006, 63, cited in Bartunek 2008, 86) or when conflicts of interest 'violate objectivity and jeopardize [the researchers'] ability to generate truth' (Bartunek 2008, 86). They result in methodological suggestions like to 'get away from frozen positions, irrespective if they are grounded in personal experiences or shared frameworks' and to 'work systematically with a notion of reflexivity, in which one tries to change the level of interpretation so that one's favored interpretations in a first instance is the target of interpretation from a meta-level position, inspired by another standpoint' (Alvesson 2003, 184, 186). The researcher should 'exercise extreme caution not to let his or her research focus fade out of awareness in the face of other pressing and enticing engagements in the field' and 'assiduously pursue other insiders' interpretations, attitudes, and feelings as well as [one's] own' (Anderson 2006, 389). This requires the researcher to specify, switch or change roles or to engage in collaborative modes of insider/outsider research (Bartunek 2008).

Our activities enabled collaboration between different kinds of insiders, like 'newcomers', 'longer-time members' and 'veterans', and drew on prevalent diversity among all participants in this respect (see Alvesson 2003). In the empirical material, self-identification or (assumed) identification by colleagues as indigenous-insider ('perceived by significant others and opinion leaders within the community as a legitimate member of the community' [Banks 1998, 72]), indigenous-outsider (who has 'experienced high levels of desocialization and cultural assimilation into an outside or oppositional culture or community' [Banks 1998, 72]) or external-outsider ('socialized within a community different from the one in which he or she is doing research', with only 'a partial understanding of and little appreciation for the values, perspectives, and knowledge of the community he or she is studying' [Banks 1998, 73]) emerged as a research theme in itself, leading to a paper on inter- and transdisciplinary identity constellations in TA (Kastenhofer and Bauer 2023). Disciplinary diversity and professional self-understanding thus proved not only an important topic *of* reflection, but also a great resource *for* reflection.

But what about all the expectations, ambitions, hopes and visions that go beyond the epistemic dimension? How to outline what kind of change our internal reflexive projects were equipped to push for? How and when to decide what kind of change they ought to push for? When and how to link up to these initial expectations? With a self-understanding as predominantly epistemic professionals, such questions did not come naturally when embarking on the projects. As TA practitioners, expectations mostly related to the kinds of output we envisioned, foremost, practical recommendations. Throughout the process, individual quests for better (professional) self-understanding also came to the fore.[5]

In contrast, much further reaching expectations are voiced in action research, transformative research, organizational learning or feminist scholarship: 'Action research aims at both taking action and creating knowledge or theory about that action' (Brannick and Coghlan 2007). For transformative scholarship, Banks (1998, 83) envisions the 'tremendous challenge but essential task' of 'helping to construct a democratic public community with an overarching set of values to which all [members] will have a commitment and with which all will identify'. Alerasoul et al (2022, 1) depict organizational learning as 'based on the individual learning of members who make up the organization', influencing 'the capacity of the

---

[5]   Anderson (2006, 390) points at autoethnography being 'particularly likely to be warranted by the quest for self-understanding'.

whole organization to stimulate learning and to generate new knowledge'. For using mind scripting with communities-of-practice, Allhutter and Hofmann (2010) refer to a team's aspiration to reflect on the normativity and political implications of their practices, which in turn shall expand an organization's capacity to strategically reconfigure processes and structures. In epistemic communities, reflecting normativities shall moreover lead to politico-theoretical transformations (Allhutter 2021).

In our two projects, we never explicitly discussed alternative or additional goals, like making ITA/TA more liveable, or positioning ourselves more clearly in regard to TA and/or other scholarly and advisory communities. In hindsight, it seems all too likely that alternative expectations, hopes and visions were present throughout the projects, even if they did not gain visibility or obtain priority. Moreover, our activities very likely linked to and resonated with change beyond our initial expectations: shifts in (self-)perception, (self-)positioning and (self-)identification; shifts in how we presented the institute to external audiences like the scientific advisory board; and, last but not least, spanning several years, our activities accompanied changes in personnel, with new colleagues joining the institute, colleagues leaving it or changing their position within the institute.

## 5. The political and psycho-social dimension of internal projects

<hr>

Vignette 2
Karen on Pol[ITA] (spring 2017, spring 2023)

My plan had originally been to co-conduct semi-structured interviews of max. 90 minutes in tandem with my colleague, asking my fellow TA colleagues about their experiences with policy advisory activities. Interviewing in tandem, with one lead interviewer and one secondary interviewer, in a field and organization I belonged to, was a situation I felt prepared for, given that I had already followed a similar approach two decades earlier when researching socialization processes in my initial field of study, biology. I remembered how it had been awkward at times, especially when my tandem interviewer (socialized in a very different academic field) had asked questions that touched on themes I had learned to treat as taboo or when she had acted in ways that I had learned to better avoid in this scientific community. And how I had learned to also see this as an interpretative resource. I remembered that it could be challenging to not presuppose what certain answers might be, to still ask even if I thought I already knew the answer or that I should actually signal to the interviewee, a former peer, that I of course knew the answer. And I felt all too familiar with

90-minute interviews. Along my experience, there were several categories of interviews: those up to 30 minutes, those between 45 and 90 minutes and those that constantly fell back into conversations, not really evolving over time. The first and the third kind I tried to avoid as I felt that they stayed rather superficial, reproducing common wisdom along pre-packaged anecdotes. The second kind was the one I preferred, promising the most intense examination of the research theme. In short, I felt that I could foresee and bear what the next 90 minutes would have in store for me when I embarked on our first session.

We had decided that my colleague would take the lead because she had been at the institute for a shorter time, had researched the topic before and might thus ask in a more open, while still more informed, manner. We were meticulous about assuring and safeguarding informed consent, confidentiality and anonymity from the very beginning. Along my recollection, what we had not really settled on was the actual length of interviews we envisioned and how fast we would finish this series of interviews. My colleague took the organization of interviews in her hands, scheduling interview after interview. All ITA members were already informed about the process and willing to contribute. At this stage, I remember worrying whether I would be able to keep up with this pace: two or even three lengthy interviews per week!

The first interview was to serve as a calibration interview, but also as a sensitizing exercise for the both of us: my colleague would start with interviewing me and we would afterwards reflect on the double experience and adapt our strategy and interview guidelines accordingly. Afterwards, one interview followed the next with practically no room for further reflection and exchange in between. And then, there was the mere length of the interviews! I had expected 60 to 90 minutes, while the actual interviews lasted up to three hours. As secondary interviewer I could render the interviews only longer by adding further questions at distinct points in the interview.

I remember very vividly when in the midst of the interview series the thought (or feeling) crossed my mind that until then I had always wanted to know more, understand better, but that then, with all these many pieces adding up to pictures that I found partly enchanting but partly also rather frustrating or frightening, I knew more than enough, saw more than I wished for, while my options of leaving this picture, or the scenery it represented, seemed limited. It was, after all, a research-from-within endeavour. I started reconsidering my plan to take part in as many interviews as possible and to select which ones I would take part in and which ones I would skip. Was it possible to know too much as an STS researcher, even about very mundane academic working contexts? We had put much effort into safeguarding our interviewees and their well-being and agency. But maybe I had overestimated my own ability to cope with the process and the answers it brought to the fore to questions unasked.

Literature on autoethnography and research from within points at several epistemological but also psycho-social challenges that relate to the power dimension and hegemonies at play in such projects. Trowler (2011, 2) points at a specific form of interview bias that comes with stronger social ties between interviewer and interviewee, as 'respondents who know you may have pre-formed expectations of your alignments and preferences in ways which change their responses'. Other scholars hint at individual (career) as well as institutional (reputational) risks. Brannick and Coghlan (2007, 70) point at potential role conflicts resulting from the insider researchers' need to 'sustain a full organizational membership role' while researching this same organization, 'find[ing] themselves caught between loyalty tugs, behavioural claims, and identification dilemmas' (see also Bartunek 2008, 86). Alvesson (2003, 181) highlights 'the problem of ... omitting some "dark" or "tabooed" aspects of the home culture' and 'the want to avoid upsetting colleagues' (that comes with social ties and local dependencies), a matter likely to be more pressing and stressful for the newcomer (or 'the outsider within'). She also draws our attention to 'the potential opposite problem of motivation coming from negative feelings and an urge to get "even"' (Alvesson 2003, 181).

Brannick and Coghlan (2007, 71) conclude that '[f]or insider action researchers, politics is more explicit, and so they need to be prepared to work the political system, which involves balancing the organization's formal justification of what it wants in the project with their own tacit personal justification for political activity'. Alvesson (2003, 191) approaches the political dimension of research from within academia from yet another angle when stressing the importance of 'relatively prestigious groups such as professionals [also] get[ting] their share of in-depth exposure' and of ethnographic researchers 'address[ing] not only the organizations and works of groups of people [e.g., natural scientists] that we [social scientists], in some sense or another, are competing with, but also ourselves'. Yet another political angle is addressed by Banks (1998). This author reminds us of heated discussions in the 1960s and 1970s of questions such as 'Who should speak for whom? Whose voice is legitimate? Who speaks with moral authority and legitimacy?' (see Collins 1986).

All these issues and considerations played also a role in our own projects. We sought to diversify the group of principal insider researchers, for example, combining a practitioner who had spent a longer period of time at ITA with one who had joined only shortly before the start of the project and had researched TA already from the outside. Most of the interviews were thus conducted in tandem and results were developed jointly. With ITA's multidisciplinary scientific personnel and interdisciplinary culture, the project teams were also quite diverse in this account and potential interdisciplinary differences and hegemonies were a topic we discussed.

Moreover, we established internal feedback rounds when preparing publications, including the director (with a view to consider the institute's vital interests), senior colleagues (with a view to capture their experiences) as well as the most junior cohort of colleagues (with a view to safeguard the interests of those who were probably most vulnerable) and put intergenerational, interdisciplinary, gendered and intersectional differences concerning perspectives, vulnerabilities and ambitions up for discussion (see Kastenhofer and Bauer 2023). Our projects had a broad reflexive scope due to the disciplinary richness of ITA, but with the relative cultural homogeneity of ITA staff (the vast majority of members at this time coming from European countries and universities), we were not able to establish diversity in this respect. We also had to acknowledge that research-from-within could not make existing power asymmetries (foremost intergenerational inequities, linked to different employment situations) and relating vulnerabilities disappear.

This links closely to yet another aspect of our research-from-within: the detailed investigations into our own institute inevitably brought situations and mechanisms to the fore that were sometimes hard to bear and bore on different members with different weight and consequences. 'Doing self-ethnography', Alvesson (2003, 183) wisely reminds us, 'is difficult and I don't think this a method for everybody to use, at least not at any time in one's life and career'. Our experiences support this appraisal. We additionally suggest that the individual and collective burden possibly correlates directly with the room to manoeuvre such projects are afforded with (thereby connecting this issue closely to the management of expectations and the organizational options at hand): can burdensome circumstances (that will come up in any institutional context, albeit with different force and of different quality) be addressed not only analytically but also be acted upon? What room is there for constructive discussions, alternative becomings and organizational change? The earlier this question is raised during the project's life cycle (from initial project design to compilation of project results and formal ending of the activity) and the more resulting answers are tied to the management of expectations regarding the project (section 4), the less (unforeseen) conflict is likely to arise on the individual as well as the collective level.

## 6. Contracting, being on board, authorship and auctorial voice in research-with-within

---

Vignette 3
Doris on TAN (spring 2019, spring 2024)

The first step in starting the mind-scripting process was to present the method and what it can do. From previous experiences I knew that people were sort of unfamiliar with the idea of having their stories deconstructed, of looking at their own memories from an observer position and trusting in a collective process that would try and question the narratives of each and everyone, not to criticize their viewpoints but to learn to see our shared sense-making. Moderating such a process while being part of the same constellation and its dynamics presented a unique opportunity, but was also challenging. While nobody questioned (or maybe nobody even assumed) that my position in this process was that of a neutral outsider, I felt that sometimes it was hard for my colleagues to acknowledge that the method did not focus on the individual even though we worked with individual memories. Some reacted in a defensive way, questioning the method and voicing concern about what the outcome of such a process could be. Years later, this concern seems more understandable to me. It was after all me alone who had ultimately been in charge of writing up the results of our collective process. And although I had sent my report to all participants to countercheck the adequate representation of their TA practices, our projected reflexive process didn't make any room for further negotiating the practice of collective reflexivity itself.

---

Internal projects can be awkward as they run counter to the standard project situations we are used to and learned to cope with. External review of the initial project plan has to be organized to secure quality (in our case, we had the opportunity to present our plans and, later, our results to the institute's scientific advisory board), contracting can be fuzzy (directorates and the collective will have to take and define this role), on-boarding and staying on board is multilayered, multi-phased and possibly more flexible than in standard projects.

Fuzziness, multiplicity, flexibility and openness can be productive forces in internal reflexive projects in our experience. But they can also trigger confusion and misrepresentation. Literature on research-from-within especially addresses issues with authorship and auctorial voice. If all collaborate, albeit in different roles at different times, if all contribute to the empirical data and their interpretation, if collective interpretation itself turns into an empirical method and a method to facilitate change, who should be the authors or owners of the results? How is authorship to be defined and what constitutes 'results' (see section 7 for the distinction between out-come and in-come)? How is quality defined? What does internal validation look like and who has a say in it? interpretation (see section 5 on feedback loops)? How is a project team defined in an internal reflexive project? When and how does team membership start, when and how does it end?

Many of these issues we did not discuss throughout our two projects in too much detail or even not at all. We did touch on what kinds of outputs the projects should deliver and who the primary and secondary addressees were. We hardly discussed how to deal with authorship and auctorial voices (for this debate, see, for instance, Murris et al 2022). The method of mind scripting 'conceives of human beings in collective and cooperative terms' (Allhutter 2012, 689) and the analytical process itself is collective. This collectivity renders the method especially beneficial for researching and reflecting on the implicit normativities of shared work practices. In our two projects, however, authorship and auctorial voice were organized around projected time and division of labour.

Experimenting with our own writing approach in this chapter, we decided to integrate different types of text that speak to each other and invite the reader to join into a multilogue of experiences, concepts and approaches. But, yet again, we are confronted with a further challenge: formally, both projects have ended, the project teams dissolved. Who can be authors, now? How do we deal with the various kinds of repurposing collective reflexive processes are prone (and, actually, expected) to trigger? While projects end, individual and collective processes of reflection do not. Are we allowed to repurpose empirical material as the questions with which we address this material change? Who are the authors then? These questions lead us to the next, and last, theme we want to put up for discussion.

## 7. Temporalities of internal reflexivity: ensuring lasting contributions to liveable worlds

Ensuring scientific impact traditionally comes with a publication strategy: planning the epistemic set-up, producing new insights and getting the results of a project 'out there' into the relevant scientific communities via their central publication outlets. Our projects were no exception in these respects. But what about the other, more-than-epistemic expectations that had triggered our internal projects, like the professionalization of our own advisory practices at ITA and the professional handling of the normative implications of TA? As to this layer of internal organizational learning (constituting rather an in-come, than an out-come), three interdependent aspects proved especially relevant: the definition of what counted as worthwhile outcomes; the collectivization of outcomes among staff members that had figured also as (more or less) active participants in the two projects; and the collectivization of outcomes among colleagues who joined the institute after the projects had formally ended and, thus, among further generations of TA practitioners at ITA.

With our variant of research-from-within that was as much a research-with-within and a research-for-within, the more-than-epistemic process was sustained by multiple persons in varying roles during different phases and its effects (out-comes and in-comes) were part of ongoing individual as well as collective processes of professional being and belonging, performing and becoming (see Vignette 4). Not all participants were at all times part of every effect to the same degree; they would not necessarily support all interpretations to the same extent or agree on their scale of relevance. Moreover, personnel at ITA changed with time while the internal, reflexive projects formally ended as all projected activities are supposed to do. Some staff members who had been part of the joint projects left, while new colleagues joined the institute who lacked this participation. During discussions, every now and then, one or the other theme would come up that touched on the thematic scope of the two projects. 'Us', who had been part of the two projects, would realize this and could connect the discussion to our own memories or look into the relevant documents. But how could we bridge the gap between 'us' and 'them', how should we present these experiences and insights to new colleagues? Should we make them 'read up' on our results? Or should we keep the central discussions going forever, translating the two reflexive projects into two streams of constant internal reflection?

---

## Vignette 4
### Karen on the ITA triangle (around 2010, spring 2017, spring 2024)

It must have happened during a recess early on during my membership with ITA, that is, some ten or 15 years ago. All of us discussed the primary orientations and tasks of TA at ITA, probably as part of an exercise to prepare for the next mid-term research programme. These primary orientations and tasks, as much was clear, were multiple, that is, not only epistemic. The model that was presented to depict ITA's specific set-up was painted on a flipchart: it was a triangle connecting the three poles of 'Wissenschaft' (science), 'Gesellschaft' (society) and 'Politik' (German for both 'policy' and 'polity'). I still remember this triangle vividly and it still holds definitional status in my imagination of TA.

The triangle was not meant to be the only graphic depiction of TA. Polygons followed, replacing the triangle, as did other creative illustrations. But the triangle, for me, kept being the most convincing and the most attractive characterization.

During the series of interviews that were part of Pol[ITA], when we asked interviewees about their definitions of TA, I mentioned this triangle to several interviewees who had been around as long or longer than me. To my surprise, not all of them could remember it. Was I mistaken, did the triangle never happen? Or did it not resonate with others to the same extent as it did with me?

Just a few days ago, the triangle resurfaced again in a conversation with two colleagues. It did happen, after all, and others did remember! But what about those who hadn't participated in the same recess more than a decade ago?

Should we present them with the triangle? Why would we, now? Would we be open to alternative visions of and for TA?

---

(Collective) memory is not a simple archive of what has actually happened. Remembering is a dynamic relation and a relational dynamic – and, in this spirit, a rich analytical resource for collective memory work and mind scripting. Memories are constantly reworked in our everyday actions and are therefore context sensitive, fragmented and contradictory (Allhutter 2021, 432). The temporality of (collective) memories itself is entangled with values and norms in our practices. As Barad (2007, 393) suggests, remembering is embodied historicity deeply rooted in our (collective) becoming. That means, what is remembered at a certain moment in time and forgotten another time establishes the grounds for what collective practice has as a common reference point and who is included in or excluded from this collectivity.

## 8. Conclusions: looking back ahead

Looking back at the two internal reflexive projects from some (temporal) distance, reliving and rethinking this research-from-within, we have no final answers to all the questions we raised. However, our 'critical-dialogical engagement' (Jandrić et al 2023, np) scrutinizes some of the expectations, challenges, shortcomings and results that the overall process came with for individuals and collective(s) at ITA.

Throughout the two projects, different meanings of and expectations for the reflexive processes had to be balanced: reflexivity as a means to open up debates and showcase diversity on the one hand and reflexivity as a means to find closure by informing best practice guidelines on the other hand; reflexivity as a critical self-examination aiming for more just relations and liveable professional worlds on the one hand and reflexivity as a means for professionalization, aiming for stabilizing the organization rather than questioning it on the other hand. These different meanings and expectations were not necessarily at odds; still, an understanding of TA, of the institute, its collectives and its environments that would make room for both would have to be actively sought first. This requirement clearly transcended the scope and capacity of both projects from within ITA, with our institute being one element in a much larger organization and academic landscape. It did inform and motivate further-reaching engagements in these larger, science policy contexts, though, that transcended and outlived the two projects.

The second theme that we have addressed here and that we keep pondering is the question of how to secure the outcomes from the two reflexive projects from-within, with-within and for-within: just as the outcomes of the two processes transcended the initial expectations regarding the two projects by far for those who were directly involved, it also proved challenging to convey the outcomes to new staff members who had not yet taken part in the two projects. Other than with state-of-the-art research projects, active engagement in the process seemed just as important as taking account of the written outcomes. The reflexive projects' afterlife took on a twofold character: the results published in peer-reviewed journal papers on the one hand, and the stories remembered and told among ITA members at various occasions on the other hand. The temporality of the two reflexive projects thus was rather peculiar: for those who had joined the institute after Pol[ITA] and TAN had formally ended, they had somewhat never started, for the others, they have probably never ended. But it also seems that reflexivity, broadly speaking, will never end at the institute, as a next collective critical discussion is underway; this time regarding the use of generative artificial intelligence in TA practice. Reflexivity hinges, after all, on a collective project and process in the short run, but also on individual attitudes and institutional capacities in the long run.

## References


Acker, S. (2000) In/out/side: Positioning the Researcher in Feminist Qualitative Research. *Resources for Feminist Research* 28(3/4): 153–172.

Alerasoul, S.A., Afeltra, G., Hakala, H., Minelli, E. and Strozzi, F. (2022) Organisational Learning, Learning Organisation, and Learning Orientation: An Integrative Review and Framework. *Human Resource Management Review* 32(3): 100854.

Allhutter, D. (2012) Mind Scripting: A Method for Deconstructive Design. *Science, Technology & Human Values* 37(6): 684–707.

Allhutter, D. (2021) Memory Traces in Society-Technology Relations: How to Produce Cracks in Infrastructural Power. In R. Hamm (ed) *Reader Collective Memory-Work*. Sligo: BeltraBooks, pp 155–181.

Allhutter, D. and Hofmann, R. (2010) Deconstructive Design as an Approach for Opening Trading Zones. In J. Vallverdú (ed) *Thinking Machines and the Philosophy of Computer Science: Concepts and Principles*. Hershey: IGI Global, pp 175–192.

Allhutter, D., Bargetz, B., Brøgger, K., Cielemęcka, O., González Ramos, A., Meißner, H., et al (2024) The Politics of Feminist New Materialisms: Insights from Experimenting with Academic Practices. In F. Colman and I. van der Tuin (eds) *Methods and Genealogies of New Materialisms*. Edinburgh: Edinburgh University Press, pp 384–406.

Alvesson, M. (2003) Methodology for Close Up Studies: Struggling with Closeness and Closure. *Higher Education* 46: 167–193.

Anderson, L. (2006) Analytic Autoethnography. *Journal of Contemporary Ethnography* 35(4): 373–395.

Banks, J.A. (1998) The Lives and Values of Researchers: Implications for Educating Citizens in a Multicultural Society. *Educational Researcher* 27(7): 4–17.

Barad, K. (2007) *Meeting the Universe Halfway: Quantum Physics and the Entanglement of Matter and Meaning*. Durham, NC and London: Duke University Press.

Bartunek, J.M. (2008) Insider/Outsider Team Research. In A.B. Shani, N. Adler, S.A. Mohrman, W.A. Pasmore and B. Stymne (eds) *Handbook of Collaborative Management Research*. Thousand Oaks: SAGE, pp 73–91.

Brannick, T. and Coghlan, D. (2007) In Defense of Being 'Native': The Case for Insider Academic Research. *Organizational Research Methods* 10(1): 59–74.

Coghlan, D. and Brannick, T. (2005) *Doing Action Research in Your Own Organization*, 2nd edn. London: SAGE.

Collins, P.H. (1986) Learning from the Outsider Within: The Sociological Significance of Black Feminist Thought. *Social Problems* 33(6): 14–32.

Delamont, S. (2009) The Only Honest Thing: Autoethnography, Reflexivity and Small Crises in Fieldwork. *Ethnography and Education* 4(1): 51–63.

Dutton, J.E., Worline, M.C., Frost, P.J. and Lilius, J. (2006) Explaining Compassion Organizing. *Administrative Science Quaterly* 51(1): 59–96.

Fujiwara, L.H. (2020) Racial Harm in a Predominantly White 'Liberal' University: An Institutional Autoethnography of White Fragility. In Y.F. Niemann, G. Gutiérrz y Muhs and C.G. González (eds) *Presumed Incompetent II: Race, Class, Power, and Resistance of Women in Academia*. Logan: Utah State University Press, pp 101–116.

Hess, D.J. (2001) Ethnography and the Development of Science and Technology Studies. In P. Atkinson, P.A. Coffey, S. Delamont, J. Lofland and L. Lofland (eds) *Handbook of Ethnography*. Thousand Oaks: SAGE, pp 234–245.

Jandrić, P., Luke, T.W., Sturm, S., McLaren, P., Jackson, L., MacKenzie, A., et al (2023) Collective Writing: The Continuous Struggle for Meaning-Making. *Postdigital Science and Education* 5: 851–893.

Jubas, K. and Seidel, J. (2016) Knitting as Metaphor for Work: An Institutional Autoethnography to Surface Tensions of Visibility and Invisibility in the Neoliberal Academy. *Journal of Contemporary Ethnography* 45(1): 60–84.

Kastenhofer, K. (2004) Reflexion und Reflexivität in der Biologie. In M. Arnold and G. Dressel (eds) *Wissenschaftskulturen - Experimentalkulturen – Gelehrtenkulturen*. Wien: Turia + Kant, pp 137–149.

Kastenhofer, K. and Bauer, A. (2023) 'Are You a TA Practitioner, Then?': Identity Constructions in Post-Normal Science. *Minerva* 61(1): 93–115.

Knuuttila, T. (2002) Signing for Reflexivity: Constructionist Rhetorics and Its Reflexive Critique in Science and Technology Studies. *Forum Qualitative Sozialforschung / Forum: Qualitative Social Research* 3(3): 15.

Lynch, M. (2000) Against Reflexivity as an Academic Virtue and Source of Privileged Knowledge. *Theory Culture Society* 17(3): 26–54.

Maruyama, M. (1978) Endogenous Research and Polyocular Anthropology. In R.E. Holloman and S.A. Arutiunov (eds) *Perspectives on Ethnicity*. Mouton: De Gruyter, pp 79–126.

Merton, R.K. (1972) Insiders and Outsiders: A Chapter in the Sociology of Knowledge. *American Journal of Sociology* 78(1): 9–47.

Murris, K., Taylor, C.A., Kuby, C.R., Fullagar, S., Malone, K., Zhao, W., et al (2022) Writing Together-Apart: Introduction to the Glossary. In K. Murris (ed) *A Glossary for Doing Postqualitative, New Materialist and Critical Posthumanist Research Across Discipline*. Abingdon, Oxon and New York: Routledge, pp xix–xxvii.

Sikes, P. and Potts, A. (2008) *Researching Education From the Inside: Investigations From Within*. London and New York: Routledge.

Smith, D.E. (2005) *Institutional Ethnography: A Sociology for People*. Lanham: AltaMira Press.

Trowler, P.R. (2011) Researching Your Own Institution. *British Educational Research Association (BERA) On-line Resource*. Available at: https://www.bera.ac.uk/publication/researching-your-own-institution-higher-educat ion [Accessed 25 June 2024].

# 21

# Reflexivity in Co-Evaluation: From Challenges to Principles of Participatory Research Evaluation

*Katja Mayer*

Research evaluation is a systematic process used to measure the quality, relevance and impact of research activities across various levels from scientific to socioeconomic or environmental impacts, employing both quantitative and qualitative methods. Evaluation procedures have become more important with the increase of the promotion of transparency and public accountability in public services in general. Formative research evaluation, conducted during the research process, seeks to improve the methodology and execution of ongoing research through iterative feedback. Conversely, summative evaluation occurs post-research and focuses on assessing the project's outcomes or impacts, often informing decisions about broader dissemination of findings or future resource allocation. Both evaluations together should provide a comprehensive assessment of research processes and results (Gibbons and Georghiou 1987).

My exposure to formal research evaluation remained limited until we wrote the proposal for the research project CoAct (Codesigning Citizen Social Science for Collective Action, 2020–2022, Horizon Europe). Citizen Social Science is a collaborative research approach, where non-scientists actively participate in the scientific process, contributing to data collection, analysis, dissemination and translation to address social issues and initiate social change (Albert et al 2021). As we were planning the project design, I was struck by the conspicuous absence of literature on specific evaluation approaches suited for participatory research projects, not only within the realm of Citizen Science but also in participatory action research more generally. While evaluating research performance and impact has become so essential for research funders and administrators to ensure effective resource allocation, and also for the scientists to demonstrate the quality and effectiveness of their research, the research participants typically had no stake in the evaluation process aside from ex-post assessment survey participation.

Our project was designed to be highly participatory across all phases of the research cycle. The team was thus compelled to challenge this apparent exclusion of participation from the realm of evaluation, making it imperative to involve a multiplicity of voices in the evaluation process and to empower them in shaping the evaluation methodology itself. We were and still are convinced that evaluation can be so much more: it can be designed to provide concrete places and times in a research project where participation and inclusion are not only enacted but also put to the test and be reflected, where future visions of research, innovations and social change can be negotiated within the scope of the research topic. In our case, participation in the making and 're-making' (Chilvers and Kearnes 2016) involved various stages, from aligning different imaginaries of participation to structuring collaboration in contextually sensitive ways. Understanding participation 'in the making' shifted the focus to the situative arrangements necessary and required us to engage in 'tinkering' (Mol et al 2010), as we organized reflexivity along co-created research paths. This approach emphasizes a flexible, adaptive process of continuous adjustments and improvisations, tailored to the specific needs and contexts of our research environment. By integrating participation in the design and implementation of the evaluation process, we wanted to encourage critical self-examination and responsiveness, ensuring that all research practices remained ethically attuned and empathetic to all stakeholders involved. Even though we were not able to fully embrace the participatory opportunities in evaluation – due to the many constraints that came with the COVID-19 pandemic – this framing of co-evaluation as a tinkering process became a dynamic and collaborative learning experience, fostering a space where collective insights and mutual growth were prioritized.

## Developing a participatory approach to research evaluation

In general, co-creation processes require careful coordination and expectation management as well as attention to community building processes. In other words, they require 'some a priori conceptualization of which internal and external people need to work together, what they want to do together, and what value they will create as a new community' (Gouillart 2012, 11). In the process, it is imperative to orchestrate different normative systems in a manner that ensures an equitable distribution of benefits among all participants. Evaluation procedures of such participatory processes therefore must consider not only the expectations towards the results and benefits, but also the expectations towards the ways knowledge is produced – towards the epistemologies of participation. We thus tried to move evaluation away from its traditional image as an inevitable burden at the end of a research process and to embrace it as a fully-fledged element of the participatory research process in the tradition of feminist epistemology and participatory action research (Crupi and Godden 2023).

The evaluation process we consequently set up became an exercise in organizing collective reflexivity during a pandemic with severely limited face to face contact and necessitated a lot of improvisation. Our aim was to create a co-evaluation approach that not only complements rigid quantitative performance metrics (Key Performance Indicators [KPIs]) but also focuses on the inclusive and three-dimensional representation of participants. Such assessments would actively involve all engaged actors (or their representatives) in the scientific process as competent co-evaluators, negotiating how project developments could be measured against different interests and jointly defining what (proof of) success might look like. We understood early on that this could not be achieved by a summative, ex-post evaluation structure. Instead, we had to start to collaborate on the evaluation from the beginning of the project and utilize it as a formative feedback cycle to reflect not only on the project goals, but also on the modes of participatory knowledge production – that is, how we (want to) collaborate to create new knowledge.

As you can imagine, this operationalization of the 'reflective practice' of co-evaluation requires continuous adjustments in how we organize and implement the different forms of knowledge production that make up a research process. In this context, co-evaluation should help to improve not only the reflexivity but also the social robustness of the process and the knowledge it produces. We therefore employed a diverse toolbox, consisting of methods such as surveys, discussion formats, group reflection sessions, feedback exercises and workshops, which in most cases had to be held virtually due to global lockdown regulations. The tools were chosen in a responsive manner and tailored to the respective case studies (Kieslinger et al 2022a; Mayer et al 2022).

## Challenges of co-evaluation

Co-evaluation is an iterative participatory evaluation process that engages all relevant actors in a scientific research project. It involves collaboratively discussing, documenting and revisiting project goals, objectives, understandings of success and impacts throughout the project's life cycle and beyond, ensuring transparency and inclusivity in assessment practices.

Overall, we faced three considerable challenges in realizing our co-evaluation approach:

1. adapting to the virtual situation imposed by the COVID-19 pandemic;
2. balancing the benefit of engaging participants in the evaluation with the added burden of deeper engagement; and
3. constructively handling the blurring boundaries between the research and its evaluation.

The shift to online interactions impeded the implementation of shared hands-on research activities, and in turn encumbered the development of trustful relationships between the different involved actors. It also exacerbated existing challenges such as time constraints and maintaining motivation among participants who volunteered their limited time to the project. Additionally, the pandemic constraints meant that we could never fully include all stakeholders in the manner we initially envisioned. As such, any activity to collaboratively implement needed to be chosen with care. Our tailored toolbox allowed for iterative adjustments and measures responsive to the specificities of each situation. However, despite these efforts, the virtual environment complicated our ability to build trustful relationships, and privacy concerns limited data sharing, making it difficult to conduct follow-up activities effectively. We found that multiple pre- and post-evaluation meetings were necessary, and we had not anticipated how language barriers required strong collaboration and continuous adaptation between core research teams and the evaluation team.

In addition, the dominance of social issues over scientific goals inherent to Citizen Social Science made it difficult to assess scientific objectives collectively with participants, especially when we had to meet predefined criteria set by research funders. For instance, the metrics of scientific publications or citations failed to align with the success criteria of non-scientist participants who prioritized the extent to which their voices were heard and whether their participation in Citizen Science led to meaningful social transformation. Consequently, most participants showed little interest in co-authoring scientific papers; while the scientific community could certainly be helpful in addressing their issues, they are not the primary audience to initiate effective social change. So, we grappled with the need to integrate both scientific and social evaluation criteria, often questioning

**Figure 21.1:** Collage illustrating the tinkering process in the development of the principles for co-evaluation (2024)

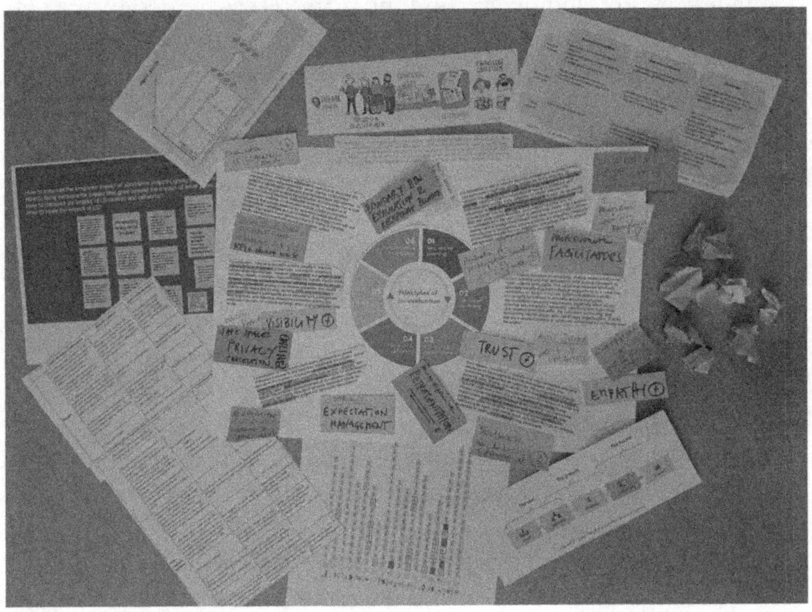

whether it was necessary or beneficial to combine these disparate aims. In the end, we decided that sometimes it is better to separate these evaluation activities completely. Additionally, we realized the critical importance of being supported by professional facilitators and moderators. We also found it too difficult, if not futile, to co-create a tailor-made representation model useful for all co-evaluators across the whole project. Instead, we co-developed more individualized approaches addressing the unique needs of each case study, while still trying to achieve some comparability. In part, this was also due to the problem of creating a sense of 'community' online when face to face meetings were not possible.

## Our guidelines for the design of co-evaluation

While co-evaluation aims to enrich evaluation criteria and foster social change, it demands a lot of commitment besides flexible project management and robust planning. Our resources were limited, and the flexible, iterative nature of co-evaluation required more engagement than we initially anticipated. The sticky notes in Figure 21.1 illustrate some of the challenges we encountered while implementing co-evaluation. They are placed across a set of principles that we have developed in a collective learning process together with our project partners and an external consultation process (Kieslinger et al 2022b), based on our definition of co-evaluation.

These principles align with the values of Citizen Social Science and participatory social science, such as inclusiveness, collective benefit and horizontality, equity, and quality and integrity. They are designed to guide the design and implementation of co-evaluation processes. By adhering to these principles, we aimed to create evaluation frameworks that empower all participants, enhance the robustness of knowledge production, and foster meaningful engagement throughout the research process.

In summary, the principles are as follows:

- *Responsible planning*: Engage participants early in co-evaluation, ideally during research question negotiation and methodological design, to respect their time and align with project activities.
- *Participant ownership*: Carefully shift evaluation responsibilities to participants, fostering a collective perspective on project outcomes and supporting co-evaluation advocates within the community.
- *Inclusivity and responsiveness*: Ensure all voices are heard through empathetic, open and flexible co-evaluation activities, promoting non-hierarchical relationships and using skilled facilitation.
- *Flexibility and reflexivity*: Adapt evaluation instruments and outcomes to the project's context, establishing regular reflexive milestones to assess the appropriateness of objectives, methods and timing.
- *Openness and transparency*: Implement transparent co-evaluation processes, balancing data privacy with the need for open science practices and educating participants on data management best practices.
- *Transformative perspective*: Use participatory methods to co-create and document project achievements for social change, engaging civil society organizations and decision-makers early to influence sociopolitical uptake.

These principles – although they emerged rather late in the process – enabled us to systematically identify existing and prospective challenges and risks, while exploring the potential solutions they required. By critically examining our practices through these principles, we were able to pinpoint some specific areas of difficulty and develop targeted strategies to address them, ultimately enhancing the effectiveness and inclusivity of our co-evaluation efforts.

Reflecting on the overall research and evaluation process, we were successful in building trust, and with it also inclusive and empathetic relationships with and among co-researchers. We also enhanced the political visibility of social issues by leveraging the entire participatory research process and focusing it from the beginning in a collaborative way on the transformation of scientific results into political action. To a large extent the project was able to initiate processes of social change and engagement beyond the project's end and gave involved communities new modes of knowledge production and dissemination, but also some tools to critically monitor and reflect on their activities (Kieslinger et al 2022a; Mayer and Schürz 2022).

Co-evaluation has a lot of strengths and benefits, and our field of Citizen (Social) Science would do well to leverage this approach on a broader basis. At the same time, it is important to weigh up the multitude of processes we ask our participants to collaborate on and be mindful of how much time and energy they can and want to invest. So we need to negotiate very carefully on the concrete formats and the breadth and depth of our collaboration. While formative co-evaluation is an important part of this negotiation process, summative co-evaluation is more involved and needs to be approached with additional care. Here, our basic principles of 'responsible planning', 'responsiveness and flexibility', and 'reflexivity' really loom large. (Stefanie Schürz in a personal conversation)

Despite the significant challenges involved and efforts required, co-evaluation as a methodology highlights the benefits of engaging non-scientists in research for social change. Through it, evaluation criteria are enriched, making them much more robust towards both scientific and social objectives, and genuinely participatory processes are fostered. If implemented carefully, co-evaluation supports the valuation of all stakeholders' contributions, and in turn promotes trust, adaptability and inclusivity, which are essential to achieve meaningful and impactful research outcomes. By embracing participation in evaluation, we honour the collaborative spirit that is necessary to drive social change and contribute to creating liveable futures that participatory research aims to achieve.

## Materials in the collage

- SDG table taken from Fraisl, D., Campbell, J., See, L., Wehn, U., Wardlaw, J., Gold, M., et al (2020) Mapping Citizen Science Contributions to the UN Sustainable Development Goals. *Sustainability Science* 15. Available at: https://doi.org/10.1007/s11625-020-00833-7
- Virtual sticky notes: Schuerz, S. (2022) Citizen Science for Social Transformation: Measuring the Impact of Citizen Science Initiatives. Available at: https://eu-citizen.science/blog/2023/06/01/citizen-science-social-transformation-measuring-impact-citizen-science-initiatives/
- Principles diagram: Kieslinger, B., Mayer, K., Schaefer, T. and Schuerz, S. (2022) *Whitepaper on Co-evaluation of Citizen Social Science*. Zenodo. Available at: https://doi.org/10.5281/zenodo.7139025

- Impact House co-evaluation methodology: Schuerz, S. and Mayer, K. (2022) *Citizen Social Science Impact House for Co-Evaluation*. Zenodo. Available at: https://doi.org/10.5281/zenodo.7457933
- List of achieved Key Performance Indicators in CoAct: Kieslinger, B., Schuerz, S., Mayer, K. and Schaefer, T. (2022) *CoAct D7.4 Final Impact Assessment Report: Evaluation Results, Overall Impact Assessment and Final Reflections on Co-Evaluation*. Zenodo. Available at: https://doi.org/10.5281/zenodo.7468546

## Funding statement

This research was supported by funding from: European Commission: Horizon Europe CoAct – Co-designing Citizen Social Science for Collective Action (Grant No. 873048); Austrian Science Fund (FWF) Elise Richter Fellowship (Project No. V699-G29).

## Acknowledgements

I would like to express my gratitude to Sarah Davies and Stefanie Schürz for their valuable comments and for reviewing this chapter. I also extend my thanks to Barbara Kieslinger, Teresa Schäfer and the entire CoAct community.

## References

Albert, A., Balázs, B., Butkevičienė, E., Mayer, K. and Perelló, J. (2021) Citizen Social Science: New and Established Approaches to Participation in Social Research. In K. Vohland, A. Land-Zandstra, L. Ceccaroni, R. Lemmens, J. Perelló, M. Ponti, et al (eds) *The Science of Citizen Science*. Cham, Switzerland: Springer International Publishing, pp 119–138. https://doi.org/10.1007/978-3-030-58278-4_7

Chilvers, J. and Kearnes, M. (2016) Participation in the Making. In *Remaking Participation: Science, Environment and Emergent Publics*. London: Routledge, pp 31–63.

Crupi, K. and Godden, N.J. (2023) Feminist Evaluation Using Feminist Participatory Action Research: Guiding Principles and Practices. *American Journal of Evaluation*. https://doi.org/10.1177/10982140221148433

Gibbons, M. and Georghiou, L. (1987) Evaluation of Research: A Selection of Current Practices. In Organization for Economic Co-operation and Development (OECD) (ed) *OECD Report*. Titel.

Gouillart, F. (2012) Co-Creation: The Real Social-Media Revolution. In S. Jackson and A. O'Connell (eds) *Putting Social Media to Work*. Harvard Business Publishing. https://www.sas.com/content/dam/SAS/bp_de/doc/studie/imm-st-harvard-business-putting-social-media-to-work-2273597.pdf

Kieslinger, B., Schürz, S., Mayer, K. and Schaefer, T. (2022a) Participatory Evaluation Practices in Citizen Social Science: Insights from Three Case Studies. *Fteval Journal for Research and Technology Policy Evaluation* 54: 10–19. https://doi.org/10.22163/fteval.2022.567

Kieslinger, B., Mayer, K., Schaefer, T. and Schürz, S. (2022b) *Whitepaper on Co-Evaluation of Citizen Social Science*. https://doi.org/10.5281/ZEN ODO.7139025

Kieslinger, B., Schürz, S., Mayer, K. and Schaefer, T. (2022) *CoAct D7.4 Final Impact Assessment Report: Evaluation Results, Overall Impact Assessment and Final Reflections on Co-Evaluation*. Centre for Social Innovation, Vienna: Zenodo. https://doi.org/10.5281/ZENODO.7468546

Mayer, K., Schürz, S., Kieslinger, B. and Schäfer, T. (2022) Transformation Messen und Verstehen: Partizipative Evaluationsansätze für Citizen Science. In J. Howaldt, M. Kreibich, J. Streicher and C. Thiem (eds) *Zukunft Gestalten mit Sozialen Innovationen: Neue Herausforderungen für Politik, Gesellschaft und Wirtschaft*. Frankfurt: Campus Verlag. https://doi.org/ 10.12907/9783593451268

Mayer, K. and Schürz, S. (2022) *Policy Report: Opportunities and Challenges of Citizen Social Science*. Centre for Social Innovation, Vienna: Zenodo. https://doi.org/10.5281/ZENODO.7466620

Mol, A., Moser, I. and Pols, J. (eds) (2010) *Care in Practice: On Tinkering in Clinics, Homes and Farms*. Bielefeld: transcript Verlag.

Project CoAct (2022) Available at: https://coactproject.eu/ [Accessed 1 May 2025].

# 22

# Reflexivity, Avoid it Like the Plague?

*Annie Y. Patrick*

What is reflexivity, and what does it mean within the collection of tools we refer to as reflexive methodologies? Numerous scholars have provided well-detailed accounts outlining the various beliefs and applications of reflexivity within Science and Technology Studies (STS) (Ashmore 1989; Bourdieu and Wacquant 1992; Lynch 2000). For some scholars, reflexivity is a powerful tool that can be used to support each other, foster solidarity and increase the reach of our work (Bourdieu and Wacquant 1992). Yet, for some scholars, reflexivity has no use in our field. Instead, it is a disruptive menace to our work and scholars should 'avoid it like the plague' (Fuller 1988, 188). I would contend that comparing reflexivity to a plague is somewhat of a stretch. For STS scholars, whose work centres on understanding and exploring the realms of knowledge and its production, reflexivity is an inherent standard of our scholarly work. Yet, it is also a personal standard that calls for and reminds scholars of a critical self-reflective awareness and honesty of themselves as a scholar and a person (Bourdieu and Wacquant 1992; Pels 2000).

Early in my career, I drew from sociology and STS, and took these thoughts about reflexivity as a given and followed these broad frameworks instructing me to be a part of the research, share my experiences with my readers, be compassionate to my subjects and develop my situatedness (Rose 1997; Cutcliffe 2003; Pillow 2003; Berger 2015). I did this with the belief that my work would be stronger and more rigorous, less biased, and would protect my research participants. In my traditional, normative role of researcher-scholar, I discussed this as my positionality, limitations and situated role within the work. In other words, I described the research process in relation to the power, authority and expertise associated with my titles (researcher, post-doc, and so on), my expertise (STS scholar, qualitative researcher), and my personal and social identities.

However, the limits of these tools became much more apparent as I took on the role of an engaged and participating STS scholar. As the 'data collector', I researched and investigated a community and as the scholar I connected my findings through a succession of STS theories and shared them with the broader academic community.

As an engaged scholar, I drew from scholars exploring engaged STS, action-oriented STS, critical participation and situated intervention that pointed to STS scholars that are interested and involved in transforming knowledge from its traditional critiques into various pragmatic applications.

I examined my findings to locate the places where I could respond to the identified challenges through a lens of responsible and ethical engagement (Puig de la Bellacasa 2011). I carefully crafted community-centred and data-driven interventions that brought visibility to hidden and overlooked communities and concerns.

Yet, being embedded within the community beyond the scope of the researcher and scholar, shifted and challenged the scope of my reflexivity. No longer was it enough to be mindful and conscious of my positionality and ensure an accurate and unbiased representation, but as I become involved in the community, my work became more responsive to action, consequences, and impacts upon others and myself. It was when *this* reflexivity encountered resistance and left me without an answer, that my own reflection opened the door to another concept. Though I draw generally from several discussions of reflexivity (Bourdieu and Wacquant 1992; Lynch 2000; Pels 2000; Ashmore 2015), the primary subject of this chapter, *self-confrontation*, draws upon Pillow's (2003) work of the 'reflexivities of discomfort', to challenge the threat of a repetitive and superficial reflexivity. Self-confrontation was my response when I came to the metaphoric end of my reflexive rope. Self-confrontation posits an active purposeful step beyond reflexivity to investigate and clarify my motivations, feelings and actions, that result from reflexivity, so that I may move forward, pause or even reorganize my approach. Self-confrontation pushed me past the knowledge that reflexivity gave me so that my actions as an engaged scholar not only protected the research and the 'participants', but forced me to reconcile my fears, my hesitations, my own visibility and protect the people trusting me.

In this chapter, I share how my application of reflexivity shifted accordingly to my roles as a strict methodologist, STS scholar and, finally, an engaged STS practitioner. I begin this chapter describing my work as part of a national engineering education change initiative in the United States. I was initially brought on as the graduate research assistant during my STS studies to conduct a culture and climate study of an electrical and computer engineering department. My findings, though providing evidence of the need for a culture change, eventually piqued my interest in doing something different by incorporating action-oriented STS practices within my work.

## Reflexivity as representation and potential alternatives

*Data collecting for change in an Electrical and Computer Engineering Department*

In 2016, Virginia Tech's Department of Electrical and Computer Engineering (ECE) became a recipient of a National Science Foundation Revolutionizing Engineering Departments (RED) grant with its proposal titled, 'Radically Expanding Pathways in the Professional Formation of Engineers'. In response to the national initiative calling for universities across the United States to change the landscape of engineering education, the ECE department proposed to change a half-century-old engineering curriculum to create an easier pathway for students to shift between the department's two majors: computer engineering and electrical engineering. The team hypothesized that these changes would attract and produce engineers of a diverse background who would be equipped with the technical and professional depth and breadth to address a wider array of technological and social challenges.

However, the team recognized that their understanding of the department's culture was based on assumptions and anecdotal observations. Therefore, one of the first steps was designing a culture and climate study to expand the team's understanding of the department, its people and its culture. Though supported by the entire RED grant team with recruitment and other necessary resources, the team's social scientist co-principal investigator (co-PI), a historian of innovation and an STS graduate student (myself) oversaw the majority of the research study. We interviewed 50 members of the department, collecting their thoughts on the necessary knowledge to become a successful engineer, identifying the challenges limiting the growth of the department, and gathering stories of struggle mixed with the pride of 'pushing through'.

Some of my findings simply confirmed the assumptions of the department.[1] For example, the team was not surprised of the high regard for rigour and analytical thinking voiced by many of the faculty, students and alumni. As one faculty member stated, 'The foundation of [engineering] knowledge boils down to the basics of mathematics, physics, logic, reasoning.' Likewise, at a research-intensive university, the 'research above the teaching' atmosphere was not a novel finding, as one undergraduate student quipped, 'It goes around that the professors tend to be here for research, and they're forced

---

[1]   The quotes are sourced from my research interviews.

to teach a class.' Lastly, as a field of 'nerdy White boys', the lack of diversity was not shocking. An academic advisor shared, 'If you're African-American you're probably lonely, if you're Hispanic you're probably lonely.'

Yet, the team learned that the department was much more complex and nuanced than assumed. The department's advisors, comprised of four women overseeing over 1,500 students, worked tirelessly to ensure that students met academic benchmarks, while providing invaluable emotional and mental care. A student shared, 'My advisor was the first person I talked to when having hesitations about succeeding in a class, she always believed in me and encouraged me to stay.' Yet, this work was unrecognized, and the advisors felt invisible and undervalued. An advisor shared, 'I don't know any of the professors ... I'd like to grow that relationship.' Also, most of the students graduated and obtained jobs in either the defence sector or the tech industry. Yet, in the student interviews, there was interest in 'non-traditional careers'. A student hoping to become a patent attorney shared:

> I have a pretty unique background in the fact that I still am thinking about going to law school. I don't know if I've met someone as interested in seeing the other side of ECE. I have one friend in computer science, who's double majoring in music technology. That's like the closest.

I presented this data to the team. The findings provided a better perspective of the department, its strengths and its challenges. However, the curricular change objectives of the project began to take the majority of the team's resources and time, and the data slowly moved to the background. I put the data aside and supported the team in its curricular re-design.

In this interim, as my STS knowledge grew, I reflected upon the data and my role as researcher and emerging scholar. In the rote procedures of being a qualitative researcher, I did what I was trained to do: I obtained the institutional review board (IRB) approvals, I recruited, interviewed, analysed and reported the findings. Likewise, my reflexivity was a mental checklist ensuring that my power and position as a researcher was not negatively coercing students' perspectives and that my own judgements and beliefs did not taint my findings. In other words, reflexivity ensured objectivity of myself and my work. Thus, I was a 'good researcher'. Yet, when I had completed my findings and reported out, a constant nagging crept into my psyche and I had to examine myself beyond the 'good researcher' and inquire of my personal interests and attitudes of what I had learnt, coupled with a desire to respond. As a nurse, I too had felt the sting and hurt of being ignored and devalued for work that wasn't as important as that done by the physician. Likewise, as an underserved and minority student, I related to the challenges of being a woman in a male-dominated field as a graduate student in information technology. If I had not had these experiences both lived and chosen, would I have wanted to intervene? What part of my shared experience and empathy played a part in how I considered the research? Additionally, I was coming out of a career in nursing in which our very framework of providing care was termed as 'nursing interventions'. In all these moments, my reflexivity turned deeply inward and began to reveal things about myself that I had not considered (Bourdieu and Wacquant 1992) and thus shaped a reflection of my personal and scholarly identities (Pels 2000) and an eventual call to action on behalf of others (Taylor and Patzke 2021).

## From interviews to intervening

My 'call to action' was three projects. The first project to 'go live' was the podcast, *Engineering Visibility*, which brought the experience of various communities to the forefront of the ECE department. Lesser-known experiences were made public, ranging from the community college transfer student explaining that though they were classified as juniors, they were technically freshmen on campus to the first-generation student sharing how their family's legacy and future depended on their ability to graduate and obtain a lucrative engineering job. The 'Expand Your ECE Career' seminar presented four ECE alumni who explained how their ECE degree led to successful careers in law, finance, fashion and entrepreneurship. 'Engineering Care: The Vital Role of Academic Advisors in ECE Undergraduate Student Success' was a white paper that 'translated' the care work of the undergraduate academic career advisors. Translating the qualitatively derived themes of personal, professional and academic care work into quantitative data was necessary to communicate the significance of the advisors' work to be valued and seen by the ECE faculty who valued numeric data. The podcast, white paper and seminar brought visibility to its respectful audience and respectively challenged the department to see beyond the research and rigour.

Upon reflection, designing and implementing three projects placed me deeply within the ECE department, not as a detached observer sitting in the corner listening and taking notes at faculty meetings nor as the graduate research assistant conducting anonymous interviews. In these roles, and within such a large department, I moved almost invisibly within the waves of students passing in the halls. In meetings, ECE professors couldn't care less about the quiet student sitting in the corner. In this role, my reflexivity was centred among my notes, my analysis and the tangibles that I shared with the team or public as reports, papers and presentations. In this, reflexivity created a boundary that corralled me with my data to produce the traditional and expected products of my work such as the critiques, the descriptions, the papers, the ideologies and the facts.

Yet, as the engaged scholar, things changed. For example, as the collaborator working with the advisors to bring attention to them and their connections to student success, my reflexivity had to do more than tune into myself as a researcher, but I had to become cognizant of what my work could do to the advisors and their relationship with the faculty, both immediately and long after I was gone. Reflexivity was not only a self-awareness, but it expanded into an 'other-awareness' which brought other untapped feelings, concerns and considerations to me and the people I worked to support.

## When reflexivity reveals

Tuning onto myself and to the project allowed me to consider alternatives and additions to my traditional research identity and stance (Taylor and Patzke 2021). Prior to the actual work of intervening, I was guided by a critical self-reflection that was purposed to protect myself, my participants, the department and the project (Lynch 2000). However, something different happened once I moved into the field and stood among the participants with a desire to engage. Some argue that scholars that decide to engage must first find the point of frictions between themselves and the people in the field and explore these connections and open oneself to different possibilities (Kember 2003; Zuiderent-Jerak and Bruun Jensen 2007). Yet, for me, the friction between myself and my participants was nothing compared the friction I felt within myself when I decided to break through the protection of anonymity bestowed through the IRB and decided to make people and myself very, very public through a podcast. Or the feelings of doubt, if the ECE alums I contacted rejected my invitation to share their non-traditional career paths. Or the thought that what if my project between the advisors and faculty only increased their gap of recognition? The many potential futures of what could happen, both good and bad, greatly shaped myself and the projects.

Thus, my reflexivity upon my experience brings me to a confession: I was scared. Though I wanted to be an engaged scholar, I was scared of being an engaged scholar. I was terrified of moving from behind the protective wall of the researcher. As the researcher, I observed, collected the requisite data, ensured the proper confidentiality and wrote the paper. I was protected by the title of researcher and my impact upon my field of study was limited with 'few' consequences. Yet, as an engaged scholar, I was more responsible for success and failure. I was the point of contact for consequences.

Yet, I had to address my innate feelings of discomfort, primarily my fears. Am I allowed to mention fear or discomfort? I could use hesitation or apprehension, but those words perpetuate a politeness of my true feelings.

I was scared of 'breaking' the ECE department. I was afraid of failing. I was scared of putting people in harm's way. I was also scared of what I did not know and did not understand. Do participating scholars discuss hesitation, apprehension or doubt? Yes, though it does not come across as strongly as fear. Therefore, I shall discuss my fear.

All fear is not bad fear. I experienced fear about the podcast to the point that I asked my dissertation advisor if I could do another project in which I would not be front and centre as the host. Obviously, if you listen to the podcast, that project did not receive the green light. It isn't that I didn't think the podcast was a good idea. I think the podcast is (and has been) a great idea, but I didn't want to be the host. I didn't want to be a heard voice. I didn't want to listen to my voice. I didn't want to be seen. Ironically, the person fighting invisibility wished to remain invisible. Also, as I began to edit the podcast episodes, I realized that my podcast guests were not protected by IRB anonymity. Even if I used pseudonyms, voices could be recognized, and complete anonymity could decrease the personal connection of the guest's experiences to listeners. I found myself stuck with a series of audio files. Should I blanket all the podcast guests in anonymity? Would that decrease the connection to listeners? Would it imply shame? However, visibility could lead to harassment, both in the classroom and on social media. After I recruited alums for the career seminar, I was concerned that students would not attend and this would only emphasize that students really just wanted to work in the tech industry and the defence sector. And would the alums feel undervalued?

To acknowledge my fear took time to understand that I was experiencing this research in a different way than when I solely interviewed participants as the 'data collector'. My interviews were private and anonymous, and once I stopped the recording, I rarely interacted with the participants again. However, intervening meant that I became a public-facing entity with my guests. I came to understand that being an engaged scholar meant visibility and lots of it. To be engaged meant to be visible and scattered throughout not only the research, but the people, the ideas, the community, and the possible backlash. I felt a responsibility to protect each participant's identity yet honour their stories.

How did I come to these realizations? First, the scholar must consider one's relationship to the public and simultaneously examine their own identity to the community at large (Zuiderent-Jerak 2015). Reflexivity serves the larger purpose of ensuring just and objective work (Lincoln and Guba 1985; Berger 2015). However, how did this apply to public-engaged work? This so-called objectivity that some argue comes along with reflexivity barely covers the surface in engagement. Let's talk instead of a deep profound need to protect participants, communities, and to think far into the future for impact, both positive and negative. A reflexive 'turning onto myself' revealed that I was fearful, but the question remained, 'What did I do with this fear?'

## A responsive and responsible reflexivity: self-confrontation

Reflexivity reveals and the revelations are not always comfortable. They can be difficult, especially when they reveal things that one is not yet prepared to accept or, worse yet, one does not know how to face. Wanda Pillow hints towards these feelings of discomfort. She summarized most theories of reflexivity into four categories: recognition of self, recognition of the other, reflexivity as truth, and reflexivity as transcendence (Pillow 2003, 181–186). However, she argues that these four categories of reflexivity are too superficial for the emotional and mental taxation of involving oneself within a different community. She proposed the idea of 'reflexivities of discomfort' to bring attention to the uncomfortableness of thinking within a different language and culture, how scholars must embody a different shape and identity, how we must engage and disengage with a community, and the work of not 'othering' those that are studied (Pillow 2003, 187).

If we address and acknowledge the 'reflexivities of discomfort', the need for alternative paths, and different methods, we can start with addressing the discomfort within ourselves. My alternative path for my discomfort was confrontation, or more specifically, *self-confrontation*.

Practising reflexivity as an engaged scholar brought me not only through a critique of the personal and professional aspects of my work, it brought me to the self-confrontation that forced me to deeply investigate myself, clarify my intentions and even reorganize my approaches.

Did I confront myself? Yes, I had to. Either I confronted my fears, or my projects would potentially fail. Self-confrontation allowed me to acknowledge the potential realities stemming from my fear. I faced each fear, reflected on its potential reality, and either addressed it or put it to the side. In each of my podcast episodes, I carefully thought of what would become the permanent public voice of each guest. I didn't want anything to be misconstrued and possibly damage their image or future. A reflection of this was not only an internal response but an awareness of the cruelty of the public. I confronted myself and found care and compassion for my guests, yet the ability to see the potential hurt bestowed by social media trolls and ill-intentioned listeners. For the white paper showcasing the work of the academic advisors, I ensured that it did not take a 'finger-pointing' stance but was meant to inform.

In my self-confrontation, I grew as a person, as a researcher and as an engaging scholar. Concisely, what is self-confrontation? Instead of listing and reflecting upon the various aspects of my social, political and cultural identities, I had to move beyond acknowledging those reflexivities of discomfort. I took responsibility for those feelings and responded to them. Self-confrontation takes bravery, and it takes honesty. I imagined what it would be to be a student facing backlash from sharing their perspective. I walk into them, and I experience the discomfort and responsibly responded to them. When we are allowed to doubt, to feel the fear and experience the empathy, we can create space for more thought, more experimentation, more attempts of trial and error, and more conversation (Zuiderent-Jerak 2015, 180).

## Conclusion

Qualitative research is replete with scholarship discussing the need to include positionality, reflexivity and reflection of our research and the researched. And these tools are invaluable for self-analysis, political awareness and doing research differently (McDowell 1992; Pillow 2003). However, as I moved from my interview data and analysis, and became an engaged scholar, these tools were not enough.

Recently, I have worked on another RED grant at the Georgia Institute of Technology. Due to the requirements of my position and the focus of the grant, I have not had the opportunity to be as engaged as I hoped. However, I find myself in moments of self-confrontation of myself, the research and the climate of social change mingled with apprehension and hopefulness. Currently in this space, topics of diversity, inclusion and equity are hot words of political and cultural misalignment and weaponization. This shift has happened at a rapid pace that makes me both nervous yet determined to not set aside or mute my research. Those around me encourage me to tell these stories. However, as I confront the changing dynamics of my local world, I must protect those who shared their stories and face the possibility to pay more through their visibility than myself. Am I paranoid? In a couple of months or years, will this apprehension and fear have been for nothing? Once again, I find myself facing fears for not only my participants and myself, but for research's continued position as a voice for the invisible. In this, self-confrontation provides an avenue to move more purposefully, strategically and intentionally within the politics and power that surround us and the academic institutions that provide the shelter to do so. Thus, it is not enough to just be reflexive when so much is at stake.

Scholars should practice reflexivity. And this reflexivity should cause discomfort. I would gather to say that if your reflexivity does not make you uncomfortable, you probably are not doing it correctly. However, if it does cause discomfort and you question your next steps, I suggest you confront those feelings and locate the sources of discomfort. It is only in the self-confrontation that our research spans beyond our scholarship and we move to become a more thoughtful and responsive researcher.

## References


Ashmore, M. (1989) *The Reflexive Thesis: Wrighting Sociology of Scientific Knowledge.* Chicago: University of Chicago Press.

Ashmore, M. (2015) Reflexivity in Science and Technology Studies. In James D. Wright (editor-in-chief), *International Encyclopedia of the Social & Behavioral* Sciences, 2nd edn, Vol 2. Oxford: Elsevier Ltd, pp 93–97. ISBN: 9780080970868. https://doi.org/10.1016/B978-0-08-097 086-8.85018-7

Berger, R. (2015) Now I See It, Now I Don't: Researcher's Position and Reflexivity in Qualitative Research. *Qualitative Research* 15: 219–234. https://doi.org/10.1177/1468794112468475

Bourdieu, P. and Wacquant, L.J.D. (1992) *An Invitation to Reflexive Sociology.* Chicago: University of Chicago Press.

Cutcliffe, J.R. (2003) Reconsidering Reflexivity: Introducing the Case for Intellectual Entrepreneurship. *Qualitative Health Research* 13: 136–148. https://doi.org/10.1177/1049732302239416

Fuller, S. (1988) *Social Epistemology.* Bloomington, IN: Indiana University Press.

Kember, S. (2003) *Cyberfeminism and Artificial Life.* London: Routledge. https://doi.org/10.4324/9780203299159

Lincoln, Y.S. and Guba, E.G. (1985) *Naturalistic Inquiry.* Beverly Hills: SAGE.

Lynch, M. (2000) Against Reflexivity as an Academic Virtue and Source of Privileged Knowledge. *Theory, Culture & Society* 17: 26–54. https://doi. org/10.1177/02632760022051202

McDowell, L. (1992) Doing Gender: Feminism, Feminists and Research Methods in Human Geography. *Transactions of the Institute of British Geographers* 17: 399–416. https://doi.org/10.2307/622707

Pels, D. (2000) Reflexivity: One Step Up. *Theory, Culture & Society* 17: 1–25. https://doi.org/10.1177/02632760022051194

Pillow, W. (2003) Confession, Catharsis, or Cure? Rethinking the Uses of Reflexivity as Methodological Power in Qualitative Research. *International Journal of Qualitative Studies in Education* 16: 175–196. https://doi.org/ 10.1080/0951839032000060635

Puig de la Bellacasa, M. (2011) Matters of Care in Technoscience: Assembling Neglected Things. *Social Studies of Science* 41: 85–106. https://doi.org/ 10.1177/0306312710380301

Rose, G. (1997) Situating Knowledges: Positionality, Reflexivities and Other Tactics. *Progress in Human Geography* 21: 305–320. https://doi.org/ 10.1191/030913297673302122

Taylor, P.J. and Patzke, K. (2021) From Radical Science to STS. *Science as Culture* 30: 1–10. https://doi.org/10.1080/09505431.2020.1857351

Zuiderent-Jerak, T. (2015) *Situated Intervention: Sociological Experiments in Health Care, Inside Technology*. Cambridge, MA: MIT Press.

Zuiderent-Jerak, T. and Bruun Jensen, C. (2007) Editorial Introduction: Unpacking 'Intervention' in Science and Technology Studies. *Science as Culture* 16: 227–235. https://doi.org/10.1080/09505430701568552

*Section IV.2*

# Place

# 23

# Coming Home to STS: Liminality of Research Positions as Mode of Reflexivity

*Nikolaus Poechhacker and Sarah Schönbauer*

## Introduction

Reflexivity enables researchers to understand their own positioning in relation to their research and research practices. This is important, since empirical researchers are often fully immersed in their research contexts, especially when conducting qualitative research. Creating reflexivity has thus been a major mode of engaging with empirical work and data in Science and Technology Studies (STS), a research field with a strong tradition of 'getting one's hands dirty' and becoming involved in the doing and making of technoscience as a social endeavour. The need for reflexivity has become ever more important in the last decades of doing research. This is tangible in the often-heard demand to 'be reflexive'. In this chapter we want to problematize and discuss reflexivity with and within STS, especially with fieldwork that is accomplished by many STS-related scientists. In our fieldwork, we engage with our field or community of interest and immerse ourselves in the practices and the understandings that are part of these. And while this allows us to take specific positions within the field or community under study that otherwise would not be accessible to us, this also means that we are in a mode of engagement that distances us from our academic disciplines. Thus, our empirical engagement has to be met with another form of engagement: *coming home* to STS.

Engaging with the empirical field and community as well as with our academic home creates an ongoing irritation, an irritation between field-based assumptions and accountability to our scientific home. With that, the empirical researcher, or as Hackett and Rhoten (2011) call it, the 'engaged researcher' occupies a liminal status between two worlds: the world which is under study and the world to which researchers come home to. However, *coming home* specifically to STS is not an easy task. Differently to other long-established disciplines, STS resembles more of an *un-disciplined*[1] field, where many different perspectives, disciplinary backgrounds and epistemological commitments are coming together to take a closer look at the relationships between science, technology and society. This *un-disciplined* nature of STS begs the question: What does it mean to come home to STS? And specifically: What does it mean to come home to STS as an *engaged researcher* who inhabits a liminal status?

We argue that reflexivity in STS requires multiple liminal positions that not only include a boundary between the empirical field and the discipline, but also extend within STS with its diverse disciplinary, methodological and epistemological engagements. Liminal positions can be very productive, such as when an ongoing irritation provokes new perspectives and insights in the studied phenomena. At the same time, and in order to become productive, liminal positions demand spaces in which tensions between different positions can exist and are valued. In the following, we discuss some implications of this positioning work: the methodological and epistemic merit of liminal positions, of our engagement with the studied field and community and the home discipline as a double movement of *coming home* to different places; how *coming home* poses a challenge for STS scholars; and what being an 'engaged researcher' with liminal positions means for reflexive spaces.

## Having multiple homes: from reflexivity to liminality

Many scientists in STS have touched upon reflexivity. It has been opened up along different schools, programmes and perspectives. Michael Lynch (2000) summarizes the different agendas and explains the degree of radical or less-radical characteristics of reflexivity, such as: systemic reflexivity in cybernetics, organizational reflexivity of late modernity, or reflexivity as a means of social objectivation. In many of these agendas, reflexivity is understood as a virtue. Understanding reflexivity as a virtue is based on conceptualizing researchers as creating subjective perspectives and as observing, writing and speaking from an identifiable position (Harding 1991; Bourdieu and Wacquant 1992). Reflexivity should neutralize the problems that come with subjectivity in research, by turning researchers' observations not only on their own research fields, but also on themselves. With this move, the researcher shall create a symmetry in observation, thus negating

---

[1] We are thankful to Jan-Hendrik Passoth who brought this idea to our attention.

the effects of one's positionality. Charmaz (2014) provides methodological examples in her constructivist grounded theory for such a reflexivity. She urges researchers to work on their methodological self-consciousness, which she deciphers as a 'deeply reflexive gaze on how our perspectives, privileges, and priorities affect our data, actions, and nascent analyses' (Charmaz 2014, 167). An epistemological practice that has been criticized by Bourdieu (2015). Instead, Bourdieu argues that we should understand reflexivity as the ability to dialectically relate the experiences and observations of the field with a scientific view of the world, that is, with a disciplinary gaze. And while we too aim to align field-observations and disciplinary classifications, we argue that reflexivity needs specific attention in STS.

The need to dedicate specific attention for reflexivity is based on our own professional development and positioning work. We both are scientists with a professional socialization that is not exclusively STS, a résumé which is not uncommon among STS researchers. Sarah was a microbiologist before starting her PhD in STS, and Nikolaus worked as an IT professional prior to his studies in STS. In our PhD and postdoctoral research projects we studied our former home disciplines among other things. Our professionalization in STS is thus tied to our former epistemic home(s). This constellation creates the need for a reflexive process that is specific to different positions. In this regard, Hackett and Rhoten have argued that the engaged scholar 'occupies a liminal status which entails commitments to values that are sometimes in conflict with one another' (Hackett and Rhoten 2011, 835). One solution they identify as integral to STS is to build symmetrical relationships with 'our subjects in science and engineering communities' and to build 'trust and confidence that transforms access into engagement' (Hackett and Rhoten 2011, 836). Hence, engaged scientists represent a liminal status, a status in between the agenda of the studied field or community and expectations for researchers. This liminal status is integral to a reflexive research process: When scientists produce knowledge, they not only accomplish research and create data, they also position themselves as scientists in the knowledge production process. This positioning work is important to reflect on what one is studying but also and importantly how one situates oneself as scholar when they come back home to their discipline.

Amann and Hirschauer (1997) as well as Breidenstein and colleagues (2020) argue that every field immersion and intense field-phase has to be accompanied by the practice of returning to one's own discipline or in other words, by *coming home*. They argue that the researcher – in a double movement – needs to adapt to their scientific peers as well as to their peers of the field or community under study. This double movement creates opportunities for reflexivity, as the accounts we produce are situated (Haraway 1988) and challenged in and by both communities, our home community and the field community. Similarly, Fuller (1999) argues that the researcher is always challenged to move between different identities. He discusses this movement in relation to the bifurcation between the academy and activism. Moving between these different identities does not only mean 'going native',[2] as it is traditionally discussed, but also, as named by Fuller with a question mark, 'going academic?' (Fuller 1999, 224). One important conclusion of Fuller is that the 'constant reassessment, renegotiation and repositioning of a researcher's various identities' (Fuller 1999, 226) is necessary as it creates important frictions between our academic self and ourselves as members of the field under study who become reciprocally reflexive. Following this, we open up our research process along tensions in our liminal status as STS researchers who study a different field or community of their former epistemic home and *come home* to STS.

## Being home before *coming home?*

In our research, positioning work was the result of a journey. When accomplishing empirical data gathering, specifically participant observations, co-working routines, or ethnographic interviews, we experienced multiple epistemic homes. In her research on plastic and its social, political and ethical dimensions, Sarah aimed to understand how different actors, such as scientists, non-governmental organizations (NGOs) or plastic-free activists, problematize plastic.

FIELD NOTE 1

*Sarah*

In my first postdoctoral position, I continued the journey I started in my PhD. I became an STS scholar. Meanwhile, I was employed in a research project in which I analysed the social and political dimensions of plastic in today's societies. This project was part of an extensive funding initiative in Germany, featuring interdisciplinary research groups researching plastic objects of all sorts. I was part of one group involving biologists, some of them concentrating on urban water management. Having been a microbiologist before my PhD and also focusing among other things on wastewater infrastructures and wastewater microorganisms allowed me to connect with the biologists in the group.

It was in one of the first meetings that I realized that the biologists spoke my former language. I was able to follow their presentations and made notes of the discussions. At the same time – and this was more difficult – I entered

---

[2]  'Going native', besides its colonial history, also has a problem of insinuating that there is a homogeneous 'nativeness' that one can have, instead of acknowledging the multiple positions that 'being native' addresses.

the group with a different background: I was the social scientist of the group. And this was not necessarily easy. Not only did I have to gain credibility among a group of biologists, I also had to find my position as post-biologist and STS scholar. In many of my interviews I agreed with the interviewed actors, be they zero waste activists or concerned NGO representatives or scientists with an activist background: plastic could potentially have severe effects on human and environmental harm. This led to the following: soon after data gathering and in the middle of the project I too reduced my plastic consumption, intake and use. I became what Roberts (2010) calls a 'plastiphobe', a person who is well aware of the potential effects of plastic-related chemicals and tries to avoid these. Being a 'plastiphobe' fostered my feminist positionality and allowed me to think along concepts such as environmental justice. Such a positionality is indeed helpful to research power, unequal relationships and injustice as part of environmental problems. But it also creates partial blindness to other interpretations.

Sarah *came home* to her former epistemic home in her fieldwork. While this situation is not exclusive to researchers in STS, it is a specificity of STS's tradition and its scholars. Sarah's *coming home* was not easy but had its merits. She was able to follow and translate the language of biologists. And – based on her upbringing as biologist – she could also contextualize the often less concerned tone about environmental microplastics in meetings with biologists. At the same time, she also created alignments with activists in her community of interest, such as zero waste activists or activist scientists. Researching plastic thus represents contradictory understandings, for example from scientists, organizations, activists, companies, understandings that account for a complex positioning of the researcher in the analytical process. This is reflected in the shifts and tensions of Sarah's position: she was at the same time an observer of the technical specificities in the scientific debates and an observer of and ally in the emotional and political debates on plastic in the environment.

Second, Nikolaus was involved in a project which aims to democratize algorithms in a public broadcaster. While the matter seems very technical at first, becoming quite literally a member of the development team enabled him to get a new understanding of what it means to develop such an algorithm. By sharing the problems, the expectations, and to some degree also the hype around that technology, he experienced first-hand what it means to make a recommender system and how it is linked to technical and organizational issues.

## FIELD NOTE 2
### *Nikolaus*

With my PhD I also started a journey with the development team of the software department of a public broadcaster. The aim of the project was to research the possibilities for developing a machine learning powered recommender system that was in line with the legal and political requirements of a public service broadcaster.

However, the start was not easy, as I entered the field as the project's sociologist. A notion that would also be brought up during meetings when I was introduced. One could see that the connection between social science and development was not obvious to the people I was introduced to – including the developers of the public broadcaster. I explained my research interest and the interdisciplinary nature of the project, yet I was the person responsible for the 'people' questions. That is, until I took the initiative and developed a mathematical approach to analyse old user data to see if there were filter bubbles to be found. The approach was not revolutionary and the R script I developed was rather short, but it entailed some knowledge about coding, higher algebra, databases and network analysis. After I presented the results, my role in the project changed, and I became involved in rather technical discussions. By becoming a team member, I shared a common understanding with the other developers, not only of the technology, but especially about the situation in which the development took place. As a result, I was able to discuss and understand matters and issues that were buried deep within the disciplinary and organizational reasoning, including questions of access to internal information infrastructures, the social impact of singular parameters in the algorithms optimization function, or the struggles of interpreting data that has been used for the algorithm from an internal project perspective.

In these vignettes, we illustrate our field-immersion journey and show a glimpse into how we became competent members of our fields of concern (again). We argue that field-immersion is an important step in the *coming home* process, not only when doing ethnographic fieldwork, but for understanding a scientific field or community. Thomas Kuhn (1970) already argued that adequate competence in the field under investigation is a prerequisite for the study of the empirical field and its paradigms. He argued that 'one must go native, discover that one is thinking and working in, not simply translating out of, a language that was previously foreign' (Kuhn 1970, 204). However, we were not going native, with all its difficult connotations, but we were – in a way – *coming home*. Field-immersion as part of *coming home* also requires a change in perspective, in which the researcher tries to take the perspective of the field participants (see also Goodwin 2000): Sarah became a *plastiphobe* and allied with activists and Nikolaus became a member of the team, knowing and working along the same problems and challenges. We would not have been able to observe, understand and experience the field, if we would have chosen to just observe from a distance.[3] We came *back home* to our study-fields and immersed ourselves in them. And while this does not have to be the primary choice of methods, for us and our research, it was (and still is).

## *Coming home* from home

In the first part, we have shown our field-immersion and the opportunities it provided us with. However, field immersion comes with a price. First, it creates blind spots for common-sense elements that are part of everyday field practices. The more we are part of a social situation, the more we tend to overlook its specificities. Second, the field carries its very own normativities and assumptions expressed in the field's practices. Reflexivity as a virtue should act as a remedy to these issues. So, we gained important insights through field-immersion, but how to communicate that to our professional home and what does field-immersion imply when *coming home* to STS?

Let us start with mapping out some core concerns post field-immersion: the researcher is in a position that is not always easy to navigate. On the one hand they should become familiar with the field and learn its often implicit knowledge of how to interpret and understand their field without misrepresenting it or just applying pre-defined categories to the observation. On the other hand, they are called to create an analytical distance to the very same field to avoid analytical blind spots and not lose themselves. In other words: it is important to become a member of the field of study, but at the same time it is crucial to be able to find a way home to one's own research community. Creating distance makes an analytical view possible that can provide more than just a mere description (Law 2004). The ongoing alienation of the research field is especially important for researchers who are proficient in their fields of study. This would counter the dangers of creating too many blind spots for an analytical approach to the field (see, for example, Latour and Woolgar 1986). As a result, immersion to and distance from the field are both necessary for an informed analysis which exceeds mere description. So, while immersing ourselves in the field is essential in our studies, we also need to reflect on the processes we engage in, the normativities we inherit from the field and how to find a way to *come home* to our research community.

For example, Sarah was challenged with normativities in the field and when bringing them back home. She experienced different interpretations of the potential effects of plastic and microplastics, which characterized her

---

[3]  This should not be a critique of other research strategies, but each approach puts the researcher in a different position from where they can see different things. The standpoint from which we are reporting and analysing matters.

field experience. Sarah also experienced a shift in her own interpretations and valuations of plastic material since a focus on activist initiatives framed her way of seeing and interpreting the collected material.

## FIELD NOTE 3
### *Sarah*

Plastic research, and more generally research on environmental harm, comes with a few challenges, such as: what does it mean to address and analyse environmental problems along a specific positioning and what kinds of positions are regarded as relevant or even valid in STS communities? For example: What does it mean to concentrate on activists and scientists' voices and leave out voices from industry? I started to compare findings from my different research projects on plastic. I revisited the conversations I had with scientists working on plastic, with NGO representatives, with activists, and revisited my media analysis and observational notes. When I started to re-engage with material, I was reminded of the heterogeneity of valuations in interpretations of plastic and its potential danger. For example, scientists disagreed and still remain indifferent on the risk potential of small plastic particles. Similarly, different interpretations appear in the media portrayal of microplastics (Schönbauer and Müller 2021). Meanwhile, activist narratives, such as from zero waste activists, largely represent a homogeneous interpretation of plastic and its risk potential. The zero waste and activists' interpretation of small and big plastic objects in relation to environmental and health concerns have meanwhile entered my life. When I started my journey of *coming home*, I became fond of the plastic-free communities' debates, debates that resembled many of the critiques coming from STS communities too, specifically related to environmental justice and the construction of risk. These heterogeneous interpretations were thus present and absent in the debates at *my home*. So, while I found similarities between the STS debates and some debates from the field, I felt that there was something missing.

Nikolaus started his research by coming back to the world of software development. He was fascinated by algorithms and code fragments and very keen to observe how social values and imaginaries would be inscribed in the actual software product. Over this, however, critical questions of the broader context seemed to move to the background. Understanding and adopting the centrality of recommender systems for a democratic discourse seemed to be self-evident. So, while this position allowed a very clear perspective on how different algorithmic designs would impact the broader sociotechnical context, paradoxically these broader questions also seemed to be missing in the assessment.

## FIELD NOTE 4
### *Nikolaus*

During my research, however, I became not only a researcher of the algorithmization of public broadcasting, but instead also became a proponent for public broadcasting in general, and the specific approach of a public service recommender system specifically. In discussions with friends and colleagues, I defended the public broadcasting system (PBS), argued for the necessity of a digital PBS, and gave presentations in front of political stakeholders emphasizing the democratic necessity of such systems. As a result of that new ways to approach digital infrastructures for such algorithms were developed – especially to counter the emergence of filter bubbles (Poechhacker et al 2024). However, I was no longer just an observer, but I became convinced that public broadcasting needs recommender systems, and that this should also take priority over other processes within the organization. Of course, this was also part of the very premise of the project I was a part of, but still. It created tensions that could not be resolved in my role as a project member. Questions like: What logic are we importing into the PBS when we utilize algorithms that are being developed by Netflix? What understanding of diversity is important for the public broadcaster? And is it more important to stay relevant, measured in clicks, or provide relevant content in terms of democracy? And how would one balance that?

In our vignettes, we exemplify the challenges to create distance and closeness from the field under study. Realizing this interplay as part of our research process was an essential step in our reflexive process. Breidenstein and colleagues (2020), for example, debate the role of closeness and distance in research processes. Through creating distance and closeness, the position of the researcher oscillates between becoming familiar with the field under study and alienating themselves from it. This way, the researcher aims to get to grips with the observed practices they analyse, but also becomes able to interpret it in a way that is adequate for the field. Helen Verran (2002), for example, uses this perspective change in her conceptual work on alternative firing regimes in Australia. She focused on the *sameness* between environmental scientists and Aboriginal landowners. The concept of sameness however demands plurality and allows differences to be collectively enacted in the research process. With her conceptual approach, distance and closeness are tied into a common sensibility. These examples resonate with our own experiences. First steps into the interplay of distance and closeness allowed us to detect frictions and with that to identify normativities in our research processes that we reflected on in later steps.

Our reflexive process and our *coming home* certainly didn't stop with the first detection of frictions and normativities. We started to think and work along with them. In Sarah's case, working along and with frictions is tangible in the construction of different positionalities in the microplastic community.

## FIELD NOTE 5
### *Sarah*

Let me share some frictions from my empirical examples that are worthwhile to unpack: Marine litter is indeed a problematic material in and for the environment, for example when swallowed by or even directly harming marine life. Marine litter is also an activist matter of concern, it challenges environmental justice, specifically in highly polluted areas, it mirrors postcolonial infrastructures and a lack of collective and transnational responsibilities. In informal conversations but also in interviews I realized that marine litter also stands for a research topic, a popular research agenda, and that it has reached substantial media attention, which in return helps scientists with funding applications (Schönbauer 2024). So, when thinking about marine litter along dominant conceptual terrains, I miss debates on how marine litter has become a buzzword, an important trend in scientific research and a research identity for some marine and even social scientists. Similarly, plastic waste as taken up by zero waste activists represents environmental care, health concerns, individual empowerment and puts emphasis on missing environmental justice. At the same time, plastic waste for zero wasters often catalyzes normative gender dimensions (Müller and Schönbauer 2020; Wilde and Parry 2022) and individualized responsibility tied back to partially problematic do-it-yourself action. Zero wasters, however, are also effective in steering empowerment and thinking beyond capitalist practices, reflections important to challenge dominant waste discourses. What does this mean? It means that more than one position is important; it also means that shifting positions and creating frictions for ones' field-related normativities is inevitable, even more so when intending to accomplish research on environmental justice. While my feminist positionality clearly equips me to attend to unheard voices, postcolonial and colonial relationships, and power imbalances, this positionality has however not unpacked the frictions of researching or interviewing social groups in power.

Nikolaus was learning about the broader societal dimension of the context of his work. While the project was clearly aimed at something that could be called 'public good', he realized that there is a need for discussions around the 'platformization' of society and how public institutions tie into it (van Dijck et al 2018).

## FIELD NOTE 6
### *Nikolaus*

Recommender systems as part of the PBS is a hotly debated topic. As such, scholars were also thinking about the question how we can ensure a diverse information diet for citizens via these algorithmic approaches – and to realize the democratic function of these institutions (Napoli 2011; Helberger 2015, 2018, Poechhacker 2024). However, this led to conceptual differentiations between diversity on the supply side and diversities on the consumption side. While the first aims to provide the possibility to gather diverse information, the latter seeks to implement diversity also in the actively consumed content. And while both are absolutely valid approaches to realize the democratic value of information diversity, the latter leans towards digital paternalism (Sørensen and Schmidt 2016), while the first is better suited for a liberal understanding. It is interesting to observe, however, that the notion of diversity on the consumption side is only debatable because modern digital environments allow for a dense and stringent surveillance regime. At conferences that are especially focused on data protection and privacy, the question whether such a system would not do more harm than good came up. A close second question was why have algorithms in the first place? When we import algorithms into central democratic institutions, are we not changing the logic of public broadcasting according to an overall narrative from surveillance capitalism (Zuboff 2019)? Especially if the argument for algorithms is that we need to keep users on our platforms to make them better citizens. In a strange way, capitalist notions of operating digital platforms and democratic ideas of 'making' citizens are entangled in these systems. Being part of only one of these communities – my empirical fields, recommender systems community, and critical algorithm studies scholars – would not have made me aware of these tensions, as the reflexive modes of normal interpretations would have created blind spots on the intersection of these issues.

With our fieldnotes, we show that it is important to return to one's research community, a necessary step which immerses the researcher back in their home discipline in order to reformulate the observations made in a broader network of assumptions, sensibilities, and well-established theories and knowledge (Amann and Hirschauer 1997). Without confronting the learned assumptions, evaluations and practices with a disciplinary and disciplined way of thinking, the researcher risks being lost to the field or to their research community. This also means that researchers are in need of renegotiating the meaning of their observations (see also Passoth and Rowland 2013).[4] Thus, creating reflexivity in our research practices in the cases presented does not mean another view from nowhere or a subjective evaluation of the situation, but taking (again) the position of a disciplined researcher – a position that can be identified, but that is also placed in the middle of a disciplined community.

---

[4]   We do not miss the irony that this argument is applying social theory concepts reflexively on our own research practices.

However, *coming home* to our research communities is a step that follows *coming home* to our fields of study. This is specific to our research as we inhabit the positions of former professionals in our research areas. Through continuous reflections on the research process and engagement with the fields of study, we immersed ourselves in the field to learn but we also came back 'armed' (Wacquant 2011). Law (1994) argues that we always are part of what we study, but that we also have to choose what 'collective' we are joining. The answer would be that we do not choose, but we are always part of both collectives, our colleagues and friends, from the field under study as well as the colleagues and friends from our home discipline. We are always both, and this positioning can create (productive) frictions. Thereby, we abandon an artificial boundary between being 'inside' the field and 'outside' (see, for example, Yanow 2014) but rather argue that our positioning as researchers is a liminal process of always renegotiating one's own position. Reflexivity in that sense does not mean that we become reflexive about our biases and blind spots by our virtue or trained skills, but that reflexivity is a process full of tension in which we oscillate between different fields and the positions that we inhabit in them. Thus, we never *are* reflexive, but we are constantly *becoming* reflexive. Becoming reflexive in that sense means to allow for friction between positions in communities and allowing them to irritate our thinking.

## On *coming home* to Science and Technology Studies

We started by asking: What does it mean to come home to STS as an 'engaged researcher' and who inhabits a liminal status? The liminal status is a specific position that we inhabit as researchers with an STS background and other professional backgrounds, such as biology and computer science. This status allows for reflexivity by being part of two collectives that irritate each other in terms of assumptions, values and perspectives. However, the liminal status is also important – and potentially challenging – when coming home to an *un-disciplined* research community such as STS. So far, we discussed reflexivity as *coming home* to two distinct collectives. But where do we come home to in STS?

STS is and has always been an incredibly interdisciplinary field, whose scholars are travelling from and between different disciplines, theories and approaches. This is tangible in the many STS conferences that exist around the globe, and which host a wide variety of disciplinary approaches like anthropology, sociology, engineering, media studies, history, art and design – to name just a few. But if STS exists in a multiplicity, where do and can we *come home* to? Who is the community we are speaking to? These questions are becoming especially important if we think of reflexivity as a liminal status that resides between collectives and their various modes of operation.

As there are a variety of paradigms, perspectives and approaches in STS, becoming reflexive, and crafting a liminal status, must also be designed accordingly. Liminality is not only between *two* 'homes', but between *multiple* ones. As a result, the frictions that are important for reflexivity are also multiplying. This multiplication leads to a constant (re-)negotiating of the material and observations we bring back from our field studies – and thus to the multiplication of reflexivity. In the context of this multiplication, the researcher is confronted with many forms of reflexivity, with many forms of disciplining and disciplined ways of researching, analysing and giving accounts of their observations. However, multiplicity demands a price.

In his work, Nikolaus was confronted with scholars from infrastructure studies, critical algorithm studies, and even computer science. However, when he tried to present his work to sociologists (with a connection to STS) the questions asked were very different – and challenged his approach to think about his empirical observations fundamentally. Nikolaus' experience indicates the limited capacities of inhabiting a liminal position and staying reflexive as part of different communities. Sarah had similar experiences, specifically when translating her research on plastic to the biologists of the research group, to sociologists or political science scholars, to STS scholars and others. The plastic research project also included a multidisciplinary collaboration space that Sarah was co-leading with a wide variety of other social science scholars, all with different backgrounds. Hence, Sarah struggled to translate her findings into other neighbouring disciplines but also to reflect on the normativities when coming back home to STS, a community with a diverse approach towards plastic and waste, such as considering the ever-growing sub-genre of waste studies.

Taken together, the multiplication of reflexivity complicates the picture of being reflexive within one's research as an STS scholar. If we lack the spaces to engage with the different situated reflexivities, we also lack the ability to speak about, with, and potentially for the phenomena that we study. STS and its community have to be aware of these issues. Acknowledging the multiplicity of STS is as important as providing a place to come home to. As such, STS faces the challenge to strike a balance between establishing places, institutions and communities that are tied together, but also allowing for diversity of perspectives that inform each other. This way, reflexivity can create spaces that inform us about our blind spots and normativities, but also does not necessarily discipline its scholars into uniformity. Situated reflexivity is informed by multipositionality – and therefore also by multiple roles we take, and multiple homes we come back to. We strongly suggest that the analysts' positionality – also within STS – can or maybe even should be one that is under continuous construction. Instead of being reflexive, we rather want to speak about an ongoing *becoming* reflexive that not only oscillates between the empirical field and our home discipline, but also between the different sub-communities and thought collectives that found their home under the roof of STS.

Being able to live in different research collectives and to stay reflexive, however, needs designated spaces. We argue that scholars in STS, especially when situated in different homes, such as former professional homes or along multidisciplinary positionalities, need collective spaces that serve reflexivity. In these spaces, different research traditions and communities could collectively do reflexivity beyond traditional disciplinary boundaries. We also argue that such spaces can allow different ways of seeing that extend for example team meetings, project meetings, conferences or hierarchical constellations that we live and work with, such as meetings along the PhD-supervisor relationship. While establishing such spaces is crucial, it is also hard. For one, allowing for different perspectives is a considerable time and energy commitment. Research in academia specifically is largely based on third-party funded projects and limited to time and qualification processes. These qualification processes, such as doing a PhD or working as a postdoctoral scholar, are limited in time, competitive and oriented towards the individual. And, second, allowing for different ways of seeing and different frictions requires some epistemic humility. It calls for being open to other perspectives, other approaches, and engaging with them from our own position, as well as engaging with others on their grounds. In this line, we call for a mode of reflexivity that channels productive irritation, an irritation that adds a different perspective to a debate and thereby multiplies frictions. We find it crucial to root for reflexive spaces and create engagements that enable a liminal status as STS researcher and that allow us to come home to STS in many different ways.

If we value the multiplicity of our positions – and thus also lose the privileged position of a singular 'home', we need to question the idea of *going native* followed by *coming home*. These terms become meaningless as we level the playing field: we are always at home – and we have to leave that home eventually. Where we go, and where we come from, is a choice – and a question of the problems we ought to solve. The productive element is in the in-between of these homes and the (ongoing) liminality of our positions. We are researchers, we are activists, we are democrats, we are computer engineers, and we are environmental scholars. There is multiplicity to our researcher positions that we base in different communities. And this multiplicity of positions also allows us to multiply the ways in which we can formulate critique. Critique that is based on different situated reflexivities can be more, it can be different, and it can be surprising.

## Acknowledgements

We would like to thank the editors of the book for the extraordinary workshop they created in 2023 and for creating a community that deeply cares about reflexivity in research. The order of the authors is alphabetical. Both authors have contributed equally and are therefore both 'first' authors.

## References

Amann, K. and Hirschauer, S. (1997) Die Befremdung der eigenen Kultur. Ein Programm. In S. Hirschauer and K. Amann (eds) *Die Befremdung der eigenen Kultur. Zur ethnographischen Herausforderung soziologischer Empirie*, Frankfurt am Main: Suhrkamp, pp 7–52.

Bourdieu, P. (2015) *La misère du monde*. Paris: POINTS.

Bourdieu, P. and Wacquant, L.J.D. (1992) *An Invitation to Reflexive Sociology*. Chicago: University of Chicago Press.

Breidenstein, G., Hirschauer, S., Kalthoff, H. and Nieswand, B. (2020) *Ethnografie: Die Praxis der Feldforschung*. München: UTB.

Charmaz, K. (2014) *Constructing Grounded Theory*, 2nd edn. Thousand Oaks: SAGE.

Fuller, D. (1999) Part of the Action, or 'Going Native'? Learning to Cope with the 'Politics of Integration'. *Area* 31(3): 221–227.

Goodwin, C. (2000) Action and Embodiment within Situated Human Interaction. *Journal of Pragmatics* 32(10): 1489–1522.

Hackett, E.J. and Rhoten, D.R. (2011) Engaged, Embedded, Enjoined: Science and Technology Studies in the National Science Foundation. *Science and Engineering Ethics* 17(4): 823–838.

Haraway, D. (1988) Situated Knowledges: The Science Question in Feminism and the Privilege of Partial Perspective. *Feminist Studies* 14(3): 575–599.

Harding, S. (1991) *Whose Science? Whose Knowledge? Thinking from Women's Lives*. Ithaca, NY: Cornell University Press.

Helberger, N. (2015) Public Service Media: Merely Facilitating or Actively Stimulating Diverse Media Choices? Public Service Media at the Crossroad. *International Journal of Communication* 9: 1324–1340.

Helberger, N. (2018) Challenging Diversity: Social Media Platforms and a New Conception of Media Diversity. In M. Moore and D. Tambini (eds) *Digital Dominance: The Power of Google, Amazon, Facebook, and Apple*. New York: Oxford University Press, pp 153–175.

Kuhn, T.S. (1970) *The Structure of Scientific Revolutions*, 2nd edn. Chicago: University of Chicago Press.

Latour, B. and Woolgar, S. (1986) *Laboratory Life: The Construction of Scientific Facts*, 2nd edn. Princeton: Princeton University Press.

Law, J. (1994) *Organizing Modernity: Social Ordering and Social Theory*. Cambridge, MA: Wiley-Blackwell.

Law, J. (2004) *After Method: Mess in Social Science Research*. London and New York: Routledge Chapman & Hall.

Lynch, M. (2000) Against Reflexivity as an Academic Virtue and Source of Privileged Knowledge. *Theory, Culture & Society* 17(3): 26–54.

Müller, R. and Schönbauer, S.M. (2020) Zero Waste—Zero Justice? *Engaging Science, Technology, and Society* 6: 416–420.

Napoli, P.M. (2011) Exposure Diversity Reconsidered. *Journal of Information Policy* 1: 246–259.

Passoth, J.-H. and Rowland, N.J. (2013) Beware of Allies! Notes on Analytical Hygiene in Actor-Network Account-making. *Qualitative Sociology* 36(4): 465–483.

Poechhacker, N. (2024) *Democratic Algorithms: Ethnography of a Public Recommender System*. Lüneburg: meson press.

Poechhacker, N., Burkhardt, M. and Passoth, J.-H. (2024) Recommender Systems beyond the Filter Bubble: Algorithmic Media and the Fabrication of Publics. In J. Jarke, B. Prietl, S. Egbert, Y. Boeva and H. Hendrik (eds) *Algorithmic Regimes: Methods, Interactions, and Politics*. Amsterdam: Amsterdam University Press, pp 207–228.

Roberts, J.A. (2010) Reflections of an Unrepentant Plastiphobe: Plasticity and the STS Life. *Science as Culture* 19(1): 101–120.

Schönbauer, S. and Müller, R. (2021) A Risky Object? How Microplastics Are Represented in the German Media. *Science Communication* 43(5): 543–569.

Schönbauer, S.M. (2025) Environmental Care: How Marine Scientists Relate to Environmental Changes. *Minerva* 63: 93–113. [Preprint]. https://doi.org/10.1007/s11024-024-09538-y

Sørensen, J.K. and Schmidt, J.-H. (2016) An Algorithmic Diversity Diet? Questioning Assumptions behind a Diversity Recommendation System for PSM. In *RIPE@2016*. Antwerpen, Belgium. Available at: http://ripeat.org/library/2016/7015-algorithmic-diversity-diet%C2%A0questioning-assumptions-behind-diversity-recommendation [Accessed 12 August 2020].

van Dijck, J., Poell, T. and de Waal, M. (2018) *The Platform Society: Public Values in a Connective World*. Oxford: Oxford University Press.

Verran, H. (2002) Transferring Strategies of Land Management: Indigenous Land Owners and Environmental Scientists. In M. de Laet (ed) *Research in Science and Technology Studies, Knowledge and Society*. Oxford: Elsevier & JAI Press, pp 155–181.

Wacquant, L. (2011) Habitus as Topic and Tool: Reflections on Becoming a Prizefighter. *Qualitative Research in Psychology* 8(1): 81–92.

Wilde, M. de and Parry, S. (2022) Feminised Concern or Feminist Care? Reclaiming Gender Normativities in Zero Waste Living. *The Sociological Review* 70(3): 526–546.

Yanow, D. (2014) Neither Rigorous nor Objective? Interrogating Criteria for Knowledge Claims in Interpretive Science. In D. Yanow and P. Schwartz-Shea (eds) *Interpretation and Method: Empirical Research Methods and the Interpretative Turn*, 2nd edn. London; New York: Routledge, pp 97–119.

Zuboff, S. (2019) *The Age of Surveillance Capitalism: The Fight for a Human Future at the New Frontier of Power*. New York: PublicAffairs.

24

# A Better Place for Science and Technology Studies? The Art Studio as Heterotopia

Elaine Goldberg

*White walls, white ceiling, bright light due to large windows that allow a view over Vienna. Strong industrial look. Everything found here is either a tool, paint, some sort of working material, or something indefinable made of metal. Everything here has a concrete function. Everything here is a tool for creating objects. But it is also a wide space that leaves much opportunity for imagination, reflection and exchange.*

*I am sitting on the sixth floor of the University of Applied Arts Vienna. It is 28 degrees Celsius outside, windows are open. I am sitting on a sofa in a corner of a huge chaotic, dirty place. Dirty is not the right word though – more 'used'. People work here. Marcia, a painting student, is lying next to me on the sofa. She wants to take a small nap before her 'band meeting' in a conference room next to the art studios here. A minute ago, another painting student came to the sofa on which I am sitting, looked at me for a while – in his face the expression 'What is she doing here? I think I have never seen her' – but he doesn't say anything but 'Hi'. He gets his music speaker, turns on loud hip hop music, and starts spraying on one of the walls on the other side of the room. Marcia and I are laughing because it was just the moment when she wanted to fall asleep when the music started to play very loud.*

*Wind is blowing through the studio. Music is loud, you hear how people work with different materials. It smells like wood and fresh colour. But the atmosphere is very relaxed. I am pretty calm and feel comfortable even though I am a stranger here. I just wanted to take a few notes, but this place inspires me to write a text. However, this is also the case because Marcia is lying next to me. She is my excuse for being here. She will leave in a few minutes, and I will stay. I am curious how this will change my comfort here.*

*Marcia left. People are working around me. I asked a few of them if it's OK that I am sitting here. Without asking why I am here, they answered with 'Yes, yes, totally.' So, maybe it is just my fear of being detected as an outsider that makes me question if it is OK to sit here. Now, I hear weird sounds, underwater sounds, experimental music. People next to me are using a drill for fixing something on the wall – it is really loud.*

For me, the place I describe here is not just an art studio where painting students have their workplaces. I want to argue that the art studio can also be a place for Science and Technology Studies (STS). The art studios of the University of Applied Arts Vienna (*Angewandte*) are a very concrete, real place, where I could make my observations and develop my thoughts, but they are only an exemplification – though a particularly exciting one as these are shared studios, spaces in which work is done collectively and in exchange. Through this experience, I want to reflect on how the art studio might be a place for STS.[1]

STS often finds itself in the conflict of being a detached observer, an authority of reflection and critique independent of worldly processes, while at the same time wanting to be an engaged and activist part of society, intervening and collaborating rather than merely observing (Calvert 2024). These two strands of STS – the theoretical, academic strand which prefers to inhabit an ivory tower, and the activist strand which wants to enter the policy room and to intervene in public spaces – continue to generate discussions about what place STS should occupy in society. My suggestion is that the art studio can *both* be an ivory tower outside society that enables reflection and intellectual isolation, while at the same time it is a critical, activist and formative part of society. In that sense, the art studio spatializes what STS wants: it is a utopia for STS, but very different – a heterotopia.

## Entering

I visited the studios of the painting students at the University of Applied Arts in Vienna with the idea to take a look at the art studio from an STS

---

[1] By 'places' I mean concrete physical locations with coordinates and names (Casey 1996; Gieryn 2000), by 'spaces' I mean a more abstract idea of 'simultaneity of stories-so-far' (Massey 2005, 130), 'a set of relations' (Foucault 2002 [1967], 231) that are not determined by a concrete location. In other words, there can be many spaces at one place and, conversely, places are realized, unique events of spaces. In addition, there is the concept of 'rooms' (Calvert 2024), a subset of places which require a certain discipline – the rules inherent to them are effective on the activities taking place in them. I also use other terms such as 'spatiality' or 'locality', which for me refer to ideas of spaces and ideas of what a place could be.

perspective. The idea was not to do an elaborate ethnographic study, but just to collect impressions, to perceive the atmosphere there, to get ideas, to think, observe, see, listen, feel. Ethnography, if I may call this exploration as such, is for me in this context an experiential approach (Pink 2013) that allows theories to be developed inductively in the space of inquiry. I went there, observed and experienced, made notes, and thought about the potential of this place for STS. How could the art studio be a place for STS? What attracts and fascinates me about this place? It was at this place, where I came up with the idea of the art studio as a heterotopia for STS.

The first step of my fieldwork was that I needed to get invited into this place. Even though it is a public building which is actually open for everyone, it would be strange and intrusive to walk around there as a stranger without an explicit point of connection. It is also important for your personal well-being to have a contact person with whom you feel comfortable because they give you the 'right' to be there. Luckily, I have a friend, Marcia, who is working there and who invited me in.

At the same time, the optic of the room expresses explicit openness: it is very bright due to large windows, there are sofas for hanging out, people are walking around, some students are playing table tennis, others are standing together at the windows and are smoking cigarettes. But I entered this room in a different way: I did not know the people there and was not using the room like all the other persons present. As a visitor, despite my physical presence in the room, I remained outside – on the surface. For this reason, I would describe these studios as an *opened and closed* space at the same time. They are open to my presence, but not to my participation.

When I entered the studios, I first walked around with Marcia who introduced me to this place and showed me everything. The studios are basically one large area, divided by paravents and flexible walls. The entrance area belongs to the first-year students, the rearmost area to the graduates. Each area is again separated by partitions. Marcia works together with another student in one area. The place is, among others, characterized by the work materials that are lying around everywhere, by a chaotic and messy look that still seems to promise productivity, and by a lot of empty space that allows for imagination and creativity. Unfortunately, I was not allowed to take pictures of this. For copyright reasons, I could only take pictures in which none of the artworks could be seen, which was hardly possible.

Figure 24.1 shows my workplace within the studios. I sat down there with my laptop, observed, and made notes. The beginning of this chapter describes the situation I found myself in. My aim was not to intervene or collaborate but to 'only' observe. However, I would like to argue that observation is not necessarily a distant practice opposed to intervention and collaboration. In observing, I am part of my research assemblage. I am changing this place with my presence. People behave differently: they speak to me and might do

**Figure 24.1:** My workplace in the studios of the *Angewandte*

things differently, feeling that they are watched by someone. In that sense, observation is always already intervention and collaboration. In Anna Tsing's (2015) terms it could be described as an 'art of noticing', to be sensitive for the environment in which one finds oneself, to be attentive and open for any kind of interaction.

Apart from my presence there, these studios are in general a place for collaboration. The students there are working together even if they do projects on their own. They help each other, reflect on their work together, and receive feedback from each other. The time I went there, they worked together on an exhibition. From observing the communication habits there, I can definitely say that the art studio is not necessarily, or actually never, as Farías and Wilkie (2015) would argue, a place where a lonely genius works in isolation on their masterpieces. It is a collective place, a place where creative ideas and material practices emerge in interaction with other human and nonhuman actors. Art emerges from situations that are shaped by the space and the actors who construct it and not only from individual imaginations.

On the other hand, the strong collectivity of this place also has its downside: I assumed that the studios would be an intimate space, but I was told that unfortunately this was not the case. The fact that so many students work together here can also make the artists feel uncomfortable and exposed, which makes creative work impossible. However, this is mainly the case in the front part of the studios. As soon as the students have reached higher semesters, they get separated places for themselves in the back part of the premises. From these impressions I can suggest that a balance between collectivity and privacy is a necessary condition for the studio to exist as such.

## Heterotopias

Now that I have visited the art studio, I will address the question of how the studio could help us think about places for STS. Initially, I turn to Foucault to show the qualities of the studio as a heterotopia, and then relate these findings to the studio as a working place for STS scholars, which is perhaps more attractive than the university office.

Heterotopia is a neologism by Michel Foucault who describes heterotopias as:

> [S]omething like counter-sites, a kind of effectively enacted utopia in which the real sites that can be found within the culture, are simultaneously represented, contested, and inverted. Places of this kind are outside of all places, even though it might be possible to indicate their location in reality. Because these places are absolutely different from all the sites that they reflect and speak about, I shall call them, by way of contrast to utopias, heterotopias. (Foucault 2002 [1967], 231)

Heterotopias, as realized utopias, are outside society. They are *other places*, isolated but accessible. Foucault mentions gardens and cemeteries as examples. These places are different from those they reflect – they have a relationship to places within society, refer to them, but are outsourced. When I enter a garden or visit a cemetery, I feel this sense of 'being outside'. Usually, it is precisely the reason for the visit: to want to be somewhere else, outside. Foucault describes five principles of such places. And I argue that these principles are not only applicable to the studio (as Anderwald and Grond also argue in Chapter 17), but also to STS as an other place in academia. And, therefore, to the studio as a heterotopia *for* STS.

The first principle is that all cultures build heterotopias but two different kinds: *crisis heterotopias* for people in a state of crisis that therefore need a place outside society; and *heterotopias of deviation* for those whose behaviour is deviant from the norm. While the first is more meant as a stationary stay for individuals, for example, in their adolescence, the latter is the one that would apply to the art studio. Here, people find refuge who think differently about society and seek expression in creative activities. Breaking with the norm is part of the artistic habitus. STS scholars are also constantly questioning or breaking norms in academia, trying to develop alternatives, and generally adopting a different habitus that is at odds with what is taken for granted in academia. In this sense, the studio could be a *heterotopia of deviation for STS scholars.*

Second, when society changes, so do its heterotopias. They are not static but vary in their function according to what is needed at the time. An art studio in the 18th century looked differently than an art studio in the 19th century, which is illustrated very nicely by Svetlana Alpers (1998). Today, studios again look very different and also their function has changed. They are far more present in society as experimental, creative spaces, and more collectively organized than the art studios of the previous millennium. At this point, we also see its paradoxical quality: the studio as heterotopia is simultaneously outside and inside society, constructed by it as an other place and yet in constant interaction. STS is such a place in science: *always different and yet part of the system it critiques.*

Third, spaces that are usually incompatible are juxtaposed within one single space. For the art studio this is easily imaginable through the different artworks and practices present there that could be incompatible in reality, but complementary in the art studio. For STS it should be possible to have such a *space, where paradoxical, contradictory, and incompatible things and thoughts are allowed to coexist.* This is one of the arguments of STS: There are different kinds of knowledge claims, of discourses, methods and research practices. Which one is currently accepted is decided by the social context. These are the first origins of STS in the thinking of Ludwig Fleck (1979 [1935]). While this is and has often been perceived as provocative in the natural sciences (science wars), we need a place where such thinking may be freely practised; where different forms of knowledge are allowed to stand side by side, and where it is not a matter of having to decide on a pattern of action, for example, like in the political sphere. The studio promises to be such a room for STS thinking.

The next point is that heterotopias have a *different kind of temporality.* Temporality in academia is a much-debated topic in STS (Felt 2021). Not only as an object of research, but STS scholars also experience it in their own career paths. Publishing as much as possible in as short a time as possible is also a must for STS scientists to make a career – to somehow survive in academia. And this is absurd: we talk about situated and local knowledges, criticize representationalism and capitalist tendencies in academia, and yet we run in the same direction. We must have more time or have time differently. I suppose this is a desire of many scholars. The possibility to deal with topics over long periods of time, and not having to rush from appointment to appointment, from office to office, Zoom conference to Zoom conference. To be liberated from these pressures, we need a different place: the studio with white walls, light and lots of space (and I am not saying that this may not be true for other sciences as well).

And finally, heterotopias are, on the one hand, an isolated place, and, on the other, penetrable. They have a system of opening and closing, meaning that they are not accessible for everyone, but a sort of permission is needed to get in. Again, this is what I have experienced in my ethnography in the art studios of the *Angewandte*. Although open and penetrable, art studios are also closed spaces: they need a special reason or invitation to be there. Ultimately, this principle can also be applied to STS demands: On the one hand, STS wants to be open and accessible to all parts of society. Everyone should have the opportunity to come into contact with STS. It wants to be politically activist and socially reformist. But at the same time, it is important that the access is not completely unlimited: not everyone can be active in the field of STS. It requires a certain higher education and social attitude. It requires analytical skills, intellectual capacities and creative ideas. It needs the ability to reflect critically. This must be learned. In this sense, the field is open to everything, but real access is limited. Qualities that the studio as a heterotopia embodies.

## A better place for Science and Technology Studies?

After visiting the art studios at the *Angewandte* I wondered together with my STS colleagues if this would not actually be a better place for studying STS, for doing research in the way we want to do it. Also, if it is a more inspiring and welcoming place, where students and lecturers like to hang out with each other, spend their breaks together and work collaboratively. It is an experimental site where we could playfully try out different research methods and multiple presentational forms of our research. My central question here is: Do we want in STS what the art studio enables, that is, collaboration, imagining and practising how things could be otherwise, working inter-/transdisciplinarily, inhabiting an ivory tower that is open for the public and brings publics into being, being activist and academic at the same time?

A colleague of mine, Anastasia Nesbitt, once said: 'As researchers, we are working creatively. We are supposed to have ideas. But we are creating a surrounding and work conditions in which it is impossible to have ideas.' This goes to the heart of my concerns about places for STS. In contrast to offices in university buildings, art studios are spaces designed to develop ideas. In my perception, university offices are not. In a digital environment of databases, Zoom meetings and Google Drive folders, I have a hard time developing creative ideas of how to approach my research fields. I think we have the imagination that social scientists need nothing more than a table and a computer, than Microsoft Word and the World Wide Web. Maybe a library and a seminar room, but in COVID-19 pandemic times this was also abolished. No one can work creatively and develop ideas and new research methods in such an environment because the spaces in which we work shape our thinking in them.

I realize how demanding that sounds, and that with all these access points and infrastructures around us, we probably have one of the most privileged positions in the world. However, this is not about complaining, but about rethinking what STS could be and how this could be locally conditioned. In this sense, I am arguing that STS is in need for places that truly allow for transdisciplinary exchange, that enable making and doing STS, that is, approaches to search for and create different forms of knowledge expression and travel (Zuiderent-Jerak and Downey 2021). There are approaches, especially in the field of Art and STS, to use forms of knowledge production and presentation that are not written or verbal (Rogers and Halpern 2022). The call for a plurality of research methods and knowledge forms becomes louder – and not only for epistemic reasons. It also provokes, questions and shifts power relations in science (Rogers and Halpern 2022). But this must be accompanied by a change of location. Places are performative. Therefore, we need to work in those that are constitutive for such a plurality. Against this backdrop, I would like to suggest that the studio is a better workplace for STS scholars and students than the offices in which we languish.

I think the *why* of my argument has now become clear. But the *how* is still unclear. What exactly do STS people want to do in these art spaces and who is going to finance it?

I would like to demonstrate this briefly using my own work as an example: I am currently working as an STS researcher at the Anthropology department. Although there are close links between these disciplines/fields, I can seriously say that I am not an anthropologist. But only this department within the Faculty of Social Sciences allows me to make films. For me, visual ethnography is an important method that I consider suitable for my research areas. That's also the reason why a research funding organization asked me to collaborate on one of their projects – although I'm an early career researcher, the funders wanted someone who brings STS and visual ethnography together, and there aren't many of those in Vienna. But I wouldn't have been able to do it at the STS department: it lacks the infrastructure, the space, the equipment, the expertise of other filmmakers to support and supervise the project. As an STS researcher, I want to use artistic methods to approach certain fields of research. When I enter a studio, I can stand in front of a large white wall and sketch ideas, I can sit on the floor and spread out objects in front of me that were powerful actors in my field of research. And build a sculpture out of them if I see epistemic sense in doing so. And grow a bacterial culture on it. And then photograph it and exhibit it. It's about creating possibilities, different ways of thinking. And for me, who is just starting to gain a foothold in research, it is precisely about finding new approaches to contemporary issues. Even if it may sound too optimistic, I think that research funding will flow into this – and it may need this sort of naivety to enter academia. When I think of relevant research, the first image that comes to mind is not a database server on which hundreds of new papers are uploaded every day. In my context, I'm thinking of building an installation of film clips from my visual ethnographies, where I can invite people into, allow them to experience, and talk with them afterwards about how we perceive and display things differently and, therefore, only arrive at verification processes for certain phenomena by overlaying disparate media formats – forensic architecture works like this. STS, a discipline that puts technoscience and society together in a context of critical and activist reflection, is for me a place where I want to practice these things. This may be a utopia, but it is a realizable one. A place where I can be somewhere else. A place to think about how things could be otherwise. A place to reinvent epistemic practices. As a researcher this is my heterotopia.

## Exiting

What could be places for STS? This question was the starting point of a reflection on where and how STS can be practised. Fundamental to this is the question of whether STS should be an activist, intervening part of society that aims to change academic and wider political structures, or a rather distant, observing and theoretical authority? The current consensus is that it should be and may be both. Lucy Suchman (2014) suggests 'to combine theoretically informed, scholarly analysis with critical, transformative interventions within technoscientific worlds'. Fair enough, probably all STS scholars of today would agree on this conception. But it still does not answer my question: What is the actual, physical place for STS then? Where can STS practise this combination?

The workplaces of STS scholars are usually university offices with occasional trips to laboratories, conferences and policy rooms. Within this text, I proposed another option: What if we not only think of a place for STS in conceptual terms, but if we think of a different workplace for STS? More specifically, could the art studio be a place for STS, and if so, in what way could it be such? My thesis is that the art studio as a creative workplace *spatializes* what STS seeks to be in society: a critical and reflective entity that can investigate the entanglements of society and technoscience from a certain distance, while at the same time being an activist and formative part of society. The art studio is an ivory tower which allows for intellectual isolation, and at the same time a room for intervention through sociomaterial practices. It is a space that enables what Suchman (2014) believes is the mission of STS in the world. And in this sense, it is certainly a utopia, but a real one. The art studio could be a place for STS, a realized utopia that speaks and reflects on other places in academia and society, but at the same time is external to it. A counter-site to the university or the policy room. A space in which other sites are represented, contested and inverted. This place is what Foucault (2002 [1967]) calls a heterotopia. And after the preceding discussion of the art studio, I would like to conclude here: The art studio is a heterotopia for STS – at least how I perceive it and would like to practice it.

This work has been a playful exploration, but still I have come to end with a call for breaking out of the university departments to find new places to work at. If we don't want to stagnate, we should find new places that pose new challenges to the field of STS. If social processes and material practices are so important to us, let's exit the office and find new companions!

## References


Alpers, S. (1998) The Studio, the Laboratory, and the Vexations of Art. In C.A. Jones and P. Galison (eds) *Picturing Science, Producing Art*. Routledge, pp 401–417.

Calvert, J. (2024) *A Place for Science and Technology Studies: Observation, Intervention, and Collaboration*. The MIT Press.

Casey, E.S. (1996) How to Get from Space to Place in a Fairly Short Stretch of Time. Phenomenological Prolegomena. In S. Feld and K.H. Basso (eds) *Senses of place. School of American Research Press*; distributed by the University of Washington Press, pp 13–52.

Farías, I. and Wilkie, A. (2015) *Studio Studies*. Routledge.

Felt, U. (2021) The Temporal Fabric of Academic Lives: Of Weaving, Repairing, and Resisting. In F. Vostal (ed) *Inquiring into Academic Timescapes*. Emerald Publishing, pp 267–280.

Foucault, M. (2002 [1967]) Of Other Spaces. In N. Mirzoeff (ed) *The Visual Culture Reader*, 2nd edn. Routledge, pp 229–236.

Fleck, L. (1979 [1935]) Introduction to Thought Collectives. In *Genesis and Development of a Scientific Fact*. University of Chicago Press, pp 38–51, 154–165.

Gieryn, T.F. (2000) A Space for Place in Sociology. *Annual Review of Sociology* 26(1): 463–496. https://doi.org/10.1146/annurev.soc.26.1.463

Massey, D.B. (2005) *For Space*, SAGE.

Pink, S. (2013) Visual Ethnography across Disciplines: Ways of Seeing, Knowing and Showing. In *Doing Visual Ethnography*, 3rd edn. SAGE, pp 13–48.

Rogers, H.S. and Halpern, M.K. (2022) Introduction: The Past, Present, and Future of Art, Science, and Technology Studies. In H.S. Rogers, M.K. Halpern, D. Hannah and K. de Ridder-Vignone (eds) *Routledge Handbook of Art, Science, and Technology Studies*. Routledge, Taylor & Francis Group, pp 1–46.

Suchman, L. (2014) Society for Social Studies of Science 2014 Presidential Election: Candidate Bio and Statement, May 17. https://www.research. lancs.ac.uk/portal/files/362263892/4S_Pres_Statement.pdf [Accessed 10 March 2025].

Tsing, A. (2015) *The Mushroom at the End of the World: On the Possibility of Life in Capitalist Ruins*. Princeton University Press.

Zuiderent-Jerak, T. and Downey, G.L. (eds) (2021) *Making & Doing: Activating STS through Knowledge Expression and Travel*. The MIT Press.

25

# Why Bogotá? The Local, the Global and the Interesting, Reflexively, or: STS – Here and There

Malcolm Ashmore and Olga Restrepo Forero

It is not worth the while to go round the world to count the cats in Zanzibar.

Henry David Thoreau, Walden, 271

It is not worth it, as Thoreau said, to go round the world to count the cats in Zanzibar.

Clifford Geertz, The Interpretation of Cultures, 16

- Malcolm (M): So let's begin by examining this pair of epigraphs.
- Olga (O): They are not the same.[1]
- M: On the contrary.[2] Despite superficial appearances, and despite their

---

[1] Yes, this is a dialogue between the authors, voiced as in a performance; which is indeed the origin of this text, which started out as a conference presentation complete with a witty PowerPoint full of interesting images, some of which you will find here. And this dialogic format continues to the end, relieved only by a few footnotes (of which this is the first), the epigraphs and the references.

[2] Dialogic texts have been used for centuries to accomplish many distinct textual tasks. Prominent among these is pedagogy (Plato, Galileo, Marcet). Another use, which flourished briefly in the sociology of scientific knowledge (SSK) among 'the reflexivists' (Ashmore, Mulkay, Woolgar) of the late 1980s, is as one of several 'New Literary Forms' (NLFs) devised with the political purpose of dis-author-izing, of reducing the authoritarian effects of the Plain Style (Shapin 1984), by writing self-insisted 'fiction' and, yes, by conducting dialogues between strange characters (D. Phil Candidate; The Third Author; The Spirit of Bertrand Russell – all from Ashmore [1989]); for a sample of these experiments, see Woolgar (1988a). (See also the extraordinary yet, in our field,

322

**Figure 25.1:** The locality of Concord and Walden Pond

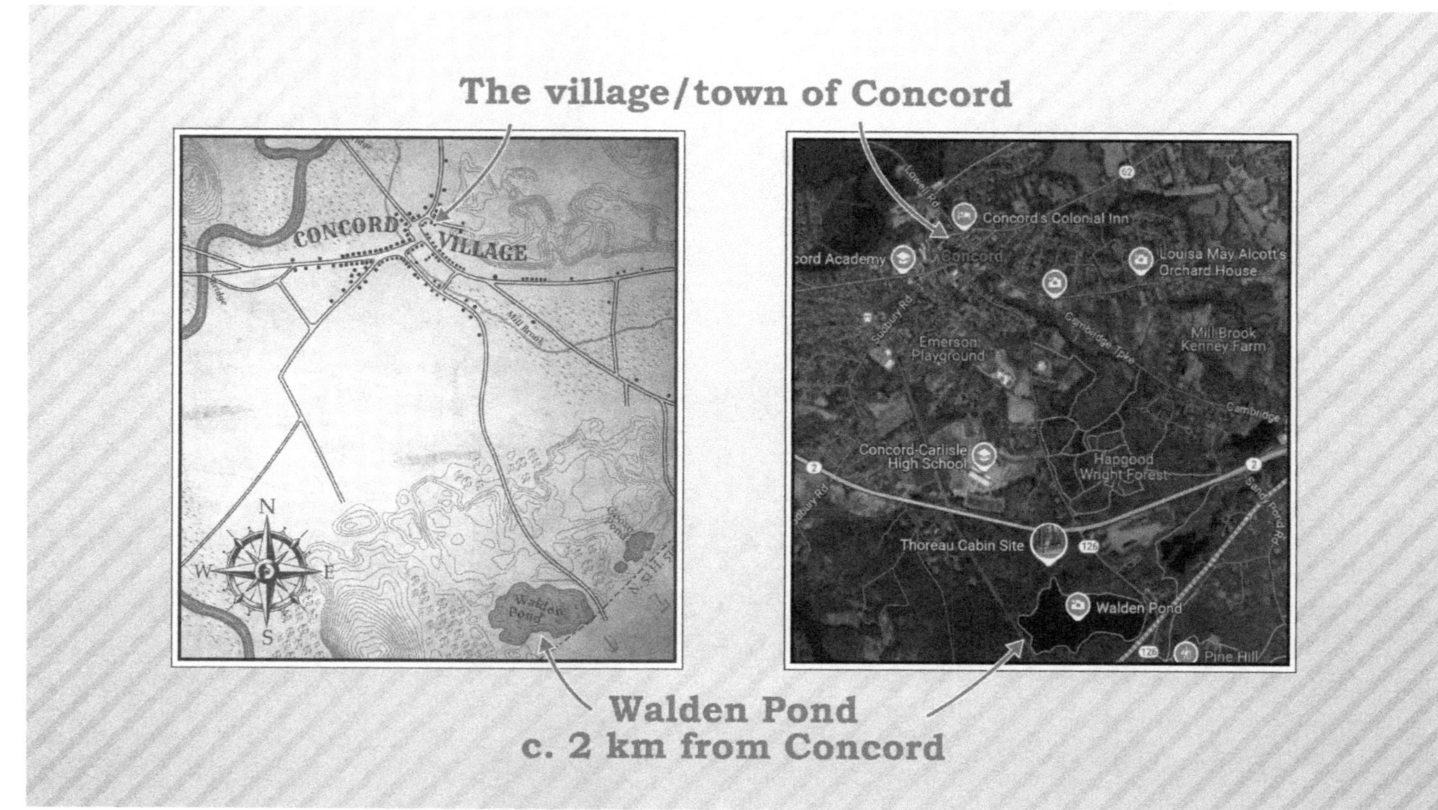



Source: Left: historical map © Monica Navarro Aranda; right: Google map, 2024. Authors' annotations. Total image design © Monica Navarro Aranda.

agreement on 'it not being worth it', they are not even similar.[3]

- O: Indeed not.[4] Thoreau was arguing against travel of any kind which entailed physical movement. The only travel 'worth the while' was self-exploration, the journey inside oneself. The journey Thoreau undertook to Walden Pond, which was, even in the 1850s, very close indeed to his starting point, the town of Concord in Massachusetts, was accomplished only in order to better enable this inner journey (see Figure 25.1).

- M: Geertz, on the other hand, is saying that mere cat-counting is trivial, and not the job of the proper ethnographer: 'It is not against a body of uninterpreted data, radically thinned descriptions, that we must measure the cogency of our explications, but against the power of the scientific imagination to bring us into touch with the lives of strangers' (Geertz 1973, 16). Simply counting cats or anything else anywhere else, even at home in California, Chicago or Princeton, is not worth the while. And, I think, implied in Geertz's usage is an attack on those who may see anthropological ethnographers as self-indulgent tourists (see Figure 25.2).

- O: It's interesting that neither of our epigraphists appear to know anything about Zanzibar ...

- M: ... well, to be fair, we had to look it up ... I thought it was an old colonial name for modern Madagascar ...

- O: ... a perfect name isn't it (at least in English): steeped in the popular exotic imaginary ...

- M: ... but I was wrong. It is the contemporary name for a semi-autonomous region of Tanzania, an archipelago in the Indian Ocean ...

- O: ... or the main island ...

- M: ... or the main town ...

- O: ... or even the channel between the mainland and the main island (see Figure 25.3).

---

entirely ignored work of Bernard Sharratt [1982] and Avital Ronell [1989].) These two purposes of dialogue, the pedagogic and the NLF-ic have been beautifully linked, analysed and exemplified by Greg Myers (1992).

[3] For two nested analyses of the significance of the differences to be found in superficially identical texts, see Michael Mulkay's (1988) analysis of Jorge Luis Borges' (1970) analysis of (the fictional) Pierre Menard's rewriting of portions of Cervantes' *Don Quixote* (1605 and 1615; Borges' Menard's version, c. 1930s).

[4] Olga: Hello. Sorry to introduce a personal voice into this collection (of almost anonymous footnotes), but ... as you will notice later on, dear reader, this dialogue is not performed only for stylistic (or theoretic; or politic) reasons: it forms part of a constant back-and-forth in our mutual effort to understand each other's points of view. It is real and fictional, and recreated and transformed over and over again. At times very seriously, often in jest, and sometimes in an accusatory/defensive mode/mood. Watch for these shifts as we proceed ...

**Figure 25.2:** Snorkelling in Zanzibar

Source: Original image © Monica Navarro Aranda. Authors' annotations.

- M: The point is that what might be interesting in Zanzibar cannot be known before we go there. Perhaps there is an extraordinarily unusual cat population, for example.
- O: Or perhaps cat-counting is a highly significant local activity upon which much of the rich, thickly describable, cultural life of Zanzibarians rests …
- M: … like cock-fighting in Bali.
- O: Another thing is that both of our authorities assume that Zanzibar is 'around the world'. Neither, that is, are addressing the poets …
- M: … or the ethnographers …
- O: … or the cat-counters …
- M: … of Zanzibar,
- O: … or Tanzania,
- M: … or East Africa.
- O: Instead, their addressees, their assumed audiences, consist of 'folk like them', denizens of 'here' rather than 'there', of 'home' rather than 'away', of those places relative to which Zanzibar is 'around the world'.
- M: Finally, before we leave Zanzibar, we must note that Geertz's 'anti-appropriation' of Thoreau's dictum is frequently used to indicate what a proper ethnography should be; not Thoreau's introspective journey into oneself, but a journey into the interpretation of interpretations.
- O: So Geertz's 'Zanzibar' becomes this influential moral tale about how to conduct ethnographic research; but only if you are not a local – here, of course, a Zanzibarian (autoethnography being implicitly outlawed).
- M: Quite. Now, leaving our esteemed epigraphists behind I suggest we begin again with some introductions. It's only polite. So I'm Malcolm …

**Figure 25.3:** The Zanzibar multiple

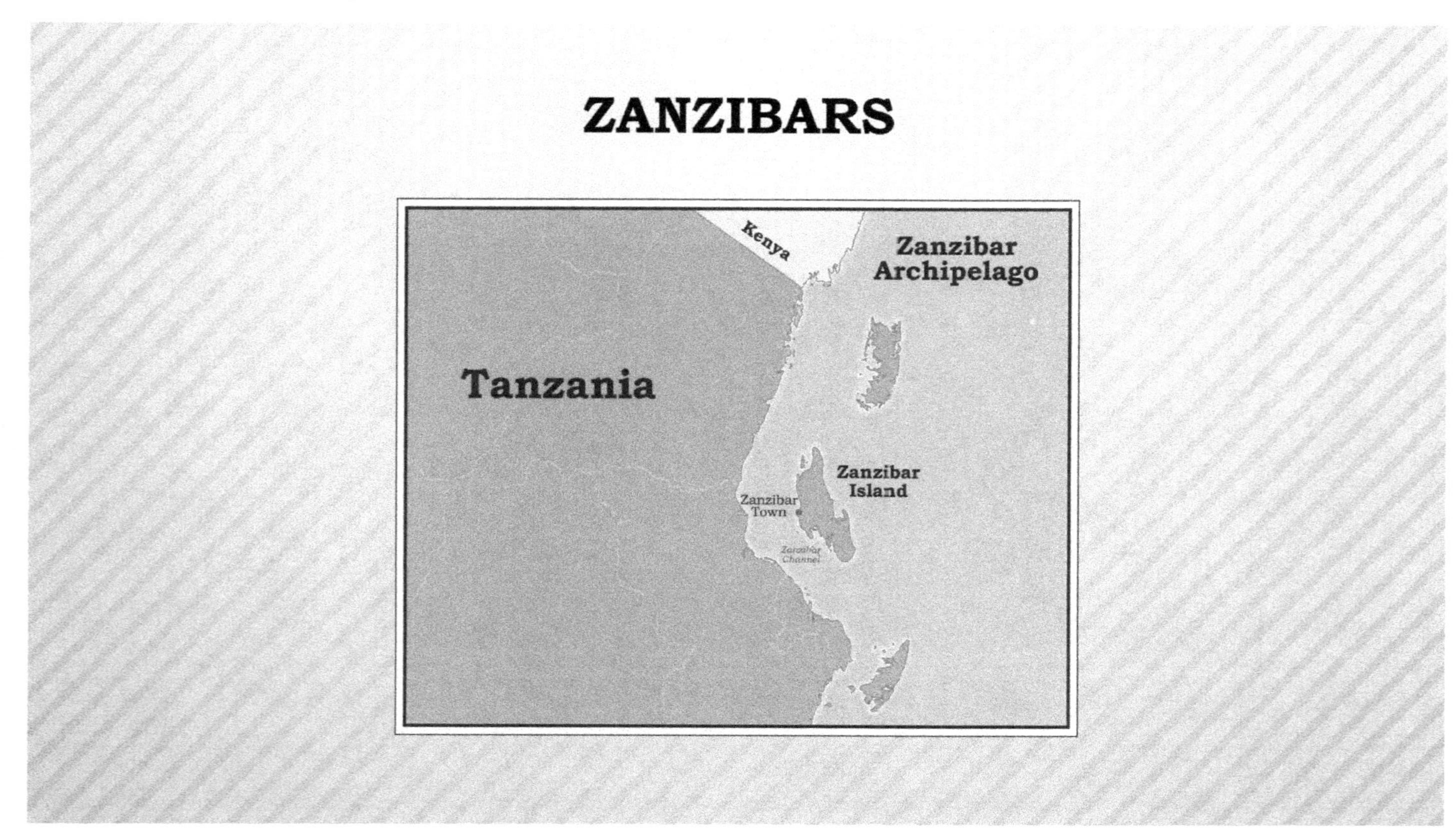


Source: Image © Monica Navarro Aranda

- O: … and I'm Olga.
- M: We're both sociologists and published STSers[5] of long standing …
- O: Though almost all my stuff is stubbornly in Spanish …
- M: … while mine is in the fortunate tongue, English, the master *idioma*
- O: And we're both from Bogotá …[6]
- M: Indeed we are. But the meaning of 'from' is very different for each of us.
- O: I am a native. A *Bogotana*, a *Colombiana*. With a large family and other extensive networks …
- M: … while I am fairly recently arrived. An ex-pat Brit. With very little Spanish and few connections.
- O: I have wanted to write on the place of place in STS for some time … and I have been trying to enroll you on this project for almost as long. … Of course, I have done work on this topic (for example, Restrepo Forero 1998), but I wanted to do something more dialogical, more of a North–South dialogue, as the 2014 ESOCITE/4S Meeting in Buenos Aires wanted to be performing.[7]
- M: I am persuaded. My new place has made it seem so pertinent …
- O: … do you mean personal?
- M: Not only that, but also *crucial* for the field, as it always has been. The *inevitability* of situatedness, the *inescapability* of locality …
- O: Yes, this concern has been there in STS since the beginning – or before the beginning if we take into account Ludwik Fleck's (1935; 1979) work on the localized and historical and contingent production of a scientific fact.[8] But the question is that situatedness and locality don't mean the same thing nor act in the same way when you ({M: Who?}) are talking

---

[5]  Practitioners of the messy and multiple field(s) of Science and Technology Studies (STS).

[6]  We were (living there) when we began this piece. We now live three hours down the mountain in 'tierra caliente'. We blame it on COVID-19. We give embarrassing thanks to the pandemic.

[7]  4S (Society for Social Studies of Science)/ESOCITE (Associación [Sociedad] Latinoamericana de Estudios Sociales de la Ciencia y la Tecnología) Meeting, 'Ciencia en contexto(s): Sur(es) y Norte(s)', August 2014. This was the first time that 4S had travelled 'South of the (USA) border'.

[8]  O: Note this. Fleck was the *real* pioneer in and of STS.
M: The *real*? The *only* or the *genuine*?
O: Both! It should never be forgotten that his work (1935) was unknown and invisible (in 'central-canonical' academic circles) until Thomas Kuhn cited it in his very famous *Structure* (1962, 1974, 1996, 2012). And Kuhn did not just cite Fleck, but also *downgraded* him to the role of 'precursor' by stating that his book 'anticipates many of my own ideas', ideas that, however, needed 'to be set in the sociology of the scientific community', in what to me counts not so much as an acknowledgement (see Hacking 2012, n29), but as a cover-up.

about Bogotá (a Third World city, as you constantly say ({M: I do not!}[9]), than when you ({M: Me? We?}) are talking of London or Edinburgh …

- M: Well, that's fairly obvious, what's so interesting about that? So, what are you really saying?
- O: I mean that if I were to do a laboratory study in Bogotá, of an actual laboratory in Bogotá, I could not treat it as, for example, Bruno Latour and Steve Woolgar did in *Laboratory Life* (1986), or as Karin Knorr-Cetina did in the *Manufacture of Knowledge* (1981).
- M: Oh well, of course not, because it would be a different laboratory. And, actually, in *Laboratory Life* not a lot is said about its locality … apart from the fact that we are shown a lot of photographs of the specific place, including its roof!
- O: Of course, we both know that that is not a placing device, but a joke played on readers who care too much for proper representation (the 'ideology of representation', as Woolgar later called it [1988b]) or on readers that wanted a truer picture, if you know what I mean. … But that aside, in Chapter 1 we are told: 'we attach particular importance to the collection and description of observations of scientific activity obtained in *a particular setting*' (Latour and Woolgar 1986 [1979], 28; original emphasis).
- M: Yes, but a few pages later, Latour and Woolgar tell us that one of the members of this laboratory was awarded the Nobel Prize for Medicine in 1977, just as they were writing the manuscript for the first edition to be published in 1979 (1986 [1979], 31). So that, in a sense, works paradoxically as both a localizing and a delocalizing device.

---

M: Strong words indeed. But I think justified when compared to the case of Gregor Mendel, which, according to the conventional historical account (for example, Barber 1961), has three features: '(a) … [that Mendel was] the original founder of … genetics; [and] that (b) the announcement of his discovery in 1866 was … confounded, distorted, misunderstood or simply lost … but that (c) his contributions were [rediscovered] simultaneously … in 1900' (Brannigan 1981, 89). This triple accounting leaves Mendel with a very different status to Kuhn's Fleck: as an 'original founder' of a science rather than as a mere anticipator of 'many of my own ideas' whose ill-formed theses needed to be reframed to be useful. Brannigan, whose own work in STS seems to have suffered a similar eclipse over a similar period of time, proceeds to refute all three of these Mendelian (mis)understandings by emphasizing the changing contexts of reception: '[t]he status of the discovery was not a simple function of the *contents* of the paper, as much as the *contexts* in which it appeared' (Brannigan 1981, 89, original emphases). Perhaps it is time for the rediscovery, if not the reification, of Gus Brannigan!

9   O: Shall we move this interjection to this footnote?
M: No, let's leave it as we had it in the presentation.

- O: It localizes by telling us what specific laboratory they are talking about (in case one happened not to have read the acknowledgements, or the Introduction, written in La Jolla, California, by the founder of the Institute, Dr Jonas Salk[10]), and …
- M: … it delocalizes by pointing to that specific consecratory device for universalizing, the Nobel Prize. A work done in a particular place that precisely gets to come from nowhere as it becomes universal.
- O: Precisely, and they also stress, in early STS Kuhnian terms, that their laboratory was doing 'normal science',[11] 'routinely dull work', the kind of work, they stress, 'which is relatively free from obvious sociological events' (Latour and Woolgar 1986 [1979], 31). And this is exactly the point. I could not write about a laboratory in Bogotá without radically localizing it, whether to explain how it is that this laboratory works so well, *in spite* of its location; or to describe its shortcomings as due to, *precisely*, its location. … And this takes us back to what you said before: 'not a lot is said' about the locality of the Latour and Woolgar laboratory, except to say that it is a proper laboratory, one where nothing 'obviously sociological' happens.
- M: Yes, but that was written appallingly long ago. You seem to forget how early that book was in the history of STS. Since then, the interest in locality has become much more focalized even to the point that geographers and historians are theorizing the spatial construction of scientific knowledge (Smith and Agar 1998; Livingstone 2003).
- O: Yes, but this emphasis on 'spatial construction' arose in the wake of long held and very problematic understandings of the 'diffusion of knowledge', a model according to which science spreads all over the world simply by virtue of its intrinsic superiority to all other knowledges, aided by the work of missionaries, colonizers and explorers, and bit by bit, the colonized build their own more-or-less independent scientific institutions (Basalla 1967).
- M: Science as a precious gift from the West to the Rest.
- O: A gift that keeps on giving fully-formed, developed and proven ideas, paradigms, or research practices. Initially, 'reception' studies registered the histories of early or late adoptions, local distortions or local obstacles to the proper diffusion of ideas (Glick 1974). It took a long while to unpack these stories, and to challenge their understanding of the role

---

[10] Or possibly by some ghost writer authorized to do just that, as some gossips have it.

[11] O: This simplistic term never goes away. (We must remember not to use it in the chapter.) I agree with Thaddeus Trenn (co-editor, co-translator of Fleck) that 'Kuhn's sharp distinction between so-called normal and revolutionary science has no direct counterpart in Fleck's theory' (Fleck 1979, xiv).

of different localities and places in the making of science (Blaut 1993; Chambers 1993). And in working with particularly prominent scientific revolutions, such as Darwinism, it took a lot of time and a lot of work to question the diffusionist-receptionist approach (Restrepo Forero and Becerra Ardila 1995; Puig-Samper et al 2002; Restrepo Forero 2002; 2009). As you very well know, this has been one of my obsessions. I even recruited you once to present a paper with me on the topic of 'Moving Darwin' (Restrepo Forero and Ashmore 2009) where we found ourselves criticizing the diffusionist agenda in a session organized by the 'father of receptionism' himself, the very patient Thomas Glick …

- M: … I remember it well. But to return to our main theme, the place of place in STS, localism is also crucial epistemically. Listen to Tom Gieryn on the paradox of place and truth: 'The passage from place-saturated contingent claims to place-less transcendent truths is achieved through the geographic, architectural and rhetorical construction of a "truth-spot" (i.e., the place of provenance). Place allows claims to escape place, to transcend its suffocating particulars; place achieves placelessness' (Gieryn 2002, 113). Let's have some bullet points on Gieryn's example of Thoreau in Figure 25.4:

- O: According to Gieryn, Walden is for Thoreau a truth-spot 'device', or a 'register of authenticity', allowing Thoreau's claims to stand firm outside the confines of this particular place, paradoxically by virtue of being well-grounded just there. As Gieryn shows, Thoreau makes a point of displaying himself as local and knowledgeable of this particular place, therefore achieving 'credibility from nativity' (2018, 115).

- M: And at the same time the credibility of his inward journey is enhanced by his lack of commerce with fellow country people from Concord, which Gieryn calls 'credibility from isolated skepticism'. And these deeply localized devices are contrasted with the unnecessary journey to Zanzibar, for Thoreau can find the universal in the local, through a profound understanding of the typical, not the exotic.

- O: And, finally, there is credibility coming from the authenticity that is to be found in Nature itself, as rendered by a skilled writer.[12]

- M: Thoreau's 'registers of authenticity', as Gieryn rightly points out, are part of the repertoire that has been available to social scientists as they do the field work upon which their credibility is based. Other such resources are distance, as represented in Simmel's (1950 [1908]), and Schuetz's

---

12   O: Is this skilfully written?

　　M: Maybe remove this question?

　　O: Will it make readers sigh? If so, what's wrong with a bit of fresh air?

　　M: [sighing] OK, leave the question, but cut the rest.

**Figure 25.4:** Gieryn's Thoreau's *Walden's* authenticities

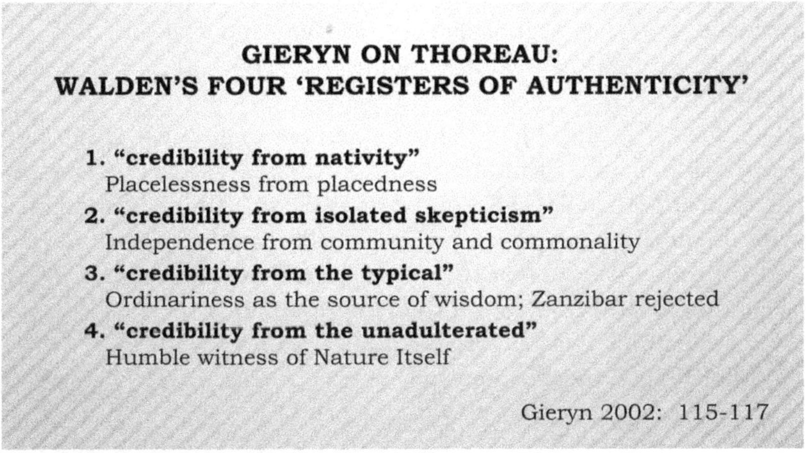

**GIERYN ON THOREAU:**
**WALDEN'S FOUR 'REGISTERS OF AUTHENTICITY'**

1. **"credibility from nativity"**
   Placelessness from placedness
2. **"credibility from isolated skepticism"**
   Independence from community and commonality
3. **"credibility from the typical"**
   Ordinariness as the source of wisdom; Zanzibar rejected
4. **"credibility from the unadulterated"**
   Humble witness of Nature Itself

Gieryn 2002:  115-117

Source: Authors' PowerPoint design; modifications © Monica Navarro Aranda.

(1944) *The Stranger*, or the inherent exoticism of a particular place, or its remoteness …

- O: Back to Zanzibar, eh? But, more comprehensively, there is the 'credibilizing transit', as discussed by Gieryn in his fascinating study from 2019, embodied by Carl Linnaeus, that takes him from his very long collecting walks in Lapland (even posing for a portrait dressed as a native), to the Leiden 'centre of calculation' becoming there an author, not a simple collector, and, finally, to the Uppsala 'pulpit', where he demonstrates his system, and trains and anoints his apostles to preach it around the world. But this last move is not simply consecratory, it is not just a matter of 'spreading the word', however important that might be in terms of the accumulation of credit in the whole cycle of scientific production. This 'mundialization transit', as we might call it, does much of the openly epistemic and invisibly ontic work of producing an orderly (a classifiable) natural world.[13]

---

[13] For examples from this South side of the Atlantic, see Amaya (2005) and Nieto Olarte (2006). These authors differ on the issue of locality in quite important ways despite sharing a similar topic. Amaya explains the apostolic work of a colonial scientist, José Celestino Mutis, as the task of producing a local scientific elite, while using his direct correspondence with Linnaeus to by-pass Spanish intermediaries, at least in part in order to centre himself and Bogotá (though mediated through his correspondence with the Big Scientist). In contrast, for Nieto Olarte, drawing and inscribing local Flora using Linnaeus' taxonomic system was for Mutis a means to make these inscriptions legible and amenable for transportation in the form of remedies for the (Spanish) Empire. But in either case, in this 'mundialization transit', Linnaeus' taxonomic system was being locally

- M: So reporting about some specifics in cat-counting in Zanzibar could be construed as one of those successful rhetorical devices well-connected to place, that can be transported, moved, and made of the world, *mundializado*. As Mike Mulkay might put it, both of *The Word and the World* (1985).

- O: Indeed. All this is good and very interesting, but it is still far too general a concern. Given my place, on the so-called periphery, in the Third World, the Global South, a relative exotic (though among fellow tribe-members here, of course) we need something more pertinent, more specific. We can start by noticing that there are two loci of 'place', according to the geographer David Livingstone …

- M: … the (in)famous Victorian colonial explorer?

- O: Idiot![14] First, there is the venue …

---

validated, no matter how tightly that corset stiffened and pinned down the local tropical Flora (Restrepo Forero 2000). Mutis, it should be noted, remains a local hero, as the Botanical Expedition (1782–1808) that he led has been consistently associated with the origins of the enlightened and elitist 'national' project of Independence, heavily freighted with Eurocolonial 'dreamscapes of modernity' (Jasanoff and Kim 2015).

[14] O: That's not even funny. Do you really want to joke about that Imperial civilizing nightmare that never goes away?

M: The joke is about the coincidence of name and, given the two-century gulf, near-enough profession. But there is a case for the power of ridicule, at least in the satiric mode with its strong literary heritage.[#] Fairly recently, there has been a debate of sorts on the 'progressive' or 'regressive' character of (political) satire among various writers, with the starting gun fired by Jonathan Coe (2013), Middle English novelist, often characterized as 'satirical' (for example, *What a Carve Up!* [1994]), by recanting his youthful enthusiasm for satire as an effective progressive, left, project, 'speaking truth to power' or, better, 'kicking power's arse': finding it now, in Middle Age, 'one of the most powerful weapons we have for preserving the status quo' (Coe 2013). Coe's argument is picked up and wholeheartedly endorsed by Malcolm Gladwell (2013) in a podcast episode entitled 'The Satire Paradox'; which endorsement is then contested by Jeff Bercovici (2013) who puts forward a more attractive theory of how satire works: 'satire turns ideas into memes, allowing them to spread through the culture and influence behavior in a way more complex, "serious" arguments seldom can' (Bercovici 2013, 3). Weighing in on the anti-satire side is Will Self (2015) another English (ex-)satirical novelist, who, by discussing France, at least succeeds in relieving the intense little-england parochialism of this footnote.

O: I'm glad you are owning up to this *Middle England* (Coe 2018) intermezzo of a footnote – though I agree with you on disagreeing with Coe's recantation.

M: Lovely word!

O: But are you sure he is being earnest?

M: In the Wildeian sense? The US academic humor-ist James Caron (2016) raises the bar by articulating a very fancy form of satire's paradoxicality. The 'dilemma of ethical ridicule' rests on this quantum-like paradox: 'Satire is … committed ethically to promote the process of social change, yet also committed comically to use the symbolic violence of ridicule and artful insult' (Caron 2016, 157). From this point of view, 'ethical ridicule' can and should be used to raise all those

- M: … which is where Gieryn's 'truth-spots' and all the lab studies belong …
- O: … but there is also culture. Annemarie Mol, for example, writes frequently in *The Body Multiple* about 'Dutchness'. She also says 'only exotics are required to culturally localize themselves' (Mol 2002, 173). According to this, we, the *real* exotics, the inhabitants of the tropics, the Third-World-dwellers, should resist this imperative for self-localization … shouldn't we? We should avoid at all costs being put in our place!
- M: You're saying that for Mol, a northern European, to claim an exotic identity is far-fetched …
- O: …well, though centres and peripheries are relative and fractal, being from Bogotá is surely more exotic, and more peripheral, than being from Maastricht …
- M: … not with reference to the locality of Colombia, where Bogotá is Paris, nor for the Netherlands, where Maastricht is a just an insignificant border town (see Figure 25.5).

- O: Maastricht as just an 'insignificant border town', sounds provocative and funny as said from Bogotá. Yet I have had students wanting, sensibly, to do their PhD studies in STS at Maastricht University. So in certain global networks Maastricht becomes another matter, a different place. But I see your point. Certainly, it is the case that *us* Latin Americans ({M: Me too?}) tend to see Europe as a unity, a monolith representing proper 'modernity', proper science, and more unified in these accomplishments than the porous European Union. And the same goes for all the doubled terms such as The Developed/Developing World, The Global North/ South, The West/Rest and, of course the bogus distinction on which

---

awkward questions that the agents of power would much rather remain unasked, and better yet, unheard-of.

The state of Israel in 2024 is not funny and neither is the Western endorsement of its actions; but it certainly is absolutely available for satiric treatment: for a strong dose of 'ethical ridicule'. As the Egyptian/American surgeon/comedian Bassem Youssef performs so perfectly when charged every day with being antisemitic: '**WHOOO HOOO** [hands upheld in classical position of surrender, but wiggling, either side of mock-scared face]!!'.

# In the English tradition it starts right at the beginning of The Novel in the 18th century with Sterne's *Tristram Shandy*, Fielding's *Tom Jones* and Swift's *Gulliver's Travels* – this last mysteriously shelved for generations as a children's book.

O: *À propos* (thanks to Mr Google) here is a Swift quote for you: 'Satire is a sort of glass, wherein beholders do generally discover everybody's face but their own.'

M: How very kind! More-or-less skipping the s(t)olidly Realist 19th century, satire blooms again as a major cultural current in late 20th-century television (for example, [of course] *Monty Python's Flying Circus*) and film (for example, Wilder's *The Apartment*, Kubrick's *Dr. Strangelove*). And once again in the novel (for example, Heller's *Catch 22*, Coe's *Already Cited*). Thank you Mr Coe.

**Figure 25.5:** The relativity of locality

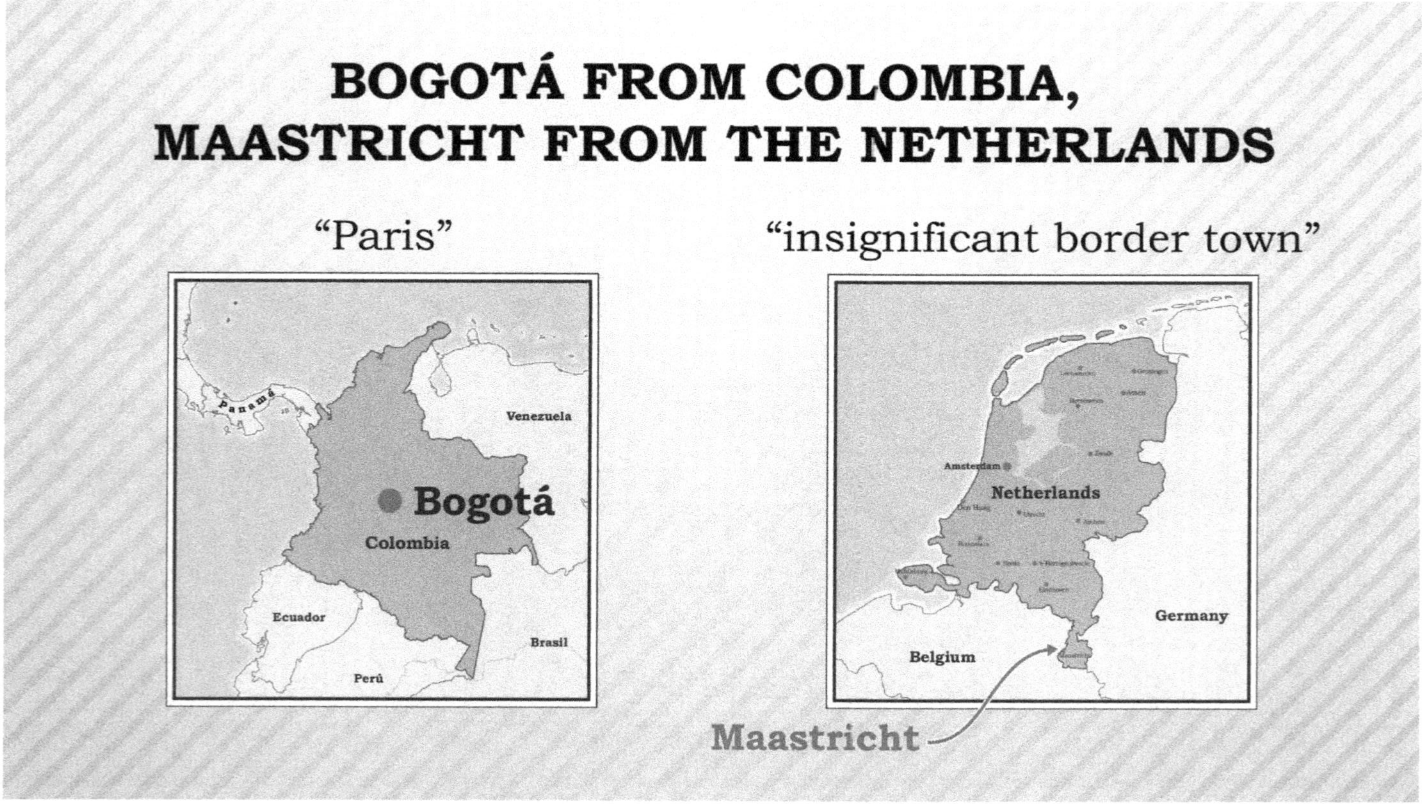

Source: Design © Monica Navarro Aranda. Authors' annotations.

they all depend of The Centre and its Peripheries. All these create more problems than they solve particularly because they serve as convenient simplifications that work as ready-made explanations for what should instead be studied by introducing finer textures, denser narratives and more complex stories.[15]

- M: Yes, I agree entirely. When we ({O: Who?}) say 'The Global North' what are we ({O: 'All' of 'us'?}) saying? I was born in *England*. I am a *British* citizen. I hold a passport issued by the *United Kingdom of Great Britain and Northern Ireland*. When I write and publish I do so of course as a subject of this unholy political trinity. In the same way as Being There (for 60 years) has formed most of my tastes and preferences. This is merely ordinary inescapable cultural determinism (if we must use ready-made explanations!). But do I have to carry that load (the present and past politics of those overlapping places) all the time? Yes, of course, I do understand the privileges[16] that come with being a native speaker of the master language (though Here, these are rather less than obvious), or, more proximately relevant, of being in closer contact with some of the members of the nascent field of SSK/STS, which allowed me even to conceive and then write *The Reflexive Thesis* (Ashmore 1989), that so-advanced albatross. … But reflexivity was only a passing fling, and what was central for one minute became marginal the next …

---

[15] O: For examples of more polyphonic narratives that do not use these stereotypes see Medina et al's *Beyond Imported Magic (2014)*. This book presents STS case studies from many different Latin American countries, and in that sense expands the truncated versions of the continent as comprising only Mexico, Brazil and Argentina, with the rest of the countries being only the local 'fly-over states'. For examples from one of these countries (guess which!), see Restrepo Forero (2013).

[16] On the subtle issues of privileges and responsibilities, politically framed, we know of no better writing than Sven Lindqvist's beautiful self-account of being a Swede with the guilt – or innocence – attendant upon the official neutrality of Sweden during the Second World War, thus facilitating the transport of German troops across Sweden to Norway and those soldiers' terrible effects on that other country. Encountering 'as a very young man' (in 1951) some Norwegians, the following exchange took place:

'At last the great-grandmother said: "Swedish, eh? Well what about the 1942 transits then?" … I tried to make light of it: "I was ten in 1942. They didn't ask me." "But big enough to share the booty" said the great-grandmother. … [Later] I silently composed a grand speech in my defence. "It's wrong to burden children with blame for their parents' actions. Every new generation is born free of guilt." But of course that wasn't strictly true. … Simply by being born Swedish, I was born rich. … It was my own country's cowardly appeasement policy I had to thank. … Yes, the great-grandmother was right. I'd had my share of the booty, so I had to take my share of the responsibility, too' (Lindqvist 2007, 10–12).

We urge you to read the whole story as written. And the whole book. And all his other books.

- O: Why marginal? Because you were not prepared, as Latour put it, 'to talk *about* something'? Or because you didn't follow the lead 'to get out of academic circles and to tie our work to the many current struggles to resist being known, explained, studied, mobilized or represented'? (Latour 1988, 173, 175). And also, why a 'passing fling'? You always put down reflexivity in the courses you taught much later in Bogotá. Always citing the 'navel gazing' superficial criticisms rather than coming out waving your reflexive wand!
- M: Flag?
- O: No, wand! I don't think the magic of reflexivity can be dismissed so lightly, for it comes back to force you to have another look!
- M: To bite you on the arse, you mean. Strike that. OK, if we understand reflexivity as an ethical position, the first requirement is to treat it with its own skepticism by refusing to accept it as an ethical position.
  'Do not make an exception on your own behalf.'
  'You *cannot* be serious' (McEnroe c. 1980).
  It is a practice not a position. Accept nothing.
- O: You were certainly thorough, though, lecturing and elaborating with full periodic tables and critical taxonomies of reflexivity,[17] even going so far as proclaiming it to be suicidal (following Latour 1978).
- M: Let's get back on track, shall we, by telling our promised 'Why Bogotá?' story.
- O: Of course. But before we do, shouldn't we tell your own personal 'why Bogotá?' story? Didn't you have to explain many times the *reasons* for your move to Bogotá in 2010? Certainly, you would not have been asked that question in those terms if you had moved to Maastricht. ... Remember when one of your very close friends and dearest colleagues in STS joked about whether you were going to establish the 'Bogotá school in STS'? I didn't find it funny. Apart from anything else because the establishment of such a school didn't require your 'centre-ist' intervention as it already existed; if, admittedly, only locally.[18] And who was it that seemed so surprised to discover your new whereabouts?

---

[17]  O: Your lecture presentations included ambivalent critiques by Lynch (2000), Pels (2000), Pinch and Pinch (1988) and Pollner (1991). One of your many damning bullet points on reflexivity read: 'It has no soul (to bare) and no wisdom (to distribute), just an overdose of clever-clever irony.' You worked so hard at putting your students off reflexivity!
M: Just trying to be honest. There's nothing I despise as much as self-promotion. But perhaps that wasn't what was required. Less 'honesty' more 'passionate advocacy', no? And, to be fair (to myself) the final time I did that session (Ashmore 2022) I included Bouzanis' (2017) 'For Reflexivity' as a counter to Lynch's (2000) 'Against Reflexivity'. Six of one, half dozen of the other ...

[18]  O: And only locally was/is totally fine! What is this ambition of speaking from Bogotá in the name of Latin America, the Global South or the Entire Periphery?

- M: That would be name-dropping ...
- O: So somebody with a name to drop, some big fish, huh? In any case, going back to Annemarie Mol's book, she does 'show resistance' when one reviewer of her book, a North American, as Mol is determined to inform us, 'saw *Dutchness* running as a thread through every page and [he or she] challenged me to acknowledge this' (2002, 171). In fact, running through her book there are many references to the Dutch language and culture and to Dutchness, but they always come with a question mark attached, many times jokingly. Because location is but one of many contexts and modes of adjudicating relevance, there are endless possibilities, and in a sense each story, like her ethnography of atherosclerosis and her understanding of *The Body Multiple*, can equally be moved up or down, like with a series of Matryoshka-dolls, in a hierarchy of relevancies, determinants and particularities. Following a Matryoshka principle, we can either free *The Body Multiple* from any specific context, understanding it as an 'alternative metaphysics of enacted fractionality' (as John Law does [2004: 67]); or, in the other direction, *The Body Multiple* can be laden with so many specificities that it won't be able to move out of its utter individuality: 'piled up to the point where the material analysed here can be said to come from hospital Z and hospital Z alone' (Mol 2002, 177) (see Figure 25.6).
- M: But this points to a much more general, even global, concern. Here is Marisol de la Cadena:[19]

Universal in appearance, western forms of knowledge and their practices are not confined to Europe or the United States – they have exceeded those territories for almost six centuries now. Articulated by a vocation to spread reason the modern geopolitics of knowledge both established a center (the north Atlantic) and surpassed it thus constituting regional academic (and intellectual) formations with their own centers where the institutions of reason accrued, and peripheries, where rational logic had a weaker established presence. These regional formations comprise a complex configuration of multiple, hierarchically organized, centers some of which are 'peripheral' in relation to other 'more central' ones. (de la Cadena 2005, 202)

So, place and locality, should perhaps be better studied praxeologically, as they are multiply practised and enacted. If so, then our 'Why Bogotá?'

---

[19] M: Do you think we might add a long quotation here? O: I don't like them as you know. M: But it's a good one, and the second, coming up in less than a page, is even better. O: How very unlike you to argue for content over form!

**Figure 25.6:** I (do not) contain multitudes

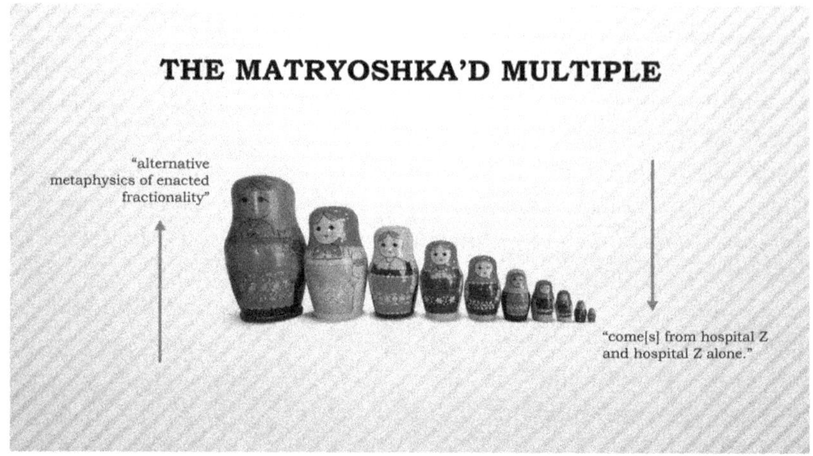


Source: Authors' photograph. Design © Monica Navarro Aranda.

story becomes relevant to these ideas of the 'enacted fractionality' of the 'modern geopolitics of knowledge': all these issues around centres, peripheries, places, localities …

- O: Yes, yes, we'll get to it. … But another issue connected with localizing is comparing – the act of comparing, the practice of making comparisons. This has all kinds of political stakes attached to it, because in order to compare you have to frame and this framing is often done following the taken-for-granted parameters of what has come to be construed as the normal, the proper, the standard; the unmarked products of all the self-attributed centres …

- M: Yes indeed! Which reminds me of the anthropologist Tim Choy's wonderful book on 'ecologies of comparison'. Focusing on environmental politics in Hong Kong, Choy reminds us that:

Franz Boas, the nineteenth-century anthropologist … famously repudiated the discipline's 'comparative method' of distinguishing and locating cultures in a racially segregating evolutionary ladder. … In other words he cautioned us about the frame in which anthropologists emplotted the various cultural specificities they encountered in their work. A century later I wonder how Boas would respond when American colleagues express surprise that I would study environmental politics in Hong Kong, ask whether environmental politics have caught on 'yet', or seek insight into why certain places are more 'environmentally backward' than others. Comparison, my time-travelling companion might remind me, is not in itself the problem. But we need to make explicit the stakes and politics that attend particular lines of comparative thinking, bound up in the very concepts and scales through which, seeking an example, we think to draw a comparison.

(Choy 2011, 6–7)[20]

- O: So now, following Choy's 'Why Hong Kong?' account, we finally come to our 'Why Bogota?' story.
- M: At last! I'll introduce it. At one of the weekly seminars of the STS group in *Bogotá, Colombia*, a native of *New York City, USA*, currently studying for her PhD in *Edinburgh, Scotland*, following her acquisition of a Masters degree in *Amsterdam, The Netherlands*, presented her work (see Figure 25.7). She was studying in vitro fertilization (IVF) practice in Bogotá; that is, she was studying IVF practice, and she *just happened to be* studying it in Bogotá.
- O: But maybe this was not the right way to understand it. For immediately the question arose and persisted: *Why Bogotá?* Why study IVF *here*? What is so interesting, so specific, so specifically interesting, about IVF in Bogotá, in Colombia? She replied, first, in an intellectual frame, that she wanted to understand the particular meanings attached to IVF in the Colombian context. And, when pressed, that Bogotá had been the first place in Latin America to pioneer IVF. And finally, when this second account failed to halt our motivational enquiries, that there were very many IVF clinics in Colombia.
- M: An odd sequence, this, moving from the stronger to the weaker response.
- O: So of course we persisted with our questioning: 'But surely you must be comparing (implicitly exotic) IVF practice in Bogotá to how it is (implicitly standardly) done elsewhere, in, say, Edinburgh, Amsterdam or New York?' Maybe someone even suggested that some kind of 'hypernormal'[21] work was going on in Colombian IVF clinics. But I'm not totally sure we went there.
- M: The trope of exoticism, if you recall, is one of the devices for producing an authentic place noted by Gieryn. So it is not surprising that it was being drawn upon as a possible explanation for the *Why Bogotá?* conundrum.

---

[20] O: I do like this quote, despite its length. I agree with the need to 'make explicit the stakes and politics that attend particular lines of comparative thinking' which are usually implicit, hidden or even painfully unacknowledgeable.

[21] A concept transported by Pablo Kreimer from France to Argentina, to characterize the type of work typical in situations of what he calls 'subordinated science', where the research agenda for many local 'peripheral research scientists is set in mainstream central institutions' (2006, 205; see also both his older [1997] and more recent work [2019]).

**Figure 25.7:** Programación, GESCTM Seminario Permanente, abril 1(!), 2013

Source: New design of GESCTM members' email advertisement © Monica Navarro Aranda.

- O: True, but how many locals do you know who would like to be portrayed as exotics? Exoticism, which is a 'distanced normalizing mode of ethnographic discourse' as Renato Rosaldo (1987, 93) has argued, was found wanting when it began to be assessed by some of the subjects whose actions or feelings were described in this mode. In a dramatic way this form of exoticism was parodied and criticized back in 1956 by Horace Miner in his famous paper on the body rituals of the Nacirema.

- M: Of course, it's obvious that those strange Nacirema people depicted by Miner didn´t like their well-crafted hygienic practices being turned into irrational ritual. But, apart from the exotic, what other repertoires were suggested by seminar participants as alternative rationales for the Bogotá choice?[22]

- O: Well, another line of questioning or interpretation referred to the lack of regulations as something that could account for an interest in IVF in Bogotá. But this was not based on specific knowledge possessed by the seminar participants regarding the local normative conditions for IVF practice. Instead, this suggestion was doubly speculative: first it articulated an unstated interest on the part of the researcher, and second, it displayed a commonplace understanding that would be prepared to describe some areas of local scientific research as unregulated, possibly rogue, and therefore interesting for someone coming from a place with contrastingly well-regulated practices.

- M: Ah, but this possible 'rogueishness' is a different concern, even less flattering than the exoticism account. It makes me think of the Hwang Woo-Suk story I was working on with that student of yours a few years ago. You know, about this superstar Korean stem-cell scientist, his debunking as a fraud, and his precipitate fall from grace. In that case even before the fraud allegations were made there were serious doubts raised concerning the ethical character of his research (Ashmore and Guillot 2009).

- O: This same argument is put forward in a book called *Local Cells, Global Science* (Bharadwaj and Glasner 2009) about stem cell research in India. One of the topics analysed is how India is 'routinely "othered" as a locale

---

[22] Olga: Here I turn to doing something that I have to do all the time. I am the native, Malcolm is the alien – you understand, do you, that he was not even present in this seminar; all 'his' comments are actually mine – and I constantly translate, and sometimes I get it wrong, and he gets it wrong, and we go about, round and round, misunderstanding and dispelling misunderstandings, and sometimes creating interesting things out of misunderstandings.<br>
Malcolm: Sounds like 'normal' academia to me.<br>
Olga: Where did you come from? This one was mine, my safe footnote space! But … I actually agree. That is what we academics do all the time – in, dare I say it, *any* locality?

involved in unethical and/or maverick science' (2009, 6). Contrary to this imagined dis-location, or departure from some ethical or regulatory standard, the authors discuss the 'hyperethicality' entailed in the production of 'healthy experimental subjects' as problems that need to be analysed from the point of view of a critical ethnography of the constitution of these 'shining examples of gold standard research' (2009, 28), rather than from some decontextualized comparison with other supposedly standard localities. On reflection none of us thought of the possibility of particularly good IVF practices, of the sort of technoscience described beautifully by Marcos Cueto when he coined his well-crafted 'scientific excellence on the periphery' (1989). More recently Anna Tsing reflects on the fact that even though the science of Masutake is well-established and developed in Japan, and therefore one would expect it to be the 'modern tradition that inspires new science', scientists elsewhere (except Korea) are busy at work, not in honouring this tradition but creating their *own* new 'traditions', which inspires her insightful coda: 'This is not the universal science we are taught to expect. Following its uneven development shows us science as postcolonial translation' (Tsing 2015, 218).

- M: It's interesting to consider that the seminar participants were all trapped in the standard view from a normalized 'centre', trailing a 'periphery' where practices are seen as hypernormal, or fraudulent, or self-deluded, or defective; in short, just not right … trapped – and lost – in the 'postcolonial translation'.
- O: Which reminds me, when we gave our most successful joint paper in a 4S/EASST Conference in Copenhagen, what was the title? And is it a coincidence that it got us rather more attention than other very sparsely attended talks?
- M: Oh yes, it was *Mundane technologies of distrust: Colombia, the future of the world?* And it probably sent shivers up and down some attendees' spines. Of course. Obviously it did …
- O: In that case, were we placing ourselves as envoys from some dystopian future with a moral tale to share?
- M: Of course we were. Though I'd much prefer to talk in terms of the interesting rather than the moral. Maybe at some (other) point we should go back to this 'Colombia the future of the world' proposal. But let's get back right now to that evening in Bogotá …
- O: During the *Why Bogotá?* seminar we discussed seriously the possibility of some rogue practices going on in IVF clinics or with surplus embryos. Indeed, this became a very strong candidate for making sense of what was interesting about IVF clinics in Bogotá.[23] This was also connected to work

---

[23] O: One thing has to be made clear. All our speculations and prejudices were ours only. They do not reflect Malissa Shaw's fine work on IVF clinics in Colombia, which she completed as her PhD dissertation (2016), and in several subsequent publications (2018; 2019; 2021).

by Charis Thompson (2009; 2013) on medical tourism in Colombia, work that we all knew and appreciated as an eye-opener on some disturbing practices that, as in the Indian and Korean cases, connect the global and the local.[24] But still, we explored other possibilities, as the questioning went on and on … until, of course, some 'uninteresting' 'personal' reasons were found, and then everything made sense, it all came into focus. … As if the personal were not always there …

- M: Yes of course, there are always personal reasons and personal connections that get written out of the official narrative of how a place was chosen for a research site. Going back to *Laboratory Life*, for example, Bruno Latour (2013: 290–292) has told us (later, after the fact, in autobiographical mode) how he came to the Salk Institute to do his ethnography. But at the time nobody was asking Bruno the 'Why La Jolla/California/United States?' question.[25]

- O: Because, crudely and obviously, that place is the Centre of Centres.

- M: So now, for us, there arises a different question: is Bogotá/Colombia *un*interesting enough to sustain any kind of 'place/space-disinterested' approach? Or are we, out here on the edge, condemned to the particular, tied into Place, if, that is, we want to be Interesting?

- O: We do, oh we do. But Annemarie Mol has already said it best: 'only exotics are required to culturally localize themselves' (2002, 173). But where does the force of this requirement come from? Can we not, and should we not, resist this compulsion?

- M: Alternatively, we should all become equally exotic, equivalently located, similarly placed. Let's all unmask the unmarked! Can we not take this from STS's ethical trajectory? And make it, at last …

- O: … or maybe put a stop to these why, why, why questions and carry on telling good carefully crafted stories? They might travel far; they might stay close to home. Maybe we should all cease speaking in the name of the unvoiced and undervalued peripherals, all the subalterns, the marginals, the *latinoamericanas* – and withhold our urge to appropriate the voice of the 'Other', the indigenous, the colonized – and really listen to them (whoever they/we might be) as we do our own work of being ourselves?

---

[24] In Thompson's work her problem is not with the medical procedures themselves, which she claims are of a very good standard. Thompson's concern is with the Colombian industry of health tourism, and with the worrying, and probably macabre, easy availability of so many young organs for transplant.

[25] And interestingly, Bruno's Choice also entailed some 'uninteresting' 'personal' elements: 'A scientist friend from Dijon, Roger Guillemin (a cherished priest uncle's former altar boy!) had suggested that I join him at the newly-established Salk Institute in San Diego, if I could come up with funding' (Latour 2013: 290).

- M: Michel Callon's prescient warning should be taken very seriously: 'To speak for others is to first silence those in whose name we speak' (1986, 216).
- O: Some of us will produce our own works, some others will tell their own stories, without appropriations or (mis)representations. Would this be part of the work of decolonizing academia that has been called for by Zoe Todd (2016)? Will it be part of the ongoing work of 'provincializing STS' (Law and Lin 2017) not only from the centre, but in the spirit of a decentred world?
- M: And, finally, may some of us allow ourselves to carry on struggling to understand (and to voice) our stubborn resistance to the so-seductive call to speak in the name of others?
- O: Or to practice some silence for a while?
- M: Hush now. … Is that what you mean?
- O: Not exactly. I mean the silence performed in the art of listening, of giving up the desire to have the last word. So let Anna Tsing's words close our conversation: 'No one thought this meeting was unproductive. We practiced arts of listening: the recognition of differences as the beginning of work together' (Tsing 2015, 224).

## References


Amaya, J.A. (2005) *Mutis, apóstol de Linneo: Historia de la botánica en el virreinato de la Nueva Granada (1760–1783)*. Bogotá: Icahn, 2 vols.

Ashmore, M. (1989) *The Reflexive Thesis: Wrighting Sociology of Scientific Knowledge*. Chicago: University of Chicago Press.

Ashmore, M. (2022) Session 5. Stepping Back: Epistemic Reflexivity and 'New Literary Forms'. Lecture in course, *Perspectivas en los estudios sociales de ciencia y tecnología, 2*. STS Masters Program, UNAL Bogotá, March–June.

Ashmore, M. and Guillot, J. (2009) Seeing Double and Finding Fraud: Hwang Woo Suk and His Stem Cell Photographs. Paper presented at 4S annual conference, Washington, DC, October.

Barber, B. (1961) Resistance by Scientists to Scientific Discovery. *Science* 134: 596–602.

Basalla, G. (1967) The Spread of Western Science. *Science* 156: 611–622.

Bercovici, J. (2013) Malcolm Gladwell is Wrong about the Power of Satire. *Forbes*, 11 December. Available at: https://www.forbes.com/sites/jeffbe rcovici/2013/12/11/malcolm-gladwell-is-wrong-about-the-power-of-sat ire [Accessed 13 March 2025].

Bharadwaj, A. and Glasner, P. (2009) *Local Cells, Global Science: The Rise of Embryonic Stem Cell Research in India*. London: Routledge.

Blaut, J.M. (1993) *The Colonizer's Model of the World: Geographical Diffusionism and Eurocentric History*. New York: The Guilford Press.

Borges, J.L. (1939, 1944, 1974, 1994 [20th edition]) Pierre Menard, Autor del Quijote. Publication details: 1939 in *Sur* [Argentinean journal]; 1944 in J.L. Borges, *Ficciones*. Buenos Aires: Emecé Editores; 1974 and 1994 in *Jorge Luis Borges Obras Completas, Volumen I*. Buenos Aires: Emecé Editores, 444–450.

English translation (1970) Pierre Menard, author of the *Quixote*, translated by James E. Irby. In J.L. Borges, *Labyrinths*, London: Penguin, 62–71.

Bouzanis, C. (2017) For Reflexivity as an Epistemic Criterion of Ontological Coherence and Virtuous Social Theorizing. *History of the Human Sciences* 30(5): 125–146.

Brannigan, A. (1981) *The Social Basis of Scientific Discoveries*. Cambridge: Cambridge University Press, pp 89–119.

Callon, M. (1986) Some Elements of a Sociology of Translation: Domestication of the Scallops and the Fishermen of St. Brieuc Bay. In J. Law (ed) *Power, Action and Belief: A New Sociology of Knowledge?* London: Routledge and Kegan Paul, pp 196–223.

Caron, J.E. (2016) The Quantum Paradox of Truthiness: Satire, Activism, and the Postmodern Condition. *Studies in American Humor* 2(2): 153–181.

Cervantes Saavedra, M.d. (1605 and 1615) *El Ingenioso Hidalgo Don Quijote de la Mancha*. Madrid: Francisco de Robles.

Chambers, D.W. (1993) Locality and Science: Myths of Centre and Periphery. In A. Lafuente, A. Elena and M.L. Ortega (eds) *Mundialización de la ciencia y cultura nacional*. Madrid: Doce Calles, pp 605–617.

Choy, T. (2011) *Ecologies of Comparison: An Ethnography of Endangerment in Hong Kong*. Durham, NC: Duke University Press.

Coe, J. (1994) *What a Carve Up!* London: Penguin.

Coe, J. (2013) The Paradox of Satire (I) & (II). In *Marginal Notes, Doubtful Statements: Non-fiction, 1990–2013*. London: Penguin e-book.

Coe, J. (2018) *Middle England*. London: Penguin.

Cueto, M. (1989) *Excelencia científica en la periferia: actividades científicas e investigación biomédica en el Perú 1890–1950*. Lima: GRADE.

De la Cadena, M. (2005) The Production of Other Knowledges and Its Tensions: From Andeanist Anthropology to *Interculturalidad*. In G. Lins Ribeiro and A. Escobar (eds) *World Anthropologies: Disciplinary Transformations within Systems of Power*. Oxford: Berg Publishers, pp 201–224.

Fleck, L. (1935) *Entstehung und Entwicklung einer wissenschaftlichen Tatsache. Einführung in die Lehre vom Denkstil und Denkkollektiv* [Genesis and development of a scientific fact. Introduction to the study of thought style and thought collective] (in German). Basel: Schwabe.

Fleck, L. (1979) *Genesis and Development of a Scientific Fact*. Edited by T.J. Trenn and R.K. Merton. Translated by F. Bradley and T.J. Trenn. Forward by T.S. Kuhn. Chicago: University of Chicago Press.

Geertz, C. (1973) *The Interpretation of Cultures*. New York: Basic Books.

Gieryn, T. (2002) Three Truth Spots. *Journal of the History of the Behavioral Sciences* 38(2): 113–132.

Gieryn, T. (2018) *Truth-Spots: How Places Make People Believe*. Chicago and London: University of Chicago Press.

Gladwell, M. (2013) The Satire Paradox. Episode 6 of the podcast 'Revisionist History'. Available at https://www.pushkin.fm/podcasts/revisionist-history/the-satire-paradox [Accessed 13 March 2025].

Glick, T.F. (1974) *The Comparative Reception of Darwinism*. Austin: University of Texas Press.

Hacking, I. (2012) Introductory Essay. In T.S. Kuhn, *The Structure of Scientific Revolutions*. 50th anniversary edn, 4th edn. Chicago: University of Chicago Press, pp iv–xxxiii.

Jasanoff, S. and Kim, S.-H. (2015) *Dreamscapes of Modernity: Sociotechnical Imaginaries and the Fabrication of Power*. Chicago: University of Chicago Press.

Knorr-Cetina, K. (1981) *The Manufacture of Knowledge*. Oxford: Pergamon Press.

Kreimer, P. (1997) Understanding Scientific Research on the Periphery: Towards a New Sociological Approach? *EASST Review* 17(4): 13–21.

Kreimer, P. (2006) ¿Dependientes o integrados? La ciencia latinoamericana y la nueva división internacional del trabajo. *Revista Nómadas* 24: 199–212.

Kreimer, P. (2019) *Science and Society in Latin America: Peripheral Modernities*. New York: Routledge.

Kuhn, T. S. (1962) *The Structure of Scientific Revolutions* (2nd expanded edition, 1970; 3rd edition, 1996; 4th edition [50th anniversary], 2012). Chicago: University of Chicago Press.

Latour, B. (1978) *Observing Scientists Observing Baboons Observing …* New York: Wenner Grenn Foundation for Anthropological Research.

Latour, B. (1988) The Politics of Explanation: An Alternative. In S. Woolgar (ed) *Knowledge and Reflexivity: New Frontiers in the Sociology of Knowledge*. London: SAGE, pp 155–176.

Latour, B. (2013) Biography of an Investigation: On a Book about Modes of Existence. *Social Studies of Science* 43(2): 287–301.

Latour, B. and Woolgar, S. (1986 [1979]) *Laboratory Life: The Construction of Scientific Facts*, 2nd edn. Princeton: Princeton University Press (1979, *Laboratory Life: The Social Construction of Scientific Facts* 1st edn. SAGE).

Law, J. (2004) *After Method: Mess in Social Science Research*. London: Routledge.

Law, J. and Lin, W.Y. (2017) Provincializing STS: Postcoloniality, Symmetry, and Method. *East Asian Science, Technology and Society: An International Journal* 11(2): 211–227.

Lindqvist, S. (2007) *Terra Nullius: A Journey Through No One's Land*, translated by S. Death. London: Granta.

Livingstone, D.N. (2003) *Putting Science in its Place: Geographies of Scientific Knowledge*. Chicago: University of Chicago Press.

Lynch, M. (2000) Against Reflexivity as an Academic Virtue and Source of Privileged Knowledge. *Theory, Culture and Society* 17(3): 26–54.

McEnroe, J. (c. 1980) You *Cannot* Be Serious. Available at: https://youtu.be/_8lWS_iOhfM [Accessed 13 March 2025].

Medina, E., da Costa Marques, I. and Holmes, C. (eds) (2014) *Beyond Imported Magic: Essays on Science, Technology, and Society in Latin America*. Cambridge, MA: MIT Press.

Miner, H. (1956) Body Ritual among the Nacirema. *American Anthropologist* 58(3): 503–507.

Mol, A. (2002) *The Body Multiple: Ontology in Medical Practice*. Durham, NC: Duke University Press.

Mulkay, M. (1985) *The Word and the World: Explorations in the Form of Sociological Analysis*. London: George Allen & Unwin.

Mulkay, M. (1988) Don Quixote's Double: A Self-exemplifying Text. In S. Woolgar (ed) *Knowledge and Reflexivity*. SAGE, pp 81–100.

Myers, G. (1992) History and Philosophy of Science Seminar 4:00 Wednesday, Seminar Room 2 'Fictions for Facts: The Form and Authority of the Scientific Dialogue', *History of Science* 30: 221–247.

Nieto Olarte, M. (2006) *Remedios para el imperio: Historia natural y la apropiación del Nuevo Mundo*. Bogotá: Universidad de los Andes.

Pels, D. (2000) Reflexivity: One Step Up. *Theory, Culture and Society* 17(3): 1–25.

Pinch, T. and Pinch, T. (1988) Reservations about Reflexivity and New Literary Forms or Why Let the Devil Have All the Good Tunes? In S. Woolgar (ed) *Knowledge and Reflexivity*. SAGE, pp 178–197.

Pollner, M. (1991) Left of Ethnomethodology: The Rise and Decline of Radical Reflexivity. *American Sociological Review* 56: 370–380.

Puig-Samper, M.Á., Ruíz, R. and Galera, A. (eds) (2002) *Evolucionismo y Cultura. Darwinismo en Europa e Iberoamérica*. [Madrid]: Doce Calles; [Extremadura] Editora Regional de Extremadura; [México]: Universidad Nacional Autónoma de México.

Restrepo Forero, O. (1998) En busca del orden: Ciencia y poder en Colombia. *Asclepio* (Madrid) 50(2): 33–75.

Restrepo Forero, O. (2000) La sociología del conocimiento científico o de cómo huir de la 'recepción' y salir de la 'periferia'. In D. Obregón (ed) *Culturas científicas y saberes locales*. Santa Fe de Bogotá: CES- Universidad Nacional de Colombia- Programa Universitario de Investigación en Ciencia, Tecnología y Cultura, pp 197–220.

Restrepo Forero, O. (2002) Leyendo historias sobre el darwinismo. In M.Á. Puig-Samper, R. Ruíz and A. Galera (eds) *Evolucionismo y Cultura. Darwinismo en Europa e Iberoamérica*. Madrid: Doce Calles; Extremadura: Editora Regional de Extremadura; México: Universidad Nacional Autónoma de México, pp 21–45.

Restrepo Forero, O. (2009) La mundialización del Darwinismo como proceso y como texto. *Acta Biológica Colombiana* 14(4S): 41–62.

Restrepo Forero, O. (ed) (2013) *Ensamblado en Colombia*. Tomo 1. *Ensamblando Estados*. Tomo 2. *Ensamblando Heteroglosias*. Bogotá: Universidad Nacional de Colombia, Facultad de Ciencias Humanas, Centro de Estudios Sociales (CES), Grupo de Estudios Sociales de la Ciencia, la Medicina y la Tecnología (GESCMT).

Restrepo Forero, O. and Becerra Ardila, D. (1995) El darwinismo en Colombia. Naturaleza y sociedad en el discurso de la ciencia. *Revista de la Academia Colombiana de Ciencias Exactas, Físicas y Naturales* 19(74): 547–568.

Restrepo Forero, O. and Ashmore, M. (2009) Moving Darwin: Tales of the Travels of Darwinism. XXIII International Congress of History of Science and Technology. Budapest, 28 July–2 August.

Ronell, A. (1989) *The Telephone Book: Technology, Schizophrenia, Electric Speech*. Lincoln: University of Nebraska Press.

Rosaldo, R. (1987) Where Objectivity Lies: The Rhetoric of Anthropology. In J.N. Nelson, A. Megill and D.N. McCloskey (eds) *The Rhetoric of the Human Sciences: Language and Argument in Scholarship and Public Affairs*. Madison: Wisconsin University Press, pp 87–110.

Schuetz, A. (1944) The Stranger: An Essay in Social Psychology. *American Journal of Sociology* 49(6): 499–507.

Self, W. (2015) A Point of View: What's the Point of Satire? *BBC*, 13 February. Available at: https://www.bbc.com/news/magazine-31442441 [Accessed 13 March 2025].

Shapin, S. (1984) Pump and Circumstance: Robert Boyle's Literary Technology. *Social Studies of Science* 14(4): 481–520.

Sharratt, B. (1982) *Reading Relations: Structures of Literary Production. A Dialectical Text/Book*. Brighton: Harvester.

Shaw, M.K. (2016) *Embodied Agency and Agentic Bodies: Negotiating Medicalization in Colombian Assisted Reproduction*. Doctoral thesis, Department of Sociology, University of Edinburgh.

Shaw, M.K. (2018) The Familial and the Familiar: Locating Relatedness in Colombian Donor Conception. *Medical Anthropology* 37(4): 280–293.

Shaw, M.K. (2019) Doctors as Moral Pioneers: Negotiated Boundaries of Assisted Conception in Colombia. *Sociology of Health & Illness* 41(7): 1323–1337.

Shaw, M.K. (2021) Exploring the Multiplicity of Embodied Agency in Colombian Assisted Reproduction. *Body & Society* 27(4): 55–80.

Simmel, G. (1950 [1908]) The Stranger. In K. Wolff (ed and trans) *The Sociology of Georg Simmel*. New York: Free Press, pp 402–408.

Smith, C. and Agar, J. (1998) *Making Space for Science: Territorial Themes in the Shaping of Knowledge*. Basingstoke: Macmillan.

Thompson, C. (2009) Medical Tourism, Stem Cells, Genomics: EASTS, Transnational STS, and the Contemporary Life Sciences. *East Asian Science, Technology and Society: An International Journal* 2(3): 433–438.

Thompson, C. (2013) Sujetos humanos colombianos y consentimiento en biomedicina en idioma inglés. In O. Restrepo Forero (ed) *Proyecto Ensamblado en Colombia. Tomo 2. Ensamblando heteroglosias*. Bogotá: Universidad Nacional de Colombia, Facultad de Ciencias Humanas, Centro de Estudios Sociales (CES), Grupo de Estudios Sociales de la Ciencia, la Medicina y la Tecnología (GESCMT).

Thoreau, H.D. (2006 [1854]) *Walden*, edited by J.S. Cramer. New Haven: Yale University Press.

Todd, Z. (2016) An Indigenous Feminist's Take on the Ontological Turn: 'Ontology' Just Another Word for Colonialism. *Journal of Historical Sociology* 29: 4–22.

Tsing, A.L. (2015) *The Mushroom at the End of the World: On the Possibility of Life in Capitalist Ruins*. Princeton and Oxford: Princeton University Press.

Woolgar, S. (ed) (1988a) *Knowledge and Reflexivity: New Frontiers in the Sociology of Knowledge*. London: SAGE.

Woolgar, S. (1988b) *Science: The Very Idea*. Chichester/London: Ellis Horwood/Tavistock.

PART V

# Revisiting Reflexivity

# 26

# Snapshots of Reflexivity

*Sarah R. Davies, Elaine Goldberg, Andrea Schikowitz
and Fredy Mora-Gámez*

This section has had a number of different titles over the period we have
been working on this book, ranging from 'Concluding' to 'Reflecting' and
now, finally, 'Revisiting Reflexivity'. These changes reflect the ways in
which its content has shifted, sometimes from month to month, and our own
hesitations about what it means to close a volume like this one. In the end,
the section is perhaps best understood not as offering a conclusion to the ideas
and themes raised in the preceding sections (though Chapter 30, 'Whose
Worlds Are More Liveable Now? Abandoning the Alienated "Blah"', does
make an effort to draw some of these together), but as centring contributions
that exceed and spill over the temporalities and concerns of the rest of the
volume. These contributions take us back in time, presenting texts and
material from earlier Science and Technology Studies (STS) discussions of
reflexivity, and point us forward, by introducing new ideas and expanding
the languages of reflexivity on which we have been relying. This section
*overflows* what has gone before.

Of course, this distinction (earlier coherence versus this section's excess)
is not entirely valid. The chapter that precedes this one – Malcolm
Ashmore and Olga Restrepo Forero's text 'Why Bogotá?' – has a similar
prehistory to some of the material in this section, in that it has been
circulating for some time in different forms (as a reviewer of the book
wrote, 'Malcolm and Olga's chapter has circulated for a while as an
[almost legendary] draft, so I'm very glad to see it finally published!'). In
this section, Steve Woolgar's exchange with Fredy Mora-Gámez ('Dear
Steve', Chapter 28) and Sally Wyatt's haikus (in 'When Sally Met Steve',
Chapter 29) similarly contain material from particular moments in STS
discussion of reflexivity: 2000, in the former case, and 2021 in the latter.
The section therefore offers some snapshots of reflexivity, in the sense

of providing glimpses of what it was (how it was discussed in 2000, for instance) and what it might become (ontologized, for example, as Mike Michael and Alex Wilkie argue in Chapter 27).

What do these snapshots tell us about the trajectories of reflexivity, past, present and future? Steve Woolgar's contribution is in many ways a classic of STS engagement with reflexivity through experimentation with literary form: dense, playful and raising themes that continue to resonate today ('[some] reflexive performances seem not to provide any rules for how to respond to them', 'Brian Peabody' notes. Indeed, 'when all is said and done, I'm not at all sure that any of your fancy playfulness with presentational forms is going to be very illuminating either'). Similarly, Sally Wyatt offers a set of haikus and haibun that speak to Woolgar's work, adding further intertextuality in the shape of a set of explanatory notes. Both texts powerfully draw us into specific moments and communities: we hear about a conference in Vienna, sites of STS scholarship such as Brunel, and particular individuals (Trevor Pinch, Roger Silverstone, 'Jim Johnson'). That such references will be more or less legible to different readers is, of course, part of the game: as Woolgar notes, 'implicit assumptions about the identities for whom we perform reflexivity are deep seated ... a key requirement of reflexive practice must be to explore creative ways of confronting, challenging and disturbing our routine reliance upon assumptions of identity'.

Mike Michael and Alex Wilkie's and our own contributions engage with slightly different themes. Michael and Wilkie (Chapter 27) offer a further expansion of the notion of reflexivity, bringing it into dialogue with thinking on ontology and aesthetics. Their argument that reflexivity should be understood as 'something distributed across – or patterned within – a heterogeneous assemblage that spans human and nonhuman, including epistemic and, crucially, aesthetic processes' insists that the practice of reflexivity must incorporate attention to the nonhuman and affective. In common with others in this volume (see Chapter 5), they suggest that 'reflexive research involves sensitivity to, affective relations in, and becoming-with, the researched', and offer a rich conceptual language for considering how this might be instantiated in different sites (or, better, research events). Our own text (Chapter 30) is deliberately open-ended, but returns to preoccupations introduced at the very start of this collection: liveability, agency, the structural constraints around (particular) academics being able to realize reflexivity as 'transformative practice'. More than presenting theoretical reflections or grouping the chapters of this collection in apparently logical ways, the last chapter displays our suggestions for concrete actions and questions that can potentially materialize what 'making more liveable worlds in academia and beyond' is about.

Taken together, the contributions in this section can therefore be understood as pointing forward to how reflexivity might be continued to be thought and practised, whether that is through new languages and concepts or in the form of questions that have resonated from the earliest STS framings of the notion.

27

# Rethinking Aesthetics, Ontologizing Reflexivity

Mike Michael and Alex Wilkie

Both authors, Michael and Wilkie, are cyclists, more or less obsessive, more or less skilled. When we meet online to co-author, this research event inevitably interlaces discussion of theory, empirical cases, methodology, writing tasks, and so on, with talk about bikes, gear, terrain, routes, (near-) accidents, and so on. Even if we don't subscribe to the Atomic Theory in which frequent riding results in the exchange of atoms between humans and bicycles (O'Brien 1967), we cannot deny that we are 'attached to', and 'entangled with', our bicycles. How does the seemingly irrelevant, and at best marginal, objects and practices of cycling impact on our research collaboration? More pertinently, how might such an impact be considered a matter of reflexivity? In this short text, we outline a way of thinking about reflexivity in terms of ontology; that is to say, reflexivity can be understood as a heterogeneous process that reflects associations among, and interweavings out of which emerge, the human and the nonhuman. As we shall argue, this can be conceptualized through a version of aesthetics which addresses the heterogeneous patterns and dynamics that comprise an ontologized reflexivity.

But first, let us recount a particular and partial reading of reflexivity in the Sociology of Scientific Knowledge (SSK). At the zenith of the 1980s debates on reflexivity in SSK, Bruno Latour's (1991) contribution introduced the idea of infra-reflexivity. Instead of reflecting on how (scientific) knowledge was socially constructed, infra-reflexivity indexed the fact that we were always doing politics, and this is what we should be reflecting on. Likewise, at the height of 'classical' Actor-Network Theory's (ANT) managerialism (Michael 2017), reflexivity was yet another means of building actor-networks: whatever else reflexivity accomplished, its texts were nevertheless

356

crafted to persuade readers of the value of reflexivity, and thereby enrol them into the authors' networks. Of course, things swiftly moved on, and ANT mutated into a post-ANT that was characterized not least by a sensibility towards those who were subaltern within, or excluded from, networks. There are two things to draw from this brief episode in Science and Technology Studies. First, Latour's ANT-tinged focus on the managerialist author of reflexivity hints at a tactic – a sort of pre-planning – which in turn implies an emphasis on human agency and cognition. As we have seen in this volume (Anderwald and Grond [Chapter 17] and Goldberg [Chapter 24]), reflexivity can be expanded to incorporate the affective and the socio-spatial, but it remains by and large focused on the human. Second, ANT famously engages with the nonhuman: this too can be ascribed agency and actor-hood (or, more accurately, actant-hood). This suggests that we might wish to think about how the nonhuman can be incorporated into the processes of reflexivity. However, this is not by virtue of its impact on human agency and cognition (or consciousness). Rather, we are interested in reflexivity as something distributed across – or patterned within – a heterogeneous assemblage that spans human and nonhuman, including epistemic *and*, crucially, aesthetic processes.

We can unpack this thought via a discussion of a version of aesthetics aligned with the work of A.N. Whitehead. Reflexivity is aesthetic in various ways: some reflexivity texts are more aesthetically pleasing than others (our favourite remains Ashmore's [1989] *The Reflexive Thesis*); some reflexive practices embrace the aesthetically ambiguous, complex, variegated (Donna Haraway's work is perhaps exemplary in this respect). In contrast to this largely phenomenological perspective on aesthetics, we treat it as a matter of ontology. For Whitehead (1978), the world becomes through the unfolding of events (or actual occasions). Events are composed of heterogeneous elements (prehensions) which experience and feel each other, combining (concresce) to produce a certain cogency or actual and concrete conformation (satisfaction). As such, instead of feelings and experience being the phenomenological privilege of humans, these are generalized to all entities which respond to, and combine with, one another in the unfolding of events. These events in turn become the elements that feed into subsequent events. In essence, events are aesthetic or, as Shaviro (2014, 61) puts it, 'aesthetics are universal structures, not specifically human ones'; beauty thus becomes 'the internal conformation of the various items of experience (elements) with each other' (78), that is, 'some kind of harmony' is attained (Connolly 2013, 159). To reiterate, 'experience' (or feeling) is generalized to all entities – human and nonhuman can all 'feel' others.

How do we apply this ontologized aesthetics to reflexivity? In a typical SSK enactment of reflexivity there is the mobilization of a perspective on an event, phenomenon or entity to uncover its 'precursors' or its 'grounds'.

For instance, a standard move is to show how analytic social constructionist accounts of scientific knowledge-making are themselves socially constructed. Here, a 'disparity' or 'incongruence' is revealed between the SSK authors' object of analysis and their practices of analysis.

Drawing on these notions of 'disparity' or 'incongruence', we can say that a heterogeneous 'reflexive event' also involves 'disparity' or 'incongruence' among its constituent elements. Conformation is 'disharmonious' – it takes on the quality of, echoing Massumi's (2011) terms, a 'semblance' in which feelings are in 'tension' or 'discordant', where elements co-become in 'discrepant', unexpected ways. In the process, new potentialities become available (if not always actualized). That is to say, the ontologically reflexive event can be generative in surprising ways, and can yield unanticipated conformations in subsequent events.

Following Sehgal and Wilkie (2024), we can draw out some further useful implications of this ontologized aesthetic version of the event, not least in how aesthetic processes can be understood to relate to reflexivity and knowledge practices. The first point to note is that knowledge occurs in continuity with (non-personified) feeling and experience: knowledge and feeling are co-extensive and consistent. Accordingly, knowledge shifts from vague aesthetic association (feelings) towards a reflexive knowledge concerning something or other. Thus, knowledge of and about worlds is the upshot of aesthetic experience and concerns, rather than aesthetics being a secondary non-essential effect of knowledge practices. More significantly, this places aesthetics and aesthetic processes at the very heart of the becoming of phenomena where acts of experience and feeling set the parameters for knowing and for claims about 'truth' and facts. This raises a second, related point, or question. If feelings and experiences precede, and are necessary dimensions of, the production of knowledge, what kinds of feelings and experiences are being produced as part of the 'research event' (Michael 2021) and how does this matter? That is to say, to open up experiences and feelings is part of the necessary contents of the research event, and not simply a by-product, or 'social' effect, of knowledge practices. For the purposes of the research practitioner, this entails an opening up or attunement to the aesthetic processes and becoming of worlds, where things feel one another. This kind of opening up entails a heterogeneous reflexivity wherein reflexivity involves, drawing on Vinciane Despret (2004), an impassioned becoming-with the researched where 'passions' set the immanent conditions, not the results, of (scientific) knowledge. Effectively, researchers must learn to repassion their knowledge, rather than produce dispassionate knowledge in order to produce more partial and more 'objective' knowledge. Consequently, heterogeneous reflexivity involves the situated mangling (Pickering 1995) of the discursive and the linguistic with experience and feeling (through which they derive). In short, the reflexivity proposed here is not simply linguistic, but rather a heterogeneous process entailing a nexus of relations. Echoing the disposition of geneticist Barbara McClintock (see Keller 1983), reflexive research involves sensitivity to, affective relations in, and becoming-with, the researched. This serves to craft situated and more robust knowledges (Haraway 1988), and is fundamentally characterized by a mutual feeling for, and a co-experiencing with, phenomena – phenomena that crucially include the researcher and the tools of research as well as the researched.

Returning to our opening example of how the objects and practices of cycling impact our research collaboration, we can begin to see how this is a research event marked by heterogeneous feelings and experiences. The (spectral) presence of bicycles event-uated in our respective bodies contribute to the sort of aesthetic 'disparity' or 'incongruence' mentioned earlier. The research event is marked by a background tension between those elements that evoke the issue at hand or the matter of concern, and our corporeal drift towards matters of cycling. The upshot is that our conversation can take odd turns and unfold in unfamiliar and unusual ways. This is not a case of 'reflexivity' in the typical sense: we are not excavating our own presuppositions to produce a novel account. Rather, the research event is marked by an aesthetic discordance and an ontological reflexivity in which heterogeneous elements mis-align. Out of this there emerges an opening up, a (com)possibility of new becomings. If linguistic reflexivity held epistemic claims to epistemological account, the reflexivity of bodies (in the widest sense) proposed here points towards ontological and aesthetic potentiality.

## References

Ashmore, M. (1989) *The Reflexive Thesis: Wrighting Sociology of Scientific Knowledge*. Chicago and London: University of Chicago Press.

Connolly, W.E. (2013) *The Fragility of Things: Self-organizing Processes, Neoliberal Fantasies, and Democratic Activism*. Durham, NC: Duke University Press.

Despret, V. (2004) The Body We Care For: Figures of Anthropo-zoo-genesis. *Body & Society* 10(2–3): 111–134.

Haraway, D.J. (1988) Situated Knowledges: The Science Question in Feminism and the Privilege of Partial Perspective. *Feminist Studies* 14(3): 575–599.

Keller, E.F. (1983) *A Feeling for the Organism: The Life and Work of Barbara McClintock*. New York: W.H. Freemand and Company.

Latour, B. (1991) The Politics of Explanation: An Alternative. In S. Woolgar (ed) *Knowledge and Reflexivity: New Frontiers in the Sociology of Knowledge*. London: SAGE, p 224.

Massumi, B. (2011) *Semblance and Event*. Cambridge, MA and London: MIT Press.

Michael, M. (2017) *Actor Network Theory: Trials, Trails and Translations*. Los Angeles, London, New Delhi, Singapore, Washington, DC and Melbourne: SAGE.

Michael, M. (2021) *The Research Event: Towards Prospective Methodologies in Sociology*. Abingdon and New York: Routledge.

O'Brien, F. (1967) *The Third Policeman*. London: Picador.

Pickering, A. (1995) *The Mangle of Practice: Time, Agency, and Science*. Chicago and London: University of Chicago Press.

Sehgal, M. and Wilkie, A. (2024) Beyond the Bifurcation of Nature: Tracing More-than-Human Aesthetics in Times of Socio-ecological Crisis. In M. Sehgal and A. Wilkie (eds) *More-than-Human Aesthetics: Ventures beyond the Bifurcation of Nature*. Bristol: Bristol University Press, pp 1–26.

Shaviro, S. (2014) *The Universe of Things: On Speculative Realism*. Minneapolis and London: University of Minnesota Press.

Whitehead, A.N. (1978) *Process and Reality: An Essay in Cosmology* (corrected edn, ed D.R. Griffin and D.W. Sherburne). New York: The Free Press.

# 28

# Dear Steve: On the Contribution of Reflexivity to General Human Wellbeing and Liveability in the World beyond Research

*Steve Woolgar*

Dear Fredy

**This** is my submission for your excellent sounding proposal for a fun filled volume on reflexivity!

At the Vienna 4S/EASST conference in 2000 I gave a paper in the panel: 'Reflexivity: Is it all over now?' At the last moment I abandoned my prepared presentation and decided instead to read out a letter I had recently received. It was from the well-known industrialist Brian (subsequently Sir Brian) Peabody. The letter is unusual because, as you will see, Brian clearly articulates key issues about the potential 'interaction' between academia and the 'real world' and related issues about reflexivity. All from the standpoint of a 'non-academic'. Brian himself was a most remarkable character. A real intellectual, smart, articulate, generous and somehow, very much in touch with areas of scholarship outside his own experience.

Of course, the landscape of Science and Technology Studies (STS) and discussions of reflexivity have moved in different directions since 2000. It might be said that the fascination with reflexivity in the 1980s and 1990s was born of a concern for consistency. The main driver of all those early experiments in reflexivity – dialogues, new literary forms, textual interruption, fake histories, fictional characterization and so on – was to grapple with and explore alternatives to the potentially self-defeating character of arguments which profess the social bases of knowledge. If I show that any particular knowledge claim is socially constructed, does that not also apply reflexively to my own argument, and with what consequences? This resulted in a body of work which was creative, intriguing and an attractive alternative to routinized forms of STS analysis. In particular, the subjects of our research, the studied scientist, the technologist, acquired a more active and prominent place in our narratives. They were allowed to answer back. Yet this particular style of reflexivity failed to cut through. This was partly, I think, because it was premised on an over-sensitivity to the prospect of inconsistency and self-contradiction. Our imagined audiences were more concerned with the logic of the argument than with its impact on well-being.

So the importance of the letter is as an artefact iconic of an earlier era of reflexivity, yet which so powerfully resonates with many of our present-day concerns. Brian so clearly articulates many of the key questions about the reflexive programme: its impact, relevance, success; and, indeed, its contribution to general human well-being and liveability in the world beyond research.

The letter caused quite a stir when I read it out at the conference. Sally Wyatt reported that the person sitting next to her in the audience remarked how amazing it was that a mere captain of industry 'got it'. This remark teaches us an important lesson. The identity 'a mere captain of industry' (as opposed to say, 'a true renaissance man-polyglot'?) discursively performs a community of recipients of reflexivity, divided between those who get it and those who don't. (Conference participants do, mere captains of industry do not.) We are thus reminded that implicit assumptions about the identities for whom we perform reflexivity are deep-seated, and institutionalized in conventional practice. It follows that a key requirement of reflexive practice must be to explore creative ways of confronting, challenging and disturbing our routine reliance upon assumptions of identity.

Here then is the text of Brian's letter. I had not thought to publish it before. But your current revival of reflexivity makes its new appearance very timely. And, by the way, there should be no issues about getting permissions for publishing the letter because, sadly, Brian passed away in 2017.

All best

Steve

46 Canmoor Heath

Cullsden

Warwickshire CV5 4NE

6th June 2000

Professor Steve Woolgar

Virtual Society? Programme

Brunel University

Uxbridge UB8 3PH

Dear Steve

It was great to see you at the FEI dinner and Foresight meeting, and thanks for your various messages. Thanks in particular for the invitation to join in your interesting sounding project. An interactive approach sounds great. But as I'm sure you realize – although you are too kind actually to say so – this kind of thing is well above me, not to say about a million miles from the day to day concerns of someone like me. So I'm not at all sure I can be of much help. But I've got to admit it's a sufficiently intriguing idea to at least have a go. And I love the idea of a joint approach to the problem. So here's my first effort at answering your initial question. I do apologize in advance if my points seem just obvious or just not very academic and/or they have already occurred to you. But I think it's sometimes useful to allow someone with an entirely new perspective to comment because it sheds light on where the problem originates (or, as I think you'd say, it is sometimes helpful and illuminating to use an outsider perspective as a way of 'displacing taken for granted assumptions').

So let me recap your starting point. You say the question of the connection between reflexivity and interaction was stimulated by two incidents. The first was an inquiry from a research student. An 'Andrea Buccholz', wasn't it, who came to you at some point in late 1998. She had just discovered two of the classic reflexive texts of the late 1980s (viz Ashmore's *Wrighting the Reflexive Thesis* and Woolgar's *Knowledge and Reflexivity*). Her simple, devastating question was: 'what happened?' In other words, what became of the energy and ideas of reflexivity since the heyday of the late 1980s? Your interlocutor wasn't so tactless as to make her concern explicit: how come you weren't still writing all those dialogues and experimenting with form and so on?

As I understand it, the expectation is that innovative developments in social studies of science and technology usually spawn various mini genres. I've found a few in the literature: laboratory studies, ethnomethodological approaches, actor network theory, standpoint perspectives and so on. The expectation seems to be that each genre would train masses of like-minded students, invent acronyms (or get Trevor Pinch to do so) – we have STS, SSK, EPOR, SST, ANT, RSST (and a brand new one, SCSSK, is to be announced at Vienna I believe) – put on panels at EASST/4S meetings and generally build their own STS sub-empires. Why hasn't reflexivity managed this? What happened?

The second incident you report is when you joined that rather grand sounding European Think Tank charged with devising strategies for the communication and transfer of research findings (that does sound very grand, doesn't it?!). You were stunned when one of the Dutch academics you first met there asked if you were really the same Steve Woolgar who had written all that stuff in the 1980s about radical reflexivity? A mutual colleague apparently expressed surprise that you were involved. What on earth were you doing on an EC think tank junket? Or rather more to the point, who on earth had imagined that a radical reflexivist could be of any use to the said think tank. How could radical reflexivity help with that? She was saying that there is some major incompatibility between being reflexive and doing outreach; perhaps, worse still, that attention to the marketing of research necessitates some kind of denial of the 'true' path of esoteric scholarship and socio-philosophical style investigations of reflexivity. Or put differently, that surely grantspersonship, consultancies, fund raising, public committees and generally, mixing it with 'users' constitutes a form of 'selling out' on the higher principled, more basic research. You say there is the further implication that the person in question, that is you (!), is somehow behaving disreputedly. Or at least, inauthentically, by which I mean you are having to desert your intellectual commitments and position in order to mix it with users.

So your anxiety stems from two kinds of critical observation. First, the suggestion that nothing has become of reflexivity. Second, that there is an inconsistency, perhaps even an inauthenticity, in moving from reflexivity to interaction with users. What then, you ask, is the route from/connection between 'reflexivity' – in many ways the watchword for the radical constructivist impetus of the late 1980s – and 'interaction' – the emerging characteristic of user sensitive social studies of science and technology in the 21st century?

From what I've gathered from our conversations, there seems to me a more general issue lurking here, and it's worth spelling it out right at the start. This became clear from the email you forwarded me yesterday from Denis Oswell [I'm sure he means David!]. The alleged disjuncture between radical reflexivity and interaction with users has an uncanny parallel with Oswell's question about the place of ethics (or value) in thinking about identity and difference in social thought. In relation to childhood, Oswell says that he sympathizes with social constructionism, and with reflexive and actor network analyses, and readily buys into post-structuralist thinking about the deconstruction of the subject and the social. This quite rightly calls into question the Cartesian/foundational/ ontological perspectives on the subject (the child). Also, says Oswell, it requires us to rethink the basis for action, in the sense that intervention etc has traditionally been premised on claims about the subject (child) at the ontological level. The approximate parallel here is the alleged disjunction between the deconstructionist arguments on the one hand (social construction of the child, reflexive analyses of knowledge creation) and action and intervention on the other (action on behalf of the child, interaction with users). So the problem of connecting reflexivity and interaction is a particular case of the more general problem of relating deconstruction/ relativism etc with utility/intervention. From what I can tell, this same general problem crops up in several different versions. It is for example asking how can we intervene, act (politically), be useful, engage in outreach, interact with users etc while maintaining scepticism and anti-essentialism. It is the problem of how to have activism without objectivism (Herrnstein Smith).

I wonder if we are quite right to adopt such a rigid distinction? Is there not a danger that adoption of these analytic dichotomies will itself end up dictating and circumscribing the conventions of appropriate practice, action, ethico-political stance and so on. I'm looking forward to what you tell me is Oswell's proposed solution to this at Vienna.

But on the basis of the little reading I've done, I wonder if a more appropriate response to this would be to try to destabilize the categories, conventions upon which we depend and which implicitly delimit our pretensions to action?

So is it all over now? My first effort to get a handle on all this was to begin with your specific problem and start looking at the literature on reflexivity. If you work reasonably hard at compiling a list of reflexive analyses, it's not hard to come up with quite a few (Mushakoji, Suber etc). So there is evidence to counter the argument that the field just dried up. On the other hand, if you look at the nature, rather than just the number, of the publications, the situation is less promising. For example, I've found it hard to discover a book-length treatment anywhere as nearly as good as Ashmore's exemplar of the genre since its publication in 1989. Looking for the standard indicators of the success of the field, you might ask where are the new journals of reflexivity, the international association of radical reflexivity (IARR), the annual conferences (Reflex 2000), the newly established Chairs in Reflexivity and so on.

Of course, I realize that these off-the-cuff assessments of the fate of a sub-field use rather dubious indicators of value. We would expect reflexivists both to be alert to the problems of relying on these indicators and to be adept at arguing that they did not apply in any particular case. Reflexivists would presumably argue that these usual indicators of successful institutionalization of an academic field are inappropriate, precisely because they are not trying to emulate the usual form of institutionalization of research. They are instead trying something novel and different. To be authentic to their practice they would resist its transformation into a formulaic method. They would especially resist persuading students to take up reflexivity, and they would not wish to institute regimes of training in reflexivity. So in that regard at least, it has to be said that reflexivity has succeeded spectacularly. Reflexivity is a success because it has argued itself out of a job.

Well, yes, okay. The initial premise – that it's all over now – can itself be reflexively challenged. But it's a measure of the exasperation that some people feel with this kind of response that the sheer cleverness of the answer is unconvincing. Thus, blisteringly devastating, self-referential inversions of the initial premise excite reactions of the genre: come off it (COI) and oh for god's sake (OFGS). More than this, COI and

OFGS responses have power: they seem to carry the day. How is this possible? What's going on here?

The key, I reckon, is that the appeal of reflexivity is itself premised on implicit conceptions of truth and logical consistency. The temptation is in the appeal that nobody would want the sociology of scientific knowledge to be a standing refutation of itself. It can't absolve itself of the reflexive critique that its own claims and theories are themselves socially constructed. I won't get into all Cretans being liars and the dynamics of paradoxical relations at this point [Oh, shame really], except to note one thing. The impetus for the reflexive project is based on a rationale whose logic is unassailable, and yet as we see, large numbers of people have been able just to ignore it. I'm reminded a bit of my favourite Lewis Carroll story, do you know the one, about Achilles and the Tortoise? [Err, do we all know it?]. Carroll shows brilliantly that even though the logic is unassailable there too, the logic stills fails to persuade. Illogical, untruthful, incoherent, idiosyncratic responses of the COI and OFGS variety carry the day. They turn out to be more powerful than purity!

I reckon this carries over in a similar way to a related appeal of reflexivity, that one should be relentlessly sceptical about the grounds for truth claims. Yes, in principle, every truth claim, or even gesture, implication, hint, innuendo about reliable knowledge should be rooted out and have its constructed origins displayed in public. Yes, but one is tempted to say, what an effort, what a cost and for what? It's all very well for radical constructivism to take that stance but it seems to run counter to the other central tenet of social studies of science: viz. That what is prized in knowledge production is utility not truth. That what comes to count as truth largely does so because it's useful. Let me quote back at you that example you yourself give. Scientists don't get excited and grab at someone's lapels because this bearer of news has discovered the truth. It's because what they are saying has implications for what experiment they can set up next. Conversely, challenges to the truth status can be fairly reasonably ignored if they have little bearing on the practicalities of what to do next. From what you tell me, I think something like this happened last week. You asked Julian, in effect, what was the basis of his claims about press distortion. [For those of you who weren't there …]. I don't know what you were expecting to happen there? Did you imagine that by asking him that question Julian might throw up his hands in horror and say 'you've got me' or 'the whole epistemological foundation of my analysis is faulty' or even 'my god I give up'? No, what could he possibly do with that observation other than reply that he thought the press treatment of media studies was distorted! Yours was a clever observation and possibly true, but its truth and cleverness are (almost) entirely beside the point. Clever but entirely useless, you idiot [???]. It just made you come across as grumpy, difficult, nitpicking, and so on. And my suggesting by the way that Julian has scant regard for the truth is no denigration of his epistemological attitude. Rather it's a comment on the absurdly high value which, in spite of all your sophisticated constructivism, you implicitly attach to truth. At the heart of the much vaunted openness of reflexivity is what your colleague Christine Hine calls 'epistemological correctness'.

Despite a good hard look, I could find very few negative reviews of books on reflexivity. Perhaps, as is often said, a good way of killing new innovations and ideas is simply to ignore them. In this vein we could say that the Ashmore and Woolgar books were a critical success but a box office disaster.

There is also of course the stark possibility that reflexivity failed (if it did, right?!!) because it was simply wrong-headed or erroneous. Now I take it we can simply dispose of that one since it would be in complete violation of all post-asymmetric analyses of the truth status of science. In other words, you'd have had to read nothing about science since early Robert Merton!

The related thing to notice is the extraordinary silence that often descends after reflexive performances and analyses. The audience says absolutely nothing. Not, I think, because they necessarily agree with everything that's been said. But because (some) reflexive performances seem not to provide any rules for how to respond to them.

Or perhaps, reflexivity has just now become a tamed, watered down version of its original self. I think you told me that someone called Pollster [I guess he means Pollner!] wrote a paper called something like 'Left of Ethnomethodology', in which he described ethnomethodology as having settled down and moved out to the suburbs. The implication is that the radical elements of a new line of thought routinely get tamed and move away from where the action is. The interesting implication is that this is a recurrent feature of radical thinking; it's what happened when Garfinkelian ethnomethodology got turned into conversational analysis; it's what happened, perhaps, when Foucault got turned into the History of the Present group. Through a process of institutionalization and assimilation, the original concepts become denuded of their radical connotations, the dangerous destabilizing tendencies become calmed, threats to established academic and intellectual organizations are neutralized. It becomes reasonable to adopt mild forms of radical reflexivity, to speak (as does Jim Clifford) of being content with having reflexive moments. This fits quite well with the point about the failure of reflexivity to promote dialogue. The failure to provide clear rules for practical benefits and procedure results in silence. And the threat of silence has been finessed by those who have turned the initial sceptical move into a methodology; ethnomethodology into conversational analysis for example.

I rather imagine that reflexivists would favour this account, since it neatly attributes radical credentials and tendencies to reflexivists who are portrayed as engaged in a constant struggle with the dark forces of conservative thinking.

If I follow the reflexive formula correctly, it's at about this point in the exposition that one would expect to find the denouement, right? We would expect to have been treated to a discussion which gives credence to, and sustains respect, both for the endless (?) wit, cleverness and ingenuity of reflexivity and for the hopelessly (?) flawed (erroneous, unsupported, wrong) but nonetheless powerful genre of COI and OFGS reactions. Then the whole point of the (otherwise curious?) use of form should now be spelled out, right?

To do this, you might have one of your main character(s) suddenly realize that s/he/they could perhaps fashion an entire piece which itself experimented with the analyst-user couple, perhaps by making the whole narrative into a letter latterly recently by the author. But, as I've already intimated, I think this would be just too clever by half. And nobody is going to be convinced that the putative user voice is anything other than your own invention. On the other hand, I suppose this does at least open up the dynamic of the user relation, even if I appear as a grotesquely stilted figure in your narrative.

Anyway, like I said at the start, I'm sorry for this skimpy reading of the sources. An industrialist's attention span is certainly no more than about ten seconds! So I'm not at all sure I've got it right, and I've probably not done the arguments the justice they deserve. But I hope this may be of some help. If nothing else it's very clear to this user's point of view that (at least a form of) reflexivity is entirely compatible with, not to say rather productive for (at least a form of) interactivity. In particular, as I've suggested, there's no reason why a reflexive appreciation of the social basis of the social relations of knowledge shouldn't be of enormous help in promoting greater interactivity. It's precisely by thinking more about the social basis for interactivity that we can inform our practical interactions with users. (Gosh, I find myself slipping into your way of thinking about it.) What I mean is: it's precisely by thinking more about the social basis for interactivity that **you** can inform **your** practical interactions with users like myself.

So: in order to be interactive you clearly need to be more reflexive, not less. Not only is the route from reflexivity to interaction deserve to be lauded; it's certainly nothing to be ashamed of. Meaningful interaction may actually depend on it. Although it's probably a good idea to be clearer which kind of reflexivity is useful to this end. I'd say (and I'm sure you would agree) that what we need is a form of reflexivity which actively destabilizes the categorical distinctions which feed and sustain assumptions about identities, attributes and expectations of (in this case) users.

I had a look at the way the term is being used in social theory by the way. The authors you suggested: Beck, Giddens and Slash [He surely means Lash!]. They seem to be saying that reflexivity is happening more and more in modern society; indeed that it is a crucial dynamic of major social change (I think I've got that right). They even suggest this is a good thing and, interestingly, that it will promote greater political debate and awareness.

> We all refuse the paralysis of the political will apparent in the work of so many authors who, following the dissolution of socialism, see no place for active political programmes any longer. Something like the contrary is actually the case. The world of developed reflexivity, where the interrogation of social forms becomes commonplace, is one that in many circumstances stimulates active critique. (Beck et al, 1994, viii)

The problem of course is their selective application, in classical ontological gerrymandering fashion, of the activities and domains which they say are susceptible to this reflexive tendency. Notably absent is social theory itself. There is almost no single hint of ways in which increasingly reflexivity might be affecting the genesis, production, consumption of social theory in this new world. Nor, critically, any assessment of how this might affect what is said under the guise of social theory about reflexivity! (Gosh, I think I'm getting the hang of this now!)

But I should confess, in the end, when all is said and done, I'm not at all sure that any of your fancy playfulness with presentational forms is going to be very illuminating either. Hope this doesn't lead to silence between us! And sorry again that it's so long.

With very best wishes to all in CRICT,


Brian Peabody PhD OBE FREng


## Reference

Beck, U., Giddens, A. and Lash, S. (1994) *Reflexive Modernization. Politics, Tradition and Aesthetics in the Modern Social Order.* Cambridge: Polity Press.

29

# When Sally Met Steve: Virtual Reflexivity

*Sally Wyatt*

## Preamble

I prepared this haiku/haibun[1] on the occasion of Steve Woolgar's retirement in August 2021, in Norrköping, Sweden. The COVID-19 pandemic was still with us, and the event had been postponed at least once. It was hybrid, and I attended remotely. This version includes the haiku I read, together with some explanatory notes.

## When Sally Met Steve

meeting in writing
from *Laboratory Life*[2]
Pyro-Glu-His-Pro[3]

To meet in person, probably in late 1986, I travelled to Brunel on the tube with Bill Melody and Paschal Preston,[4] to be offered pizza and lively discussion by a very motley crew, including your good self, Roger Silverstone, Martin Cave, Dave Morley and Georgina Born. Central London to Uxbridge[5] often felt more difficult – practically and intellectually – than the journeys to further flung PICT partners.

configure users[6]
technographic approaches[7]
Access '98[8]

director at last
virtual society?[9]
purple violet[10]

Non–users. They came.[11]
Five virtuality rules[12]
nature takes a turn

Your epistolary presentation during the EASST/4S conference in Vienna was wonderful. It was part of a session you organized together with Malcolm Ashmore, called 'Radical reflexivity: Is it all over now?'.[13] You began by saying that you had not had time to prepare a paper, so instead you would read the letter sent to you by the chair[14] of the Virtual Society? Advisory Board, as a way of relativizing and situating the programme with the funders and policy makers. Afterwards, a very earnest young man told me how impressed he was with the intellectual level of the chairman. It was a reminder of the literal–mindedness of some people, and perhaps also of the reason radical reflexivity sometimes stumbled.

reflexivity
novel literary forms
light on the water

coming to Oxford
turning to ontology[15]
separate an egg[16]

Steve Woolgar, thank you
for your sense of irony
and for the ice cream[17]

ice cream that I used
to frighten IT support
into the forest

---

[1]  Haiku is three lines, of five-seven-five syllables. The final line usually invokes nature, as a contrast to the social. Haiku can be interspersed with prose paragraphs, called haibun.

[2]  Latour, B. and Woolgar, S. (1986) *Laboratory Life: The Construction of Scientific Facts*. Princeton: Princeton University Press.

[3]  Porcine thyrotropin releasing hormone, mentioned in chapter 3 of *Laboratory Life*.

[4]  Bill Melody was the first director of the Programme on Information and Communication Technologies (PICT), an interdisciplinary programme funded by the UK Economic and

Social Research Council (ESRC). Paschal Preston and I were research associates with the programme.

5    Uxbridge is at the western end of the Metropolitan line of the London Underground. Brunel University, where Woolgar worked from the mid-1980s until 1999, is in Uxbridge.

6    Woolgar, S. (1990) Configuring the User: The Case of Usability Trials. *The Sociological Review* 38(1): 58–99.

7    Woolgar, S. (1998) A New Theory of Innovation? *Prometheus* 16(4): 441–452.

8    Access was a database management system included in the Microsoft Office Windows suite of programmes. Access to the internet was a major theme of the project I was part of in the Virtual Society? programme (see note 9).

9    The Virtual Society? research programme was another interdisciplinary programme funded by the ESRC from 1997 to 2001. Woolgar was the director.

10   The branding for the Virtual Society? programme was a lurid shade of purple.

11   Wyatt, S., Thomas, G. and Terranova, T. (2002) They Came, They Surfed, They Went Back to the Beach: Conceptualising Use and Non-use of the Internet. In S. Woolgar (ed) *Virtual Society? Technology, Cyberpole, Reality*. Oxford: Oxford University Press, pp 23–40.

12   Woolgar, S. (2002) Five Rules of Virtuality. In S. Woolgar (ed) *Virtual Society? Technology, Cyberpole, Reality*. Oxford: Oxford University Press, pp 1–22.

13   My biological age does not match my Science and Technology Studies (STS) age. Vienna was the first joint EASST/4S conference I attended. I had long been a reflexivity groupie, but came to it after its heyday. My initial training was in economics, and it took me a long time even to feel comfortable writing in the first person. I have misremembered the title of the session. When giving presentations about STS to a non-STS audience, I always refer to the Vienna session as 'Radical reflexivity'. Brian Rappert and I tried to get the band back together for the 2020 EASST/4S conference in Prague. Woolgar and others had agreed to participate. We also contacted Jim Johnson (aka Bruno Latour), but were politely informed that Johnson had retired. Due to the COVID-19 pandemic, we cancelled our session as we felt it would not work online. See Johnson, J. (1988) Mixing Humans and Nonhumans Together: The Sociology of a Door-closer. *Social Problems* 35(3): 298–310.

14   I am sorry to hear that Sir Brian Peabody passed away in 2017. My condolences to Steve, and the earnest young man who sat next to me in Vienna in 2000. I fear we may never see the likes of Sir Brian again.

15   Woolgar moved to the Saïd Business School, University of Oxford, in 1999. He organized a series of workshops during his time there, including one called 'A turn to ontology in STS', held in June 2008, during which I took on the role of discussant for one session. The workshop led to a special issue of *Social Studies of Science*, 43(3).

16   My partner, not someone who bakes cakes, remains surprised at my ability to separate an egg. He is a philosopher, and finds the separation of eggs to be ontologically impossible. He has also contributed to the debate on reflexivity. See: Radder, H. (1992) Normative Reflexions on Constructivist Approaches to Science and Technology. *Social Studies of Science* 22(1): 141–173.

17   The farewell gift for everyone involved in the Virtual Society? programme was a plastic 3.5-inch floppy disk on top of which is an ice cream cup, tipped over, with ice cream spilling over the disk. For many years, I had this on my desk at work. See web version for a photo: https://bristoluniversitypress.co.uk/revisiting-reflexivity/additional-content.

# 30

# Whose Worlds Are More Liveable Now? Abandoning the Alienated 'Blah'

*Fredy Mora-Gámez, Elaine Goldberg, Sarah R. Davies*
*and Andrea Schikowitz*

We were not expecting you to read this book in an organized, linear manner – indeed, we have been counting on your engaging with it in your own messy way. As such this is not a traditional conclusion. We find it hard to draw the ideas raised throughout the contributions together in a tidy or coherent manner. Instead what we want to present here is more of a collective map of open questions.

By the time you reach this section, we expect that your chosen adventure has triggered unforeseen reflections and insights about the liveability of worlds that are of relevance to you, your teams, colleagues, participants or interlocutors. Different chapters of the book have invited us to reimagine reflexivity as a transformative practice, or perhaps as (diffr)action, engagement or embodied knowledge. Contributors have talked about the troubles involved in reflexivity, or its epistemic potential, or its connection to experimental methods. Regardless of the adventure you chose to follow or the path of contributions that you chased, we hope that it is clear that part of our collective invitation in this book has been to challenge or trouble the taken-for-granted connection between reflexivity, on the one hand, and transformation, on the other. While much scholarship takes for granted reflexivity's emancipatory potential, this volume, taken together, acknowledges but also complicates this. This is not least in part because increasingly precarious and discriminatory conditions in academic spaces, institutional practices disregarding critically oriented research, research methods that overlook the embodiment of knowledge, and an almost inevitable colonial intellectual extractivist inertia fuelling our research projects are some of the constitutive conditions shaping the academic worlds we inhabit.

At this point, it might be worthwhile to pause, and reflect: What are (y) our commitments after navigating the pieces offered by this book? Besides (y) our intellectual agreements and disagreements, how has (y)our engagement with different sections of the book triggered insights about (y)our immediate worlds, everyday academic practices, and ways of collaborating, writing or even citing? What do (we) you think now of research that takes the risk of embracing less conventional methods?

Long before the discussions around reflexivity fuelled the engines of Science and Technology Studies (STS) in the 1980s, and before we and those whom we usually cite (often, STS scholars primarily based in Euroamerican institutions) began to conceptualize the limitations and ontological implications of reflexivity, researchers in other less privileged locations had already immersed themselves in the complexities of reflexivity as a transformative practice. In his seminal work *Pedagogy of the Oppressed*, Brazilian philosopher and educator Paulo Freire delivers profound insights concerning the relation between reflection and action:

> An unauthentic word, one which is unable to transform reality, results when dichotomy is imposed upon its constitutive elements. When a word is deprived of its dimension of action, reflection automatically suffers as well; and the word is changed into idle chatter, into verbalism, into an alienated and alienating 'blah'. It becomes an empty word, one which cannot denounce the world, for denunciation is impossible without a commitment to transform, and there is no transformation without action. (Freire 1970, 84)

Abandoning a notion of reflexivity as a mere intellectual alienating 'blah', while simultaneously revisiting it constitutively as action, partially captures the invitations extended by the contributions to this collection. All of them reflect on reflexivity, documenting their experiences of it while critically examining how both positive transformation and harm or trouble are enacted through it.

As you may be aware by now, the question of how to create more liveable worlds in academia and beyond is comprised of multiple foldings. These foldings are shaped by the institutions, bodies, fields and even the geographic locations where STS and interdisciplinary social research are conducted. By recognizing this intricate complexity, we can further navigate this collection by articulating more specific questions that arise from our reading and engagement with it. These questions are pertinent to both our worlds and our commitment to transforming them, while they also point towards possible everyday life practices and entry points (in *italics*) that can potentially enact more liveable conditions. These entry points avoid the tautology of using the words *reflexivity* or *reflect on*, precisely in synchrony with Freire's quote inviting us to engage in actions.

Ewa, Maria, Mirjana, Lisa, Erika, and Ruth and Leonhard (in Chapters 12–17) took the risk of embracing unconventional formats to articulate important insights about public space, the pedagogy embedded in experimental biology research, the challenges of writing by hand in a digital era, and the possibilities of art as a reflexive mode of inquiry. In everyday life in and beyond academia, how do we *assess* articles, chapters, thesis, and so on that incorporate unconventional methods? How often do we abandon or ***embrace*** ideas involving more experimental methods for the sake of being safely assessed or not having our submissions rejected? How willing are we to ***moderate and facilitate*** safe spaces in our seminars/classes for our students and younger scholars to engage in less conventional and more creative projects?

In a related vein, Dimas and Camilo (in Chapters 9 and 10) offered us empirically grounded reflections on the implications of embodying hybrid spaces as researchers based in European universities while doing fieldwork with rural communities. In these spaces, situated forms of reflexivity become crucial to challenge normativity while configuring research as participatory collective action. How willing are we to ***care for*** the challenges of participatory research designs that allow our interlocutors to speak on their behalf? How often do we decide to abandon such a possibility to avoid institutional resistance? How do we ***support*** junior scholars who are willing to work with different communities and ***avoid*** intellectual extractivism or epistemic erasure (Dimas)?

Whereas Michael (Chapter 5) introduces us to the epistemic implications of bringing our own bodies as sites of reflexive inquiry, marissa micah (Chapter 7) invites us to ***feel–with*** *the vulnerabilities* of their (and our) own bodies and challenge the gendered/gendering worlds. Ewa (Chapter 12), Ruth and Leonhard (Chapter 17) invite us to dive into hybridized-bridging ways of knowing that combine academic knowledge and artistic methods that reify the body as an epistemic agent. In this regard, Maria (Chapter 13) reflects on the challenges of ***bridging*** worlds while trying to overcome the colonial legacies of Western academia and even art as forms of knowledge.

How do we ***appreciate*** *or disregard* research that addresses the situated struggles imposed on bodies by social, cultural and technological configurations? How ***aware are*** we of the challenges that come with academic knowledge-making practices? How often do we ***take into account*** how those challenges are magnified in the context of particular bodies and intersectional positionalities? How often do we reductively welcome decolonial thinking basically as an exoticized fashion trend within academia?

The institutionalization of reflexivity as a checklist or an accountability practice comes together with additional forms of labour that are usually invisible, reproducing existing inequalities based on gender, ethnicity or migration status (among other positionalities). In this regard, the contributions offered by Karen and Doris, Katja, Annie, and Nikolaus and Sarah (Chapters 20–23) guide us through some of the challenges and possibilities of reflexivity as a practice to be carried out within institutions. Concerning STS institutions, Elaine and Malcolm and Olga's chapters (Chapters 24 and 25) invite us to **destabilize conventional understandings** of sites and spaces in STS. How do we **actively communicate** our critical point of view about the institutionalization of reflexivity and critique? How do we **dignify and reward** the extra tasks and labour involved in reflexivity within institutional projects? How do we **acknowledge** the time and effort that reflexivity takes in research? How do we **ensure** the possibility of heterotopias (Chapter 24) despite institutionalization? But also, how can we **stop thinking** of sites outside of the Euroamerican bubble merely as exotic cases of knowledge? How do we **reify** the work of researchers who inhabit sites considered as peripheries of academic knowledge production? How do we **stop territorializing** the claims, arguments, and concepts crafted by pioneering more-than-academics, like Freire himself, by justifying our extractive practices on our own ignorance or language inaccessibility? How to make (academic) worlds more liveable for those whose knowledge we continue to prey on?

These questions, while functioning as a map to navigate this collection, also call for action. As we explained in Chapter 1, the questions inspiring the project of bringing together this collection were the outcome of collective encounters between ourselves as a research group. As you have witnessed in your own navigation of the book, however, these questions are now part of a collective collage of inquiries into the worlds we inhabit, even beyond academia. Speaking to this collective aspect of reflexivity, Freire elaborates: 'For apart from inquiry, apart from the praxis, individuals cannot be truly human. Knowledge emerges only through invention and re-invention, through the restless, impatient, continuing, hopeful inquiry human beings pursue in the world, with the world, and with each other' (Freire 1970, 72).

We believe there are important things to **discuss–share–feel** about reflexivity in the face of precarity, about learning to inhabit time and space in different ways, about solidarity and the possibility of building liveable worlds together that remain unsaid here. Such unrealized realities haunt the text – and, in so doing, we hope, also call attention to the foreclosures that haunt the production of knowledge in all material systems especially our present one. As such, for us as authors at least, the optimism of the titular slogan is thus accompanied also by a sense of loss, a lament for things we could not or did not do, and a world whose possibilities we fleetingly intuit but cannot realize.

Nonetheless, in an attempt to challenge the unidirectional format of conclusions in edited collections, we now invite you to share with us, editors and contributors, your reflections, questions and experiences around reflexivity as a transformative practice. You are welcome to become part of our collective ongoing conversations about, among other things, how reflexivity as a transformative practice will continue to shape the field of STS and interdisciplinary social research. We expect that by acknowledging the unfinished status of this collection we can together partially grasp some of those unrealized realities and expand our interactions to other modalities and digital spaces. Take this invitation as our attempt to embrace and facilitate other types of interaction that betray the conventional academic format, inevitably shaping the arena of this edited collection.

As food for thought before you do so, here are some final questions to bring to our ongoing conversations: What has reflexivity meant for you in your research (or other) practice? What has it afforded or threatened? Whose worlds and lives have been made more liveable through it (if any)? Is reflexivity a pleasure or a pain (or a bit of both)? Can it ever be institutionalized? Is it still a productive frame, or should we switch to different languages and practices (such as diffraction)? Have you experienced reflexivity as transformative? And, ultimately, (how) has reflexivity helped you explore how the world could and perhaps should be otherwise?

---

Vignette 7

*What I find exciting about this experience is that the theme of reflexivity, the use of different media and reflection on methods runs like a common thread through very different contexts. I feel as if whole worlds are being dismantled and rebuilt around me while I'm still sitting here at my desk writing or making my films. Working environments come and go in our academic system, but relationships remain – and the research itself. Perhaps a reflection on working in academia must also include this: yes, context matters, and our work is situated, but our work also remains our activity, travelling through the project worlds of the institutions that surround and fund us. While a reflection on the academic world of work always tends to agitate me, this thought calms me down: me and the writing, the filming, the photographing, the reflecting, the reading and noting, the editing and imagining – and all around the precarious world of project work. But they can't take my work away from me. This is our craft.*

---

## Reference

Freire, P. (1970) *Pedagogy of the Oppressed*. New York: Continuum. Originally published in 1968 (Portuguese).

# Index

References to figures appear in *italic* type. References to footnotes
show both the page number and note number (142n6).